MATTHEW 19:9

- A DEADLY EXCEPTION

MATTHEW 19:9

– A DEADLY EXCEPTION

Jesus said, "whoever divorces his wife,
except for sexual immorality,
and marries another, commits adultery."

David Lowe

SKM

Kalamunda, Western Australia

SKM

Published in 2020 (Paperback), 2021 (eBook) by ShowKnowMercy
www.showknowmercy.com

Title: Matthew 19:9 – A Deadly Exception

ISBN: 978-0-6450493-0-5 (Paperback)
ISBN: 978-0-6450493-1-2 (eBook)

Subjects: Marriage, Divorce, Christian Ethics, Gospel of Matthew, Religion, Family

A catalogue record for this work is available from the National Library of Australia.

ACKNOWLEDGEMENTS

Thanks be to Jesus Christ,
the son of David, the son of Abraham (Matt 1:1),
for his mercy – and anything good in this book!

And to God our perfect heavenly Father (Matt 5:48).

And to the Spirit of our Father for comfort and
words to bear witness for Jesus' sake (Matt 10:18-20).

Thanks also go to my wife, Ruth, and our three sons,
for their support and long-suffering!

I am grateful too for a scholarship from the Australian College of
Theology that covered most of my PhD course fees.

Finally, thanks go to my supervisors, who have mercifully contended
with my big ideas that challenge standard positions, and with my
(often) awkward expression! They have helped me to order, deepen
and smooth this work, but all imperfections remain,
of course, my own responsibility.

"Blessed are the merciful, for they shall receive mercy." (Matt 5:7)

CONTENTS

APPENDICES

LIST OF ABBREVIATIONS

ABRL	Anchor Bible Reference Library
Ag. Ap.	Against Apion
Ag. Jov.	Against Jovinianus
AMG	Advancing the Ministries of the Gospel
ANE	Ancient Near East
Ant.	Antiquities of the Jews
AOTC	Apollos Old Testament Commentary
ASJ	Asia Journal of Theology
B&H	Broadman and Holman
Barn.	Barnabas
BCOTWP	Baker Commentary on the Old Testament Wisdom & Psalms
BDAG	Bauer, Danker, Arndt, Gingrich (Greek-English Lexicon)
BDB	Brown, Driver, Briggs (Hebrew-English Lexicon)
BECNT	Baker Exegetical Commentary on the New Testament
B.J.	Bellum Judaicum (History of the Jewish War)
BSac	Bibliotheca Sacra
BST	Bible Speaks Today
BTCB	Brazos Theological Commentary on the Bible
CBQ	Catholic Biblical Quarterly
CGTC	Cambridge Greek Testament Commentary
CTM	Concordia Theological Monthly
CUP	Cambridge University Press
ERV	English Revised Version
ESV	English Standard Version
EVA	Evangelische Verlagsanstalt
Git.	Gittin
GTJ	Grace Theological Journal
HALOT	The Hebrew and Aramaic Lexicon of the Old Testament
Herm. *Mand.*	Shepherd of Hermas *Mandate*
Herm. *Vis.*	Shepherd of Hermas *Vision*
Hom. Num.	Homilies on Numbers
HTS	HTS Theological Studies
Hypoth.	Hypothetica
ICC	International Critical Commentary
JBL	Journal of Biblical Literature
JBQ	Jewish Bible Quarterly
JETS	Journal of the Evangelical Theological Society
JGAR	Journal of Gospel and Acts Research

Jos.	On Joseph
JSNT	Journal for the Study of the New Testament
Ketub.	Ketubot
KJV	King James Version
LNTS	Library of New Testament Studies
LXX	Septuagint
MT	Masoretic Text
NAB	New American Bible
NAC	New American Commentary
NASB	New American Standard Bible
NEB	New English Bible
NET	New English Translation
NCBC	New Century Bible Commentary
NIBC	New International Biblical Commentary
NICNT	New International Commentary on the New Testament
NICOT	New International Commentary on the Old Testament
NIGTC	New International Greek Testament Commentary
NIV	New International Version
NT	New Testament
NTS	New Testament Studies
OT	Old Testament
OTL	Old Testament Library
OUP	Oxford University Press
PNTC	Pillar New Testament Commentary
Ps.-Phoc.	Pseudo-Phocylides
RBT	Reading the Bible Today
RevExp	Review & Expositor
RNTC	Reading the New Testament Commentary
RSR	Religious Studies Review
Sanh.	Sanhedrin
SBJOT	Southern Baptist Journal of Theology
SCM	Student Christian Movement
SHBC	Smyth & Helwys Bible Commentary
Sir	Sirah
SMR	St Mark's Review
SNTSMS	Society for New Testament Studies Monograph Series
Sot.	Sotah
Spec.	Special Laws
Sus	Susanna
TB	Tyndale Bulletin
ThHNT	Theologischer Handkommentar zum Neuen Testament
ThZ	Theologische Zeitschrift

T. Jud.	Testament of Judah
TSAJ	Texte und Studien zum antiken Judentum
UBS	United Bible Society
UCP	University of Chicago Press
Ulp. *Dig.*	Ulpian *Digest*
WBC	Word Biblical Commentary
WJK	Westminster John Knox
WTT	Leningrad Codex Hebrew Old Testament
Yebam.	Yebamot
YUP	Yale University Press
ZEE	Zeitschrift für Evangelische Ethik
ZNW	Zeitschrift für die Neutestamentliche Wissenschaf

OVERVIEW

For almost 2000 years Christians have firmly upheld the permanency of marriage: God joins one man and one woman together for good! Solemn wedding vows, promising to love in sickness and in health, for richer or for poorer, were plainly seen as applying 'until death do us part'. There were no "ifs" and "buts" inserted into these vows. Love truly was love; it was everlasting and unconditional. To mention even one exit clause at the wedding altar, "*I will love you except if you...,*" would have been unimaginable – and extremely unloving.

Until only a generation ago, divorce and remarriage remained stigmatised, along with out-of-wedlock pregnancy. When problems in marriage arose, a popular resolution – in and out of the church – was to 'stick together at least for the sake of the children'. The age-old sin of adultery was always a threat, *but it was genuinely regarded as 'sin'* (and cohabitation or remarriage '*living in sin*'). Such infidelity did not necessarily lead to divorce, despite the destruction reaped. Today adultery – and generally sex outside of marriage – is commonplace and often celebrated.

Nonetheless, the high hope of enduring love is a universal constant. No love-smitten couple entertains divorce on their wedding day. However, the ideal has been greatly undermined by certain, often unspoken, offences that might offer future grounds for divorce. "Divorce for adultery or abandonment" is something of a mantra today for many Christians. This current Protestant majority view has opened the door to endorsing divorce for just about any cause. Most assume a right to remarry after divorce. Those against this view, or who simply feel uneasy with it, often remain silent – else they may be seen as unloving, judgemental and legalistic.

This book is based on my PhD thesis, '*Matthew 19:9 – A Deadly Exception*' (Vose/ACT, 2020).* It essentially found that the "sexual immorality" (Greek: *porneia*) of Matthew 19:9 does not equate with "a matter of indecency" (Hebrew: *'erwat dabar*) in Deuteronomy 24:1. **The current Protestant majority view on divorce and remarriage is therefore wrong, because it largely depends on this equation.**

This "majority view" (of late) not only clashes with the teaching of Jesus, but teaches the opposite. It perilously aligns with cultural practice that Jesus condemns. Mercy is not core to this view. As with other current views, it also misses the point of the 'exception clause' in Matthew 19:9 (and 5:32).

The "sexual immorality" of Matthew 19:9 is no trivial offence. It offers no easy escape from marriage. Instead, as written in the Law of Moses, "sexual immorality" encompasses every kind of illicit sexual intercourse: acts that attract the death penalty, even if never applied by Israel. This includes "adultery," *an evil in God's eyes* and a sin against God (cf. Ps 51:4). Applying Deuteronomy 22:22 to Matthew 19:9 has dire ramifications, especially for an "evil and adulterous generation" (Matt 12:39; 16:4). In contrast, "a matter of indecency" (Deut 24:1) is something unfavourable in a wife found *merely in a man's eyes*. Capital punishment is not applied. The matter is not connected with ritual impurity, so it cannot be a religious matter that offends God. It is a highly subjective and likely selfish judgement.

By the Law, any man who writes "sexual immorality" on his wife's divorce certificate hands her a death sentence! Does Jesus advocate this for Christians today? No. We must not rush straight to Christian application, but appreciate that Jesus was tested on a matter of Law by people seeking his death. Jesus turns the tables on his opponents: he is totally lawful and they are lawless (cf. Matt 23:28). Jesus has also taught that whoever looks with lustful intent at another woman commits adultery in his heart (Matt 5:28-30). Therefore, whoever divorces his wife for "sexual immorality" (usually "adultery" in the context of marriage) risks joining the lawless "hypocrites" Jesus condemns, and if a man divorces his wife for any other reason, then he commits adultery himself (a dire offence against God).

A deadly judgement rests on all who test God and break covenant in their unfaithfulness. If anyone does not love the person whom they see in front of them, especially the one whom God has joined them to in marriage and commanded them to always hold fast to, then how can they say that they love God whom they cannot see (1 John 4:20; Matt 7:21-23)? Christian application begins here.

This book firstly examines a legal matter, for Matthew 19:1-12 involves a question of Law. Many scholars agree that Jesus did not abolish or change the Law (cf. Matt 5:17-20), but they then contradict themselves by saying Jesus modified the Law, especially in the area of marriage. They use complex arguments to do this, but they really do not take Jesus at his word. **Jesus. Did. Not. Change. The. Law.**

Christians routinely hold that only the moral law, as represented by the Ten Commandments, remains applicable, without sure basis for neglecting the 600-odd other Old Testament commands – with their many bloody demands. Matthew's 'exception clause' is often seen as clear proof that Jesus changed the Law, for it is thought that (in keeping with contemporary law and culture) he replaced death for adultery with divorce. However, **the 'exception clause' is actually exceptionally good proof that Jesus did not change the Law at all.**

Understanding the Sermon on the Mount is critical. Rather than radicalising or internalising the Law (to include inward thoughts), Jesus simply brings out the original meanings, such as already found in the Tenth Commandment. He does not alter the Law by even a dot, but holds his Jewish audience (and all Jews under the Old Covenant) fully accountable to it. Jesus certainly kept the Law himself, to the letter. He could not be the true King of Israel or Jewish Messiah or perfect saviour if he did not. How Christians observe Jesus' commands without changing the Law – including any capital code – is another question.

This is not an appeal to reinstate the death penalty, but to **clearly understand which law and covenant Christians come under**. Observing Jesus' commands (Matt 28:20) must involve observing the context of his commands. Christians are not commanded to obey the (Old Testament) Law of Moses, but to obey the (New Testament) law of Christ. All principles of the Law endure – as do all penalties of the Law for those who remain under the Law. Yet all fall short of the Law's perfect standard (Matt 5:48), so all must rely on God's mercy and Jesus' surpassing righteousness for salvation.

When tested on grounds for divorce, Jesus used the first book of the Law to highlight a clear command on marriage. He gave a definite "No" to divorce: "What therefore God has joined together, let not man separate" (Matt 19:4-6; cf. Gen 2:24). The Pharisees continued their test by asking why Moses permitted divorce (cf. Deut 24:1-4). Jesus then charged them with "hardness of heart" (*sklerokardia*, Matt 19:8). This is usually taken to mean that God permits divorce as a concession to human fallenness. **Here is another common mistake.**

Examining every occurrence in Scripture of "hardness of heart" shows that this rare characterisation is a terminal indictment that attracts certain – deadly – judgement. *This is an irredeemable stubbornness.* It is foolish to follow the divorce practices of those in Moses' time who lived in rebellion to God and never reached the Promised Land. When we see "hardness of heart" as dire judgement, and not as some sort of gracious concession to general sinfulness, we can then better see how

Jesus' sole exception, "sexual immorality," uttered in the one same sentence, also brings dire judgement.

How Matthew uses *apolyo* (a Greek term for "divorce") is also illuminating: elsewhere it has no technical meaning invested in it, suggesting that better attention be paid to its simple verbal use within a marriage context. **"To divorce" simply means "to send away,"** and Israel has been sent away from God and his "house" (Temple / land) before in the Babylonian Exile roughly 500 years prior to Christ. Within a generation of Jesus speaking, Israel will be sent away again, this time for almost 2000 years. No wonder "Babylon" features four times in the opening of the Gospel. Matthew has good news: God will save his people; and bad news: God has just grounds for sending away his unfaithful wife (again).

The 'exception clause' of Matthew 19:9 is best understood not only in relation to the Law, but in its narrative context. Jesus has just spoken on forgiveness, and marriage is the perfect place to practice this! Reading Matthew 19:1-12 in the light of Matthew 18:21-35 reveals that an unpayable debt *to God*, as accrued say by committing adultery, can be forgiven. Thus, any debt *to a spouse* – due to indecency – that the hard-hearted hold as grounds for divorce, should be forgiven too. If divorce is ultimately about an unwillingness to forgive, then no wonder God's anger burns. God rejects those who reject his voice (Heb 3:8, 15; 4:7), who test him and stubbornly rebel against his clear command to hold fast in marriage (Matt 19:4-6; cf. Gen 2:24; Mal 2:16).

God will not forgive those who do not forgive (Matt 6:15; 18:35); he sends away ("divorces") the hard-hearted who send others away. Such people do not truly know God's ways or the Gospel. For the unmerciful and unfaithful, judgement looms, as witnessed by the binding nature of biblical blood covenants, and in the climactic fulfilment of the Hebrew narrative. Critics fear that this understanding will wreak havoc in the church, but it actually offers clear teaching and solid hope. It encourages the humble to examine their own hearts, to repent of all unfaithfulness and bitterness, and to know and show God's mercy.

God desires mercy (steadfast love, compassion, faithfulness). Strikingly, Hosea 6:6 is cited twice by Jesus in Matthew's Gospel (9:13; 12:7), but this verse is found nowhere else in the New Testament. **Mercy requires mercy (Matt 18:33).** The merciful will be united with God forever in his house – a place abounding with love, peace, security and sensational celebration. Such people are blessed with the good news of Jesus and the presence of God eternally.

Note: As the book progresses, more technical language creeps in. Please do not let that deter you! It is vital to wrestle with the original languages of the Bible. If these languages are unknown to you, then you just might learn the meaning of a few key words. Transliteration is given for some Hebrew and Greek terms to make them easier to recognise. (But do not fuss about "proper pronunciation" – the secret is out: no one knows how these words really sounded thousands of years ago!)

* Other related works by the same author:

▸ *Matthew 19:9 – A Deadly Exception; Summary*
A short book that summarises the main thesis. It is written in everyday language, without academic jargon or difficult technical terms. It does not contain any Hebrew or Greek text, although it does explain key Bible words in simple English.

▸ *A Deadly Exception – What Matthew 19:9 Teaches
on Marriage, Divorce, and Babylon*
A comprehensive book covering everything in the main thesis and much more! It delves in depth as to why Matthew records the 'exception clause' (when no one else does), with a special focus on the Judah-Babylon (Exilic) connection – which has plenty to do with the provenance of the Gospel. Some might consider this work more speculative (with too many radical ideas for a dissertation) or more prophetic. It also contains more pastoral application.

CHAPTER 1 – Introduction

In Matthew 19:9, Jesus is recorded as saying,

> Whoever divorces his wife, **except for sexual immorality**, and marries another, commits adultery.[1]

This singular exception of "sexual immorality" (Greek: μὴ ἐπὶ πορνείᾳ[2] [*porneia*][3]) has become a wellspring to justify divorce for "any cause," which is precisely what Jesus countered (Matt 19:3-6). Jesus upholds the permanency of marriage, but when pressed on the matter, many believe that because Jesus allows divorce for one serious offence (here), then he would surely allow it for additional grounds.

However, other Gospels have parallel sayings that are absolute;[4] they offer no exceptions at all:

> Whoever divorces his wife and marries another commits adultery against her. (Mark 10:11)

> Everyone who divorces his wife and marries another commits adultery, and he who marries a woman divorced from her husband commits adultery. (Luke 16:18)

To understand the teaching of the passage that contains Matthew's 'exception clause' (Matt 19:1-12), many perceive that a first-century Jewish debate is in the background, as Richard Hays reflects:

> But what exactly does *porneia* [πορνεία] mean? What is the exception that makes divorce permissible? To ask this question is, of course, to reprise the rabbinic debate about the meaning of 'indecency in anything'.[5]

---

[1] ESV: *The Holy Bible: English Standard Version*, (Wheaton: Crossway, 2002). Unless otherwise noted.

[2] Similarly Matt 5:32, "except on the ground of sexual immorality" (παρεκτὸς λόγου πορνείας).

[3] The English term *pornography* derives from this: *porneia* in graphic form.

[4] Although exceptions, particularly sexual immorality, have regularly been assumed to be implicit. E.g. D. Instone-Brewer, *Divorce and Remarriage in the Bible: The Social and Literary Context* (Grand Rapids: Eerdmans, 2002), 153.

[5] R. Hays, *The Moral Vision of the New Testament* (Edinburgh: T&T Clark, 1996), 354.

Although Pharisees raise the question of divorce with Jesus, a contemporary debate between rabbinic schools is difficult to prove.[6] Hence it may not have influenced the Pharisees' question to Jesus.

Nonetheless, two schools of thought are commonly recognised with competing views on the Hebrew phrase *'erwat dabar* (עֶרְוַת דָּבָר) of Deuteronomy 24:1 in determining grounds for divorce,

> When a man takes a wife and marries her, if then she finds no favor in his eyes because he has found some indecency [*'erwat dabar* (עֶרְוַת דָּבָר)] in her, and he writes her a certificate of divorce and puts it in her hand and sends her out of his house, and she departs out of his house.

One stance, associated with Hillel (a Jewish teacher around Jesus' time),[7] emphasized both terms *'erwah* (עֶרְוָה "indecency") and *dabar* (דָּבָר "a matter"), so that a man might divorce his wife if she offended him in any way. For example, "She burnt my dinner" could be grounds for divorce, and "I found someone else prettier" could be another reason.[8] The man could possibly give no reason at all.[9]

A more conservative stance, associated with Shammai (another contemporary Jewish teacher), interpreted *'erwat dabar* as one concept, where "a matter of indecency" referred only to serious sexual misconduct. This is often taken to mean adultery, which usually had to be proven in court. Yet David Janzen notes that it is hardly clear that "the Shammaites hold the opinion that only adultery suffices for divorce."[10] And what exactly is 'adultery'? Is it limited solely to sexual intercourse? Or did *'erwah* (עֶרְוָה, "indecency" or "nakedness" of Deut 24:1) mean that the wife showed some bare leg, let her hair down, or

---

[6] M. Bockmuehl, "Matthew 5:32, 19:9 in the Light of Pre-Rabbinic Halakhah," *NTS* 35, no. 2 (1989): 291. There is no certainty that Hillel and Shammai were even Pharisees. J. Meier, *A Marginal Jew: Companions and Competitors*, vol. 3 (New York: Doubleday, 2001), 318. A rabbinic debate here "may actually be a prime example of the anachronistic use of later texts to explain earlier ones" (where a fourth-century text is used to elucidate a first-century teaching of Jesus). *A Marginal Jew: Law and Love*, vol. 4 (New Haven: YUP, 2009), 95.

[7] Also Akiba and Josephus. *Ant.* 4.253 (cited: book number, Greek text number). F. Josephus, *The Works of Josephus, Complete and Unabridged*, trans. W. Whiston (1987; repr., 1991), 120.

[8] Cf. *m.Git.* 9:10. J. Neusner, *The Mishnah: A New Translation* (New Haven: YUP, 1988), 487.

[9] Generally a woman could not initiate divorce in OT times.

[10] D. Janzen, "The Meaning of Porneia in Matthew 5.32 and 19.9: An Approach from the Study of Ancient Near Eastern Culture," *JSNT* 80 (2000): 73.

flirted (or simply spoke) with another man? This leaves Janzen to conclude,

> The Shammaites may well have been referring to adultery, although it is difficult to say which particular definition of *'rwh* [עֶרְוָה] they meant; and that is why the claim that the Matthean Jesus' use of *porniea* [πορνεία] put him in agreement with a group of Pharisees is suspect.[11]

The school of Hillel dominated after 70CE, while the school of Shammai was slightly earlier and initially more influential.[12] However, the views of these two pre-70CE leaders and any link with Shammai may have been suppressed by the "ultimate triumph of the Hillelites."[13] David Instone-Brewer writes that "by the second century the Shammaites had almost all disappeared, and the Hillelites had won the day."[14] This thesis will focus on critiquing the Shammaite interpretation, for if the sexual immorality (*porneia*) of the Matthean 'exception clause' is found to not equate with a strict Shammaite understanding then the more liberal Hillelite understanding may be dismissed as well. Given that Jesus forbids divorce and remarriage in the Synoptic parallels to Matthew 5:31-32 (cf. Luke 16:18) and Matthew 19:1-9 (cf. Mark 10:1-12), it is difficult to fathom why Matthew would report that Jesus was openly permissive about the matter.

Today's Protestant "majority view"[15] basically believes that Jesus opposed the popular easy-divorce view of Hillel and supported the stricter view of Shammai (even though we cannot be sure of the details). For instance, William Heth states: "We can be sure that Jesus had the same ground for divorce in mind that the Shammaites did."[16] However, Leon Morris rightly points out a great problem: "This is surely an incorrect understanding of Scripture, for the punishment for adultery was death."[17] The Decalogue clearly prohibits adultery ("You shall not

---

[11] Ibid.

[12] After Shammai and Hillel came Gamaliel I (cf. Acts 5:34) and Simeon I, both of whom Neusner connects with the House [school] of Shammai. J. Neusner, *The Rabbinic Traditions About the Pharisees before 70: The Masters*, vol. 1 (Leden: Brill, 1971), 344-45, 86-87.

[13] Meier, *Marginal Jew*, 3, 378-79.

[14] Instone-Brewer, *Social and Literary Context*, 112.

[15] W. Heth, "Remarriage for Adultery or Desertion," in *Remarriage after Divorce in Today's Church: 3 Views*, ed. M. Strauss, Counterpoints (Grand Rapids: Zondervan, 2006), 59.

[16] Ibid., 70-71.

[17] L. Morris, *The Gospel According to Matthew*, PNTC (Leicester: IVP, 1992), 120.

commit adultery," Exod 20:14; Deut 5:18), and Mosaic legal codes plainly prescribe the death penalty:

> If a man commits adultery with the wife of his neighbor, both the adulterer and the adulteress shall surely be put to death. (Lev 20:10)

> If a man is found lying with the wife of another man, both of them shall die, the man who lay with the woman, and the woman. So you shall purge the evil from Israel. (Deut 22:22)

Equating "sexual immorality" (Matt 19:9) with "a matter of indecency" (Deut 24:1) is therefore highly problematic because it confuses capital and non-capital offences of the Old Testament (the "matter of indecency" in Deut 24:1 is clearly not treated as capital).

In an attempt to solve the problem, Protestant Reformers such as Martin Luther and John Calvin settled for a metaphorical death to allow remarriage (**i.e. pretend your spouse is dead!**),

> The temporal sword and government should therefore still put adulterers to death, for whoever commits adultery has in fact himself already departed and is considered as one dead. Therefore, the other [innocent party] may remarry just as though his spouse had died.[18]

This meant that the person one had promised to love in sickness and in health, 'until death do us part', could effectively be treated forevermore as an untouchable leper!

Would Jesus really have taught anything like this? Deep down this does not resonate with the characteristic great love and compassion of Jesus, nor is it true to our wedding vows. Current views need testing, for they tend to skirt true death and true reconciliation.

Determining the "innocent party" is also an ancient problem.[19] Many today have settled for 'no-fault' divorce, believing that this might make matters easier. However, marital breakdown appears greater than ever before and no less hurtful. *With confusing grounds and the almost impossible task of deciding guilt or innocence, a completely different direction may be in order.*

---

[18] M. Luther, *The Christian in Society, the Estate of Marriage, Part 2, Luther's Works,* vol. 45, 32.

[19] "Even Origen realized that adultery can sometimes be blamed on the partner who refused conjugal rights rather than on the partner who was unfaithful." Instone-Brewer, *Social and Literary Context,* 286.

CHAPTER 2 – Christian Views

Christian views on divorce vary widely but coalesce around four main positions all claiming scriptural authority. Only the fundamentals of these extensive positions will be covered here, with key conflicts and gaps noted. It is the third position that comes under most scrutiny, but they all have a common legal fault that needs addressing.[1]

1. No Divorce Permitted

In the first view under consideration, marriage is seen as a permanent or indissoluble union that can be broken only by death.[2] "Indissolubility of the bond (*vinculum*)" has served more recently in Roman Catholic doctrine as a rigid theological foundation for this position.[3] Against newly established Reformation views, the Council of Trent in 1563 affirmed marriage's sacramental character, stipulating that "the bond of marriage cannot be dissolved by the adultery of one of the married parties" and that neither spouse, even the "innocent one," can contract another marriage while their spouse is still living without committing adultery.[4] In particular, every *ratum et consummatum* (consummated baptised believers') marriage is considered indissoluble.

Kenneth Himes and James Coriden find that the early Christian writers insisted on the permanence of marriage, but the language of "indissolubility" is neither biblical nor patristic.[5] Even so, Ulrich Luz, a Protestant scholar, maintains that the almost unanimous history of interpretation in the ancient church speaks for the Catholic interpretation, where

---

[1] This is not a full-orbed review, but mainly a critique of how each view relates to the Law.

[2] A 'marriage' or marriage-like union may be declared invalid under the Catholic practice of annulment, but this is a separate issue for it is deemed that no marriage, and thus no divorce, has taken place.

[3] According to Himes, a specialist in Catholic social teaching, and Coriden, a professor in canon law, "The first time that the term 'indissoluble' was employed... in official teaching was at the 16th-century Council of Trent in the doctrine and canons on the sacrament of marriage." K. Himes and J. Coriden, "The Indissolubility of Marriage: Reasons to Reconsider," *Theological Studies* 65, no. 3 (2004): 457-58.

[4] Anyone promoting a contrary position was anathematised. N. Tanner, *Decrees of the Ecumenical Councils: Trent to Vatican 2*, vol. 2 (London: Sheed & Ward, 1990), 754-55.

[5] Himes and Coriden, "Indissolubility," 457-58.

The 'divorce' of the wife in the case of adultery is for all practical purposes a 'separation'. In such a case the husband must send his wife away. This Matthean possibility of separation, however, is completely different from the Jewish divorce whose purpose is to make remarriage possible. …marriage is part of the created order and reflects "Adam's" primal existence (Gen 1:27), and as such it may not be annulled. It remains indissoluble, even when the husband must send his wife away because of unchastity.[6]

Luz accepts that this separation was not normal Jewish practice, but it did become normal Christian practice for centuries. Himes and Coriden explain the historical basis, pinpointing Jerome's "eisegesis" that influenced Augustine's treatment of the Gospel text, where Jerome upheld the ban on divorce *and* the Matthean 'exception clause':

His [Jerome's] solution was to insist that what was being considered in the exceptive clause was not divorce, and certainly not remarriage, but separation from bed and board without divorce. There is, of course, no basis for such an assumption and a notion of permanent separation without divorce would have made no sense to a first-century Jew.[7]

Contra Himes and Coriden, this type of separation does match select instances of divorce in Scripture, such as the case in 1 Corinthians 7:10-11 where a separated wife "should remain unmarried or else be reconciled to her husband." It also hardly accounts for the response of Jesus' disciples, questioning marriage altogether (Matt 19:10).

It remains doubtful on a practical level that marriages are "indissoluble." In everyday life and by all human measures, marriages disappear and new unions are established. The same was true in Jesus' social context, as the account of the Samaritan woman who had five previous husbands makes clear (cf. John 4:18). Heth writes,

As many have observed, Jesus' statement, "Therefore what God has joined together, let man not separate" (Matt. 19:6), does *not* mean "no one *can* separate," but rather it means "it *is* possible to separate, but you should not."[8]

The Pharisees' question on divorce is not "Is it possible…?" (which could be answered with "No, because marriage is indissoluble"), but "Is

---

[6] U. Luz, *Matthew 8-20: A Commentary*, Hermeneia (Minneapolis: Fortress, 2001), 494.

[7] Himes and Coriden, "Indissolubility," 470. For more on the historical development see: T. Mackin, *Divorce and Remarriage*, Marriage in the Catholic Church (New York: Paulist, 1984), 187-223.

[8] Heth, "Remarriage for Adultery or Desertion," 62. (Italics original.)

it lawful...?" (Matt 19:3; cf. Mark 10:2). This presents a specific legal probe where what is ruled unlawful must be entirely possible – just as murder, theft, adultery, and other transgressions are all unlawful but possible. If no one committed these offenses, why have laws governing impossible activities? Laws are routinely broken – many very easily, including capital ones – and Israel has a long history of violating the Law.

A Matthean question on "any cause" might still be met with "No cause is lawful," but even then, unlawful causes can be found that are possible and probable. The surprise here is that succeeding what appears to be an absolute "No" from Jesus (Matt 19:4-6), there is a single affirmative: "except for sexual immorality" (Matt 19:9). This lawful cause should be assessed in terms of the Law itself,[9] not philosophically rejected outright as impossible.

J. Carl Laney champions an evangelical 'no divorce' position, but prefers the covenantal language of permanency and a "lasting one-flesh union which does not terminate with divorce."[10] He rejects the common evangelical view that equates the "sexual immorality" of Matthew 5:32 and 19:9 with "adultery,"[11] seeing that πορνεία is not the normal word for "adultery" (μοιχεία) and that Matthew makes a distinction between the two (Matt 15:19).[12] However, Laney does not then accept a broader view of πορνεία, for he fears that Jesus would be taking a more lenient stance than Shammai, and "internal contradictions in Matthew's text" would result.[13] Instead, Laney takes πορνεία in "a specialized sense to refer to incestuous marriage"[14] – but this is an unlawful union, so the Matthean 'exception' cannot be a real exception at all.

In a similar manner, Ben Witherington III undermines his own proposition that πορνεία means incest. He strives to "recognize that in Mt 5.32, as in Mt 19.9, we have a real exception, whatever the meaning

---

[9] This includes upholding every legal implication (every demand, small or dire, for covenant violation), without abolishing the least part.

[10] J. C. Laney, "No Divorce & No Remarriage," in *Divorce and Remarriage: Four Christian Views*, ed. H. W. House (Downers Grove: IVP, 1990), 24. See also J. Boice, *The Gospel of Matthew* (Grand Rapids: Baker, 2001). A. Cornes, *Divorce and Remarriage: Biblical Principles and Pastoral Practice* (Grand Rapids: Eerdmans, 1993). J. D. Pentecost, *The Words and Works of Jesus Christ* (Grand Rapids: Zondervan, 1981). J. Piper, "Divorce and Remarriage," (Minneapolis: Bethlehem Baptist Church, 1986). C. Ryrie, "Biblical Teaching on Divorce and Remarriage," *GTJ* 3, no. 2 (1982).

[11] Laney, "No Divorce & No Remarriage," 34.

[12] Ibid.

[13] Ibid.

[14] Ibid.

of πορνεία might be."[15] Yet he later concedes that his view does not even recognise that Jesus addresses *lawful marriage*, for "Marriages which violate God's laws in relation to human relations are not true marriages, since God has not joined them together."[16] There can be no real divorce if there is no "real marriage,"[17] for it would only be a separation of what God *has not joined together*. Hays' rebuttal is that this position, favoured particularly by Catholic interpreters,

> has much to commend it in terms of what it affirms (...*porneia* can refer to incestuous marriage), but is problematical in what it denies (...adultery might also constitute legitimate grounds for divorce under the Matthean exception clause).[18]

In terms of application, this first view appears to be "an absolute prohibition of divorce no matter what the circumstances," which makes Heth question if Laney would strictly enforce it were a husband to beat his wife or commit incest with the children.[19] The narrow interpretation is also dubious because its main proof text (Lev 18:16-18) relates to *illicit sex* rather than to "incestuous marriage." Thomas Edgar well refutes the position and highlights that "incestuous marriage" cannot simply be a Jewish challenge, relevant solely to Matthew's main audience.[20] Indeed, Matthew's Jewish audience, presumably familiar with the Torah's prohibition of incest, would hardly need a reminder. If this was the sole intended meaning of πορνεία, one might wonder why the 'exception clause' is absent from the divorce texts of Mark and Luke when incest was also a large Gentile problem.

A logical flaw also appears in the "incestuous marriage" view in that the husband (or "male partner," if this is not really marriage) would be held innocent in Matthew 19:9.

---

[15] B. Witherington III, "Matthew 5:32 and 19:9 - Exception or Exceptional Situation," *NTS* 31, no. 4 (1985): 571.

[16] Ibid., 574.

[17] "Jesus, at least according to Matthew, acknowledged that some marriages were not real marriages." L. W. Countryman, *Dirt, Greed and Sex: Sexual Ethics in the New Testament and Their Implications for Today* (London: SCM, 1989), 261. Countryman's approach is similar to Witherington's, but he sees the Matthean 'exception clause' as referring to pre-marital sex, noting that if a woman "were not a virgin, she would not be suitable for marriage." (ibid., 158.) This is an extreme understatement for he has just noted the lawful death penalty for pre-marital sexual offences (Deut 22:23-27) but neglects to apply this to the Matthean 'exception clause'.

[18] Hays, *Moral Vision*, 355.

[19] W. Heth, "Divorce, but No Remarriage," in *Divorce and Remarriage: Four Christian Views*, ed. H. W. House (Downers Grove: IVP, 1990), 59.

[20] T. Edgar, "Divorce & Remarriage for Adultery or Desertion," ibid., 177-87. See also Janzen, "Porneia," 69-70. C. Blomberg, "Marriage, Divorce, Remarriage, and Celibacy: An Exegesis of Matthew 19:3-12," *Trinity Journal* 11, no. 2 (1990): 176-77.

The tone of the passage implies that because the wife is guilty
of *porneia*, the husband who divorces her is blameless, but in
an incestuous marriage both would be guilty.[21]

Here Edgar does not carry his good Old Testament contextualisation
to its full scriptural conclusion however. Incest certainly constitutes one
case of πορνεία, but mere "divorce" or "separation" *from each other* is
not the lawful demand. All who commit the incestuous acts of Leviticus
18:6-18 "shall be cut off from among their people" (Lev 18:29).[22] This
means execution (cf. Lev 20:11-14) or extirpation,[23] and such practices
pollute the land, inducing national expulsion.[24] In claiming that πορεία
must mean "adultery" instead of "incestuous marriage," Edgar also does
not carry his fine Old Testament analysis to its logical end. As with
incest, the penalty for adultery is not divorce with a freedom to remarry,
but far more grievous. Furthermore, there are no convincing reasons
why πορνεία cannot refer to other capital sexual offences along with
adultery.

In summary, while the permanency of marriage is to be expected,
the concept of "indissolubility" is questionable. It is also now generally
accepted that covenants can be broken,[25] but are the covenants then
"dissolved"? Closer attention needs to be paid to covenant stipulations
for any violation. Finally, Matthew 19:9 most naturally provides a real
exception for a valid marriage.

---

[21] Edgar, "Divorce & Remarriage for Adultery or Desertion," 178.

[22] Cf. Lev 7:20, "The precise nature of the punishment... is no longer known."
Nonetheless, "this phraseology depicts one of the worst fates for a person who has been a
member of the covenant community." J. Hartley, *Leviticus*, ed. J. Watts, WBC (Dallas: Word,
1992). Kiuchi considers the absolute isolation "virtually no different for the offender from
the death penalty." N. Kiuchi, *Leviticus*, ed. D. Baker and G. Wenham, AOTC (Nottingham:
Apollos, 2007), 140.

[23] J. Milgrom, *Leviticus: A Book of Ritual and Ethics*, Continental Commentary
(Minneapolis: Fortress, 2004), 66.

[24] "Progressive pollution of the land ultimately leads to its regurgitation of the pollution
together with its inhabitants." Ibid., 211.

[25] "Covenants may be both violated and dissolved" premises the Protestant majority
view. W. Heth, "Jesus on Divorce: How My Mind Has Changed," *SBJOT* 6, no. 1 (2002): 6.

2. Divorce with No Remarriage Permitted

According to this view, divorce is a separation or full severance that bears no freedom to remarry. Following the approach of Henri Crouzel,[26] Jacques Dupont,[27] and Quentin Quesnell,[28] Gordon Wenham believes, "On the no-remarriage view, Jesus always means 'separate' when he uses *apolyein*."[29] This separation is possible and (usually) permissible as a concession to fallen humanity, but not desirable.[30]

Wenham restricts the application of the Matthean 'exception clause' such that πορεία (*porneia*) only warrants divorce but never remarriage. He recasts Jesus' teaching in Matthew as:

(i) Divorce plus remarriage equals adultery (5:32b; cf. Mark 10:11-12; Luke 16:18);
(ii) Divorce alone (except for πορνεία) equals adultery (5:32a); and in combining these,
(iii) Divorce (except for πορνεία) plus remarriage equals adultery (19:9).[31]

However, Wenham's "exegetical gymnastics"[32] here are awkward to say the least. Edgar regards this interpretation as "grammatically impossible," and after making this charge three times on the one page, he further judges that Wenham

> makes the grammatically and logically impossible claim that Matthew 19:9 (and 5:32) can be divided into two propositions: (A) to divorce except for *porniea* is adulterous and (B) to divorce and remarry is adulterous.[33]

---

[26] H. Crouzel, *L'eglise Primitive Face Au Divorce* (Paris: Beauchesne, 1971).

[27] J. Dupont, *Mariage Et Divorce Dans L'evangile. Matthieu 19, 3-12 Et Parrallèles* (Bruges: Desclée de Brouwer, 1959).

[28] Q. Quesnell, "'Made Themselves Eunuchs for the Kingdom of Heaven' (Mt 19.12)," *CBQ* 30 (1968): 335-58.

[29] G. Wenham, "No Remarriage after Divorce," in *Remarriage after Divorce in Today's Church: 3 Views*, ed. M. Strauss, Counterpoints (Grand Rapids: Zondervan, 2006), 88. Also G. Bromiley, *God and Marriage* (Grand Rapids: Eerdmans, 1980), 44-45. This overlaps the no-divorce view, especially if separation without a right to remarry is not seen as full divorce, or the separation is of an illicit union.

[30] The main distinction from the 'no divorce' view is that here divorce is possible, even if discouraged. Some (not Wenham) interpret the "hate" in Mal 2:16 as God's absolute prohibition of divorce.

[31] G. Wenham, "Does the New Testament Approve Remarriage after Divorce?," *SBJOT* 6, no. 1 (2002): 36.

[32] Witherington III, "Exception or Exceptional," 571.

[33] Edgar, "Divorce & Remarriage for Adultery or Desertion," 157.

Notwithstanding Wenham's strained syntactical argument, the 'no-remarriage' position has enjoyed majority support for the major part of church history.[34] Wenham writes,

> It is my contention that, in their original context, all the Gospel divorce texts should be understood as condemning remarriage after divorce. ...Among the Greek-speaking fathers both pre- and post-Constantine there is total unanimity. ...The evidence of the Latin fathers is equally impressive. There is only one dissenting voice in the West, who cannot be identified, but... totally ignored by subsequent fifth-century Latin writers. ...The witness of the early church thus points unequivocally to a no-remarriage understanding of the Gospel divorce texts.[35]

Wenham acknowledges a first-century cultural assumption that divorce provided a freedom to remarry, and that the Old Testament tolerated divorce and remarriage, but remains unconvinced by the "Evangelical Consensus"[36] that sexual immorality dissolves a marriage to permit remarriage. He provides three compelling lines of argument:

(i) Multiple dispute stories count against Jesus only teaching contemporary beliefs;
(ii) The Pharisees try to prove that Jesus deviated from their reading of Moses; and
(iii) Even interpreters who hold that Jesus permitted remarriage after divorce for sexual immorality admit that he did not always allow remarriage.[37]

On this third point, Wenham (along with Murray[38]) shows that according to Matthew 19:9, Jesus expressly rejects remarriage after divorce for "non-πορνεία": "not even the husband is free to remarry without committing adultery."[39] Thus it simply cannot be true "that *apolyein always* means 'divorce with the right to remarry'."[40] He extends Jesus' argument that remarrying after divorce is equivalent to

---

[34] The 'no-divorce' position is backed by the same consistent witness of church fathers.
[35] Wenham, "Remarriage?," 30-31.
[36] Heth, "Jesus on Divorce," 9-10.
[37] Wenham, "Remarriage?," 33-34.
[38] J. Murray, *Divorce* (Phillipsburg: Presbyterian & Reformed, 1961), 25.
[39] Wenham, "No Remarriage," 34. If a wife separates, she must remain unmarried or reconcile (cf. 1 Cor 7:10-11).
[40]Ibid.

committing adultery even to the case where the spouse has been legitimately divorced for committing *porneia*. This contrasts with contemporary ways that encourage, even mandate, divorce for these most grievous grounds and that permit remarriage.[41]

Wenham perceives a problem with the cultural norm,

> According to Jewish law, "the essential formula in the bill of divorce is 'Lo, thou art free to marry any man'" (*m. Git 9:3*). The implication of Jesus' pronouncement is that the essential declaration in the divorce formula does not work. A woman is *not* free to marry any man after divorce. If she does, she commits adultery.[42]

Jesus rejects the normal divorce tradition! Jesus' pronouncement implies that a divorce certificate originally did not confer a right to remarry, but Deuteronomy 24:1 demonstrates how it assumed this authority. This is despite the fact that adultery was committed with this cultural practice, which Jesus makes explicit in the first century – when the divorce certificate was still thought to carry such authority. However, a right to remarry would *always ensue* whenever the capital demands of the Law were fully applied to cases of sexual immorality, including adultery, even though in Jesus' day there may have been no ability or inclination to carry out the capital sentence enshrined in the biblical law codes.

Markus Bockmuehl commends Wenham's exegetical analyses of the Matthean divorce texts, but rather than supporting divorce with no freedom to remarry, sees this

> as supporting a divorce only *a mensa et thoro*; this (and the hope for repentance and reconciliation) is also the preferred reading of the fathers beginning with Justin (*Apol* II 2) and Hermas (Mand. iv 1.6).[43]

Bockmuehl notes a patristic trend against second marriage in general (even after the death of a spouse) as a possible related matter, present in Origen, Tertullian and others, and scripturally implied at least for church officers and widows (1 Tim 3:2, 12; 5:9-12; Titus 1:6 cf. Lev 21:13-15; Luke 2:36-37).[44] Bockmuehl finds additional evidence for a required divorce for adultery (and rape) in his study of 1QapGen 20.15, but concludes that it is not definitive as to how Matthew's church dealt

---

[41] D. Instone-Brewer, *Divorce and Remarriage in the 1st and 21st Century* (Cambridge: Grove, 2001), 7.

[42] Wenham, "No Remarriage," 26.

[43] Bockmuehl, "Halakhah," 295.

[44] Ibid.

with it. He does find it clear, however, that Matthew's Gospel is indebted to this pre-rabbinic exegetical tradition, where *porneia* "makes husband and wife unfit for continued conjugal union."[45] Other "probable support" is found in Proverbs 18:22, "He that puts away a good wife puts away a good thing, and he that keeps an adulteress is foolish and ungodly" (LXX, omitted in the MT), and Matthew 1:19 (Joseph's resolution to divorce his betrothed) that Tertullian, Origen, Ephrem and other early writers often cite as requiring separation though not divorce.[46]

On Deuteronomy 24:1-4, Bockmuehl shows that the state of a remarried woman in relation to her first husband is described using the same term for defilement (טָמֵא) that Leviticus 18:20 applies to cases of adultery (cf. Num 5:13, 14, and 20). This suggests the impossibility of restoring a disrupted first union after remarriage (cf. Jer 3:1; Ezek 16:38, 40),[47] and points to a serious matter of "sexual immorality" (cf. *porneia*, Matt 19:9) that was forbidden under Moses, as distinct from another "matter of indecency" that was permitted (cf. *'erwat dabar*, Deut 24:1). That there were stricter regulations for priests (Lev 21:7, 13-15) bolsters the seriousness of this defilement, along with more generally "the prescribed... death penalty for adultery" (Lev 20:10; Deut 22.22; cf. Ezek 16.38, 40; John 8:5).[48]

In summary, that the Matthean 'exception clause' only allows for divorce but not remarriage is determined more by theology than rules of Greek language construction. Traditionally, divorce always provides a right to remarry, but Jesus rejected this. Early Christianity held a no-remarriage view for hundreds of years. Although the death penalty is acknowledged for adultery "(though *apparently* rarely enforced),"[49] divorce for sexual immorality (*porneia*) could also point to a separation that supporters of this position have not yet contemplated: a separation by death that does allow for remarriage.

---

[45] Ibid.
[46] Ibid., 292. See also Crouzel, *L'eglise*, 47-51.
[47] Bockmuehl, "Halakhah," 292.
[48] Ibid., 292-93.
[49] Ibid., 293.

3. Divorce for Adultery or Abandonment

The third view considered assumes that in keeping with Jewish, Roman, and Greek culture, divorce provides a freedom to remarry. Bockmuehl cites "rabbinic injunctions *prescribing* divorce in case of infidelity."[50] Under Roman law, divorce was mandated for adultery,[51] although Instone-Brewer holds that

> divorce for adultery did not become compulsory, even among the rabbis, till after 70 C.E. when the rite of the suspected adulteress fell into disuse.[52]

The church long prohibited remarriage, but it became popular Protestant practice from the time of Desiderius Erasmus. In the Reformed tradition, adultery or deliberate desertion are "sufficient reason for dissolving the bond of marriage"; the innocent may remarry *and the guilty party treated as if dead.*[53] Heth rightly denounces such "legal-fiction exegesis."[54] This crafty commutation of the Old Testament death penalty clutches at the Law's severity, but nevertheless relaxes the written legal requirements. It also subverts Matthew's purpose.

Calvin realised the gravity of the Matthew 19:9 'exception clause' but his application, lamenting woeful magistrates who would not implement capital punishment,[55] will not be followed in this thesis. Heth, once a champion of the no-remarriage position in everything he published from 1982 to 1997 (including a joint publication with Wenham[56]), changed to support "the majority view among evangelicals today" advocating "two grounds that would permit divorce and remarriage, namely, marital unfaithfulness and desertion by an unbeliever."[57] The weight of the 'Evangelical consensus' helped convince him, along with pastoral concern for the "innocent parties" of divorce. A narrow understanding of "sexual immorality" (such as

---

[50] Ibid., 292. (Italics original.)

[51] The *lex Julia de maritandis de ordinibus* 18BCE and *lex Papia Poaea nuptialis* 9BCE. Instone-Brewer, *1st and 21st Century*, 7.

[52] *Social and Literary Context*, 272.

[53] D. Milne, *The Westminster Confession of Faith for the 21st Century* (Strawberry Hills: PCA, 2001), 43-44.

[54] Heth, "Divorce, but No Remarriage," 110.

[55] J. Calvin, *A Harmony of the Gospels: Matthew, Mark and Luke*, vol. II, Calvin's Commentaries (Grand Rapids: Eerdmans, 1972), 247.

[56] G. Wenham and W. Heth, *Jesus and Divorce*, BTCL (Carlisle: Paternoster, 1984; repr., 1997).

[57] Heth, "Remarriage for Adultery or Desertion," 59.

incest) involving a specific situation in Matthew's church proved to be "no longer a viable interpretive option."[58]

However, the Protestant majority view[59] that equates the "sexual immorality" (*porneia*) of Matthew 19:9 with "a matter of indecency" (*'erwat dabar*) in Deuteronomy 24:1 also has viability problems. Other biblical commandments condemn adultery as a capital offence (Lev 20:10; Deut 22:23-24; cf. Jer 29:23), without any lighter alternative of divorce and remarriage, and it seems unlikely that Matthew would have used the term *porneia* for a lighter "matter of indecency" rather than a serious legal offence such as adultery. Richard Davidson, knowing that the Law would be conflicted in commanding capital punishment *or* permitting the writing of a divorce certificate *for the same crime*, distinguishes between offences:

> Since adultery (and other illicit sexual intercourse), however, receives the death penalty (or that of being "cut-off" from the congregation) according to the law (Deut 22:22; Lev 20:10-18), the indecent exposure referred to here in Deut 24:1 must be something short of these sexual activities.[60]

This only raises more problems, for if "a matter of indecency" is an offence short of adultery, then how far short? Does adultery or any other serious sexual offence then *not* provide grounds for divorce and remarriage? Davidson rightly recognises the death penalty for illicit sex, yet he makes no connection of the illicit sex mentioned in Matthew 19:9 with the Law's capital meanings. Why must "sexual immorality" even be a matter short of adultery, let alone short of other sex acts that belong to the category of *porneia* that are capital offences? In Matthew 19:9, if Jesus intended to specify sexual offences in the same order as adultery, then is not *porneia* the best word to use? ***What better word should he have used?***

Along with the theological problems, the pastoral dilemmas with the current Protestant majority view are great. Craig Keener confesses,

---

[58] "Jesus on Divorce," 5.

[59] Other proponents of this view include J. Adams, *Marriage, Divorce and Remarriage in the Bible* (Grand Rapids: Zondervan, 1980). C. Blomberg, *Matthew* (Nashville: Broadman, 1992). J. MacArthur, *Matthew 16-23*, The Macarthur New Testament Commentary (Chicago: Moody, 1988). P. Wiebe, "Jesus' Divorce Exception," *JETS*, no. 32/3 Sept (1989): 327-33. D. Pao, "Adultery, Divorce, and the Hard-Hearted People of God: The Function of the Matthean Exception Clause (Matt 19:9) in Its Literary Context," *Paradosis: A Journal of Bible and Theology* 1 (2014): 70.

[60] R. Davidson, *Flame of Yahweh: Sexuality in the Old Testament* (Peabody: Hendrickson, 2007), 391.

The lack of absolute certainty on where best to draw the line in some cases is an admitted problem of my position, one I feel keenly. Yet this is often a problem when we must move from explaining the original meaning of biblical passages to applying them to unexpected situations today. ...I wish these exceptions were much rarer than they are today.[61]

Heth and Keener concede there are problems knowing "where best to draw the line," but this is not only for "tragic marriage situations,"[62] "extreme examples," or "unexpected situations."[63] There are widespread difficulties in assuming that "sexual immorality" (Matt 19:9) equals "a matter of indecency" (Deut 24:1), for "indecency" is so nebulous. It could mean just about anything! In ancient times, it seems to have meant whatever a husband wanted it to mean, and the wife who was divorced for it had no right of reply.

However, in "the original meaning of biblical passages," the Law offers no "lack of absolute certainty on where best to draw the line." "Adultery" is never a trivial offence,[64] nor are other instances of illicit sex. Jesus provides absolute certainty too: "What therefore God has joined together, let not man separate" (Matt 19:6).

In summary, treating an ex-spouse "as if dead" is completely at odds with Matthew's narrative context of mercy and forgiveness. A right to remarry presumes that Jesus agreed with the culture, and goes against centuries of early Christian practice. There is also a troubling lack of clarity on the grounds for divorce,[65] and perhaps an impossibility in determining the "innocent party."[66] Crucially, equating "sexual immorality" or "adultery" (Matt 19:9) with "a matter of indecency" (Deut 24:1) jars with the extreme penalty in the Law for illicit sex: death.

---

[61] C. Keener, "Remarriage for Adultery, Desertion, or Abuse," in *Remarriage after Divorce in Today's Church: 3 Views*, ed. M. Strauss, Counterpoints (Grand Rapids: Zondervan, 2006), 115.

[62] Heth, "Remarriage for Adultery or Desertion," 130-31.

[63] Keener, "Remarriage for Adultery, Desertion, or Abuse," 115.

[64] Roberts reasons that the first husband who divorced his wife in Deut 24:1 "must have dismissed her for trivial reasons, as proved by the fact that he later wanted to marry her." B. Roberts, *Not under Bondage: Biblical Divorce for Abuse, Adultery and Desertion* (Ballarat: Maschil, 2008), 67-68.

[65] E.g. can "adultery" be committed by flirting, or only by sexual intercourse? Can "desertion" include emotional neglect and lack of financial support, or only physical abandonment?

[66] Instone-Brewer, *Social and Literary Context*, 286.

4. Divorce for a Variety of Reasons

Some cautiously move beyond the Protestant majority view, with its two standard grounds for divorce (i.e. adultery and abandonment), by appealing to Scripture to include abuse (which could otherwise be grouped under 'abandonment') and additional serious offences.[67] For others, the key interpretative framework significantly shifts from the text to (purported) scriptural trajectories and situational ethics.[68] For example, despite warning against being ill-swayed by sympathy for hurting people, Larry Richards' introductory personal anecdotes of a neighbour with an abusive husband and another nearby home with suspected child sexual abuse signals a certain bias, however compassionate.[69] Restudy of the topic of divorce after repeated requests from a leader of a Bible study group that included young women undergoing divorce, also suggests that Richards' change from "a relatively hard line on divorce and remarriage" might not be primarily driven by what "Scripture teaches."[70]

Richards rightly sees that "Is it lawful...?" (Matt 19:3) was "the issue that consumed the attention of the Pharisees," where this "group of dedicated Jewish men was committed to keep each and every statute of the Mosaic Code."[71] However, it was not that "The Pharisees asked the wrong question," as Richards asserts,[72] for to note this first is to jump to pastoral concerns without doing full justice to the actual question asked. It also overlooks that it could equally be said of Jesus and his disciples that this "group of dedicated Jewish men was committed to keep each and every statute of the Mosaic code" (cf. Matt 5:17-20).

Richards' approach denigrates the Law as a legalistic *"lowered standard"* indicative of God's accommodation to humanity's weaknesses,[73] but a better approach recognises that Jesus completely upheld the Law as God's good and perfect standard. In the conversation that follows Matthew 19:3, Jesus might (indirectly) address the

---

[67] Keener, "Remarriage for Adultery, Desertion, or Abuse." *And Marries Another: Divorce and Remarriage in the Teaching of the New Testament* (Peabody: Hendrickson, 1991).

[68] A proponent of this very open position is J. Sprinkle, "Old Testament Perspectives on Divorce and Remarriage," *JETS* 40, no. 4 (1997): 529-50.

[69] L. Richards, "Divorce and Remarriage under a Variety of Circumstances," in *Divorce and Remarriage: Four Christian Views*, ed. H. W. House (Downers Grove: IVP, 1990), 216-17.

[70] Ibid., 237-38.

[71] Ibid., 221.

[72] Ibid.

[73] Ibid., 223. (Italics original.)

problems that Richards raises of "spiritual pride" and the "shallowness of every Pharisee-like approach to faith," but to say that his intent was "to dispose of their legalism"[74] suggests that Jesus was not interested in legalities. Yet Jesus does not condemn the Pharisees for "strict obedience" to the Law, which could be termed "legalism" in a non-pejorative sense, but only their selective hypocritical practice of it (cf. Matt 23:23).

Richards confirms the sinfulness of divorce,

> Jesus makes it clear that, while it is permissible to divorce, it is not *righteous*. …In view of God's ultimate standard for us, divorce, while permissible, is still sin. And remarriage, while permissible, involves an act which measured against the ideal must be acknowledged as adultery.[75]

Matthew does not, however, make it clear that divorce is "not *righteous*," for it would not have been "sin" for Joseph, a righteous man, to divorce Mary (Matt 1:19). The Old Testament also pictures God as righteously divorcing, or at least having a right to divorce (cf. Isa 50:1; Jer 3:8; Hos 2:2). For capital offences, in particular sexually immoral acts, Jesus certainly makes it clear that divorce can be righteous and lawful. Yet divorce "is still sin" for trivial grounds, such as those that may have been cited in relation to Deuteronomy 24:1-4.

Richards acknowledges the Law's capital implications,

> On the one hand, the Law's penalty for adultery is death by stoning, not divorce (Lev 20:10). On the other hand, the way to treat a wayward spouse, as illustrated by God's treatment of adulterous Israel and Hosea's treatment of his adulterous wife, Gomer, is to seek reconciliation (see Hos 1, 11). Adultery may be grounds for forgiveness, but it is not grounds for divorce![76]

This points in a good direction, for Scripture, particularly the book of Hosea and Jesus' teaching, certainly presents mercy as more desirable than capital punishment, and this is especially so for the guilty party! Waywardness, whether of a capital nature or not, never necessitates divorce if forgiveness is sought and mercy granted. If, however, forgiveness for an act such as adultery is not sought, then the Law's death penalty could in itself be considered "divorce," where the judgement involves sending away the guilty party to destruction. This

---

[74] Ibid., 221.
[75] Ibid., 233. (Italics original.)
[76] Ibid., 229.

concept will be investigated to see if it biblically applies to judgement for sexual offences both on a personal and a national level. If so, then divorce *can be righteous* (contra Richards), and this includes the ultimate manner in which God deals with an adulterous wife (Israel) who stubbornly spurns reconciliation.

Richards flatly rejects that adultery is on par with the "sexual immorality" of Matthew 19:9, but his position suffers for he never clearly defines "sexually immorality." Despite citing one old (1975) New Testament dictionary that provides a sufficient semantic range for *porneia*, and ignoring other scholars who provide solid reasons for favouring one definition, Richards concludes "Actually, attempts to define *porneia* do not seem to help us clarify Jesus' meaning"![77] He settles merely with,

> But since we cannot be sure what *porneia* involves, it is best
> to affirm that any divorce involves sin. And that any
> remarriage involves an act of adultery.[78]

With a nebulous idea of "sexual immorality" and an admission of "adultery" for any remarriage, Richards evades serious matters of the Law in support of a direction that he believes is unrighteous and yet excusable. If remarriage is permissible but involves an act that "must be acknowledged as adultery" (as Richards contends), the Law's grave prohibition of "Do not commit adultery" which Jesus has reinforced in Matthew 5:27 would surely apply.

Instead, Richards reframes Jesus' teaching basically as a call "to confess our failure," "not to assume that divorce and remarriage are trivial things," but "in this age of grace" to commit adultery anyway:

> The physical consummation of the new union may technically
> and in reality be an adulterous act. In such a case it must be
> acknowledged as sin and dealt with as sin. It must be brought
> to the Lord in confession, with the expectation that the Lord
> will keep his promise and forgive.[79]

It is not that adultery is unforgivable, but **would Jesus really teach anyone to act unrighteously and to sin wilfully (*commit adultery!*) with the expectation that God will simply forgive?** Richards' revisionist reinterpretation consciously relaxes Jesus' commands on marriage. His view, built on vague grounds for divorce, contradicts the

---

[77] Ibid., 231.
[78] Ibid., 233.
[79] Ibid., 236.

text that treats adultery as a serious offence to be avoided at all costs (cf. Matt 5:27-30).

Such a position, driven by pastoral concerns, tends to privilege a personal dimension over the spiritual dimension of sexual offences. Yet we are dealing with no mere earthly matter, for in Scripture

> adultery is defined not primarily as a private matter, a sin against the spouse, but was regarded as an absolute wrong, a sin against God.[80]

Jesus would not endorse any wilful act of adultery – any great evil that is a direct sin against God (see Joseph's words to Potiphar's wife, Gen 39:9; and David's prayer, Ps 51:4) – with or without a presumption of forgiveness. This is seen especially so when Jesus judges his generation as "evil and adulterous" (Matt 12:39; 16:4).

In summary, instead of inspiring believers to flee from evil and adultery at all costs (cf. Matt 5:27-30; 1 Cor 6:18), this position on divorce downplays the gravity of sexual sin, and presumes upon the grace of God. Grounds for divorce are highly subjective, with even greater questions than the current Protestant majority view on where to draw the line. It is a logical extension of that view however, except now there is little or no attempt to characterise some divorces as righteous: they all are sinful, but simply excusable.

A New – or An Old – Interpretative Direction

Luz notes that Matthew attaches no importance to a rabbinic debate based on Deuteronomy 24:1-4,[81] and Janzen believes the '*erwat dabar* of Deuteronomy 24:1 "was as poorly understood in the first century as it is in ours"![82] The vast range of views noted above tends to attest to this. Yet a charge of "sexual immorality" (*porniea*) or "adultery" (*moicheia*) need not be so poorly understood, for the application of a Hebrew Scripture such as Deuteronomy 22:22 to the "sexual immorality" of Matthew 19:9 produces a straightforward, lawful and awful conclusion. In keeping with what Jesus taught on the Law (Matt 5:17-19), the early church may have possessed this radical

---

[80] B. Rosner, *Paul, Scripture and Ethics: A Study of 1 Corinthians 5-7* (New York: Brill, 1994), 126-27.

[81] Luz, *Matthew 8-20*, 488-90.

[82] Janzen, "Porneia," 73.

understanding, which would explain why it overwhelmingly opposed divorce.[83]

Granting the full force of the biblical laws is not to champion capital punishment or to infer Jesus' disciples must follow the legal codes in the Pentateuch (as forever strictly determinative for Christians),[84] nor does it lead to altering biblical commandments in the least. Simply, Jesus' sole grounds for divorce in Matthew 19:9, namely "sexual immorality, " and the consequent breach of committing "adultery, " have dire ramifications for those appealing to Moses (Matt 19:7) and what is written in the Law. Irrespective of whether the death penalty was (ever) implemented,[85] the immense legal gravitas should impact our understanding of what Jesus teaches. The interpretative framework here upholds all legalities without necessarily being legalistic. Instead, anyone applying such grounds could be judged legalistic – and hypocritical, for who has not committed sexual immorality in their own heart (cf. Matt 5:28)?

A straightforward interpretation of Matthew 19:9 rests on the premise that Matthew depicted Jesus as living in complete obedience to the Torah, in a way that was distinct from the oral traditions of the Pharisees, and his teachings were not controlled by the Roman laws regulating the institution of marriage. Jesus was thoroughly tested for his Law-allegiance, but never does he relax the least part of the Law, or else by his own confession he would be called least in the kingdom of heaven (Matt 5:19). In this context, Jesus gave a timeless deadly exception where under the Law if a husband writes "sexual immorality" (Matt 5:32; Matt 19:9) on his wife's divorce certificate, he writes her a death sentence. However, if he does not terminate his marriage for this cause and he remarries, the husband commits adultery, also a capital offence by the Law. Nonetheless, given the restorative context (Matt 18:21 to 19:2) and permanency command (Matt 19:5-6), God desires mercy (Matt 9:13, 12:7), not divorce and destruction.

---

[83] The *Shepherd of Hermas* (c.140CE) did demand a wife be put away for adultery, yet even then, if she repented, the husband must take her back. If the husband remarried anyone else while she was alive, Hermas considered it adultery. Mandate 4.1.29. M. Holmes, *The Apostolic Fathers: Greek Texts and English Translations* (Grand Rapids: Baker, 1999), 380-81.

[84] Yet the Law "is still of value for Christian conduct as Scripture and *as wisdom.*" (Italics original.) B. Rosner, *Paul and the Law: Keeping the Commandments of God* (Downers Grove: Apollos, 2013), 160.

[85] "Biblical law required the execution of both parties (Lev. 20:10; Deut. 22:22), though it is unclear to what extent this was carried out in the first century, when Jewish authorities lacked the authority to do so." W. Loader, *Sexuality in the New Testament: Understanding the Key Texts* (Louisville: WJK, 2010), 61.

Central Question: A Deadly Exception?

The central question of this thesis is: ***Does Matthew 19:9 contain a deadly exception that permits divorce and remarriage?*** Specifically, should "sexual immorality" (*porneia*) in the 'exception clause' be understood as a dire offence that attracts the Law's death penalty (cf. Deut 22:22), in no way equivalent to a "matter of indecency" ('*erwat dabar*) found in Deuteronomy 24:1? If this is true, a second question follows: *Does Matthew 19:9 contain another dire matter*, such that whenever the 'exception clause' is not satisfied, the resultant "adultery" is to be understood as a capital offence?

If the nature of these offences is capital, then a call to abstain from sexual immorality (cf. Acts 15:29; 1 Cor 6:18) is certainly one end. Yet where sexual immorality does occur, is the Law to be mercilessly employed, ignored, or changed, even though it endures (Matt 5:17-19)? **What can Christians, *who are not under the Law* (Rom 6:14-15; Gal 3),[86] learn from this matter of Law**, knowing that all Scripture is profitable (2 Tim 3:16)? Exploration of a strictly legal reading of Matthew 19:1-12 shall be the principal aim of this thesis, with some ethical application simply gleaned in the process.

Prophetic fulfilment is another area considered, for Jesus came to fulfil both the Law and the Prophets (Matt 5:17). As marriage is instituted by God (Matt 19:4-6) and for God (Eph 1:10; cf. Col 1:16),[87] then its social purpose is penultimate and a larger theological question is raised: *Is a God-human marriage metaphor at work in Matthew 19:1-12, one that entails prophetic warning of divine judgement?* Are Matthew's texts on marriage part of the "escalating indictment against Jerusalem and its stewards"?[88] For God is in a marriage covenant with Israel (Isa 54:5-7; Ezek 16:8; Hos 2:19-20) and the imminent catastrophic judgement of 70CE is comparable to ***God's divorce*** of the Northern Kingdom of Israel in the Assyrian Conquest; and ***God's separation*** from the Southern Kingdom of Judah in the Babylonian Exile (Isa 50:1; Jer 2-6; Hos 2:2).

---

[86] "If you are not under the Law, you cannot transgress it," so "while Jews *transgress* the law, Christians do not." Rosner, *Paul and Law*, 97.

[87] Paul connects the Creational command of Gen 2:24 (cf. Matt 19:5) with the profound mystery revealed: "it refers to Christ and the church" (Eph 5:31-32).

[88] M. Spadaro, *Reading Matthew as the Climactic Fulfillment of the Hebrew Story* (Eugene: Wipf & Stock, 2015), 2.

CHAPTER 3 – Methodology

Reading Matthew's Gospel as a Biography

When Matthew 19:1-12 is examined within the genre of a biographical account,[1] and in the light of what can be "read" in Scripture (especially the Torah, that Jesus directs his immediate audience to in Matt 19:4), this may then inform us concerning the Gospel's provenance. Matters made explicit in the text about Jesus' setting, actions, and teachings are given priority, over and above implicit or conjectured matters concerning the author. This runs against twentieth-century redaction criticism that made much of implied historical settings seen in possible editorial changes between the Gospels, but aligns with recent scholarly efforts keen on "hastening the demise of an approach that has held back Matthean studies for far too long."[2]

The Greek text of Matthew 19:9 is accepted as reliable; the 'exception clause' appears in all early manuscripts.[3] A starting point of: "Which of the various versions of the prohibition contained in the NT most likely reflects Jesus' original teaching?"[4] proves to be the wrong question to ask when we see that Jesus' view on divorce is consistent across all witnesses. Within the text of Matthew 19:1-12, there is no hint of a textual debate (conflict never arises over variant manuscripts or differing law codes), even if the Pharisees misread the text of Deuteronomy 24:1-4 as suggesting that Moses was an advocate for divorce. Although the evangelists paint four distinct pictures of the same historical figure,[5] they all take for granted that Jesus cites and fulfills the same Mosaic Law comprising the same Mosaic penalties.

In exegeting Matthew 19:1-12, key Greek terms will be examined in their context and in the light of how they are used in other parts of Matthew and the New Testament. Study is made of the same terms in

---

[1] R. Bauckham, *The Gospels for All Christians: Rethinking the Gospel Audiences* (Grand Rapids: Eerdmans, 1998), 1-2. See also Appendix 1.

[2] B. Cooper, "Cedric E. W. Vine. The Audience of Matthew: An Appraisal of the Local Audience Thesis," *JGAR* 1, no. Sept 2017 (2017): 102.

[3] B. & K. Aland et al, *The Greek New Testament*, Fourth ed. (Westphalia: UBS, 2001), 71.

[4] Meier, *Marginal Jew*, 4, 96.

[5] M. Strauss, *Four Portraits, One Jesus: An Introduction to Jesus and the Gospels* (Grand Rapids: Zondervan, 2007).

the Septuagint and, where appropriate, similar terms or concepts in Hebrew/Aramaic. This aligns with William Mounce's basic methodology in defining Greek New Testament words:

> it is the word's background in the OT via the Septuagint that is the most important background... not its general usage in the first century.[6]

This is not to imagine that the Septuagint is perfect, for concern is raised in some places, but the principle remains that the Old Testament meaning is primary, not first-century usage that may be little more than a theoretical reconstruction based on limited documentation.[7] Even when historical reconstruction of early tradition is trustworthy, including that of Jewish culture preserved *within* Matthew's Gospel, care must be taken to determine whether this is upheld or challenged by Jesus. Cultural understandings of any term (such as "divorce") that Jesus opposed should not skew Jesus' own teaching on divorce. At the same time, "A Jesus fundamentally discontinuous with the Jewish tradition could not have been Israel's Messiah."[8]

The Gospel of Matthew, with our focal passage of Matthew 19:1-12, is well-connected to the Old Testament that Jesus constantly appealed to as he taught. Matthew has 62 quotations from the Old Testament; Mark is a distant second with 31, followed by Luke with 26 and John with 16.[9] A striking emphasis in Matthew is on the fulfilment of "what the Lord had spoken" (Matt 1:21) by the Hebrew prophets. Jesus did not uncritically defer to "authoritative interpreters" (prior or contemporary; e.g. he never mentions Hillel or Shammai by name), although he "clearly cherished the Jewish religious tradition."[10] Matthew presents Jesus as the authoritative expositor of the Law, the "premier source of authority."[11]

---

[6] W. Mounce, *Mounce's Complete Expository Dictionary of Old & New Testament Words* (Grand Rapids: Zondervan, 2006), xxi.

[7] E.g. Instone-Brewer cites a few extant Jewish and Graeco-Roman divorce certificates to show that a right to remarry post-divorce was assumed, but even if 1000 of such deeds were unearthed, this still would not guarantee accurate reconstruction of *Christian practice* in the first century. D. Instone-Brewer, "1 Corinthians 7 in the Light of the Jewish Greek & Aramaic Marriage & Divorce Papyri," *TB* 52, no. 2 (2001). "1 Corinthians 7 in the Light of the Graeco-Roman Marriage and Divorce Papyri," *TB* 52, no. 1 (2001). Indeed, in many areas centuries of early Christian practice runs counter to Jewish practice.

[8] D. Allison, *The New Moses: A Matthean Typology* (Eugene: Wipf & Stock, 1993; repr., 2013), 272.

[9] Aland et al, *Greek New Testament*, 888-9.

[10] G. Stassen and D. Gushee, *Kingdom Ethics: Following Jesus in Contemporary Context* (Illinois: IVP, 2003), 85.

[11] Ibid., 84.

Synoptic Matters

Textual concerns such as the date and authorship of Matthew's Gospel are not vital to this thesis, but presuppositions of modern scholarship do come under question.[12] Even a position of Markan priority (the idea that Mark wrote his Gospel first) does not bar Matthew from having had access to another early and historically reliable oral or written tradition of Jesus' words that preserved the 'exception clause' (of 5:32 and 19:9). It is erroneous to suppose that Matthew must have invented any non-Markan material.

In considering the effective history (*Wirkungsgeschichte*) from the earlier impact of Jesus, James Dunn sees Matthew not simply as the voice for his community, but as a faithful reteller of traditions from wide-ranging Christian gatherings in a predominantly oral society.[13] He well questions whether literary dependence is the best solution for parallel material which is not close, and contends that the twenty-two doublets in Matthew's Gospel (which includes 5:32 and 19:9) points to multiple oral versions, rather than purely two written sources (Mark and Q).[14] This does not imply unlimited diversity, for

> the doublet tradition itself is testimony to tradition being the *same* in subject and emphasis even when *different* in wording and detail.[15]

Instead, such differences may be "the result of different versions which Jesus *himself* used. After all, what teacher gives his instruction only once?"[16] In other words, Jesus' teachings that we now have in written form could have come from a lot of different sources (oral and written),

---

[12] Spadaro similarly raises concern that "The consensus dating of this work (AD 80) has been influenced by a limited set of presuppositions" Spadaro, *Matthew*, 15. Dunn reacts against an over-dependence on a 'literary paradigm' that assumes a high reliance on written sources. J. Dunn, *The Oral Gospel Tradition* (Grand Rapids: Eerdmans, 2013), 122-23. See also Appendix 1.

[13] *Oral Gospel*, 120-37.

[14] Runesson also notes that the existence of Q is disputed and it is highly unlikely that Matthew would have known about traditions in Mark's Gospel only from Mark's Gospel. A. Runesson, *Divine Wrath and Salvation in Matthew: The Narrative World of the First Gospel* (Minneapolis: Fortress, 2016), 20. Matt 19:1-12 shares much vocabulary with Mark 10:1-12 nonetheless, which implies some literary dependence. This holds true for the Matt 19:9 / Mark 10:11 parallel: ὃς ἂν ἀπολύσῃ τὴν γυναῖκα αὐτοῦ is identical, as is καὶ γαμήσῃ ἄλλην μοιχᾶται. However, the crucial clause μὴ ἐπὶ πορνείᾳ (Matt 19:9) has no close Markan parallel – indeed no parallel at all; the introductory words differ: λέγω δὲ ὑμῖν ὅτι (Matt 19:9) / καὶ λέγει αὐτοῖς· (Mark 10:11); and the closing words of Mark 10:11 add a remarkable element μοιχᾶται ἐπ᾽ αὐτήν· ("he commits adultery against her") absent from Matt 19:9.

[15] Dunn, *Oral Gospel*, 135. (Italics original.)

[16] Ibid., 136. (Italics original.)

but this does not mean that they contradict each other. Different versions may serve different purposes, not only of the final author, but of the original teacher who taught many things in many ways at many times.

Primary Hermeneutic

In understanding Matthew 19:1-12, *permanency of the Law* will serve as the primary hermeneutic rule (method of interpretation), based on Matthew 5:17-20. Scot McKnight calls this "the most significant passage in the entire Bible on how to read the Bible,"[17] although a tighter focus "on how to read the Law and Prophets" better appreciates the Jewish context. This principle conspicuously precedes Jesus' first teaching on divorce (Matt 5:31-32) and has direct bearing on Jesus' second teaching, for it follows a question of lawfulness brought by stewards of the Law (Matt 19:3) and it upholds God's command on the permanency of marriage, reasserted by Jesus (Matt 19:4-6). It is therefore vital to understand what Jesus teaches *concerning the Law* when speaking within a Torah-observant Jewish context before any Christian ethic of marriage is formulated for those who do not practise the Jewish Torah.[18]

Although this thesis intends also to discover the purpose of a Christian writer's record of what Jesus taught about divorce, it has the same starting point as John Meier in asking:

> only what a particular Palestinian Jew named Jesus taught other Palestinian Jews about divorce ca. A. D. 28. This point must be stressed because the halakic teaching of Jesus *the Jew*, addressing *other Jews*, is usually not the sole or even the major focus of most of the countless modern books and articles on 'Jesus and Divorce' or 'Divorce in the NT'.[19]

As such, effort is made to avoid "a facile relevance, a rush to 'what does this mean for us today?'"[20] Strict application of this hermeneutic risks being misunderstood as urging Law-reliance for Christians. However, Jesus' teaching on God's desire for mercy (Matt 9:13; 12:7), especially as illustrated in a story immediately prior to Matthew 19:1-12, paves another way.

---

[17] S. McKnight, *Sermon on the Mount*, The Story of God Bible Commentary (Grand Rapids: Zondervan, 2013), 66.

[18] Rom 3:19 is consistent with this hermeneutic, with a notable receptor-focus, "whatever the law says it speaks to those who are under the law."

[19] Meier, *Marginal Jew*, 4, 75.

[20] Ibid.

The Jewish legal concern here must not simply be superseded with a Christian precept. "Mosaic Paradigms"[21] and "The Transfiguration of Torah"[22] may facilitate mission and the founding of other well-ordered societies, but this is not Matthew's original concern. Anders Runesson brings some corrective,

> Readers of Matthew as a normative text should consider theologically the fact that this narrative endorses life as a follower of Jesus within Judaism, with strict law observance... This does not mean that mainstream Christianity today, which has moved in other directions, should adopt a Matthean way of life.[23]

More precisely, Matthew's narrative endorses strict Law observance for all followers of Judaism – including Jesus – prior to Jesus instituting a "new covenant" (unmentioned by Jesus in Matthew). Certainly "the narrative context of Matthew and the broader prophetic and theological contexts... have been largely overlooked,"[24] and David Pao maintains this connection in his literary study to argue that

> Matthew is locating this legal exposition of Deut 24:1-4 within a wider prophetic interpretation of the passage: God's covenant people have been unfaithful to their covenant partner, and therefore God has the right to divorce them.[25]

However, Pao's framing of Matthew 19:1-12 as a "legal exposition of Deut 24:1-4"[26] does not fully capture Matthew's purpose, for Jesus quickly moves beyond this passage with references to capital offences that are legislated on elsewhere (such as Lev 18:6-30; Deut 22:13-24). A "legal exposition of what is written in the Law" is a better descriptor, embracing the Creation ideal for marriage, plus prescribed curses for rebellion and blessings for obedience (cf. Deut 28). Critically, God's legal "right to divorce" unfaithful people must be understood in relation to Jesus' mission to "save his people" (Matt 1:21) and instances of mercy as found written in the Law and Prophets.

In this thesis, the Law will be focussed on mainly due to space constraints, but legal and prophetic fulfilment belong together. Jesus was emphatic that he came to fulfil both the Law and the Prophets (Matt

---

[21] P. Kuntz, *The Ten Commandments in History: Mosaic Paradigms for a Well-Ordered Society* (Grand Rapids: Eerdmans, 2004).

[22] R. Hays, *Echoes of Scripture in the Gospels* (Waco: Baylor, 2016), 186-90.

[23] Runesson, *Divine Wrath*, xxv.

[24] Pao, "Literary Context," 64.

[25] Ibid.

[26] Ibid.

5:17). "Fulfil" (πληρόω) connects with numerous other fulfilment texts in Matthew,[27] which suggests that

> Matthew wants us to see Jesus' teachings in the Sermon on the Mount as the salvation-historical fulfilment and climactic completion in Jesus' own teachings.[28]

Jesus' salvific work follows his teachings, and legal fulfilment can be seen in his own death by capital punishment, which itself implies that the Law's capital demands have not been abolished (cf. Matt 26:59-66).[29] H. Wayne House notes, "The New Testament ...assumes the Old Testament concept of retribution," and thus

> discussion of the sacrifice of Christ [cf. Heb 2:2] will make no sense unless ...readers agree on the concept of retribution as established by the Mosaic Law.[30]

At the same time, that Jesus did not abolish (καταλύω) the Law (Matt 5:17) differs from him abolishing (καταργέω) the law of commandments (Eph 2:15).[31]

Jesus and the Law

In Matthew's Gospel, Jesus is not portrayed as a "revolutionary"[32] wanting to overthrow everything in the religious order of his day, for he upheld every element of the Law, and taught other Jews to do the same (Matt 5:17-19). If Jesus does not follow the commandments or he makes Israel depart from them, then according to Deuteronomy 13:1-5, he must be put to death as a false prophet or dreamer. He would not be the expected prophet or Messiah who is "one like Moses" (Deut 18:15-19).

---

[27] "The idea that what God has promised in the Old Testament scriptures is fulfilled in Christianity runs throughout this Gospel." Morris, *Matthew*, 3.

[28] S. McKnight, "Matthew as 'Gospel'," in *Jesus, Matthew's Gospel and Early Christianity: Studies in Memory of Graham N. Stanton*, ed. D. Gurtner, J. Willitts, and R. Burridge, LNTS (London: T&T Clark, 2011), 71.

[29] This is the case at least for blasphemy. There is no scriptural record of any individual being executed for adultery, including David for his infidelity with "the wife of Uriah" (Matt 1:6). However, when confronted by Nathan (2 Sam 12), David knows that the crime *deserves death* and finally a "son of David" does die for it. In the original setting: David's firstborn son to Bathsheba dies; in the Matthean setting: "Jesus Christ, the son of David" (Matt 1:1) dies, to "save his people from their sins" (Matt 1:21).

[30] H. W. House, "In Favour of the Death Penalty," in *The Death Penalty Debate: Two Opposing Views of Capital Punishment*, ed. J. H. Yoder and H. W. House (Dallas: Word, 1991), 29.

[31] Refer to exegesis of Matt 19:9.

[32] A. Lindsley, "C.S. Lewis on Chronological Snobbery," *Knowing & Doing* Spring (2003): 2.

Matthew presents Jesus as perfectly Torah-obedient; "Matthew's readers would not have thought that Jesus was opposing the law at all."[33] The first miracle Matthew places immediately after the Matthew 5-7 discourse specifically demonstrates Jesus' strict lawfulness. Jesus directs a leper he has healed to show himself to the priest and offer the gift that Moses commanded (Matt 8:4; cf. Lev 14:2-32). This would have involved a long journey to the Jerusalem Temple to make elaborate ritual sacrifices. Such instruction is inapplicable to a post-70CE audience. That the leper disobeyed Jesus is immaterial to Matthew's purpose (he omits this fact) but it does suit Mark and Luke's purposes (Mark 1:40-44; Luke 5:12-14).[34] Any internalisation of the Law[35] has not negated the normal external application of the Law, with outward proof of obedience still required. This "proof to them" (Matt 8:4) can have multiple meanings: pertaining to healing and social restoration, but also substantiation of Jesus' Law-allegiance.[36]

Matthew records other meticulous legal points such as Jesus paying the Temple tax (Matt 17:24-27), highlighting how Jesus abided by the Law even in a place remote from Jerusalem. Jesus upheld the Law in his very clothing: a tasseled garment fringe (Matt 9:20) for the wearer "to look at and remember all the commandments of the LORD, to do them" (Num 15:39a).[37] By contrast, the Pharisees also wear tasseled garments (Matt 23:5), but do not uphold the Law. They are "blind guides" (Matt 23:16) "full of hypocrisy and lawlessness" (Matt 23:28) who neglect the "weightier matters of the law: justice and mercy and faithfulness" (Matt 23:23).

The Torah is vital for interpreting Matthew 19:1-12, for Jesus cites Genesis (Gen 1:27; 2:18, 21-24; 5:2) in Matthew 19:4-5, the Pharisees call upon Moses (Deut 24:1-4) in Matthew 19:7, and Jesus then responds with why Moses permitted what he did in Matthew 19:8. If the question in Matthew 19:3 is a trial of Jesus' Torah-piety, if "sexual immorality" and "adultery" of Matthew 19:9 pertain to written

---

[33] Keener, *And Marries Another*, 120.

[34] Torah-allegiance is not vital to evangelisation of Gentiles. The Jerusalem Temple, even if still standing for the first readers, has no role for Gentile inclusion or in the new covenant.

[35] Internalisation is nothing new. Rosner provides examples of Psalms that back up every one of the Ten Commandments with evidence of internalising the Law, including exhorting "actions of the hands and heart" beyond mere cultic conformity. Rosner, *Paul and Law*, 167-74. "The law was meant to be interiorized, taken into the heart and observed naturally because one's heart is right" (Deut 6:4-9 and Lev 19:17 intend this). E. Sanders, *Judaism: Practice and Belief 63BCE - 66CE* (London: SCM, 1992), 231.

[36] Morris, *Matthew*, 190.

[37] Israel's requirement for tasseled garments immediately follows the demand to execute a Sabbath-breaker (Num 15:32-36), suggesting both are to be taken seriously.

commandments of the Law, and if "eunuch" (Matt 19:11-12) has its primal meaning in the Pentateuch (cf. Lev 21:20; Deut 23:1), then the whole debate (Matthew 19:3-12) centres on the Torah.

Torah-piety sets Jews apart from other peoples. Prior to both divorce passages (Matt 5:31-32 and 19:1-12), Matthew stresses that Jesus has not come to abolish the Law or the Prophets (Matt 5:17) – a clear proclamation absent in other Synoptics. This is unsurprising, because for Mark and Luke the Law's permanency is less relevant for evangelistic efforts toward the Gentiles. Non-Jews are simply not under the Law, and many would be ignorant of Torah demands even if their own law codes had some commonality.[38]

Jesus has an emphasis on both *teaching* and *doing* the Law (Matt 5:18-19). Contra Hans Hübner, fulfilment does not include modification of the Law, nor does Matthew incorporate traditions here for "'rejudaising' the Jesus tradition" in an effort to reverse a trend.[39] Furthermore, Jesus' challenge to "be perfect" (Matt 5:48) surely cannot be achieved by Gentiles observing the Law in greater detail than the finest Jews. For Matthew's purposes the Law is what Jesus follows perfectly as a Jew, in contrast to others who "break the commandment of God" for the sake of tradition (Matt 15:3). All those under the Law must likewise follow it perfectly in every detail.

Matthew stylised Jesus as "a new Moses figure,"[40] possessing astonishing authority, keeping and teaching the Law of Moses, and making declarations (Matt 5-7) that Israel must listen to (cf. Deut 18:15-19).[41] Andrew Cornes holds that "Most commentators... see Jesus in Matthew's Gospel as the new lawgiver, surpassing Moses,"[42] and Robert Gundry reasons that Matthew does this to "accentuate the authority of Christ's law,"[43] although Matthew mentions nothing about

---

[38] This explains why Mark and Luke have extra notes to help the reader understand points of Law. E.g. Mark 7:3-4 explains Jewish food law; Matt 15:2 does not. Luke 23:56 contains an explanatory note about the Sabbath, "they rested according to the commandment," totally unnecessary for a Jewish reader.

[39] H. Hübner, *Das Gesetz in Der Synoptischen Tradition: Studien Zur These Einer Progressiven Qumranisierung Und Judaisierung Innerhalb Der Synoptischen Tradition* (Gottingen: Vandenhoeck & Ruprecht, 1986), 196. "To interpret Matthew on the basis of 5:18 should really be a thing of the past" (ibid., 206.) only holds true when "heaven and earth pass away" (Matt 5:18).

[40] McKnight, *Sermon*, 22.

[41] Entrance to the kingdom of heaven depends on hearing and doing the very words of Jesus (Matt 7:21-29).

[42] Cornes, *Divorce and Remarriage*, 36.

[43] R. Gundry, *Matthew: A Commentary on His Literary and Theological Art* (Grand Rapids: Eerdmans, 1982), 7.

a "new Torah" for a "new people."[44] Matthew nowhere took over Mark's strong expression, "new teaching" (1:27)."[45] The new Moses supports the old Moses.[46]

Thus Wesley Olmstead's "new nation"[47] is not entirely new. The Abrahamic ἔθνος μέγα ("great nation") that he connects with Matthew 21:43 supports Matthew's emphasis on Israel's continuity: judgement falls on rebellious people but others will lead the *same* great nation in following the Jewish Messiah, tending the *same* vineyard of God.[48] Israel is made great again: a revitalised nation that includes people of all nations. These fruitful citizens "respect" God's Son and share "his inheritance" (Matt 21:37-43) in a nation or Davidic "house" that cherishes God's promises (2 Sam 7:16 dominates in Matthew's fulfilment scheme) and is forever a nation before him (cf. Jer 31:31-37).

Donald Hagner rightly observes, "The law as expounded by Jesus is not a 'new' law... but the true or intended meaning of the Mosaic law."[49] However, a "dynamic tension" between "the grace of the kingdom and the demands of the law"[50] is more dynamic than many envisage, for in Israel's history *amazing grace* has long preceded the arrival of the messianic king, and the *exceedingly high demands* that avail righteousness (cf. Matt 5:20) – for the recipients of the Mosaic Law – endure long after. The king's departure and fulfilment of the Law also brings more tension, especially between the subjects of the Law and those who are not, or who remain no longer, subjects.

---

[44] Contra McKnight, "Jesus, the new Moses, taught his disciples the new Torah." McKnight, *Sermon*, 24-25. Likewise Stanton's "New People," which he admits does not correspond with Matthew's terminology in 21:43, does not sum up Matthew's intentions. G. Stanton, *A Gospel for a New People: Studies in Matthew* (Edinburgh: T&T Clark, 1992), 18.

[45] Allison, *New Moses*, 272.

[46] C. Keener, *The Gospel of Matthew: A Socio-Rhetorical Commentary* (Grand Rapids: Eerdmans, 2009), 160-63.

[47] W. Olmstead, "A Gospel for a New Nation: Once More, the Ἔθνος of Matthew 21.43," in *Jesus, Matthew's Gospel and Early Christianity: Studies in Memory of Graham N. Stanton*, ed. D. Gurtner, J. Willitts, and R. Burridge, LNTS (London: T&T Clark, 2011), 115-32.

[48] Matt 21:43 refers to the kingdom of God being taken away from the leaders of Israel, as evidenced two verses later. It is not given to "the nations" or "the Gentiles," for the Greek is an anarthrous singular substantive: ἔθνος (Matt 21:43); it is simply given to "people producing its fruits" (Matt 21:43). "A [single] nation" other than Israel can hardly be in view, nor is this the normal terminology for "nations" or "Gentiles," as elsewhere ἔθνος is always in the plural (Matt 4:15; 6:32; 10:5,18; 12:18, 21; 20:19, 25), except for in one verse where it occurs as a general reference to any nation, which could include Israel, "For nation will rise against nation..." (Matt 24:7), along with a general reference to any earthly kingdom (βασιλεία), "and kingdom against kingdom," which could also include Israel.

[49] D. Hagner, *Matthew 1-13*, WBC 33A (Dallas: Word, 1993), lxii-lxiii.

[50] Ibid., lxiii.

Many scholars adamantly claim that Jesus completely upheld the Law, but then employ sophisticated nuancing to see Jesus finally fulfilling and changing multiple elements of legal codes that are considered unpalatable (such as capital punishment, ritual cleanliness, or food law), impossible to implement (under foreign rule, or beyond 70CE), or seemingly un-Christian (such as the Jewish Sabbath or Passover). For example, Don Carson resolves:

> Jesus confirms the law, even its jot and tittle, by his life and his teaching... one marvels that the early church, as the other NT documents testify, misunderstood Jesus so badly on this point; and even the first Gospel, as we shall see, *is rendered inconsistent*. ...in both Matthew and other NT documents *some abolition is everywhere assumed*.[51]

Similarly, in commenting on Matthew 5:17-20, Gundry insists:

> No careless inattention to the details of the law here! No easy resting in the spirit of the law or even in the pervasive principle of love!"[52]

Simultaneously, he contends, "The law changes, however"![53]

Douglas Moo suggests that "Jesus simply intends to encourage absolute truthfulness," but then questions Jesus' absolute truthfulness by finding "one possible abrogation of the Law – that having to do with divorce and remarriage – occurs in the antitheses."[54] Whereas the Matthean 'exception clause' is often perceived as clear proof that Jesus altered the Law,[55] it just might be that Jesus' word in this area *is clear proof that he did not change the Law at all.*

Moo further asserts,

> In attempting to assess the applicability of OT commands to Christian believers... virtually all Christians at all times have accepted the abrogation of *some* OT commandments – those relating to the sacrificial system, for example.[56]

---

[51] D. Carson, Matthew, (Grand Rapids: Zondervan, 2017). 142-43. (Bold and italics added.)

[52] Gundry, *Matthew: Literary and Theological Art*, 82.

[53] Ibid., 7.

[54] D. Moo, "Law," in *Dictionary of Jesus and the Gospels: A Compendium of Contemporary Biblical Scholarship*, ed. J. Green, S. McKnight, and I. H. Marshall (Downers Grove: IVP, 1992), 456.

[55] "In contrast to the first two antitheses, it is commonly asserted that in the third antithesis Jesus revokes the OT law concerning divorce." "Jesus and the Authority of the Mosaic Law," *JSNT* 6, no. 20 (1984): 19.

[56] Ibid., 14. (Italics original.)

Yet distinguishing audiences is vital: Jews (and this includes the immediate audience listening to Jesus being tested by the Pharisees, plus those later reading Matthew's Gospel as a whole) hear Jewish leaders striving to uphold and not abrogate the Law; Christians hear Jesus' lessons on the Law, but are not necessarily bound by the Law and find freedom to abrogate or reapply it. Fulfilling the Law does not require abrogating or changing it, even when a new covenant is ushered in with different law (cf. Acts 15).[57]

Certainly there has been development *within the Old Testament* (e.g. from Tabernacle to Temple), but even then, any cultic development did not change the moral law of Israel and the corresponding death penalty prescribed for serious infractions such as murder, adultery and Sabbath-breaking. The New Testament does not further develop the Law, for when the Cross is reached, a completely different covenant comes into being, with a chasm far too great to leap for the notion to persist that "...the precise form of the Mosaic law may change with the crucial redemptive events to which it points."[58] At stake is something more than keeping the canon as canon,[59] for questions of lawfulness in Matthew's Gospel never raise one question for Jews about keeping Scripture as Scripture. Lawfulness concerns the Law, which sits in tension with the Gospel due to its historical nature, but even when considered the older in "two successive eras,"[60] this does not mean one dot of it is abandoned to the past. What must be determined is the place of Law in Jesus' time and beyond the Cross, and how to obtain a righteousness that enables entrance to the kingdom of heaven without any abolition or alteration of this Law until heaven and earth pass away (Matt 5:17-20).

Keener is one of many scholars who affirms that Jesus viewed the Law as eternal:

> Even the least noticed parts of God's word are eternally true
> and valid. ...Jesus' readers would have no doubt understood:

---

[57] Here, sensitivity to those under the Mosaic Law is upheld, but it is not the case that *the Law itself* is changed so that circumcision is no longer demanded and Gentile believers must keep an abridged version. Such believers are not ordered to keep the law of Moses at all, but good morals remain vital nonetheless.

[58] D. Carson, "Matthew," in *The Expositor's Bible Commentary Matthew & Mark*, ed. T. Longman III and D. Garland (Grand Rapids: Zondervan, 2010), 178.

[59] Ibid., 175. "'Law' almost certainly refers to the entire OT Scriptures." Ibid., 178.

[60] D. Moo, "The Law of Christ as the Fulfillment of the Law of Moses: A Modified Lutheran View," in *Five Views on Law and Gospel*, ed. G. Bahnsen (Grand Rapids: Zondervan, 1999), 322.

he was upholding the veracity of even the smallest details of God's word.[61]

Here Keener is right, but he does not take Jesus precisely at his word when interpreting a debate on divorce and the Law. Details are routinely jettisoned, including the death penalty for adultery – which is not even one of "the smallest details"! Keener writes, "when Matthew speaks of 'except for the cause of infidelity', his audience would have understood this as a legal charge,"[62] which is entirely true. He continues, "Jewish and Roman law, in fact, both *mandated* divorce for these grounds."[63] This is likely true too, whether these new laws were applied or not, but misses the point. The legal charge wholly relates to ancient God-given laws written in Scripture, independent of other human-made laws – recent or not.[64] Matthew presents Jesus as giving a real legal exception that is not a compromise in keeping with contemporary law, Jewish or Roman, nor teaching only for a later situation (though it may profit any new situation), but this is Jesus' own teaching on a matter of Law.

Matthew's positioning of Jesus' declaration of dependence on the *written* Mosaic text in guiding his attitude to the Law (Matt 5:17-20) is noteworthy. It comes shortly after the famous Beatitudes (Matt 5:1-12) and a passage on salt and light (Matt 5:13-16), but precedes passages on anger (Matt 5:21-26), lust (Matt 5:27-30) and divorce (Matt 5:31-32). Jesus' refrain "You have heard" (Matt 5:21, 27, 33, 38, 43) does not attack the perfect Law itself (Ps 19:7) to promote lawlessness, but highlights the inadequacy of a verbal tradition that neglects the heart and settles instead on misinterpretation or superficial religious observance. The first three 'antitheses' involve capital crimes, where Jesus' rulings expose the shortcomings, if not lawlessness, of the human judicial system. For example, with regard to the first and most expansive 'antithesis', John Nolland insightfully summarises the situation:

> In effect Jesus is saying: If you want to apply the commandment solely within the legal framework, then you will need to feed into the legal system every case where there has been a rush of anger or words of insult; what is more, you

---

[61] Keener, *And Marries Another*, 114-15.

[62] *Matthew*, 466.

[63] Ibid., 467.

[64] The new laws were probably novel even for Rome, "Roman society went 520 years without a single divorce!" K. Harper, *From Shame to Sin: The Christian Transformation of Sexual Morality in Late Antiquity* (Massachusetts: Harvard University, 2013), 62.

will need to treat all of these as capital cases, or, more exactly, your courts will need to be able to send the culprits to hell.[65]

Even if this course of action is understood as humanly impossible, it remains that Jesus' rhetoric (however hyperbolic) upholds the radical intent of the Law. That Jesus must expound on the Law implies that the "justice and mercy and faithfulness" (Matt 23:23-28) demanded is lacking within the present system, centred on the Jewish council and Jerusalem Temple (cf. "the altar," Matt 5:23-24) and not the (post-resurrection) church – which will require the same disciplinary principles. Moreover, Jesus is not merely building a fence around the Torah to bring attention to motives that *lead to committing transgressions* such as murder and adultery, but he shows (as does the Tenth Commandment) that transgressions *are actually committed* in the human heart.

"To treat all of these as capital cases"[66] should well be remembered when considering "the case of a man with his wife" (Matt 19:10), especially in relation to charges of "sexual immorality" and "adultery (Matt 19:9). Jesus' resounding "But I say to you" (ἐγὼ δὲ λέγω ὑμῖν, Matt 5:22, 28, 32, 34, 39, 44; cf. ἀμὴν λέγω σοι, Matt 5:26; ἀμὴν λέγω ὑμῖν, 6:16; and λέγω δὲ ὑμῖν, 19:9) provides authoritative teaching, echoing Jesus' personal decree "For truly, I say to you" (ἀμὴν γὰρ λέγω ὑμῖν, Matt 5:18) that affirms the Law's permanency. What is *read* in the Law (cf. Matt 19:4) – and read precisely as Jesus reads it, and then speaks, is ultimate. This differs greatly from contemporary religious teaching, evidenced in the Jewish crowds being "astonished at his teaching, for he was teaching them as one who had authority, and not as their scribes" (Matt 7:29).

Jesus demands that Jews obey every detail of the Law (cf. Matt 5:17-19; 23:1-3). If one applies the details of the Law to Jesus' words in the Matthew 19:1-12 passage, then a deadly indictment presents for any unlawfulness. Rather than disposing of legalism,[67] Jesus holds the Pharisees and any hearer who relies on the Law accountable to the Law's high legal standards. It can even be said that Jesus loves legalism – not heartless legalism, but as Psalm 119 expresses in nearly every line, a love for God and his Law that is based on "a deeply interior spirituality."[68] How Christian readers living in a different context might

---

[65] J. Nolland, *The Gospel of Matthew: A Commentary on the Greek Text*, NIGTC (Grand Rapids: Eerdmans, 2005), 231.

[66] Ibid.

[67] Richards, "Divorce and Remarriage: Variety of Circumstances," 223.

[68] Rosner, *Paul and Law*, 172-73.

apply Jesus' instruction in Matthew, which presumes the normative authority of the Torah in the context of an intra-Jewish debate, is a separate question.

The Law does cater for lower standards (e.g. murder, theft, adultery, etc. all have rulings) than the ideal which existed "from the beginning" (cf. Matt 19:4, 8), and at times describes the practice of such lowering (cf. Deut 24:1-4), but never prescribes it. Jesus' verdict of "hardness of heart" (Matt 19:8) counts against any prescription of divorce as a general standard given by God's grace to take "the warping of humankind into account."[69] Instead, the judgement for "hardness of heart"[70] is hard and specific, aligning with Jesus' *high standard* based on the Law.

Immediately after Jesus decrees that he has not come to abolish the Law, we find evidence of his commitment to it in his statements on murder (Matt 5:21-26); adultery (Matt 5:27-30); and divorce (Matt 5:31-32).[71] In each, Jesus does not lower the standards on the legal proscriptions. Given the dire consequences, to do so would not be gracious, but terrifyingly deceptive. The seven sins are *Still Deadly*[72] and the seven abominations still abominable (Prov 6:16-19). There is certain death without certain forgiveness from certain sin.

Conversely, Ed Sanders believes that Jesus "requires a stricter code of practice," noting

> No one who observed the admonitions of Matthew 5 would transgress the law, and Jesus does not propose that any part of the Mosaic code should be repealed.[73]

Yet Matthew did not perceive Jesus as creating a heightened standard either. It is not that "Jesus' commands consistently establish a greater standard of righteousness than the law required (Matt 5:20)"[74] but they consistently explicate the great and perfect standard (cf. Matt 5:48) of righteousness that the Law required, which was a greater standard than the scribes and Pharisees ordinarily acquired (Matt 5:20).

---

[69] Richards in H. W. House, *Divorce and Remarriage: Four Christian Views* (Downers Grove: IVP, 1990), 223.

[70] See discussion on "hardness of heart" in the exegesis of Matt 19:8.

[71] Keener notes that there have been at least 36 different ways of interpreting Jesus' Sermon on the Mount. So a review will not be attempted here! Suffice it to say, Keener's comment that "a central point of the sermon is Jesus' unique authority as the supreme expositor of the law's message, a new Moses" indicates that Jesus' teachings would not be antithetical to Moses' teachings. Keener, *Matthew*, 160-63.

[72] A. Cameron and B. Rosner, *Still Deadly: Ancient Cures for the 7 Sins* (Sydney: Aquila, 2007).

[73] E. Sanders, *The Historical Figure of Jesus* (London: Penguin, 1993), 210.

[74] Blomberg, "Exegesis," 171.

Wolfgang Stegemann well challenges exegetical attempts that "stamp Jesus' relation to the Torah as radical (or, more concretely, as 'mitigating' the Torah or 'intensifying' the Torah)."[75] For example, "Jesus' interpretation of the prohibition of divorce (Exod 20:14) in the second antithesis of the Sermon on the Mount …is interpreted" (due to Matt 5:28) "as 'intensification of the Torah'" but Stegemann discerns,

> The word 'intensification' presupposes that the Torah prescription itself is more open, 'weaker', or 'more broad-minded'. …For who can say what the Torah prescription ('You shall not commit adultery') 'originally' meant, whether it was originally open to 'weak' or 'broad' interpretation?[76]

Dale Allison rightly questions the label 'antitheses',[77] and Pinchas Lapide's superlative alternative, 'supertheses',[78] is preferable only insofar as we understand that Jesus' words "deepen, intensify, and radicalize the biblical commandments" by correctly drawing out the high standard *already present*[79] and regularly flaunted by sinful people.

Jesus shocked his audiences with his teachings.[80] For example, it would confront any polite society were one condemned "to have a great millstone fastened around his neck and to be drowned in the depth of the sea" (Matt 18:6). Even Gentiles without the Mosaic Law treat certain sins more seriously than others, yet if one accepts the verdict of Scripture that the human heart is "deceptive" (Jer 17:9) and the source of "evil thoughts, murder, adultery, sexual immorality, theft, false witness, slander" (Matt 15:19), then when determining right judgement, a methodological tension between Scripture and culture is unavoidable. This is evident in Matthew 19:1-12, for Jesus anchors his leading premise in a biblical vision *completely foreign* to both his first-century culture and our culture today: the Creation perfection of "the

---

[75] W. Stegemann, "The Contextual Ethics of Jesus," in *The Social Setting of Jesus and the Gospels*, ed. G. Theissen, B. Malina, and W. Stegemann (Minneapolis: Fortress, 2002), 48.

[76] Ibid.

[77] D. Allison, *The Sermon on the Mount: Inspiring the Moral Imagination*, Companions to the New Testament (New York: Crossroad, 1999), 31.

[78] P. Lapide, *The Sermon on the Mount: Utopia or Program for Action?* (Maryknoll: Orbis, 1986), 46.

[79] "The ancient rabbis, echoed by the Pharisees, restricted the scope of the seventh commandment to the bare act of unlawful intercourse with a married woman," whereas Jesus "insists that its true intent had a much wider scope, reaching also to the inward affections." A. Pink, *An Exposition of the Sermon on the Mount* (Grand Rapids: Baker, 1979), 80.

[80] The scandal and shock here is much greater than imagined in D. Instone-Brewer, *The Jesus Scandals: Why He Shocked His Contemporaries (and Still Shocks Today)* (Oxford: Monarch, 2012).

beginning," with no guarantee that anyone who has "read" about it truly understands (Matt 19:4). The most obvious inference is that what God has said and done, as recorded in a scriptural setting far beyond our time *and* far before Jesus' discourse, is the primary reference point, not contemporary culture (ours or Jesus'). **One methodological claim is thus made at the outset when weighing Scripture and culture: human practice, however ingrained and ancient, is not definitive, for Jesus' teaching often radically challenges it.**

Testament to a strong countercultural stance of Christians taught by Jesus, divorce was completely prohibited in the early church and this stance prevailed for centuries. This is unless the church endorsed divorce with a right to remarry in the first century, similar to Shammai's understanding, and then underwent a surprisingly undocumented and perhaps undebated sudden switch in the second century. If so, as Wenham exclaims,

> What on earth could have persuaded the whole church to adopt the strict discipline of no remarriage after divorce? This was no minor adjustment to doctrine or ethics. It potentially affected the lifestyle of every member of the church and every potential convert. It does not seem likely that it could be based simply on the ignorance of Gentiles who were reading the Gospels, who did not know the Jewish customs about divorce entailing the right to remarry, for, in fact, there was plenty of interaction between Jews and Christians in the early centuries.[81]

On Instone-Brewer's theory that Christians were cut off from Jews after the first century and were ignorant of Jewish practices,[82] Wenham sees this as nonsense, citing figures such as Justin Martyr, Rabbi Akiba, and others engaged in early Jewish-Christian dialogues and debates; cities like Alexandria that were "full of Jews" and the Antiochene school that owed "much to Jewish approaches."[83] An assertion that the early church "lost touch with its Jewish roots in or before 70 CE"[84] lacks

---

[81] Wenham, "No Remarriage," 36.

[82] Instone-Brewer argues that Christian excommunication from the synagogue "marked the beginning of the loss of Jewish culture within the Church." After 70CE, "Jesus' teaching on divorce was now utterly incomprehensible to Christians, as well as to most Jews," and "Christians were no longer familiar with the terms 'any matter' and 'matter of indecency' that formed the basis of Jesus' debate with the Pharisees." Instone-Brewer, *Social and Literary Context*, 238-39.

[83] Wenham, "No Remarriage," 55-56.

[84] Instone-Brewer presupposes this in examining Exod 21:10-11. Instone-Brewer, *Social and Literary Context*, 238. It is assumed as a general premise for C. Hamer, *Marital Imagery in the Bible: An Exploration of Genesis 2:24 and its Significance for the Understanding of*

credibility as Loader properly assesses.[85] Instead, this thesis holds that Jesus and the early church were supremely in touch with their Jewish roots, and this included a close reading of Hebrew Scripture.

The recent Protestant majority view does not adequately account for the early church fathers' remarkable "unanimity on the subject of divorce and remarriage."[86] A better "understanding of the roots of Jesus' teaching in the Old Testament"[87] that (contra Heth) does not emasculate the roots but maintains the severity of capital crimes of the Law (especially for "sexual immorality" and "adultery") does, however, explain why the early church fled from divorce and remarriage, even to the extremes of asceticism and celibacy. At the same time, this does not infer that the death penalty is applicable under the new covenant; *it simply was under the old, to which Matthew 19:1-12 firstly relates.*

In writing a 'Jewish Gospel'[88] that critiques the hypocrisy of Jewish leaders, if Jesus' Law-allegiance were undermined, he too could be accused of hypocrisy. Jesus would break the Law, the very charge that the Pharisees seek to lay on him, or he would change it to suit his purposes, which could hardly "fulfill" it (Matt 5:17). Neither does "heaven and earth pass away" together with any iota or dot of the Law in the time between this declaration of the Law's enduring authority (Matt 5:17-19) and Jesus' teaching on divorce (Matt 5:31-32 or 19:1-12), even if Jewish cultural practice relaxed certain legal elements. Herman Waetjen discerns a dichotomy between the oral Torah and the Law,[89] as Jesus exposes in Matthew 15:3-9. However, based on his view of Matthew 19:8, Waetjen sees that the written Torah is also "defective," with legislation "infected by the condition of sin."[90] This cannot be so, for if it were defective Jesus would have abolished or changed it, not championed its full validity forever.

The Law itself declares its eternal nature (cf. Lev 16:29; 23:21; 24:8), with its Levitical priesthood perpetual (Exod 40:15), so that even when a new law and priesthood arises (cf. Heb 7:12), those who spurn the change remain obligated to the enduring original, despite others

---

New Testament Divorce and Remarriage Teaching, Apostolos Old Testament Studies (London: Apostolos, 2015).

[85] W. Loader, *Sexuality and the Jesus Tradition* (Grand Rapids: Eerdmans, 2005), 120.

[86] Heth, "Divorce, but No Remarriage," 97.

[87] Ibid., 102.

[88] G. Osborne, *Matthew*, Zondervan Exegetical Commentary on the New Testament (Grand Rapids: Zondervan, 2010), 31.

[89] H. Waetjen, *Matthew's Theology of Fulfillment, Its Universality and Its Ethnicity: God's New Israel as the Pioneer of God's New Humanity* (London: Bloomsbury, 2017), 204.

[90] Ibid.

relegating it to a pre-Christian past.[91] It is difficult to justify a partial change to the Law, for according to Jesus any iota or dot can only "pass from the Law" *simultaneously* with "heaven and earth" passing away, "until all is accomplished" (Matt 5:18). It is unlikely that "all is accomplished" solely references Jesus' work on the cross because the Hebrew prophets point beyond, as does Jesus, to at least the destruction of the Temple (cf. Matthew 24).

Jesus' teaching on divorce in Matthew 5:31-32 and 19:1-12 remains prior to the cross in any case (regardless of whether Matthew records it immediately or afterwards). Again, this does not mean that Christians under a new covenant must obey every minutiae of Law in the old covenant. It simply means that the Law in every detail stood intact as Jesus spoke, and it has full bearing on the legal dispute between Jesus and the Pharisees on the matter of divorce. Once the new covenant is instituted, the issue for Jesus' disciples is not that of supersession, but which covenant and what law is applicable to them.

Morris insists that in Matthew's Gospel, "The law is, of course, the Pentateuch, the heart of revelation as the Jews understood it."[92] This is *the Law* that Jesus lives under, he is challenged on, and he upholds in every detail. The context of Matthew 19:1-12 is thoroughly forensic, for Jesus is tested by legal experts specifically on a point of law (i.e. "Is it lawful...?" Matt 19:3), but interpreters routinely reframe the debate or relax the Law (cf. Matt 5:19) by commuting death for adultery into divorce and remarriage.[93]

On Matthew 19:3, the UBS Translator's Handbook sees that "**Is it lawful** has the Mosaic Law as the point of reference."[94] Perhaps only from the Pharisees' perspective, "Lawful will refer to any combination of oral and written Law,"[95] but Jesus presses for one correct reading of what is written (Matt 19:4). It would actually be impossible for Jesus to uphold all oral law alongside written Law, because oral traditions were in conflict (cf. Hillelite versus Shammaite), and given the uncertainty of details, who would know what iotas and dots were lost? The divorce debate hinges on what is written, for Jesus refers to what is *read* in Scripture (Matt 19:4-6) while upholding every *written* detail of the Law

---

[91] Moo, "Law of Christ," 321.

[92] Morris, *Matthew*, 302.

[93] Loader, *Jesus Tradition*, 76.

[94] B. Newman and P. Stine, *A Translator's Handbook on the Gospel of Matthew* (New York: UBS, 1988), 606. (Bold and underscore original.)

[95] Blomberg, "Exegesis," 165.

(Matt 5:17-19). Jesus never contradicts Scripture, so "between him and Moses there can be no real conflict."[96]

The Law features heavily in Matthew's Gospel (with eight occurrences of νόμος), and the Mosaic reference point would be intuitive for a first-century Jewish audience[97] as against the predominantly Gentile (or mixed Gentile and Jewish) audiences of Mark and Luke. This does not mean that all Christians in Matthew's audience were or should be more Law-observant,[98] but his Gospel shows that Jesus' Law-allegiance was rigorously tested *by Jesus' audience* on questions of Sabbath-keeping and taxation. How Jesus responded informs our understanding of his teaching on divorce. Sabbath-keeping is given special attention for it is core to Jewish identity, and fierce conflict over it led the Pharisees to conspire on how to kill Jesus (Matt 12:1-14).

In contrast, Mark caters more for a non-Jewish audience[99] and the "Law" (νόμος) does not appear anywhere in his Gospel, leaving Loader to conclude, "The theme of Law is not central to Mark's theology."[100] An apparent conflict between Matthew 15:1-20 and Mark 7:1-23 concerning Jewish food law can be settled in several ways.[101] It is likely that Jesus simply points to the source of defilement, teaching that food cannot be made ritually unclean by unwashed hands.[102] Mark's parenthetical statement (Mark 7:19) offers a post-resurrection revelation[103] (via Peter) that Jewish food law did not apply within the

---

[96] W. Davies and D. Allison, *The Gospel According to Saint Matthew*, vol. III, ICC (Edinburgh: T&T Clark, 1997), 481.

[97] Even if Matthew's original audience was mixed (Jew and Gentile), the Jewish Christians would readily reference Mosaic Law, and Matthew does not need extra explanatory notes.

[98] "The critical consensus wrongly sees Matthew's Gospel as promoting a much more law-observant form of Christianity than his canonical companions." C. Blomberg, "Matthew," in *Commentary on the New Testament Use of the Old Testament*, ed. G. Beale and D. Carson (Grand Rapids: Baker, 2007), 20.

[99] W. Loader, *Jesus' Attitude Towards the Law: A Study of the Gospels*, vol. 97. (Tübingen: Mohr Siebeck, 1997), 12.

[100] Ibid.

[101] E.g. J. Crossley, *The New Testament and Jewish Law: A Guide for the Perplexed* (London: Bloomsbury, 2010), 51-66. Carson gives a good appraisal of views: Carson, "Matthew," 396-402. Also R. Banks, *Jesus and the Law in the Synoptic Tradition*, SNTSMS 28 (New York: CUP, 1975), 132-46.

[102] "Impure hands by themselves cannot make food impure and so... why bother washing hands if it makes no difference?" Crossley, *Law*, 52. As with divorce law, there appears to have been a rabbinic debate over food law: "the House of Shammai say, 'They wash the hands then mix the cup' whereas the House of Hillel say, 'They mix the cup then wash the hands' (*m. Ber.* 8.2)." Ibid., 53.

[103] "A great deal of what Jesus taught became *progressively* clear to the church after the resurrection." Carson, "Matthew," 401. (Italics original.)

new covenant, whereas Matthew emphasizes that Jesus (along with his disciples) honoured it within the old.

David Garland observes, "Jesus allows what the Pharisees prohibited, eating with defiled hands, and prohibits what they allow, divorce."[104] William Countryman purports that the New Testament writers saw a difference

> between the ethics of food and those of sex; but it did not lie
> in a distinction between one kind of purity and another, for
> Levitical purity was of a piece.[105]

He contends that Christians abolished the physical purity rules regarding sex but retained "a whole realm of ethics based on property considerations," whilst the ethics of food "practically ceased to be" with "the gradual disappearance of a strong Jewish constituency from the church."[106] Undoubtedly Jewish Christians struggled with the new "socially defined reality"[107] of a new (Jewish) covenant (cf. Jer 31:31-33), but the real issue was that the first-century church had to resolve its relationship with the *indissoluble* Mosaic Law of the old (Jewish) covenant, with its *indivisible* ("of a piece"[108]) purity code that still had a hold on many sensitive consciences. This it did, as Jesus did, without abolishing one dot of the Law.

Jesus' teaching on divorce in Luke 16:18 is his first and only example of how the Law endures without the smallest change:

> In asserting, like Matthew, that not a jot or stroke of the law
> is to be discarded (16.17), Luke cites just one single
> illustration: Jesus' saying about divorce.[109]

Luke's positioning links Jesus' understanding of divorce to the *written* Mosaic text, for each "dot" (Luke 16:17) is inscribed rather than *spoken*. This basic point is crucial: *what is written* in the ancient text Jesus regards as paramount; he does not see as authoritative any contemporary Roman or Jewish traditions. The textual proximity could hardly be accidental in such an "orderly account" (Luke 1:3). Where Luke does use "Law" (ten occurrences of νόμος), he makes plain what law he references: for example, "the Law of Moses" (Luke 2:22; 24:44) and the "Law of the Lord" (Luke 2:23, 24, 27, 39). Jesus also debated with

---

[104] D. Garland, *Mark: From Biblical Text to Contemporary Life*, The NIV Application Commentary (Grand Rapids: Zondervan, 1996), 380.

[105] Countryman, *Dirt, Greed and Sex*, 139.

[106] Ibid.

[107] Ibid.

[108] Ibid.

[109] Loader, *Sexuality: Key Texts*, 92.

the "Pharisees and teachers of the Law" (Luke 5:17) and when a lawyer tried "to put him to the test," Jesus tested him on how he read "what is written in the Law" (Luke 10:26), to which the lawyer responded with a citation from Deuteronomy 6:5.

Covenant Violation

Clearly from the inauguration of the Mosaic Covenant, Israel is not to test God but to follow every one of his commands, for God has "come to test" them (Exod 20:20). In this test, the nation committed itself to an indivisible, binding-unto-death blood covenant. All the people originally gathered to hear the terms and upon unanimously confirming it, Moses sealed this covenant with the blood of their offerings, throwing half of it on the altar and the other half on the people (Exod 24:6-8). James Megivern relegates the Law to a "pedagogical function"[110] to provide a sanguine solution for dealing with very bloody texts, but downplays that God did command death for certain crimes, including slaughter of whole cities, literally not hyperbolically, and Jewish scholars such as Philo did demand the literal interpretation of capital laws (which Megivern footnotes).[111] Delineation between old and new covenants should therefore be strictly upheld when examining legal stipulations, for although the testaments uniformly condemn sexual immorality, immediate demands hinge on the covenant referenced.

When the Pharisees and Jesus both cite Moses in their debate over divorce (Matt 19:7, 8), the sanguineous Mosaic covenant-making context of Exodus 24:6-8 must pertain, where Israel formally agrees to follow *all of God's commands*. Contrariwise, **Christians routinely maintain that only the moral law, as represented by the Ten Commandments, continues to be applicable, without sure basis for neglecting the 600-odd other commands** – *with their many bloody demands*. John Sailhamer criticises covenant theologians "who believe the Mosaic Law cannot be approached as a totality," adding,

> Since nine of the Ten Commandments are repeated in the NT, this reduces the disputed territory to the question of whether Christians should keep the Sabbath.[112]

Christians commonly categorise Mosaic law codes into three groups: civil, ceremonial, and moral, and then quickly dismiss the first two. Yet

---

[110] J. Megivern, *The Death Penalty: An Historical and Theological Survey* (Mahwah: Paulist, 1997), 12.

[111] Ibid., 12, 492.

[112] J. Sailhamer, *The Meaning of the Pentateuch: Revelation, Composition, and Interpretation* (Downers Grove: IVP, 2009), 548.

the division is quite arbitrary and certainly not how Israel – or Jesus – approached the Law. It is mystifying, "For how do you decide in which 'hopper' an Old Testament law belongs?"[113] Andrew Cameron risks a charge of antinomianism,[114] but his view that considers "all parts of the Old Testament to have some bearing on Christian thought about right and wrong"[115] is well-nuanced. On divorce he is pragmatic, because "marriages do end."[116] Cameron contends that the Pentateuchal laws no longer have formal legal relevance for *Christians*[117] but fails to treat the Law as law in the context of a *Jewish legal debate* on divorce (Matt 19:1-12). He instead follows the Reformed legal-fiction where "divorce certifies the death" of a marriage.[118]

The efforts of William Luck[119] and Rousas Rushdoony[120] to apply the whole Old Testament moral legislation to the believer run counter to the purpose of the Law, let alone the purpose of Matthew. If only the moral principles of the Law are obeyed, this dismisses whole chunks of civil and ceremonial law. Luck and Rushdoony do sincerely strive to "depend on the words of Jesus that he did not come to abrogate the Law but to fulfil it" and in the face of Instone-Brewer's criticism,[121] the Old Testament moral laws do apply to Christians in principle. However, both sides miss the point that the *Old Testament Law in full – not just in moral principle, but every single detail and legal demand –* must be applied to the words of Jesus whenever a question of lawfulness arises. Legal demands cannot be divorced from law. One should not presume that Jesus is legislating a separate new law for Christians with the Matthew 5:32 and 19:9 'exception clause'. Jesus addresses Jewish concerns of Law with right legal interpretation, upholding the Law in every detail. In doing so, he defends his own righteousness and indicts an evil and adulterous generation.

It is significant that Jesus has pre-empted his teaching on divorce with, "not an iota, not a dot, will pass from the Law until all is accomplished" (Matt 5:18) and that, "whoever relaxes (λύω) one of the

---

[113] A. Cameron, *Joined-up Life: A Christian Account of How Ethics Works* (Nottingham: IVP, 2011), 136.

[114] Ibid., 137.

[115] Ibid., 139.

[116] Ibid., 241.

[117] Ibid., 137.

[118] Ibid., 242.

[119] W. Luck, *Divorce and Remarriage: Recovering the Biblical View* (San Francisco: Harper & Row, 1987).

[120] R. Rushdoony, *The Institutes of Biblical Law: A Chalcedon Study* (Nutley: Craig Press, 1973).

[121] Instone-Brewer, *Social and Literary Context*, 273-74.

least of these commandments and teaches others to do the same will be called least in the kingdom of heaven" (Matt 5:19). Here Matthew uses the verb λύω to indicate that the Law can be "loosed"; John 10:35 uses the same Greek verb to teach that Scripture cannot be "loosed," meaning that Jesus claims an unbreakable unity of Scripture. Even as the Pharisees and others break the Law and are indicted for it, Scripture cannot be broken, not even the smallest part. Like Scripture, the Law must remain unchanged, serving its purpose "until all is accomplished" (Matt 5:18), but unlike Scripture, there is the real threat and possibility of it being relaxed.

Jesus levels the accusation that the Pharisees *of his own time* have neglected the Law, and therefore violated the Mosaic Covenant. Bookending Jesus' seven woes to the scribes and Pharisees is a call to follow the Law, as opposed to the hypocritical practice of Jewish leaders (Matt 23:1-2), and an indictment of lawlessness (Matt 23:28) which includes judgement for shedding righteous blood (Matt 23:35-36). To practise and observe the Law is in full keeping with Jesus' teaching on the commandments: "whoever does them and teaches them will be called great in the kingdom of heaven" (Matt 5:19). The judgement for lawlessness is dire, and the Law condemns the shedding of innocent blood (Deut 19:3, 21:8-9; etc.), where all those who do this abomination (Prov 6:16-17) are cursed (Deut 27:5).

In the immediate context of the curse for shedding innocent blood, Deuteronomy adds, "Cursed be anyone who does not confirm the words of this law by doing them" (Deut 27:26). No wonder Jesus is so adamant, just prior to his first teaching in Matthew on divorce (Matt 5:31-32), that he has not come to abolish the Law or relax it in the least (Matt 5:17-20). One wonders, however, when interpreting Matthew 19:9, why commentators have no hesitation in referencing Deuteronomy 24:1-4, but rarely or never cite proximate verses with dire judgements for Law-breaking (e.g. Deut 22:22). Ancient Law, not contemporary culture, offers the most reliable and often terrifying reference point to interpret Jesus' teachings. The blessings for following the Law, for being careful *to do all* God's commandments (Deut 28:1), are enormous (Deut 28:1-14); the curses for disobedience are dreadful (Deut 28:15-68).

An obvious objection is that the text does not cite *any Mosaic penalties* in Matthew 19:9, so how could one be in view – let alone the most extreme? This will be addressed further in the forthcoming exegesis. Nonetheless, it begs the question about why Jesus would now hold a more lenient stance than Moses and other Old Testament prophets or himself just prior (Matt 18:5-9), where he even endorses death by drowning as a better course? If the Law is eternal and "its sanctions are executed on the day of judgment,"[122] how could the demands be only temporary or translatable with progressively lesser, kinder sanctions? Ultimately, relaxing or abolishing penalties of the Law risks nullifying any legal necessity for Jesus to die for the sins of those he came to save (Matt 1:21)[123] from a fate worse than death: hell.[124] If capital punishment is considered too extreme and not in view for "sexual immorality" or "adultery" (Matt 19:9), despite clearly being in view for Jesus' crucifixion, then what of Matthew's stress on eternal punishment? It is unlikely that the one whom Matthew presents as "King of the Jews" (2:2; 27:11, 29, 37) and "King of Israel" (27:42) is compelled by Roman law to adapt the Law in any way that does not reflect the original and final gravity of high offences ultimately against Israel's God and King.

The Law commands "life for life" (Exod 21:23; Deut 19:21); and "whoever kills a person shall be put to death" (Lev 24:21). Similarly, the death penalty is commanded for several different acts of sexual immorality (cf. Exod 22:19; Lev 20:10, 13). Yet in Matthew's Gospel, judgements of "life for life" and "shall be put to death" generally do not appear (excepting e.g. Matt 15:4). However, such omission does not automatically abolish or relax unpalatable parts of Law. Rather than asserting a change in the Law, or a move from a law to a moral teaching,[125] silence may simply mean that the Old Testament penalty remains constant: Jewish people in Jesus' time, who have no concept that there is an 'old' Old Testament, know the old penalty (even if they do not apply it). The penalty only needs to be made explicit for a more Gentile readership (cf. John 8:5).

Jesus' Sermon on the Mount has long found parallels with Moses' giving of the Law at Mt Sinai. It is unsurprising then that Jesus echoes the Decalogue pattern that omits "the violent solution" for breaches.[126] Victor Hamilton demonstrates that the first nine commandments involve obvious means for establishing guilt and bringing prosecution, where a breach of any of these commandments attracts the death penalty

---

[122] Keener, *And Marries Another*, 115.

[123] This relies on Jesus' declaration that he came to fulfil the Law (Matt 5:17), with an implication that justice is served in his blood (Matt 27:19-25) being shed for the forgiveness of others (Matt 20:28; 26:28).

[124] Matthew uses "hell" (γέεννα) 8 times, far more than other Gospel writers (Mark: 3; Luke: 1; John: 0).

[125] A. Harvey, *Promise or Pretence? A Christian's Guide to Sexual Morals* (London: SCM, 1994), 21.

[126] V. Hamilton, *Handbook on the Pentateuch* (Grand Rapids: Baker, 1982), 197.

on some or all occasions, as found beyond the Decalogue.[127] For example,

> Commandment One: "You shall have no other gods" (cf. Exod 22:20, "Whoever sacrifices to any god, save to the LORD only, shall be utterly destroyed").
> Commandment Two: "You shall not make for yourself a graven image" (cf. Exod 32, with the nearly catastrophic result after the incident of the golden calf).
> Commandment Five: "Honor your father and your mother" (cf. Exod 21:15, 17, "Whoever strikes/curses his father or his mother shall be put to death").
> Commandment Seven: "You shall not commit adultery" (cf. Deut 22:22, "If a man is found lying with the wife of another man, both of them shall die").
> Commandment Eight: "You shall not steal" (cf. Exod 22:1-3; and see Exod 21:16, "Whoever kidnaps a person... shall be put to death").[128]

Hamilton then contemplates a question that is relevant both to Jesus' teaching on "adultery" in the heart (Matt 5:27-30) and the 'exception clause' of "sexual immorality" (Matt 5:32; 19:9).

> Could the pattern be made to continue into the last commandment: "Thou shalt not covet... Anyone who covets... shall die/be put to death"? ...narratives to support the idea are not lacking. This is the story of Eve, of Achan, of Ahab and Jezebel over Naboth's vineyard, of Judas Iscariot... Perhaps this is the reason why this particular command is placed last. It is the most comprehensive of all the commandments, and it includes what is lacking in the rest of the Decalogue. And who will not recognize that behind much killing, adultery, stealing, and lying is covetousness? This is the root of the problem.[129]

For Paul it appears to be the root of the problem too, for he singles out **"You shall not covet" as the commandment that brought him death** (Rom 7:7-12). Nevertheless, Paul's claim that he was "blameless" under the Law (Phil 3:6) should be taken seriously, for no court in the land could prosecute him for his inner thoughts. Yet the Law, and in particular the Tenth Commandment, still finds him guilty, the higher heavenly court finds him guilty, and Jesus' teaching in

---

[127] Ibid.
[128] Ibid., 196-97.
[129] Ibid., 197-98.

Matthew's Gospel finds him guilty, such that inner sin attracts the death penalty.

Following the Decalogue, Moses presents possible violations with their consequences. Likewise, following the Beatitudes, Jesus addresses anger, conflict, and lust. Some of these sins make one liable to the judgement of the religious council, others could lead to prison sentences, and still others could put one in danger of being thrown into the fires of hell. **In the subsequent matter of divorce, it can be expected that "sexual immorality" and "adultery" demand no lesser consequences.**

Sabbath Law

In Matthew's Gospel, Pharisees test Jesus on what is "lawful" concerning both the Sabbath (Matt 12:1-14) and divorce (Matt 19:1-12). These matters are parallel, for if any charge of unlawfulness can be proven, Jesus could lose his popularity, his authority, and perhaps his very life. The intention of the Jewish leaders is to kill Jesus, seen directly after he declares himself "lord of the Sabbath" and heals in "their synagogue" (Matt 12:8-13), whereas, leading into this conflict, the Pharisees may have been content with publicly flogging Jesus.[130] Karl Barth considers "This breach was one of the most concrete things which made His destruction necessary in the eyes of His opponents."[131]

According to the Law, the Sabbath is holy and "Everyone who profanes it shall be put to death" (Exod 31:14). Although some churches retain seventh-day Sabbath observance, the capital demand for Sabbath violation has generally been relaxed.[132] If Jesus changed the Law, then the implication is that his followers can. This includes altering "the day of the Lord" to "Sunday," even though this can yield a legalism at odds with the Law, and obscure the judgement motif.[133] However, if Jesus did not relax the Law in the least (Matt 5:17-19), then his approach to

---

[130] D. Instone-Brewer, *Traditions of the Rabbis from the Era of the New Testament*, 2a. Feasts and Sabbaths: Passover and Atonement (Grand Rapids: Eerdmans, 2011), 35.

[131] K. Barth, *Church Dogmatics, Volume IV.2: The Doctrine of Reconciliation* (London: T&T Clark, 2009), 177.

[132] To avoid capital implications it might be said, "The Sabbath can only be meant for Israel, with whom the covenant was made." Dressler in D. Carson, *From Sabbath to Lord's Day: A Historical and Theological Foundation* (Eugene: Wipf & Stock, 1999), 30.

[133] "The 'day' of the Lord came to mean the day on which God comes to judge." F. Murphy, *Apocalypticism in the Bible and its World: A Comprehensive Introduction* (Grand Rapids: Baker, 2012), 40-41. Marriage and judgement are related: "that day" is compared with Noah's flood, where people were "marrying and giving in marriage" (Matt 24:36-38). Both are also delayed: judgement "will come on a day" unexpected (Matt 24:45-51), and only the ready virgins will "meet the bridegroom" (Matt 25:1-13).

Sabbath law should inform our understanding of his divorce teaching. Jesus' response to a legal question on divorce (Matt 19:3) must likewise be interpreted as a right interpretation of the Law, *before any re-appropriation for Christian living.*

Jesus' justification for his disciples' Sabbath action lies in what is "read" (Matt 12:3, 5), which itself supports the indissolubility of the Law. There are several arguments that explain how Jesus successfully averted a charge of lawlessness.[134] Just as the priests "profane" (Matt 12:5) the Sabbath by ministering on it in their Temple duties (cf. Num 28:9-10),[135] that involved hard physical work in sacrificing animals, so Jesus – a great high priest[136] – also ministers on the Sabbath without guilt. Jesus' disciples, as priestly assistants, are thus guiltless too, for while traversing the cornfields they gain sustenance for partaking in priestly service.[137]

This presents a lawful 'exception' to the general Sabbath rest rule, not a capricious call. It might not be an 'exception' at all, for the Law prescribes a system of charity where the poor take *peah* or the grain left at the edges of the field to eat on any day (cf. Lev 19:9-10). Such casual gleaning is differentiated from putting a sickle to it (Deut 23:25) – harvest work prohibited on the Sabbath (Exod 23:12).

That Jesus strictly upheld the Law and honoured the Temple does not necessarily translate directly to (later) Christian application.[138] If lawful exceptions were permitted simply on the basis of human need, then this would raise a rather unanswerable question, "So, what happens to Sabbath observance when human need, no matter how trivial, takes

---

[134] E.g. see: M. Casey, *Aramaic Sources of Mark's Gospel*, SNTSMS 102 (Cambridge: CUP, 2004), 138-92. Crossley, *Law*, 26-44. C. Arand et al., *Perspectives on the Sabbath: 4 Views*, ed. C. Donato (Nashville: B&H, 2014).

[135] "The first-century rabbis allowed violations of the Sabbath for at least six occasions, and temple service was one of them" Y. Yang, *Jesus and the Sabbath in Matthew's Gospel*, JSNTS (Sheffield: Sheffield Academic, 1997), 178.

[136] Spadaro expounds on 'The Priestly Subtext of Matthew', and proposes that Matthew presents the same theology as Hebrews, expressed in the form of his "historical" narrative. Spadaro, *Matthew*, 29, 188.

[137] It might be countered that the disciples are not serving Jesus at this particular time. However, purely by being "disciples" they are in his service.

[138] McIver gives an example of using the Law in a way parallel to Matt 12:1-14, but in doing so exposes his hermeneutic of direct new covenant application: "*Christians* are told not to neglect paying tithe on the mint, dill and cummin (Matt 23:23)." (Italics added.) R. McIver, "The Sabbath in the Gospel of Matthew: A Paradigm for Understanding the Law in Matthew?," *Andrews University Seminary Studies* 33, no. 2 (1995): 243. Jesus does not speak to Christians here at all, but directs a rebuke at Jewish leaders who live under the Law: they should tithe precisely as the Law prescribes *and* not neglect the weightier matters. (Christians can definitely learn from this, but it would not mean tithing herbs and spices in the Jerusalem Temple offering system).

precedence?"[139] Regarding divorce, it would set a disturbing precedent. Nonetheless, a valid question remains: may Sabbath law remain inviolate not for the sake of any human need but for *the sake of human life*, say in a time of war?[140] Essentially, since there are no clear biblical commands concerning fighting on the Sabbath, the Law could permit this, especially for self-defence. In contrast, *there are clear biblical commands* concerning all types of sexual immorality, including explicit prohibitions and penalties in the Law. This makes it difficult to justify a reinterpretation of the Law on a specific question of Law to interpret Jesus' teaching that centres on "sexual immorality" (Matt 19:9).

Morris cautions against a conclusion "that Jesus is saying that any human being is entitled to modify a divine ordinance as he chooses," for this misses Matthew's Christological emphasis.[141] Jesus, being who he is, "can declare what are the rules for observing the Sabbath," but "this does not mean simply that Jesus has the authority to relax harsh restrictions."[142] Instead there is historical, scriptural, and merciful precedent *in the Law* to justify the lawfulness. Jesus likely even saw that the Sabbath

> was a pre-eminently suitable day for the performance of such works of mercy... since such works were so completely in keeping with God's purpose in giving the day.[143]

In the parallel matter of divorce law, an exception to the rule that is unanchored in the Law and based on *human need* would open the floodgates to multiple grounds for divorce, making practically "any cause" permissible (cf. Matt 19:3). It would also void the gravity of the one and only lawful case that Jesus does specify: "sexual immorality" (Matt 19:9).

---

[139] Ibid., 242.
[140] See Appendix 1.
[141] Morris, *Matthew*, 304.
[142] Ibid.
[143] F. F. Bruce, *New Testament History* (London: Nelson, 1969), 174.

CHAPTER 4 – Context of Matthew 19:1-12

Narrative Setting

The narrative setting of Matthew 19:1-12 can be no accident; "Jesus has just talked about forgiveness, and the marriage relationship is the most intense example of that need."[1] The Pharisees' concern on the lawful grounds for breaking the most solemn of all human relationships stands in stark relief to Jesus' teaching on healing human relationships at all costs; Matthew prominently references Jesus' words exhorting forgiveness (Matt 19:1) and locates them immediately prior (Matt 18:15-35) to his discussion on marriage. With this prelude of forgiveness and a journey narrative bookended with miraculous healing (Matt 19:2; 20:29-34), the legal debate contrasts sharply with a greater compassionate context.[2]

Nolland sees that Jesus' preceding story (Matt 18:23-35) is founded on "the compassion that, in connection with the coming kingdom, flows from God through the ministry of Jesus"; and inasmuch as it "treats the forgiveness of God as creating a new situation that entails fresh responsibilities, a more fundamental level of insight is involved."[3] On this more fundamental level, Martinus de Boer perceives a "new world" that Jesus' story makes "plausible, understandable, acceptable, and real."[4] This may be Matthew's way of speaking about a new heaven-like order (cf. his characteristic use of "kingdom of heaven") or new covenant, *where debt and sacrifice give way to mercy and forgiveness.*

God's mercy has of course already featured in the Hebrew Bible, as evident in the case of David's adultery (2 Sam 12; cf. Matt 1:6), with forgiveness available for those subject to the Law in a way beyond the legal codes, without annulling these codes. Likewise, Matthew upholds the existing order, based on the Law, at times in the face of contemporary Jewish practice to the contrary. He demonstrates that Jesus has not come to abolish this order, and that it will not be abolished

---

[1] Osborne, *Matthew*, 699-700.

[2] For Jesus' journey (Matt 19:1-20:34), "These two chapters begin and end with explicit references to Jesus on the road, surrounded by great crowds and healing people." Blomberg, *Matthew*, 287.

[3] Nolland, *Matthew*, 761.

[4] M. de Boer, "Ten Thousand Talents? Matthew's Interpretation and Redaction of the Parable of the Unforgiving Servant (Matt 18:23-35)," *CBQ* 50 (1988): 231.

until heaven and earth pass away (Matt 5:17-19). This insight of God's forgiveness "creating a new situation" that is not merely about fresh personal responsibilities offers fresh light on Jesus' word on marriage that directly follows, revealing how the "new world" challenges old ways without one dot of the Law giving way.

To place the marriage pericope in its wider literary context, Jesus has embarked on his final journey to Jerusalem, having ministered "beyond the Jordan" in "Galilee of the Gentiles" (Matt 4:15; cf.19:1) for the last time prior to his crucifixion. The narrative moves from the Galilean Sermon on the Mount, containing Jesus' initial teaching on adultery and divorce (Matt 5:27-32), to the Judean Mount of Olives, where Jesus predicts that all will fall away, including his closest disciples (Matt 26:31).[5] This movement, with its intervening low points, is in keeping with the fact that not everyone will follow Jesus or receive his words (cf. Matt 19:11), even those who claim to know and obey God's commands (cf. the Pharisees in Matt 19:7, and the rich young man in Matt 19:16-22). Yet on each side of this passage on what God commands about marriage, Matthew records that those with child-like humility (Matt 18:1-6) and little children who would hardly know any commands will receive the kingdom that Jesus proclaims (Matt 19:13-15). Something in this intimates that God's commands are actually easy to understand, which also suggests that a straightforward, non-technical interpretation of Matthew 19:9 is in order.

Following the Sermon on the Mount, religious leaders oppose Jesus, attempting to undermine his authority. This echoes Moses' descent from the mount to find the people "had broken loose" under Aaron, where the "sons of Levi" (Exod 32:27-29) then delivered *and* suffered divine judgement for the "evil" committed (Exod 32:22). The Law has an emphasis on purging evil by the sword or stoning to death (Deut 13:5; 17:7-19; 21:21-24; 24:7) and one startling characteristic of Matthew is his emphasis on "evil."[6] What Jesus has decreed on the mountain concerning marriage and divorce (Matt 5:31-32) will now be challenged by people with evil intent to destroy him (Matt 12:14).

Matthew features Jesus' second teaching on marriage and divorce (Matt 19:1-12) as his first lesson en route to the cross, with two subsequent wedding parables (Matt 22:1-14; 25:1-13). All three

---

[5] "Key revelatory and eschatological moments occur on mountains." J. Brown, "Matthew, Gospel Of," in *Dictionary of Jesus and the Gospels*, ed. J. Brown, J. Green, and N. Perrin (Illinois: IVP, 2014), 572.

[6] Matthew uses πονηρός 26 times (cf. Mark: 2; Luke: 14); πονηρία once (also once in Mark and in Luke); κακός three times (cf. twice in Mark and in Luke); and κακία once (absent in Mark and Luke).

marriage-related passages function as dire warnings to opponents. This is supported by viewing Matthew's two wedding parables through a lens of fulfilling the Law and the Prophets. For example, Spadaro sees the man with no wedding garment in Matthew 22:11-13 specifically as the high priest; and Scripture has already warned against repeating this offence (cf. Zech 3). He notes that the additional information of the guests being destroyed and their "city" burned (22:7) "is almost universally accepted by scholars as pointing to the destruction of Jerusalem."[7] Spadaro also understands the Ten Virgins in Matthew 25:1-13 in relation to the Jewish leaders, for the job of the priests was to perpetually keep the lamps burning in the Temple. He observes that Solomon's Temple was furnished with ten lamps (1 Kgs 7:49), five each side of the inner sanctuary, which was a sacred space having strong Ancient Near East (ANE) parallels with royal bridal chambers.[8] Such unfaithfulness to and judgement by God informs our understanding of lawful grounds for terminating marriage.

Prior to Jesus' death, Judas returns the "blood money" to the Temple, which the Jewish leaders reject as "not lawful" to place in the treasury (Matt 27:5-6). This naturally raises the question as to why the Pharisees earlier needed to ask Jesus the question "Is it lawful…?" (Matt 19:3) when they know such fine details of the Law. Their response to Judas further underlines the religious leaders' hypocrisy, since this is *the same money* given by the chief priests of the Temple system that they now will not deposit in the Temple treasury, and their legalism of straining a gnat but swallowing a camel (Matt 23:23-24). A strict legalism suits their purposes with respect to blood money, but finds them exposed and condemned by Matthew's narrative for great injustice.

Matthew concludes his account with Jesus on another mountain, back in Galilee, resurrected and reconciled with his disciples (Matt 28:16). Remote from the central Jerusalem Temple system, Jesus inaugurates a movement with a didactic emphasis, "make disciples of all nations… teaching them to observe all that I have commanded" (Matt 28:18-20). This teaching must include Jesus' commands on marriage, likely to be passed on in similar contexts of opposition from earthly authorities, general non-receptivity, and even doubt among Christ-followers (Matt 28:17). As **Jesus directed his ministry in his earthly life only to Israel** (Matt 10:5-6; 15:24-26), the original Jewish audience should primarily be borne in mind concerning what Jesus taught and to whom the commands of the Law apply. Pre-crucifixion,

---

[7] Spadaro, Matthew, 176.
[8] Ibid., 178-80.

Jesus never commanded Gentile conformity to the Torah, nor did he stage a mission teaching Jews to go out and command it. Jesus' "observe all that I have commanded you" (Matt 28:20) must include *observing the occasion* of each command.

For example, "Go nowhere among the Gentiles" (Matt 10:5) does not preclude later Gentile evangelism. "A wise man" not only distinguishes between rock and sand (Matt 7:24-25), but hears and puts into practice the lessons learnt from what Jesus tells his Jewish audience about the Law, without presuming that the Law applies to anyone outside of the Mosaic Covenant. To "obey [τηρέω]" all that Jesus has commanded (Matt 28:20) can be read as "observe" or "pay attention to,"[9] which is a better interpretation here, for Matthew uses a different term elsewhere for exact obedience: in Matthew 8:27, "the winds and the seas obey [ὑπακούω] him."[10] So with respect to Jesus' charge, "Go nowhere among the Gentiles" (Matt 10:5), Christians must "observe [τηρέω]" that this was a real command of Jesus to his all-Jewish disciples *at that time*, but they are not to exactly "obey [ὑπακούω]" it later.

Similarly, Jesus' command "to the crowds and his disciples" to do and "observe" the Law (Matt 23:1-3) should not be seen by Christians that they must exactly "obey" the Law themselves, but **they are to observe the lesson *taught there to these Jews*.** Even on that occasion, Jesus' command is not to strictly "obey" the Jewish leaders (the term ὑπακούω is not used), but to practice and "observe [τηρέω]" whatever they say as they sit on Moses' seat – which must include observing that what they say is what Moses actually commanded. Then they should follow Moses and not what the Jewish leaders do, "For they preach but do not practice." Here the word "preach" must not be prematurely Christianised either, for it involves Jews proclaiming Moses and the Law to Jews, not Christians later preaching the Gospel. A good principle of "practicing what you preach" can be observed nonetheless!

Post-resurrection, it is striking that Jesus, with "all authority" (Matt 28:18), offers no hint that the Temple remains the focal point of authority. Barth recognises that Jesus could not ascribe any permanent significance to the Temple: "Unlike the Law in Matt. 5:17f., it was not to continue until heaven and earth passed away."[11] For Christians to restore the Temple, along with its meticulous system of legal demands,

---

[9] F. Danker, W. Bauer, and W. Arndt, *A Greek-English Lexicon of the New Testament and Other Early Christian Literature*, Third ed. (Chicago: UCP, 2000), 815.

[10] Ibid., 837.

[11] Barth, *Dogmatics IV.2*, 179.

would be "a relapse into Judaism" and "a rejection of the true Judaism."[12] At the same time, the destruction of the Temple does not mean that Israel is rejected, for the very heart of Matthew's message is that Jesus will save his people from their sins (Matt 1:21).

Jesus commanded Jews to follow the Torah in every detail under the Mosaic Covenant, but in a post-resurrection age this does not imply that Jewish and Gentile disciples are commanded to keep the Torah. Disciples will have Jesus with them always "to the end of the age" (Matt 28:20), an assurance that immediately follows his call to teach and observe all that he has commanded. This suggests that Jesus' ongoing presence will guide his disciples in applying his commands in and beyond Torah-observant contexts. Then when "all is accomplished," the Law passes away (Matt 5:18), along with Jesus' commands concerning the Law in Matthew 19:1-12.[13]

The Pharisees, in their antagonism towards Jesus, function broadly as representative of the people of Israel, where "Matthew's approach is to demonstrate that the true people of God are those who believe and obey Jesus (12:46-50)."[14] While the Jewish crowds (Matt 4:25; 13:2; 19:2) are initially drawn to Jesus' teaching and miracles, they eventually follow the Jewish leaders in rejecting and condemning Jesus (Matt 27:20-25). These leaders are largely portrayed as sceptical, unfeeling, and united against a "dangerous innovator."[15] Hagner stresses that the hostile language between Jesus and the Jewish leaders is not anti-Semitic, for the words are written by a Jew concerning Jews and should be "understood as intramural Jewish polemic."[16] Jack Kingsbury maintains that this conflict is not incidental Jewish infighting, but central to the plot.[17] If so, the conflict within Matthew 19:1-12 is also central to a narrative that builds an indictment against "an evil and adulterous generation" (Matt 12:39; 16:4).

---

[12] *Church Dogmatics, Volume II.1: The Doctrine of God* (London: T&T Clark, 2009), 44.

[13] "The time for which the Torah is valid begins with Moses and ends with the end of the world." H. Betz, *The Sermon on the Mount*, Hermeneia (Minneapolis: Fortress, 1995), 184.

[14] S. McKnight, "Matthew, Gospel Of," in *Dictionary of Jesus and the Gospels*, ed. I. H. Marshall, S. McKnight, and J. B. Green (Downers Grove: IVP, 1992), 537.

[15] Morris, *Matthew*, 413.

[16] Hagner, *Matthew 1-13*, lxxii.

[17] J. Kingsbury, *Matthew as Story* (Philadelphia: Fortress, 1986), 3.

Geo-Political Setting

Conflict in Matthew 19:1-12 is evident not only in the intense discourse between Jesus and the Pharisees, but fiercely behind the scenes geo-politically. The location has much significance, for it was from "beyond the Jordan" (Num 22:1; Josh 1:14; cf. Matt 19:1) that Israel, led by Joshua, had staged their first major battle to claim promised land under enemy rule. John the Baptist had more recently ministered in the same region, as a precursor to the new "Joshua" (Hebrew: יְהוֹשׁוּעַ; or Greek: Ἰησοῦς), with the land again under enemy rule. John's execution by Herod Antipas, the occupying king (Matt 14:1-12), occurred between 28 and 30CE. So to better understand Matthew 19:1-12, Loader avers that,

> We need to consider the matter of divorce and remarriage of Herod Antipas, which would have been 'topical' during the ministry of the historical Jesus.[18]

When Jesus journeyed from Galilee to Judea "beyond the Jordan" (Perea), the ruler over both jurisdictions, Herod Antipas, had recently married Herodias and had John the Baptist killed. Josephus records that Herodias flouted the biblical laws by initiating a divorce with her husband to then marry Herod Antipas.[19] Furthermore, Herodias parted from *a living husband*, implying something unusual, if not shocking and shameful – at least for a woman to do.[20] Normal parting would be upon death, which culturally might not be referred to as a "divorce," but it would be a "loosing" from the marriage nonetheless.[21] The offence (cf. Lev 18:16; 20:21),

> is not just the issue of marrying someone who had been divorced, but marrying someone who had been married to a blood brother.[22]

Incensed, "Herodias confirms John's identity as Elijah by acting the murderous Jezebel to Herod's sympathetic Ahab."[23] Clearly *for John, Roman law, or any authority of Herod in creating his own law or standard, did not abolish the Law of Moses.*

---

[18] Loader, *Jesus Tradition*, 107.

[19] *Ant.* 18.109-111. Josephus, *Works*, 484.

[20] *Ant.* 18.136. Ibid., 485.

[21] The same Greek terms for 'divorce' could be applied for they basically mean to loose away or separate.

[22] Loader, *Jesus Tradition*, 110-11.

[23] R. Janes, "Why the Daughter of Herodias Must Dance (Mark 6.14-29)," *JSNT* 28, no. 4 (2006): 443.

Herodias was also Herod's niece, the daughter of another half-brother (Aristobulus IV); so their relationship might be deemed incestuous.[24] Matthew describes Herodias not as Herod's wife but "his brother Philip's wife" (Matt 14:3; cf. Mark 6:17). The adulterous inference is patent, echoing Matthew's designation of Bathsheba as "the wife of Uriah" (Matt 1:6). Adultery was condemned in the Law, so this supports a broader interpretation that Herod's marriage was unlawful not solely on an understanding that it might be incestuous. The historical background also lends support to a broader definition of sexual immorality in Matthew 19:9.

The Gospels make no mention of Herod's earlier marriage to Phasaelis,[25] for John's condemnation is directed only at the Herod-Herodias relationship. Josephus records that the Herod-Phasaelis marital breakdown had destructive geo-political consequences,[26] but he does not specifically mention "divorce," only the discovery by Phasaelis of Herod's intentions.[27] This obviously centred on Herod's plan to divorce her, but Phasaelis fled *before she could be sent away* in this manner. Hence, any kind of formal divorce, one that involves a husband writing a divorce certificate, putting it in his wife's hand, and then sending her out of his house (cf. Deut 24:1), simply did not occur.

Phasaelis' flight from Herod might be construed as "divorce by desertion," but Josephus never terms it as such. In Jewish history it has even been said that "this marriage was annulled."[28] Furthermore, Josephus makes no mention of Herod finding some "matter of indecency" in Phasaelis, so any connection with the divorce process of Deuteronomy 24:1-4 is even more remote. Instead, Josephus records a matter of infidelity centred on the Herod-Herodias relationship in line

---

[24] An Essene reading extrapolates this from the prohibition of marrying nephews (cf. Lev 18:6-18). D. Chapman, "Marriage and Family in Second Temple Judaism," in *Marriage and Family in the Biblical World*, ed. K. Campbell (Downers Grove: IVP, 2003), 199. However, for the Jews, marrying nieces was not generally forbidden; indeed, this was a preferred option for many for endogamous marriages. W. Loader, *The New Testament on Sexuality* (Grand Rapids: Eerdmans, 2012), 248.

[25] Herod was long-married to an Arabian princess, daughter of King Aretas IV of Nabatea. The marriage was likely arranged by Augustus, before his death in 14CE, "to gain peace between Jews and Arabs." H. Hoehner, "Dictionary of New Testament Background : A Compendium of Contemporary Biblical Scholarship," ed. C. Evans and S. Porter Jr. (Westmont: IVP, 2000), 491.

[26] The breakdown added a personal grievance to previous disputes over territory on the border of Perea and Nabatea. Aretas invaded Herod's territory of Perea and destroyed his whole army. *Ant.* 18.114. Josephus, *Works*, 484.

[27] *Ant.* 18.111-112. Ibid.

[28] M. Stern, "The Herodian Dynasty and the Province of Judea," in *The Herodian Period*, ed. M. Avi-Yonah, The World History of the Jewish People (Givatayim: Jewish History Publications, 1975), 134.

with the "sexual immorality" of Matthew 19:9. It speaks against the betrothal (only) view too.[29] Here is a serious sexual offence (not merely a matter of indecency), explicitly recorded in the Gospels *and* by Josephus, that serves as strong historical background to the divorce debate.

"Beyond the Jordan" has another calamitous association in Matthew 4:15, for the referent (Isa 9:1) offers the geographical standpoint of the Assyrian invaders. Assyria was God's instrument to destroy the Northern Kingdom of Israel when he divorced her for idolatry and sexual immorality (Jer 3:8). Yet Isaiah is at pains to note that the Southern Kingdom of Judah was not divorced (Isa 50:1). That there were two divided "houses" of Israel, one divorced and one separated for the same crimes, may infer divided approaches to marital breakdown and only two lawful outcomes.

The setting "beyond the Jordan" in Matthew 4:12-16 cannot be the same as in 19:1-12, for in the former Jesus "withdrew into Galilee," whereas in the latter, Jesus "went away from Galilee." However, Galilee remains the narrative focal point, and its shadowy repute (Matt 4:16) has overtones of Perea's destructive history, where John ministered and lost his life over a matter of divorce. Despite seeing a "great light," the same grounds for divorce that is taught in both regions (Matt 5:32; 19:9) may foreshadow the same dark future. The south is not exempt from this future. Matthew's Gospel foretells catastrophic destruction: Matthew 23 contains Jesus' pronouncement of seven woes on the Pharisees and his lament over Jerusalem "left to you desolate" (Matt 23:38); and Matthew 24 has Jesus predict the destruction of the Jerusalem Temple, the abomination of desolation, the flight of Judeans, and the great tribulation. With the growing indictment, it is Judah with her Temple stewards who may be divorced this time, and not simply the northern tribes.

Intriguingly, both Galilee and Perea (where Jesus teaches the 'exception clause') were formerly occupied by northern tribes of Israel who were all divorced by God.[30] This adds another perspective to Jesus' claim: "I was only sent to the lost sheep of Israel" (Matt 10:5-6; 15:24), for these tribes had largely been lost since the Assyrian conquest and he ministers exclusively in their regions. Thus, Jesus is essentially speaking to children of "divorced parents": Israelites forsaken by God

---

[29] A. Köstenberger and D. Jones, *God, Marriage, and Family: Rebuilding the Biblical Foundation*, 2nd ed. (Wheaton: Crossway, 2010), 224.

[30] Galilee mainly belonged to Zebulon and Naphthali; Perea to Reuben and Gad, and possibly Manasseh in part. Both regions were subject to Assyrian conquest, deportation, and immigration.

(Deut 31:17) because they forsook God and broke his covenant (Deut 31:16).

Deuteronomy 1:1 provides another ancient connection: "the words that Moses spoke to all Israel beyond the Jordan" can be compared with Jesus' words on marriage and divorce "beyond the Jordan" in Matthew 19:1-12, especially with a passage such as Deuteronomy 24:1-4 in view. This second book of law is not a second and distinct law, but repeats "much of the legislation contained in preceding books, though the context and form of that repetition is peculiar to Deuteronomy."[31] However, it does anticipate another prophet like Moses (Deut 18:15-18), and Matthew presents Jesus as fulfilling this.

In Jesus' time and in Israel's history, marriage and divorce are grave matters, over which many lives literally have been destroyed. The very purpose of the Pharisees' test question is found in their plot to see Jesus destroyed (Matt 12:14). This may help explain why Matthew sets this as Jesus' first teaching on his last journey from Galilee to his death in Jerusalem. Somehow, against this hostile setting, Jesus did not appear to have upset the secular rulers in the same way that John the Baptist had. **This suggests that it is easy to misread Jesus' 'exception clause' in accordance with current laws, cultural traditions, and personal circumstances.**

No doubt Jesus' response was reported to Herod, for the Pharisees have conspired with the Herodians (Mark 3:6), and will continue to (Matt 22:16) in order to destroy him. However, unlike John, Jesus' wise and clever divorce teaching will not get him killed! Herod could simply reason that he has valid grounds of "sexual immorality" (cf. Matt 19:9) – his own or Herodias' – or Phasaelis' supposed unfaithfulness in deserting him, or "she finds no favour in his eyes because he has found some indecency in her" (cf. Deut 24:1), which mandated divorce by Roman law. Nonetheless, he would still stand condemned by the Law and by Jesus (as he was condemned by John).

Cultural Setting

Rival Shammai-Hillel understandings of Deuteronomy 24:1-4 have already been recognised as possible background to the Pharisees' testing of Jesus, although an alignment with one contemporary view would hardly have endangered Jesus' life. The broader cultural setting will now be canvassed to better appreciate Jewish views on marriage and divorce in the Second Temple context. This may help to determine

---

[31] P. Craigie, *The Book of Deuteronomy*, NICOT (Grand Rapids: Eerdmans, 1976), 17.

whether Jesus' teaching on marriage and divorce reflected current thinking, and Jesus sought to uphold the Law in a similar way (even if more so in tune with a Shammaite understanding). Or did Jesus profoundly challenge contemporary views?

Daniel Block recaptures ancient Israelite perspectives of family life, with a vital caveat:

> Since the narratives and laws recorded in the Old Testament derive from a time span exceeding a millennium and from periods of vastly different socioeconomic realities, it would be foolish to suppose that family and marriage customs were uniform throughout this period or even throughout the nation at any given time.[32]

This makes it hard to define what is truly "Jewish," and Loader rightly cautions: "To speak of Greek and Roman cultures is already grossly to oversimplify what was much more complex," and Jewish presuppositions mingle with these and other cultural influences for at least three centuries prior to the NT.[33] Further caution is required then if it is claimed that Jesus' divorce teaching can only be understood in relation to what are uncertain marriage customs, and a question remains as to whether the narratives and laws of the Old Testament display an enduring uniformity even as family and marriage customs change. *Is there a permanency about the Law, independent of cultural change, that Jesus could be said to have upheld (cf. Matt 5:17-19)?*

Undoubtedly Jesus lived as a Jew – heralded as "the son of David, the son of Abraham" (Matt 1:1) and even "born king of the Jews" (Matt 2:2). Nevertheless, does Matthew portray Jesus' life as the "chronological antitype of Israel's experience"[34] where, as true Israel, Jesus obeyed the Law of Moses in a way that Israel – for over a millennium, and throughout the nation at any given time – did not? This can be investigated by examining some of Israel's marriage customs.

Michael Satlow sets the general scene:

> All marriage contracts in antiquity, whether Jewish or not, focussed primarily on economic relations, occasionally giving attention to the way that spouses should treat each other. The purpose of Jewish marriage documents was not to create

---

[32] D. Block, "Marriage and Family in Ancient Israel," in *Marriage and Family in the Biblical World*, ed. K. Campbell (Downers Grove: IVP, 2003).

[33] Loader, *On Sexuality*, 74.

[34] N. Batzig, "Israel and Typology in Matthew's Gospel," https://feedingonchrist.org/israel-and-typology-in-matthews-gospel/.

marriage, but to clarify and codify economic obligations within it.[35]

Even so, what if Jesus' teaching *focussed primarily on relations*, between spouses – including Yahweh-Israel, with only indirect attention to *economic relations*? Can the purpose of Matthew's 'exception clause' simply be found in reading the most sacred Jewish marriage document – the Law – that clarifies and codifies covenant obligations concerning what God has joined together? If this is the case, great import falls on the original meaning of Scripture written in *ancient antiquity*, which might differ markedly from (Jewish and pagan) marriage contracts written *throughout antiquity* that commonly emphasize economic obligations.

The Dowry

One prominent economic obligation that deserves closer scrutiny is dowry-giving, which is well-represented in marriage documents of the Second Temple period.[36] The amount is specified, and some indicate that the husband added to the dowry.[37] Yet within Israel, significant diversity presents:

> The Judean Greek documents varied from the corresponding Aramaic certificates by the use of the Greco-Roman form of stating the date, the use of the third person and the focus on the woman's dowry as opposed to a *ketubah* promise from the husband. Further, they do not refer to the marriage being "according to the law of Moses."[38]

In Judea there is a move away from referencing the Law and traditional Jewish male practices of the *mohar* (or "bride price") and *ketubah*. David Chapman explains that the Graeco-Roman distinctives "were almost certainly influenced by Hellenistic legal procedures."[39] If one accepts that Jesus did not change the Law at all (cf. Matt 5:17-19), then **does he uphold the *mohar*, the *ketubah*, or the dowry (or all three)?**[40] Does Jesus keep abreast of the progression (perhaps Hellenise

---

[35] M. Satlow, *Jewish Marriage in Antiquity* (Princeton: PUP, 2001), 84.

[36] Chapman, "Second Temple Judaism," 193.

[37] Ibid., 192.

[38] Ibid.

[39] Ibid.

[40] *b.Ketub.*82b and Elephantine marriage documents "suggest a threefold development through the Second Temple period from (1) the *mohar* being paid to the male head of the household, to (2) a dowry supplement paid directly to the wife, to (3) a promissory amount due upon divorce or widowhood." Ibid., 196-97.

the Law), put a limit on further change, or uphold the original Law as written?

The matter is complicated by the fact that Jesus declares the permanency of the Law (Matt 5:17-19) *in Galilee*, where one would expect common use of Aramaic documents, with reference to the marriage being "according to the Law of Moses" and without dowry emphasis.[41] At the same time, by Matthew's account, Galilee is where Jesus first teaches on marriage, and the 'exception clause' first appears (Matt 5:32). His next recorded teaching on marriage, and second instance of the 'exception clause' (Matt 19:9), is away from Galilee in the "region of Judea" (Matt 19:1), where one would expect common use of Judean Greek documents that focus on dowry-giving.[42] This, along with a warning against serving money (Matt 6:24; cf. 16:26) and a refusal to even rule on inheritance (Luke 12:13-21), suggests that Jesus' teaching on marriage does not hinge on economic relations that vary across Israel.

In a 2001 paper, Instone-Brewer lists five matters "A divorce deed normally consisted of" and then lists two ancillary matters:

- a list of the dowry and property of the wife which had been returned
- an affirmation that husband and wife were free to remarry whomever they wish.[43]

Contrary to cultural rhetoric about normal Jewish practice of a "freedom to marry" after divorce, Instone-Brewer posits such freedom only as a secondary item that "might" be included in a divorce deed. Furthermore, although the dowry may be part of normal Jewish practice, in his subsequent paper, Instone-Brewer reveals how unscriptural this cultural practice is:

This shows how important the dowry had become in Jewish circles, even though it was unknown in OT law. Bickerman

---

[41] "The most startling difference... is the assumption about how the marriage will end. The Greek contracts specify what will happen in the event of divorce, while the Aramaic contracts specify what will happen in the event of death." Instone-Brewer, "Jewish Greek & Aramaic," 234.

[42] However, early second century CE Aramaic marriage contracts from the Judean desert do include "You will be my wife according to the Law of Moses." Loader, *On Sexuality*, 49. These documents specify the *ketubah* but do not mention the *mohar*. By the second century CE the *mohar* seems to have shifted in some West Semitic contexts to equate with the dowry. Satlow, *Jewish Marriage*, 203-04. This state of flux with marriage customs, and the uncertainty surrounding when the changes occurred, makes it even more difficult to determine what economic relation Jesus might have supported.

[43] Instone-Brewer, "Graeco-Roman," 103.

showed that the LXX changed some texts [Gen 34:12; Exod 22:16-17 (cf. 1 Sam 18:25)] to suggest that the marriage payment came from the bride, so a bridal dowry had already become normal Jewish practice by the second century BC.[44]

So why would a "standard Jewish divorce contract" be any more scriptural than the unscriptural dowry? Like the dowry, a freedom to remarry after divorce could have easily "become normal Jewish practice" without any jot of biblical warrant. The only "scriptural" warrant for the dowry itself was created by those translating the Hebrew Bible to Greek to "suggest that the marriage payment came from the bride."[45] One wonders whether this would have happened if any women were on the translation team.

Although dowry-giving became common practice throughout Israel and the ANE, it was never demanded by the Law, or prescribed in the Hebrew Bible narratives. The clearest illustration in Scripture of dowry-giving, cited by Chapman,[46] involves a gift of land by Pharaoh to his daughter upon marrying King Solomon (1 Kgs 9:16). Is this a case of the Law developing out of, or progressing with, cultural practice? Probably not, for the dowry is land that the Israelites already owned (it was given to them as part of the Promised Land) but they had disobeyed God and never properly possessed it (Josh 21:43; cf. 16:10). Instead, a foreign ruler gives what is not his (and perhaps violates an Egyptian treaty with Gezer), and an Israelite king receives from a pagan king what Israel has failed to receive from God her king.

Furthermore, Solomon establishes a marriage alliance with Israel's archenemy (1 Kgs 3:1) which leads to idolatry (2 Kgs 23:13; cf. Deut 7:3-4) and elicits (later) stern judgement (Isa 31:1-9). It all signals that this dowry, however culturally acceptable, was elemental to a completely inappropriate and unlawful marriage. Another troubling element is that if Solomon were to ever divorce (or pre-decease) Pharaoh's daughter, then Pharaoh could demand the dowry back. Should a city in the Promised Land ever be returned to a foreign enemy ruler on such a condition? Moreover, just as every original inhabitant of Gezer was killed to create the dowry, must every Israelite living there then be killed and the city burned (for Pharaoh to rebuild and repopulate it with Canaanites)?

---

[44] "Jewish Greek & Aramaic," 227. "It is unfortunate that several English translations render *mohar* as 'dowry' in these passage (e.g. KJV, NASB)." Chapman, "Second Temple Judaism," 195.

[45] Instone-Brewer, "Jewish Greek & Aramaic," 227.

[46] Chapman, "Second Temple Judaism," 193.

The overall narrative lesson here appears to be one of indictment, not endorsement of cultural (or kingly) practice. Such an episode hardly provides a good scriptural basis from which to assess Jesus' teaching on marriage and reduce it to a monetary concern. Even in viewing the dowry positively – say as God's providential act via Egypt after Israel failed to fully possess the land, if marriage is a blood covenant, then the slaughter of a whole city raises the stakes astronomically. Any covenant unfaithfulness (cf. the "sexual immorality" of Matt 19:9) can even more so be understood as deserving of death (cf. the covenant curses of Deut 28:15-68). Money cannot compensate such high treason; the guilty party suffers loss of life *and* land (total assets).

It may be expected that daughters from wealthy families, upon entering marriage, are well-endowed with servants and gifts (cf. Gen 29:24), and this sets a cultural norm. However, Jesus provides a basis for his marriage teaching that is independent of any cultural norm, for he references Creation (Matt 19:4-6) – a time when there was no dowry-giving whatsoever. Given that the Pharisees reference a later cultural practice of divorce in the time of Moses (Matt 19:7), great care is needed to see whether Jesus' response (Matt 19:8-9) affords hearty endorsement (as a "gracious provision"[47]) or grave indictment (cf. Solomon's culturally-accepted practice).

Given also that the Pharisees ask a specific question of Law (Matt 19:3), it is unlikely that Jesus provides an answer that hinges on a practice of dowry-giving that the Law does not require. Matthew 1:19 contains the only personal example of a divorce consideration in the New Testament. For a break of betrothal, dowry-return is most likely irrelevant.[48] Would Joseph have even received a dowry, especially if the Law does not require one, and the couple are Galilean? Matthew makes no mention of a dowry, and to read into it that Joseph's resolve to divorce Mary "quietly" concerns dowry-return overlooks the real shame feared in out-of-wedlock pregnancy.

Practically, if money was core to Jesus' teaching in Matthew 19:9, and Jesus supports the threat of no dowry-return as an impediment to divorce, does this mean that dowry-giving must be instituted in other (Christian) cultures that do not have this practice, in order to alleviate high divorce rates? If Christ did Hellenise the Law and upheld dowry-

---

[47] P. Bolt, *Matthew: A Great Light Dawns*, ed. P. Barnett, RBT (Sydney: Aquila, 2014), 56. Similarly, "God has condescended to make a concession to your hardness of heart." H. Thielicke, *The Ethics of Sex* (New York: Fortress, 1964), 109.

[48] Pre-marital contractual agreements could be made concerning the amount of dowry, but this is only what "the bride might bring to the marriage." Meier, *Marginal Jew*, 4, 140-41.

giving, then how did this set a precedent to Christianise the Law and (in most churches) reject dowry-giving, ostensibly without altering the Law? Moreover, theologically, can the withholding of a divorced woman's dowry – however large – really be considered godly recompense for an "evil," such as adultery, committed *against God* (cf. Ps 51:4)? Equally, what price should a *divorced man* pay for any evil?

Socially, dowry-giving also has troubling elements. The cultural expectation to provide a dowry can place a huge burden on families, and is long-associated with the exposure (and abortion) of baby girls. Steven Baugh notes "the grim, universal practice of infant exposure in the Greek (as well as the Roman) world" and among a "number of reasons for this cruel practice" is "the birth of a girl. (Girls needed dowries to get husbands and hence threatened the sometimes meagre resources of the *oikos*.)."[49] The problem could be somewhat mitigated by wealthier families contributing to the dowries of poor girls,[50] or a father giving his daughter in marriage without a dowry ("marry her naked").[51]

This "all too common" merciless or "pitiless death"[52] clashes with Jesus' blessing of the merciful (Matt 5:7) and God's mercy found in Matthew's Gospel (Matt 9:13; Matt 12:7), exemplified by the master's "pity" (Matt 18:27) and call for "mercy" (Matt 18:33) recorded just prior to Jesus' second Matthean teaching on divorce. Yet it does recall God's ancient decree of *no pity* (Jer 13:14; Ezek 5:11) and *no mercy* (Hos 2:4) on those who do evil and commit abominations, and God's command to show no mercy to certain enemies – hard-hearted people devoted to destruction (Josh 11:20), whom Israel is to make no covenants with, including marriage covenants, else God will bring sudden destruction (Deut 7:2-4). It also echoes parabolic words foretelling a "miserable death" for murderous "wretches" within Israel (Matt 21:41), indicting those responsible for Jesus' pitiless death, and those responsible for upholding any tradition that voids the word of God (Matt 15:1-9) and engenders more pitiless death.

---

[49] S. Baugh, "Marriage and Family in Ancient Greek Society," in *Marriage and Family in the Biblical World*, ed. K. Campbell (Downers Grove: IVP, 2003), 123. "Infant exposure was widely practised, especially of females." Loader, *On Sexuality*, 82.

[50] Chapman, "Second Temple Judaism," 193.

[51] "This must be negotiated ahead of time or he must pay a minimum dowry of fifty denarii." Ibid., 194. So if Matt 18:21-35 has any connection with Matt 19:1-12 (as this thesis will argue), then one hundred denarii (Matt 18:18) sits comfortably above the minimum dowry amount. Note also that "marry her naked" carries no sense of indecency (cf. Gen 2:25), as against "a matter of nakedness" in Deut 24:1.

[52] Baugh, "Ancient Greek Society," 125.

The Ketubah

Although Instone-Brewer acknowledges that Scripture treats adultery "extremely seriously,"[53] he prefers to take cultural norms more seriously instead by heralding practices that relax or neglect extremely serious elements of Scripture:

> The normal punishment [for adultery] was divorce without repayment of the *ketubah*. Even a man who had married a woman whom he had raped and who could not normally divorce her was permitted to put her away if she became unfaithful.[54]

In Matthew 19:1-12, Jesus is not concerned about "normal punishment" according to (Jewish or Roman) culture, but what is lawful by the Law (cf. Deut 22:22). His sole grounds for divorce: "sexual immorality," must be treated extremely seriously, as must the consequence for divorcing for any other reason: "adultery" (Matt 19:9). Emphasis should of course be put on how to avoid these crimes altogether, just as anyone should want to avoid having their whole body thrown into hell (cf. Matt 5:29) or being sent to the torturers forever (cf. Matt 18:34).

A matter of the *ketubah*, which included the "bridal dowry" that Instone-Brewer admits was "was unknown in OT law," cannot be the main lawful concern here, for not only did this "tradition" "break the commandment of God" as one of the "commandments of men" (Matt 15:3-9) concocted by men to the advantage of men, such a concern trivialises the severity of sexual crimes against people and most importantly against God. In the same passage championing "normal" practice, Instone-Brewer also mentions another tradition that trivialises the Law's treatment of rape by allowing any (trivial) "matter of indecency" (*'erwat dabar*), as found in a woman *by her rapist*, to void God's commanded consequence for this man's extremely serious matter of "sexual immorality" (*porneia*).[55] **Apparently Deuteronomy 24:1 even accords a rapist grounds for divorce!**

Jesus' indictment of "an evil and adulterous generation" (Matt 12:39; 16:4) is no trivial charge; a cultural norm of "divorce [for adultery] without repayment of the *ketubah*" is entirely inapplicable

---

[53] Instone-Brewer, *Social and Literary Context*, 94.

[54] Ibid.

[55] Ibid. Instone-Brewer cites *m. Ketub.* 3.5: "[one who has raped and has to marry his victim]….If a matter of unchastity [דבר ערוה] turned out to pertain to her, or if she is not appropriate to enter into the Israelite congregation, he is not permitted to confirm her as his wife [but, if he has married her he must divorce her], since it is said, *And she will be a wife to him* (Deut 22:29) – a wife appropriate for him."

here for the nation. Freedom to remarry and property settlement is far from view, but punishment in the order of a capital crime is totally within view, and imminent for Jesus' generation (Matt 23:36). The prophet Hosea had married an adulterous woman who continued in her adultery, yet he never pursued a cultural freedom to remarry or property settlement, but exemplified mercy, love and redemption (Hos 2:14-3:5). At the same time, fearful judgement of infidelity is a primary feature of the book of Hosea, as it is in Matthew's Gospel, not to be diluted or dismissed.

The *ketubah* also has troubling personal elements:

> Key rabbinic sources locate the origin of the *ketubah* payment (as payment retained by the husband until the marriage ends and thereafter owed to the wife) as the invention of the famous first-century B.C. rabbinic forerunner Simeon ben Shetach. This literature claims that Simeon's innovation entails dictating that a payment regularly owed to the bride's father at the inception of marriage be instead paid only at its dissolution.[56]

The motives for this change may have been

> to make marriage easier (property/money is not required upfront) and/or to make divorce harder (since the man would have to pay the woman if he divorces her).[57]

However, it might not have made marriage more attractive for the woman. The *ketubah* is an innovation that deprives the woman (and her family of origin) of a full bridal gift, and leaves the control of any promised property completely in the hands of the husband. A woman only appropriates this property, along with dowry-return,[58] upon the death of her husband or post-divorce – if (grave) fault is not held against her. Such a development and other Mishnah rules

---

[56] Chapman, "Second Temple Judaism," 196. Did Jesus uphold a recent "invention," "innovation," or rabbinic "reform"? Satlow's contention that the rabbinic *ketubah* payment is actually a late first-century CE development is also cited, but Chapman concludes that the lack of widespread early documentary support more likely indicates that the *ketubah* payment "was not yet pervasive throughout all Jewish societies." Ibid., 197-98. This begs another question as to whether Jesus promoted what might only be an incipient Hellenistic tradition, and one that was unlikely held in Galilee. Cf. *b. Ketub.* 82b, J. Collins, "Marriage, Divorce, and Family in Second Temple Judaism," in *Families in Ancient Israel*, The Family, Religion, and Culture (Louisville: WJK, 1997), 114.

[57] Chapman, "Second Temple Judaism," 196.

[58] Although, at least with the Elephantine marriage contracts, Loader finds "Some include agreement …that the dowry is irrevocable." Loader, *On Sexuality*, 49.

multiplying the justifications for divorce without compensation... tilted the scales in favour of the divorcing male.[59]

The Mohar

The *mohar* may better inform our understanding of Jesus' teaching on marriage, for this practice is scriptural – and lawful (Exod 22:16-17). Jesus' bodily self-sacrifice can certainly be construed as a bride price for a pure virgin (2 Cor 11:2), ahead of a heavenly wedding feast (Matt 22:1-14).[60] This compares well with the Roman ideal: "Self-sacrifice was praised. ...Marriage, ideally, was a lasting, faithful and happy commitment,"[61] and accords with Jesus' demand that his followers deny self and take up their cross (Matt 16:24). Paul notably exhorts men to uphold this ideal, "Husbands, love your wives, as Christ loved the church and gave himself up for her" (Eph 5:25).

In contrast to the *mohar*, the idea that Christ's bride must bring a dowry is completely absent in Scripture. God owns everything (Deut 10:14), and Jesus stresses a dependence on God for everything, including bread (Matt 6:11) and clothes (Matt 6:25-34). The New Testament never mentions dowry-giving. Whether or not God endorses the cultural development should be seriously contemplated. Such inquiry coheres with Jesus honouring what is "read" and first principles (Matt 19:4-6): "from the beginning" there was no expectation for the woman to bring anything into the marriage, let alone any thought of money.

This total absence of monetary concern in the archetypal joining of a man and a woman stands in stark contrast with an anxiety of the Second Temple period about marrying a woman with a large dowry (that might one day need returning upon divorce).[62] This in turn echoes Gentile ways (Matt 6:32) that the Jews must be set apart from (cf. Lev 19:2, "be holy"). In Matthew 6:25-34, Jesus exhorts his followers to trust in God's provision and modify their ways, not modify the Law. This follows on from Jesus' decree that he upholds every part of the Law (Matt 5:17-19), his teaching on divorce (Matt 5:31-32), his requirement to forgive others (Matt 6:14-15), and his warning that one

---

[59] Collins, "Family," 119.

[60] Adam's forfeiture of a rib may also be seen as a price paid with his own flesh and bone (Gen 2:21-23).

[61] S. Treggiari, "Marriage and Family in Roman Society," in *Marriage and Family in the Biblical World*, ed. K. Campbell (Downers Grove: IVP, 2003), 182.

[62] *Ps.-Phoc.* 199-203; cf. Sir 25:21; Josephus *Ag. Ap.* 2.200; *T. Jud.* 13:4-8. Loader, *On Sexuality*, 51.

cannot serve God and money, which includes the maxim, "For where your treasure is, there your heart will be also" (Matt 6:21-24). A heart concern shines in the immediate prelude to Jesus' second teaching on divorce, "So also my heavenly Father will do to every one of you, if you do not forgive your brother from your heart" (Matt 18:35), and appears in the same sentence as the 'exception clause', "hardness of heart" (Matt 19:8). This suggests that in relation to marriage and divorce, *Jesus' principal concern is the human heart, not money.*

Property Offences

Does Matthew's 'exception clause' relate to a property offence? Hays contends,

> In Jewish Law and tradition, adultery was a property offence, a form of stealing a man's property by "taking" his wife. Thus, adultery could by definition be committed only against a man, for the husband was not in any reciprocal sense regarded as the sexual property of his wife.[63]

While this may be generally true of Jewish tradition, "property offence" is not the concern of the Hosea-Gomer marriage as a lived-metaphor of the God-Israel union. No doubt Jesus is conscious of this relationship, and Matthew too – **especially as he is the only New Testament writer to cite Hosea 6:6 (*twice!* Matt 9:13; 12:7).** In Mark 10:11-12, Jesus certainly brings gender balance to the offence, challenging a traditional view of adultery that treated extra-marital sex only as an offence by a woman *against a married man.*[64] However, there remains a foundational equality in the Law that adultery always demanded the death of both the guilty man and woman.

Countryman's one significant difference "from other property violations," that adultery involved "the consent of the property,"[65] points rather to the fact that the woman is not property at all! There is another significant difference: the Law never demanded death for property theft.[66] If a wife were merely considered property, then like theft, financial compensation could be appropriate for an act of

---

[63] Hays, *Moral Vision*, 352.

[64] "A man, married or not, committed adultery against a woman's husband when he slept with her. But a married man did not commit adultery against his own wife by having intercourse with a woman." L. Smedes, *Mere Morality: What God Expects from Ordinary People* (Grand Rapids: Eerdmans, 1983), 158.

[65] Countryman, *Dirt, Greed and Sex*, 158.

[66] "Capital punishment is never required by Moses' law for a violation against property, though it is for the violation of human beings." Smedes, *Mere Morality*, 3.

adultery.[67] Proverbs teaches that the thief "will pay sevenfold, he will give all the goods of his house," but concerning "he who goes into his neighbour's wife; none who touches her will go unpunished"; the furious husband "will not spare when he takes revenge. He will accept no compensation..." (Prov 6:29-35).[68] A wife is worth immeasurably more than property!

This is evident in Malachi 2 where "Judah has married the daughter of a foreign god" (Mal 2:10-11) and Yahweh, like the furious husband of Proverbs 6, will "cut off" or put to death the guilty ones (Mal 2:12; cf. Exod 31:14). Faithlessness is core: Israel is "faithless to one another" and has profaned the Mosaic Covenant; an "abomination has been committed" (cf. Deut 24:4) and God will send her away. Money is irrelevant; death is the outcome.

Malachi did not endorse cultural practice; he was "a reformer arguing against the current understanding of marriage."[69] Alongside the illegal marriages in Malachi 2 was widespread divorce. The divorce here is essentially condemned, for beyond the contentious Hebrew wording of Malachi 2:16 is the prophetic insistence, "do not be faithless" to "your companion and your wife by covenant" (Mal 2:14). "Companion" is derived from the verb meaning "to unite or be joined together," pointing to God's joining together that must not be separated, which Jesus later affirms on the same topic (Matt 19:6).[70]

> This is the only time that the term ["partner"] appears in the feminine form in the Old Testament. It is normally used of men to designate their equality with one another. To use this term for a wife suggests that she is not a piece of property that may be discarded at will; she is an equal and is to be treated as such – as a covenant partner.[71]

Malachi also uses the explicit terminology of "wife by covenant," emphasizing that this is a solemn contract made before a God who does

---

[67] "Adultery as a crime against the property of another man was not completely foreign (cf. Deut 22.29)," although von Rad notes a big difference here, "The compensatory payment was to be made at the time of engagement!" and never by the Law during divorce for adultery. G. von Rad, *Genesis: A Commentary*, OTL (London: SCM, 1972), 365. As dowry-giving is not prescribed in the Hebrew Bible, there is no scriptural principle for a compensatory payment at all.

[68] Longman views Proverbs as a commentary on the Law, although he wisely avoids absolutising individual proverbs as divine promises. He provides a chart showing close connections between Proverbs and the Ten Commandments, and calls Proverbs and Law "close cousins." T. Longman III, *Proverbs*, BCOTWP (Grand Rapids: Baker, 2006), 81.

[69] Collins, "Family," 112.

[70] Laney, "No Divorce & No Remarriage," 30.

[71] D. Garland, "A Biblical View of Divorce," *RevExp* 84, no. 3 (1987): 420.

not break covenants (cf. Lev 26:40-45). It must be noted that Malachi 2 begins with "And now this admonition is for you, O priests," where the divorce teaching is directed to the religious leaders and applies nationally.[72] Covenant violation has serious ramifications and in the case of the marriage covenant, financial compensation for breaches of "sexual immorality" or "adultery" is not stipulated, but death.

Given that a "right to remarry" is now assumed in Israel's divorce ethic, then has the "chief function"[73] of a divorce certificate progressed from a life-saving role in protecting a woman from a capital charge of adultery, to a life savings role in protecting a woman's capital from a debit charge of dowry loss due to adultery?[74] Would Jesus in Matthew really endorse *chiefly a monetary function* of a divorce certificate? If a cultural change has occurred, it looks awfully like the central concern has shifted from serving God – and upholding his Law in every detail – to serving mammon (cf. Matt 6:24).

Conversely, Jesus teaches his followers to not lay up treasures on earth (Matt 6:19), to not be anxious for anything about their lives, such as food, drink, body and clothes (Matt 6:25-34), to not resist the one who is evil but to give extra to anyone who sues or demands, and to love their enemies (Matt 6:39-44), lose their lives (Matt 10:39) and deny themselves (Matt 16:24). In the narrative context of Matthew 19:1-12, the kingdom of heaven belongs to those who own nothing: little children (Matt 19:13-15) and Jesus' disciples who have "left everything" (Matt 19:23-30), but not to anyone who tightly holds on to possessions (Matt 19:16-22). In the light of this major emphasis on the virtue of personal loss and complete selflessness, it would be incredible for Jesus to champion a monetary function of a divorce certificate, especially when it also relaxes the Law. In setting our minds on the things of God and not on earthly human concerns, a better focus is needed concerning the chief function of death in the work of Jesus (cf. Matt 16:21-24) and in the words of Jesus, which includes the original capital meanings in Matthew 19:9.

---

[72] Spadaro sees that "The whole of Malachi… was a prophetic indictment against the Levitical house and priesthood." If Matthew follows this script, then "This accounts for the sustained polemic against Jerusalem, which was already an object of God's wrath according to Malachi." Spadaro, *Matthew*, 28.

[73] Loader, *Sexuality: Key Texts*, 81.

[74] Instone-Brewer summarises: "In OT law the penalty for adultery was death, but by NT times this penalty had fallen into disuse. The worst that an adulterer faced was divorce and the payment of the *ketubah*, which acted like a fine." Instone-Brewer, *Social and Literary Context*, 284.

Polygyny

Polygyny (the dominant form of polygamy) intensifies the need to clarify marital economic obligations. Loader notes that the Jews' acceptance of polygyny stands in contrast to the strict monogamy of both Greek and Roman culture.[75] Solomon offers the most famous example, with 700 wives and 300 concubines (1 Kgs 11:3), but as with his foreign marriage alliance (discussed above) this violated the Law (Deut 17:17) and turned Solomon's heart away from God. Lamech provides the earliest example in Scripture of a man taking more than one wife; his descent from Cain and boast about murder to his wives (Gen 4:19-24) also associate polygyny with ungodliness and a departure from the ideal (Gen 2:20-25).

Nowhere does the New Testament endorse polygyny, and several verses are often understood as directly proscribing it (cf. 1 Cor 7:2; 1 Tim 3:12). Matthew 19:1-12 implies a rejection of polygyny, especially with Jesus' appeal to Creation: here it was impossible for the man to take more than one wife, and Jesus stresses that solely "two" (male and female) "shall become one flesh" (Matt 19:4-6; cf. Gen 1:27; 2:24). However, does this rejection drive Matthew 19:9?[76]

Loader proposes,

> Where polygyny was a viable option, a man dissatisfied with his wife could simply take another in addition, the solution Manaoh contemplated taking according to *LAB* 42:1-3 in light of Eluma's sterility, but did not. The more polygyny was called into question on grounds of belief or grounds of economic viability, the more divorce would become the option, namely replacing one with wife another. Traditionally this appears to have been left to the man's discretion.[77]

Leaving it "to the man's discretion" to replace one wife with another aligns with the practice recorded in Deuteronomy 24:1-4, *but this may be exactly what Jesus confronts.* Just as Matthew 19:6 "assumes that marriage is something God has done and sets it in contrast to something human beings do,"[78] so it assumes that humans do not have the discretionary power to separate what God has joined.

---

[75] Loader, *On Sexuality*, 80.

[76] This could be answered straight from first principles: "the beginning" marks a time when polygyny was not a viable option, yet divorce without remarriage was possible but with (universal) deadly implications.

[77] Loader, *On Sexuality*, 58.

[78] Ibid., 272.

According to Loader, Jesus' words in Luke 16:18 illustrate the Law's continuing validity in a time of cultural change:

> One reason for divorce in those times was greed: divorcing one's wife in order to marry one who would bring a more substantial dowry, especially once polygyny had fallen out of favour. The logion... is then to be understood in this context as 'Everyone who divorces his wife in order to marry another'. This recalls Belial in CD 4.17-18, namely polygyny and greed for wealth, because it assumes the former is motivated by the latter.[79]

This could explain Jesus' absolute prohibition against divorce and remarriage for a predominantly Gentile audience (including Mark's audience), and the Lukan narrative context certainly condemns greed:

> The chapter will end with the parable of the rich man and Lazarus (16:19-31). It began with the parable of the unjust steward (16:1-8) to which are added teachings about the right use of wealth (16:9-13). 16:14-15 portrays the Pharisees as money-loving and therefore resistant to Jesus' teaching; he calls their stance an abomination.[80]

However, "in order to"[81] is not a natural rendering of *kai* (καὶ, usually "and") in Luke 16:18 – or Matthew 5:32 and 19:9.

In framing Jesus' divorce teaching within a test, Matthew 19:3 uses a present participle (πειράζοντες) to give a meaning of "in order to," as does Mark 10:2. Some English versions insert "and" for readability: "and tested him" (Matt 19:3); "and in order to test him" (Mark 10:2). A literal translation of Matthew 19:3 is, "And [καὶ] Pharisees came up to him in order to test him and [καὶ] they were saying" (or, "...and they were testing him saying"), where the first and second καὶ simply carry the narrative along; neither bear purpose. Matthew's version can even be read as a live eye-witness account: "And Pharisees are coming up to Jesus testing him" (Matthew stresses *the Pharisees' persistent purpose*), and this is how they test him: "and they are saying..." (Matthew records a core question).

Similarly, telic use of a participle in the context of Jesus being tested occurs prior to Luke 16:18: "And [καὶ] behold, a lawyer stood up [in order] to put him to the test [ἐκπειράζων], saying, 'Teacher, what shall I do to inherit eternal life?'" (Luke 10:25). Again, "and" is not telic.

---

[79] CD: Damascus Document, ibid., 258.
[80] Ibid.
[81] Ibid.

Neither is it in Luke 18:18 or Mark 10:17. In Matthew's parallel account (Matt 19:16), ἵνα is used to mean "in order to" (inherit eternal life) – as also in Mark 10:17, plus earlier (Matt 19:13) concerning children: "that" (he might lay his hands on them), and in another legal context (Matt 18:16): "that" (every charge may be established by the evidence of two or three witnesses). Prior to Jesus' first divorce saying in Matthew's Gospel, Matthew uses πρὸς τὸ (Matt 5:28) to give a sense of "in order to" (lust after), and then ἵνα to introduce a purpose clause (Matt 5:30). In Matthew 5:29 and 30, καὶ ("and") appears as a simple conjunction (it is not found in 5:28 or 31).

Therefore, the close Gospel narrative strongly suggests that "and" does not mean "in order to" for any of Jesus' divorce sayings. Furthermore, *within* Jesus' first divorce saying in Matthew's Gospel, the 'exception clause' (παρεκτὸς λόγου πορνείας) appears without any subsequent clause of "and marries another" (unlike Matt 19:9), so there is no hint of a man divorcing for such a purpose. Here Matthew only uses καὶ as a simple conjunction to another idea, "and whoever marries a divorced woman commits adultery" (Matt 5:32).

Moreover, if the whole divorce debate of Matthew 19:1-12 fundamentally concerns grounds for divorce, many grounds are completely unrelated to remarriage (indeed, "sexual immorality" is often committed with no intention to marry or remarry), and this is evidenced in the background passage of Deuteronomy 24:1-4 where "no favor in his eyes," "indecency," and "[he] hates her" are claimed with respect to a man divorcing a woman *without any mention of the man remarrying*. Also, the grounds for divorce described in Deuteronomy 24:1-4 bear no inherent connection with greed, although financial consequences traditionally arise. Reading one motive – such as greed – into Jesus' divorce sayings is not supported by the textual considerations.[82]

Confining Jesus' divorce teaching to a matter of greed also raises other questions, such as: what if a man divorces his wife *in order to* marry someone poorer (and yet in other ways more attractive), with a smaller (or non-existent) dowry? Does this man then not commit adultery? Can non-financial motives provide valid exceptions as just grounds for divorce? How would a teaching centred on dowries, that may be amassed by divorce and remarriage, apply to other cultures without dowries? (Might an equal distribution of wealth negate any

---

[82] Miller supports a greed motive, with an appeal to Malachi, but concedes "The text does not say that the divorce in mind is *in order to* marry someone else." (Italics added.) P. Miller, *The Ten Commandments*, Interpretation (Louisville: WJK, 2009), 314.

sense of committing adultery in a "no-fault" divorce; should financial support be justifiably withheld from a spouse found guilty of adultery; or would it only be considered wrong to divorce *in order to* marry someone richer?)

From Genesis, there is surprising divine tolerance of polygyny, with trends to and away from it. Nonetheless, there is one constant: polygyny was not constant across society, as Loader acknowledges, "Greed will doubtless have played a role in the practice of polygyny, an option under any circumstance only for the rich."[83] So inasmuch as the Law proscribes polygyny for kings, and has rules about captive women (Deut 21:15-17; cf. 11QT^a/11Q19 63.10-15)[84] and levirate marriage (Deut 25:5-10; cf. 4QT^b/4Q524)[85] that appear to assume polygyny, taking multiple wives was never an option for most Jewish men, and certainly not for the poor in Jesus' audience. Neither was it a viable option for Malachi's main audience:

> Although polygyny appears to have been practiced within Israel throughout most, if not all, of the pre-exilic period, it was largely confined to Israel's chieftains and royalty and only rarely attested outside this circle. ...polygyny is most commonly associated with men who enjoy considerable wealth and status, characteristics which hardly typified Malachi's beleaguered contemporaries living in the rump state of Judah. ...actual marital practice was monogamous with few, if any, exceptions, particularly in the post-exilic period.[86]

Against a first-century Graeco-Roman cultural background disapproving polygamy, the elite nevertheless did partake in polygyny, which was both pilloried and prized:

> While Josephus reflects the widespread view, attested as early as Ben Sira, that Solomon's many wives ruined him, he explains that Herod's having nine wives as reflecting Jewish ancestral custom and something to be valued. In the *Jewish War (B.J.)*, he notes that Herod very much liked the custom.

---

[83] W. Loader, *The Dead Sea Scrolls on Sexuality; Attitudes Towards Sexuality in Sectarian and Related Literature at Qumran* (Grand Rapids: Eerdmans, 2009), 353.

[84] Qumran Temple Scroll^a, *Making Sense of Sex: Attitudes Towards Sexuality in Early Jewish and Christian Literature* (Grand Rapids: Eerdmans, 2013), 50.

[85] Qumran Temple Scroll^b, ibid.

[86] G. Hugenberger, *Marriage as a Covenant: A Study of Biblical Law and Ethics Governing Marriage Developed from the Perspective of Malachi*, Supplements to Vetus Testamentum (Leiden: Brill, 1994), 120-22.

His account, however, of Herod is replete with evidence that
it could cause chaos.[87]

Hence, in Jesus' time, a general non-appropriation of polygyny
except by the rich might prove little different from what is reflected in
Israel's history.[88] Furthermore, although the Herodians practiced
polygyny, there is no indication that it was to greedily accumulate
dowries, and every indication that John the Baptist would have
condemned Herod's unlawful marriage to Herodias (Matt 14:3-4)
whether it was monogamous or not. So, is Matthew 19:9 to be
interpreted foremost in the light of a possible increasing intolerance of
polygyny,[89] or does John's recent teaching (with no judgement on
polygyny) and Israel's history (with its long scriptural record describing
but not necessarily supporting polygyny) suffice?

On the basis of attitudes to polygyny, Loader differentiates the
cultural setting of Matthew 19:9 from Matthew 5:32.[90] He essentially
sees that an oddity for Jews and Graeco-Romans concerning adultery
(that a man could commit adultery against his own marriage) is absent
in Matthew 5:32, but another oddity for Graeco-Romans – the
acceptance of polygyny – suits the Galilean setting. Rather than
preserving an original Q formulation, he finds it more likely that
"Matthew's tradition removed the oddity" about adultery (and added
what was normally assumed), but in making no reference to remarriage
in Galilee, "may also reflect a setting which accepted polygyny where
another marriage would pose no problem."[91] In contrast, Matthew 19:9
occurs in a setting that is thought to not accept polygyny, so Loader
suggests that Matthew understood the saying differently there[92] – even
though it contains essentially the same exception as Matthew 5:32.[93]

There is likely to have been greater Hellenisation south of Galilee,
as evidenced by Judean Greek marriage documents (discussed earlier)

---

[87] Loader, *Making Sense*, 51. (See *BJ* 1.477; *Ant.* 17:14.)

[88] Cf. Egypt: Polygyny was the exception (limited to the elite) in all periods of Ancient
Egypt; Old Kingdom, Middle Kingdom and Second Intermediate Period, Third Intermediate
Period. R. Westbrook, *A History of Ancient Near Eastern Law. Volumes 1 and 2* (London:
Brill, 2003), 120, 275, 800.

[89] "While polygyny was still in evidence in our period, as reflected in the advice offered
about how to handle it, it was increasingly limited to those who could afford it." Loader,
Making Sense, 51.

[90] *On Sexuality*, 263-64.

[91] Ibid.

[92] Ibid., 264.

[93] Loader claims, "The Lukan form of Jesus' saying [Luke 16:18] would have suited the
context in Matthew just as well as 5:32." Ibid., 263. Yet the Lukan form would have equally
suited Matt 19:9 if not for Matthew's consistent purpose (in 5:32 and 19:9) to indict unfaithful
people.

that omit reference to "the Law of Moses." However, Judean desert marriage documents do refer to "the Law of Moses,"[94] and Matthew 19:1-12 is usually located further east of this desert. Matthew's narrative does not lose any of its Jewishness when Jesus, a Jewish leader with a Jewish audience, enters this "region of Judea beyond the Jordan" (Matt 19:1). Indeed, direct reference is made to the Law ("Is it lawful…," Matt 19:3) and to Moses (Matt 19:7-8), and the fact that Matthew records a scene change away from Galilee whilst recording the same lawful exception as in Galilee suggests reinforcement of the same teaching. Thus, polygyny could be accepted by Jews in both Matthew 5:32 and 19:9 settings, although any negativity found regarding it is only part of a larger consistent Matthean purpose.

Different strands of Judaism had differing views on divorce, but polygamous marriages remained legal in the Second Temple period and beyond.[95] Witherington notes,

> While most early Jews could not afford to have multiple wives, and monogamy seems to have been overwhelmingly the normal practice, there are cases of polygamy in early Judaism, for instance with the brother of Rabbi Gamaliel who took a second wife because the first was barren. In fact, the Mishnah records rules for and cases of men betrothed to two women. There is no debate about the matter (*m. Yebam. 3:10*), and it is doubtful this should be seen as a purely hypothetical discussion.[96]

Only long after Christ was polygamy finally declared illegal among the Jews by emperor Theodosius I (393CE).[97] So it is improbable that Jesus responded to a contemporary question on Jewish lawfulness (Matt 19:3) based on a legal view of polygyny that would not be codified until nearly four centuries later. The legal argument would lack relevance to Jesus' immediate audience, and overlook vital scriptural past reference points.

Additionally, unlike the context of Luke 16:18, there is no condemnation of greed surrounding Matthew 19:9. Instead, the preceding context is one of debt repayment (Matt 18:21-35), and subsequently, that of hindering children – who generally lack wealth (Matt 19:13-14). This raises further doubt that Matthew 19:9 should be understood differently from Matthew 5:32. It would be best to assume

---

[94] At least from early second-century CE evidence. Ibid., 49.
[95] Collins, "Family," 121.
[96] B. Witherington III, Matthew, (Macon: Smyth & Helwys, 2006). 361.
[97] Collins, "Family," 121-22.

that Matthew 5:32 and 19:9 consistently speak to a Jewish audience about Jewish concerns of the unabolished and unchanged Law (cf. Matt 5:17-19). Although Luke 16:18 has a different emphasis to Matthew 19:9, it is best to assume that it does not void one dot of the Law (cf. Luke 16:17) either.

It makes sense that a "shift away from polygyny is also likely to have exacerbated the problem of divorce,"[98] and this applies to any time in Jewish history. "Common practice was simply to take another wife when trouble occurred with the first wife, short of adultery."[99] However, for Pharisees to raise Deuteronomy 24:1-4 as core to their argument in testing Jesus, they reference a time when polygyny was culturally acceptable, so any first-century Jewish rulings founded on what the Pharisees believe to be "Moses' command" (Matt 19:7) *in Moses' time* cannot relate to a shift away from polygyny. It might be said that the Pharisees reinterpreted Moses' command to suit their own time intolerant of polygyny, but there is no scriptural indication that they did so on this basis, and every indication that they simply did not practice what was proclaimed in the Law (cf. Matt 23:2-3).[100] More generally, Jesus does not require a context of polygyny losing favour to strongly condemn greed (cf. Matt 23:25).

Loader sees that Jesus takes the Shammaite view in a stronger direction to align with Roman law: sexual immorality, understood primarily as adultery, "necessitates divorce"[101] (without execution). Yet while Matthew's 'exception clause' "should not be seen as a modification of the [absolute] saying to bring it into line with Deuteronomy 24,"[102] this need not infer that "Once adultery has taken place the marriage cannot be restored."[103] Otherwise, a disturbing principle presents: when marital trouble occurs in the order of "sexual immorality" (Matt 19:9), there is no freedom to forgive the erring spouse (here, a wife), to reconcile, and to continue the marriage. The *Lex Iulia de adulteriis coercendis* made adultery a criminal offence, such that:

---

[98] Loader, *Making Sense*, 72.

[99] Ibid.

[100] Matt 23:3 echoes Mal 2:7-8, where Israel's leaders were judged for their instruction and corruption of the covenant. Contemporary divorce practice epitomised unfaithfulness to God and each other (Mal 2:10-16). Most scholars see that Malachi's condemnation of divorce "carries no implication regarding the practice of polygyny," and even if polygyny was tolerated, it was not the norm and was "possibly even illegal in Malachi's day (the traditional view)." Hugenberger, *Covenant*, 85.

[101] Loader, *On Sexuality*, 286.

[102] Ibid.

[103] Ibid.

A husband suspecting his wife's adultery had 60 days in which to prosecute, as did her father, after which others could, with the incentive that they could gain part of the property. The evidence suggests that prosecutions were numerous. Fathers could kill both if caught in the act. Husbands could kill the man only if of a lower class, but not his wife; and if he failed to charge his wife he could be prosecuted. He must divorce and must not receive her back.[104]

If a husband failed to prosecute, he could be prosecuted for *lenocinium* (pimping).[105]

This kind of justice has no semblance of the mercy and forgiveness that God desires, as found in Matthew 18:21-35, where any sin can be forgiven multiple times, and even the largest debt can be totally cancelled. The Roman code completely conflicts with Jesus' conflict resolution code in Matthew 18:15-20, which has no hint of secular prosecution (cf. 1 Cor 6:1) or greed inducement – "gain part of the property" is infinitely surpassed by gaining a brother or sister (especially a wife)! If Jewish law did align with Roman law in a religious court,[106] then it is unsurprising that prostitutes gain entry to the kingdom of God and Jewish leaders spurn the way of righteousness (Matt 21:31-32). God's way led prostitutes and others to leave their sinful lives, for they believed John and followed Jesus, whereas the Roman way led in the opposite direction, because **"Apparently these laws resulted in more women turning to prostitution."**[107]

Capital Punishment

Some Jewish scholars in the Second Temple period viewed acts of sexual immorality – adultery in particular – as capital offences. For example,

> Philo appears to consider that people bent on carving such a swathe of promiscuity in society are incurable and sees in that the warrant for the death penalty.[108]

---

[104] Ibid., 104.

[105] Ulp. *Dig.* 48.5.2.2. T. McGinn, *Prostitution, Sexuality, and the Law in Ancient Rome* (Oxford: OUP, 2003), 173-76.

[106] "An adulterous wife must be divorced and is forbidden to her husband; t.Sot 5.9 even considers it a commandment (מצוה) to divorce a wife who bathes with the men (cf. b.Git 90a-b)." Bockmuehl also cites m.Ned 11.12; cf. m.Sot 5.1; y.Sot 1.1 16b27; b.Sanh 41a. Bockmuehl, "Halakhah," 292.

[107] Loader, On Sexuality, 103.

[108] *Philo, Josephus, and the Testaments on Sexuality* (Grand Rapids: Eerdmans, 2011), 191.

Rather than adultery constituting an unpayable but forgivable debt (cf. the ten thousand talents in Matt 18:23-35), as this thesis will argue, Philo believes that this sexual offence puts a person beyond redemption,

> Here is it the soul which is incurably diseased. Such persons must be punished with death as the common enemies of the whole human race, that they may not live to ruin more houses with immunity and be tutors of others who make it their business to emulate the wickedness of their ways.[109]

It would be incredible if capital punishment was never applied in Israel, given the passion for it (cf. Philo), the plain way in which Mosaic commands are written – complete with means of execution, and neighbouring practice. Janzen writes,

> Adultery is obviously the worst offence, and in Babylonian and Assyrian marriage contracts and laws that span well over a millennium it is clear that adultery could legally result in the death of the woman and her lover, as it did in ancient Israel (Lev. 20.10; Deut 22:22).[110]

This coheres with Philo's description of adultery as "the greatest of sins," for it pollutes the marriage of another man, "an offence which who is there would not avenge with blood?" He asserts all nations "agree in this alone, that all men think him [the adulterer] worthy of ten thousand deaths" – and his life is in the husband's hands without trial.[111] In asking (or it seems, stating) who "would not avenge with blood?" Philo reflects on murder as common and perhaps even instinctive vengeance for adultery.

Yet a charge of adultery is not open to private vengeance by the Law, but must come before Israel's public court system. Due process must be followed, and it is not only the adulterer who might be considered "worthy of ten thousand deaths," but the adulterous wife also ("both of them shall die," Deut 22:22).[112] Only when guilt is proven can capital punishment be applied. If the punishment has already been meted out privately or by a vigilante group, and the court rules that an executable offence never occurred, then there may be blood on the "husband's hands": he could be found guilty of murder, and face execution himself.

---

[109] *Spec.* 3.11; similarly *Hypoth.* 7:1; cf. Lev 20:10; Deut 22:22. Ibid.

[110] Janzen, "Porneia," 76.

[111] *Jos.*, IX.44. Philo, *Philo*, trans. F. H. Colson, vol. VI, Loeb Classical Library (London: Heinemann, 1984), 165.

[112] "Traces of inequitable deviation to the disadvantage of women lie in Book of Jubilees (*c.*110B.C.), xxx.8,9: a man must be stoned for adultery, but the woman burned alive (cf. *Mishnah*, San. XI.3)." J. D. Derret, *Law in the New Testament* (Oxford: Alden, 1970), 164.

Conversely, if adultery is proven after a husband's bloody vengeance, then a murder charge may be downgraded or discharged.[113]

Universally, rape and murder are considered utmost crimes, and despite (modern) cultural leniency towards adultery, the Law treated adultery no less severely. *Jubilees* also testifies to this in the stern warnings which follow the account of the rape of Dinah:

> No adulterer (*zamma*) or impure person (*rekus*) is to be found [masc.] within Israel throughout all the time of the earth's history, for Israel is holy to the Lord. Any man who has defiled... is to die; he is to be stoned... For this is the way it has been ordained and written on the heavenly tablets regarding any descendant of Israel who defiles... 'He is to die; he is to be stoned'. This law has no temporal limit. (30:8-10).[114]

In telling the story of Joseph, *Jubilees* re-emphasizes the heavenly origin of capital punishment, "there is a death penalty which has been ordained for him in heaven before the most high Lord. (39:7)."[115] So even if earthly law prohibited Jews from executing for adultery in Jesus' time, there existed a strong Second Temple belief that the Law, with its capital codes, was heavenly and timeless.

Some cast the capital codes not as "mirrors of practice" but a "judicial death threat" to attract attention.[116] Even then, such a threat could help interpret Matthew 19:9. In Israel, any sexual immorality, including adultery, was not to be treated lightly. Instone-Brewer admits this, with qualification,

> Adultery, when it happened, was treated extremely seriously. Theoretically this was still a capital offense in the first century C.E.[117]

Yet even if adultery was only "theoretically" considered a capital offence in Jesus' time, in the context of what is "lawful" (Matt 19:3)

---

[113] Various jurisdictions even today take into consideration a spouse's impulsive action. If found to not be premeditated, a partial defence of 'provocation' or 'loss of control' when confronted with infidelity might result in the downgrading say of a charge of murder to manslaughter. E.g. as legislated in England, Wales, and Northern Ireland; see J. Horder and K. Fitz-Gibbon, "When Sexual Infidelity Triggers Murder: Examining the Impact of Homicide Law Reform on Judicial Attitudes in Sentencing," *Cambridge Law Journal* 74, no. 2 (2015): 307-28.

[114] W. Loader, *Enoch, Levi, and Jubilees: Attitudes Towards Sexuality in the Early Enoch Literature, the Aramaic Levi Document, and the Book of Jubilees* (Grand Rapids: Eerdmans, 2007), 200.

[115] Ibid., 201.

[116] Megivern, *Death Penalty*, 11.

[117] Instone-Brewer, *Social and Literary Context*, 94.

and what is "read" in Scripture (Matt 19:4), this is and remains according to Jesus (Matt 5:17-19) the actual legal demand of the Law. Instone-Brewer sees that the death penalty was "probably never inflicted in the New Testament era," but he adds a conflicting note that "this penalty may even have been practiced in Philo's day (*de Joseph* 44: 'the husband may kill the adulterer')" [c.20BCE to c.50CE] which completely covers Jesus' time!

Also deserving of more than a footnote is Instone-Brewer's "suggestion" that the death penalty was common knowledge of the time,

> Josephus's casual assertion that the penalty for adultery was death… and the Mishnah's references to it… suggest that this penalty was generally known.[118]

Rather than somewhat dismissing adultery as "probably rare" and "almost impossible to prove,"[119] the full weight of this penalty that was "generally known" should be applied to Jesus' teaching. Additionally, there was a question of whether to burn alive "externally" (Sadducean method) or "internally" (Pharisaic method) someone who had committed adultery,[120] although both rabbinic methods contradict that claimed when Jesus was tested on a matter related to Matthew 19:9, "in the Law Moses commanded us to stone such women" (John 8:5).[121]

An argument that it would have been a trap for Jesus to affirm the Law in John 7:53-8:11, on the premise that the Romans did not allow the Jewish people to carry out the death sentence for adultery, is refuted by J. Ramsey Michaels:

> This is unlikely in view of Pilate's two explicit statements to the Jewish leaders regarding Jesus himself after his arrest, "Take him yourselves and judge him according to your law" (18:31), and "Take him yourself and crucify" (19:6). If the Gospel writer represents Pilate as commanding them to carry out the death penalty, he must have believed they had the right to do so. Thus the intent of the scribes and Pharisees could not have been to put Jesus in a dilemma between the conflicting demands of Jewish and Roman law, but rather to trap him purely on the basis on Jewish law.[122]

---

[118] Ibid.

[119] Ibid. Yet the difficulty to convict should not alter the penalty of the Law (or any law).

[120] Meier, *Marginal Jew*, 3, 460-61.

[121] See also Appendix 2.

[122] J. R. Michaels, *The Gospel of John* (Grand Rapids: Eerdmans, 2010), 496. Crucifixion could also be a Jewish method of execution; Josephus records that the Hasmonean king Alexander Jannaeus "ordered some eight hundred of the Jews to be crucified" (*Ant.* 13.380). Ibid., 491.

In Matthew 19:1-12, Pharisees attempt the same type of trap, purely based on the Law.

For an offender not to be executed does not abolish the height of the offence (sexual or otherwise), but underscores the depth of mercy. It can be no accident that the idea of great mercy for great sinners finds great emphasis in the account of Jesus' call of Matthew (Matt 9:9-13; cf. Hos 6:6). In Jewish eyes, real "sinners" such as tax collectors and prostitutes are patently sick, for they have greatly violated the Law, whereas the healthy have no need of a physician (Matt 9:12-13; 21:31-32).[123] Diminishing penalties of the Law diminishes a person's shortfall in wellness or righteousness, and the (rabbinic) "mildest penalty possible"[124] might only attract the mildest mercy – if not reject true mercy, because the true height of sin is rejected. Maintaining the ultimate demands of the Law maintains God's ultimate mercy.

That some Jewish leaders can clearly identify "sinners" (cf. Matt 9:11) but cannot clearly rule on other grave sexual matters like "adultery" highlights their hypocrisy and negligence concerning weightier matters of the Law (cf. Matt 25:23-24). In contrast, Jesus clearly rules on sexual matters when he teaches that whoever divorces his wife without the grounds of sexual immorality and marries another "commits adultery" (Matt 19:9). Such adultery would be easy to identify – especially as Jewish weddings were public celebrations; two or more witnesses at the remarriage may confidently establish a charge (cf. Deut 17:6; 19:15), without the difficult cultural proof of witnessing an adulterous couple *in coitu*.[125] Jesus' clarity on μοιχᾶται also suggests that πορνεία ("sexual immorality") – in the same sentence – has the same clarity of meaning, as opposed to the nebulous עֶרְוַת דָּבָר ("matter of indecency," Deut 24:1) that has spawned conflicting cultural meanings and progressive changes to the Law.

Another capital Law, mentioned by Jesus in a way that assumes common knowledge – and common evasion (Matt 15:2-7), deals with a rebellious son (Deut 21:18-21). It even specifies the means of execution, although it is unlikely that this was applied in the first century (cf. adultery).[126] Even so, Jesus does not dismiss the penalty: offenders remain *liable* to judgement, irrespective of whether earthly courts refuse to or are unable to judge. Murder and adultery – even by inward

---

[123] Yet those forgiven much, love much (cf. Luke 7:47).

[124] Derret, *Law*, 169.

[125] Ibid., 160-61.

[126] Although *Sanh.* 11.1 specifies strangulation for both offences. Neusner, *Mishnah*, 607. The court had power to inflict four modes of execution: stoning, burning, decapitation, and strangulation (*Sanh.* 7.1). Ibid., 595-96.

thoughts – merit eternal death ("liable to the hell of fire," Matt 5:22; "your whole body be thrown into hell," Matt 5:29). This idea does not clash with the Law, and to bolster his teaching Jesus references contemporary court practice reliant on the Law (Matt 5:21-26).

Yet the extreme liability that Jesus teaches does clash with contemporary Jewish (and Roman) culture and legal practice. Against common expectation, a rebellious son or an adulterous spouse still deserves death, and the essential goal endures: "So you shall purge the evil from your midst, and all Israel shall hear, and fear" (Deut 21:21). The dire judgement and unabridged Law, at least in theory, should inform our reading of Jesus' words on rebellion ("hardness of heart") in Matthew 19:8 and unfaithfulness ("sexual immorality" and "adultery") in Matthew 19:9, especially as Israel is called God's son (Exod 4:22; Hos 11:1) and Jesus condemns an "evil and adulterous generation" (Matt 12:39; 16:4).

Exactly what Jesus meant by "adultery" will be examined later in the exegetical section, but generally there is a chasm between his understanding and that of contemporary culture. Jesus' concept includes inner lust (Matt 5:27-30; cf. Deut 5:21), so if Matthew 19:9 intends to harmonise the Law with Roman law, then a logical but fantastic conclusion is that Jesus teaches mandatory divorce for every lustful look. This would surely offer everyone grounds for divorce, increase the divorce rate, and offer no provision for mercy and forgiveness. By the standard of Jesus' contemporary culture, adultery destroys the marriage union and mandates divorce,[127] but by Jesus' standard, those who commit adultery are to be destroyed (at least finally and eternally) – unless mercy intervenes. Adultery need not result in the separation of spouses, or an offender and God. It need not destroy marriage. It can cause great harm and eventual destruction, but adultery (or any sexual offence) can be forgiven.

Nonetheless, sex does create one-flesh unions (cf. 1 Cor 6:16), but unlawful unions – be they extramarital or incestuous – must be severed. Paul's declaration of "such were some of you," encompassing the "sexually immoral" and "adulterers" (1 Cor 6:11), evidences that this is right and possible. Sexually immoral acts, and even adultery committed in the heart (cf. Matt 5:27-30), should end not with new unions and the severing of lawful marriages, but with forgiveness and continued covenant love.

Jesus' meaning of "sexual immorality" will be examined more thoroughly later. Suffice it for now, *porneia* covers many illicit sexual

---

[127] Loader, *On Sexuality*, 290, 492.

offences, even if "understood primarily as adultery"[128] in a marital context. The normal semantic range supports this,[129] and it would be inconsistent to divorce for adultery but not for another equally immoral sexual act such as incest or bestiality (cf. Lev 18:6-23). John's condemnation of Herod points to this, for even if we ignore Josephus' record that John complained of Herod marrying his niece, Matthew stresses that Herod's offence was in marrying "his brother Philip's wife" (Matt 14:3; cf. Mark 6:17). This is no ordinary adultery, for it involved uncovering the nakedness of a close relative, strictly proscribed in Leviticus 18:16. It comprises one of many "abominable customs" practiced by the previous inhabitants, and such "iniquity" puts Israel at risk of the same dire punishment and ejection from the land (Lev 18:24-30).

Incest was outlawed in Greek, Roman, and Jewish settings, although there were variations in what this meant.[130] "Tacitus mentions execution for incest under Tiberius."[131] So, if Matthew 19:9 were aligned with contemporary Roman law, one could avoid death for adultery (except perhaps the paramour) but incur death for incest. In contrast, the Law demanded death for both party to adultery, but it is not so clear-cut on incestuous acts: "the persons who do them shall be cut off from among their people" (Lev 18:29) which along with adultery can infer execution (Lev 20:10-16), but "if a man takes his brother's wife" then the Law's only specific penalty for this "impurity" is "they shall be childless" (Lev 20:21).

As noted earlier, Roman law concerning adultery did have capital elements, so this further complicates harmonising the Law with Roman law. For example, whilst adultery meant mandatory divorce of a wife,[132] the adulterer could be put to death.[133] Hence Matthew 19:9 might then be understood as:

> If "sexual immorality" entails incest, then a guilty wife faces execution (under Tiberius); for adultery the wife is to be divorced (*perhaps "sent away" for a time to an island separate from her paramour – who might be killed*) or killed by her father;[134] and for other sexually immoral acts the Law

---

[128] Ibid., 286.

[129] Blomberg, "Exegesis," 177.

[130] Loader, *On Sexuality*, 81. E.g. in a Greek setting, marriage between uncles and nieces might sometimes be approved.

[131] Ibid.

[132] Cf. *Ketub.* 3.5; *Sot.* 5.1. Neusner, *Mishnah*, 383, 454.

[133] *Lex Iulia de adulteriis coercendis.* Loader, *On Sexuality*, 104.

[134] Contemporary Roman law demands that the two must be exiled to different islands (if a wronged husband does not kill the adulterer, or a father kills both), but this is only for a

codes must be read to accord with current secular codes (*in the first century, Roman law takes precedence*); but for not satisfying the 'exception clause' (i.e. the wife is not sexually immoral) any husband who divorces and remarries "commits adultery" (*he deserves death by the Law; but must divorce and/or be executed by Roman law*).

To complicate matters even more, capital punishment for adultery was restored by the Romans in the fourth century CE.[135] So should Matthew 19:9 be reinterpreted henceforth as adultery mandates (divorce by) capital punishment – which would return us to the original God-ordained penalty as written in Hebrew Scripture? Or did Jesus restore this original meaning independent of contemporary Roman law, and the meaning remains forever constant independent of any secular law in any land?

If, however, Jesus reinterpreted the Law to align with Roman law of his time and commanded that not a dot more be relaxed, then what keeps churches from mandating divorce (without death) for adultery and demanding the death of the paramour? Must a modern Christian ethic be beholden to first-century Roman law? If one argues that the church must obey the state, then restoring capital punishment for adultery becomes compulsory at times: in the Roman Empire of the fourth century CE, in Geneva of the sixteenth century CE,[136] or in many Islamic nations.

If one argues for a trend to abolish capital punishment altogether, then the legal execution of a paramour can certainly be rejected. However, this relaxes Roman law of the first century (and even more so of the fourth century!) *and* the Law of Moses (that demands both parties

---

period, and applies to senators, equestrians, and well-born citizens. For non-elites, "We know little of what marriage meant for the vast majority of the population." Ibid., 103-04. Such folk may take no notice of irrelevant Roman law, and even biblical law against polygyny, targeted at the elite. An adulterous couple might marry or cohabit (possibly cf. John 4:17), especially among common Jews (Jesus' main audience) in remote Judean or Galilean backwaters of the Roman empire (exile to Mediterranean islands is most unlikely).

[135] Under Constantine the law became terrifyingly strict; it even threatened the pouring of molten lead down the throat of the nurse in charge of any girl who had pre-marital sex. Edict 9.24.1 in C. Pharr, *The Theodosian Code and Novels and the Sirmondian Constitutions* (Union: Lawbook Exchange, 2001), 245.

[136] "In the days of Calvin in Geneva, the attitude toward sexual sin was quite severe. There were two forms of torture that could be authorized by the general council to extract the truth from persons suspected of adultery. In 1566 ...the general council of the city adopted an ordinance that those caught in adultery were to be punished by the sentence of death. Women caught in the act were drowned in the Rhone River, and men were beheaded outside the city gates. *There was really no forgiveness for adultery*." R. Nydam, "The Messiness of Marriage and the Knottiness of Divorce: A Call for a Higher Theology and a Tougher Ethic," *CTJ* 40 (2005): 224. (Italics added.)

be executed). So the premise that Jesus forever upholds one set or both sets of law codes cannot be sustained. Freezing a reinterpreted Law that aligns with first-century secular law has critical problems, and relaxing the Law to suit any other time jars with Jesus' decree to the contrary (cf. Matt 5:17-19) and attracts other critical problems.

Jesus suffered capital punishment himself. Matthew's Gospel indicts Herod (Matt 2:13, 20), the Pharisees (Matt 12:14), the chief priests (Matt 21:38-45), the whole Council (Matt 26:59), and the elders (Matt 27:20) who persuaded the crowd to bay for Jesus' blood (Matt 27:23). This should caution against blending God's Law with secular law when considering Jesus' divorce teaching. As Jesus foretold his death (Matt 16:21; 26:45) and that of the "wretches" (Matt 21:41) he deems responsible for it, then irrespective of whether the death penalty was applied for sexual sins, death looms large and one should not dismiss *a priori* capital meanings within the divorce debate.

Yet forgiveness is obtainable for whoever commits capital offences such as adultery and murder. The paradox, a seemingly un-Christian but not unlawful idea that a rebellious son "must surely die" (Matt 15:4), finds resolution in Jesus' sonship, an identity emphasized in the context of his death ("Son of Man," Matt 16:13; 17:9; 26:2, 24, 45; "Son of the living God," 16:16; "Son of God," 26:63; 27:43, 54). If capital meanings are present in Matthew 19:9, then it could be said that *Jesus is an advocate for capital punishment, but only in the same vein that he is passionate about his own death,[137] or that a loving heavenly Father relishes the death of his own Son – while upholding the Law's permanently commanded penalty for a rebellious son and an unfaithful spouse.*

---

[137] Jesus was "troubled," with his soul "very sorrowful, even to death" (Matt 26:37-38).

CHAPTER 5 – The Test Question & Creation Command

Exegesis of Matthew 19:1-6

Greek Text NA28:[1]

[1] Καὶ ἐγένετο ὅτε ἐτέλεσεν ὁ Ἰησοῦς τοὺς λόγους τούτους, μετῆρεν ἀπὸ τῆς Γαλιλαίας καὶ ἦλθεν εἰς τὰ ὅρια τῆς Ἰουδαίας πέραν τοῦ Ἰορδάνου.

[2] καὶ ἠκολούθησαν αὐτῷ ὄχλοι πολλοί, καὶ ἐθεράπευσεν αὐτοὺς ἐκεῖ.

[3] Καὶ προσῆλθον αὐτῷ [a]Φαρισαῖοι πειράζοντες αὐτὸν καὶ λέγοντες· εἰ ἔξεστιν ἀνθρώπῳ ἀπολῦσαι τὴν γυναῖκα αὐτοῦ κατὰ πᾶσαν αἰτίαν;

[4] ὁ δὲ ἀποκριθεὶς εἶπεν· οὐκ ἀνέγνωτε ὅτι ὁ κτίσας[b] ἀπ᾽ ἀρχῆς ἄρσεν καὶ θῆλυ ἐποίησεν αὐτούς;

[5] καὶ εἶπεν· ἕνεκα τούτου καταλείψει ἄνθρωπος τὸν πατέρα καὶ τὴν μητέρα καὶ κολληθήσεται[c] τῇ γυναικὶ αὐτοῦ, καὶ ἔσονται οἱ δύο εἰς σάρκα μίαν.

[6] ὥστε οὐκέτι εἰσὶν δύο ἀλλὰ σὰρξ μία. ὃ οὖν ὁ θεὸς συνέζευξεν ἄνθρωπος μὴ χωριζέτω.

Textual notes: (Byzantine[2] differences)

[a] οἱ ("the") is added (a scribal tendency, for Matthew tends to treat all Pharisees as a group).

[b] ποιήσας ("to make") has a greater occurrence than κτίσας ("to create").

[c] προσκολληθήσεται has a greater occurrence than κολληθήσεται (both: "to cleave").

---

[1] Novum Testamentum Graece, Nestle-Aland 28th Edition. Bibleworks: Software of Biblical Exegesis & Research Ver. 10, BibleWorks, Norfolk. (Unless otherwise noted.)

[2] The debate over what is truly "Byzantine," and whether texts so assigned accurately reflect earlier texts, does not significantly affect this exegesis and central thesis.

Verse 1

Now when Jesus had finished these sayings [words], he went away from Galilee and entered the region of Judea beyond the Jordan.

The opening Semitic idiom: καί ἐγένετο, "and it happened," is a distinctive Matthean feature which concludes each main discourse and introduces a new phase of the story.[3] This gives prominence to Jesus' "words" (λόγοι) in five main Matthean discourses (chapters 5-7; 10; 13; 18; 23-25), demonstrating "the importance of Jesus as a Teacher."[4] Yet the new phase is not unrelated to the prior, and Peter Bolt observes a valuable "narrative-speech-narrative pattern":

> the speeches tend to educate the reader, so that once we 'hear' the speeches, we then *see* the events of the narrative sections in a new light. By this structure, Matthew helps his readers to read his Gospel properly.[5]

What we understand of the Matthew 18 discourse then significantly determines how we *see* the events of the narrative as the topic of marriage is debated. Matthew presents the "words" of chapter 18 as Jesus' and not his own.[6] Although Jesus' ministry in Galilee has finished, Matthew also presents the discourse of 19:4, 5, 6, 8, 9, 11, and 12 as Jesus', and his authority to speak such words remains contested by Jewish leaders. An introductory concern, however, is that by labelling Chapter 18 'The Church Discourse',[7] interpretation of Matthew 18 (and by default, 19) can too quickly lead towards church instruction and away from the original Jewish legal context. Thankfully Bolt does 'hear' a background legal framework; for example, in commenting on Matthew 18:16, he writes, "This is an allusion to the requirements for evidence in the Jewish courts as per the Law of God in Deuteronomy 19:15."[8]

Some scholars have compared the structure of Matthew's five discourses with the five books of the Pentateuch, though "no

---

[3] R. T. France, *The Gospel of Matthew*, TNTC (Grand Rapids: Eerdmans, 2007), 297.

[4] Morris, *Matthew*, 184.

[5] Bolt, *Matthew*, 6. (Italics original.)

[6] Allowance is made of course for Matthew or another source writer to have translated Jesus' words from Aramaic or Hebrew into Greek. This is not to suppose that the whole Greek Gospel stems from a Hebrew one, but it does appreciate that Jesus' original words were most likely spoken in Aramaic or Hebrew.

[7] Bolt, Matthew, 6.

[8] Ibid., 180.

correspondence with specific Pentateuchal books is obvious."[9] Nonetheless, Matthew has more parallels, echoes and Hebrew Bible citations than any other New Testament book, and reflections of Moses in Jesus are strong. Craig Evans writes,

> Matthew again ends a major discourse (in this case the fourth) with a phrase from the Pentateuch (cf. Deut 32:45, "When Moses had finished reciting all these words to all Israel"...), thus giving Jesus' teaching a Mosaic flavor.[10]

This Matthew 19:1-12 passage is thoroughly Jewish, evidenced in the introductory Semitic idiom, the Mosaic phrasing of the first sentence, the focus on the main character as a Jew gloriously designated by the Gospel's opening words as "Jesus Christ, the son of David, the son of Abraham," the Judean setting, and the traditional identification of the writer as one of the first followers of this Jewish Messiah. The scene is well set for a Jewish legal test by experts in Jewish law: Pharisees, who cite their most esteemed authority on Mosaic Law. At stake is whose word and authority will prevail.

An unusual verb in this opening verse, μεταίρω, found nowhere else in the New Testament except for Matthew 13:53, describes Jesus' withdrawal from the region where he has ministered most.[11] The difference between these parallel "summary statements"[12] in 13:53 and 19:1 is that earlier Jesus "finished these parables" whereas here he "finished these sayings." This does not mean that Jesus' preceding stories about a lost sheep (Matt 18:10-14) or an unforgiving servant (Matt 18:23-35) are not of a parabolic nature, but Matthew simply does not call them "parables" (cf. Matt 13:3, 10, 13, 18, 24, 31, 33, 35, 36, and 53). Jesus speaks these words *to his disciples* with the expectation that they understand, for they are blessed with seeing and hearing (cf. Matt 13:16). In contrast, Matthew has already stressed that Jesus spoke only in parables *to the crowds* in order to fulfil prophecy (Matt 13:34-35), so that they do not see, hear or understand (Matt 13:10-15).

One implication is that any disciple reading Matthew's Gospel can be expected to understand the parables and sayings of Jesus. Like Jesus' first disciples, they have been given a gift in understanding the secrets of the kingdom of heaven (Matt 13:11). Another possible implication is that anyone outside of "the crowds" that Matthew specifies can be expected to understand the parables, for the prophecy against "the

---

[9] Keener, *Matthew*, 38. Cf. Deut 31:1; 31:24. See also Hays, *Echoes*, 144.
[10] C. Evans, *Matthew* (New York: CUP, 2012), 339.
[11] Morris, *Matthew*, 364, 479.
[12] Newman and Stine, *Matthew*, 604.

crowds" was fulfilled in Jesus' time. If this expectation is incorrect, then at least Jesus' sayings in Matthew 18 might be comprehensible to anyone, because they are not designated "parables," and also by virtue of being published they now speak to anyone and not exclusively to Jesus' disciples.

Furthermore, if Matthew 19:1-12 has been located to serve as an extension of Jesus' teaching on forgiveness in Matthew 18, then universal comprehension of Jesus' teaching on marriage and divorce could also be expected. However, this expectation cannot guarantee universal agreement, as a multiplicity of viewpoints proves! In keeping with the Matthew 13 purpose of the parables, Jesus' sayings may then stand as an indictment against those who do not truly understand in their heart (Matt 13:15) and forgive from their heart (Matt 18:35).

Matthew 13 narrates a movement of Jesus going out of "the house" to tell parables to great crowds (Matt 13:1-3) and then later he "left the crowds and went into the house" (Matt 13:36). This might simply delineate between what are public and private teachings, however, the term "house" curiously has a high frequency in this Gospel.[13] Matthew has just prior mentioned two houses: "the house of God" that David entered (Matt 12:4), and "the house" that an evil spirit vacated and then reclaimed with seven other evil spirits (Matt 12:43-45).[14] One house is holy (cf. the Temple) and within it are those with hearts for God (cf. David) who eat and understand (cf. Matt 13:51), while opponents remain outside. The other house represents an evil generation in a divided and demon-filled state. Given that Graham Stanton sees the five discourses in Matthew's Gospel as a "giant chiasm" and "chap. 13 is central in every sense!"[15] then the role of houses may also be central to Matthew's purposes.

Here there is no hint of anti-Semitism, for all those of both houses are Jewish. There is no family privilege (Matt 12:46-50). There is no parochialism; no 'hometown advantage' is pressed by Matthew, at least for Jesus, because in Matthew 13:53-54 Jesus "went away" from the house to go "to his hometown," and in Matthew 19:1, Jesus "went away from Galilee" and will not visit it again until after the resurrection (Matt

---

[13] Οἰκία (and compounds of) occurs 46 times in Matthew (cf. Mark: 26 times, Luke: 58 times, John: 11 times).

[14] Cf. the house of a wise, godly man (ἀνδρός) versus that of a foolish, evil man (ἀνδρός) (Matt 7:24-27). The masculine is retained to highlight any connection with a hard-hearted man who divorces his wife and sends her out of his house (cf. Deut 24:1-4).

[15] G. Stanton, "The Origin and Purpose of Matthew's Sermon on the Mount," in *Tradition and Interpretation in the New Testament: Essays in Honor of E. Earle Ellis for His 60th Birthday*, ed. G. Hawthorne and O. Betz (Grand Rapids: Eerdmans, 1987), 190.

28:7, 16). However, when "Jesus reclined at table in the house" with many tax collector and sinners (Matt 9:10), this home is Matthew's (cf. Matt 9:28; Luke 5:29),[16] and activity within it mirrors that in the kingdom of heaven, where many "recline at table with Abraham, Isaac, and Jacob" (Matt 8:11)!

Facing criticism, Jesus defends the fellowshipping in "the house" of "those who are sick" with his first use in Matthew of "I desire mercy, and not sacrifice" (Matt 9:13; cf. Matt 12:7), cited from Hosea 6:6. This directly connects "the house" to both the earthly Hosea-Gomer marriage, and to the God-Israel marriage metaphor, where in steadfast love the husband is merciful to his adulterous wife. Also, as the second citation of Hosea 6:6 occurs in Matthew 12:7, it locates David, with his notorious sin of adultery (cf. Matt 1:6) and his controversial act of entering "the house of God" to eat the bread of the Presence (Matt 12:4), squarely in the company of sinners in "the house" too, who out of mercy recline at table with the Lord.[17] Houses are important to Matthew's narrative, for they epitomise security, fellowship, and belonging. Considering the movement to or from a house is also highly relevant to understanding Matthew 19:1-12, for according to the Law, divorce always involves a man sending a woman away from his "house" (cf. בַּיִת in Deut 24:1, where it has double emphasis, and Deut 24:3).[18]

"Galilee" is last mentioned by Matthew as the location of Jesus' passion prediction (17:22-23). There the disciples reacted intensely to Jesus' teaching that people will kill him, but appear to miss the main point that Jesus "will be raised." They react strongly again after he teaches on marriage (Matt 19:10), but this time no level of distress is recorded, so perhaps here they understand Jesus' main point. Death

---

[16] If Matthew is both the author and the tax collector Levi, and he writes about his own house, then "the house" would be well-known as a place used by the Lord. This may not only be due to the "great feast" (Luke 5:29) held there with "many tax collectors and sinners" (Matt 9:10; Mark 2:15), but such a house could easily accommodate Jesus and his apostles at other times, along with later Christian meetings.

[17] Cf. "You prepare a table before me..." (Ps 23:5); "They feast on the abundance of your house..." (Ps 36:8); "One thing have I asked of the LORD, that will I seek after: that I may dwell in the house of the LORD all the days of my life, to gaze upon the beauty of the LORD and to inquire in his temple" (Ps 27:4; cf. 65:4 – both link God's house and temple).

[18] It is implicit also in Deut 24:2 with the mention of the wife: "and if she goes [away from his house]," and in Deut 24:4 with the mention of the husband: "who sent her away [from his house]," so it could be said that the "house" is important in every verse of divorce legislation in the Hebrew Bible. It appears implicit too in the marriage legislation, such that a man "takes a wife [into his house] and marries her" (Deut 24:1). Culturally, a marriage could hardly be considered marriage without cohabitation, where a woman enters a man's house or bridal chamber with public celebration, whereas private consummation is not the defining element (cf. Matt 1:24-25).

features in this passage too, not only in the background with John the Baptist's death and the Pharisees' desire to kill Jesus, but in the capital offences of "sexual immorality" and "adultery" (Matt 19:9). Thus, in and away from Galilee, the disciples are confronted by Jesus' deadly – or death-centred – words.

"*Judea*" and "*Jordan*" stress a Jewish setting, one under Roman authority at that time. Rome regarded Judea as a province restricted to west of the Jordan, so Matthew's setting of "Judea beyond the Jordan" is problematic.[19] It could simply align with Rome's western jurisdiction, though it would have been unlikely for a Jewish writer to designate this "beyond the Jordan," or loosely refer to Jewish occupied land anywhere north or east of the Jordan River, such as Perea. Another option, in keeping with Jewish aspirations, is that the terminology was deliberately eschatological and in defiance of Rome's limited conception. To the Jews, the original land promised to Abraham (Gen 15) extended to the east far beyond the Jordan, even to the Euphrates River. A smaller area was conquered by Israel under Joshua and three tribes were allotted an inheritance east of the Jordan (Josh 13:8-32). However, there was provision that with a new prophet like Moses (Deut 18:15), God would enlarge their territory "to all the land he promised to give" in fulfilment of what was sworn to their fathers (Deut 19:8 cf. Matt 5:17). The Nabatean and Perean territorial disputes thus fade in significance, for in the Matthean scheme, both territories come under Judea! Moreover, in Jesus' scheme, his heavenly kingdom is over all the kingdoms of the world,[20] so his rule and ethics surpass any territorial and ethnic limits of the Law of Moses.

The first mention of the patronymic ancestor of Judea, Judah, is found in the Matthean genealogy. Thus the contextual setting, "Judea beyond the Jordan," of this marriage pericope connects also with the most prominent narrative setting of Matthew's Gospel, suggesting that questions of marriage may well be informed by examining Jesus' own

---

[19] Morris, *Matthew*, 479. Morris evaluates alternative ideas, but finds it more likely that Jesus' entrance into Judea was from the eastern area beyond the Jordan.

[20] The phrase "kingdom of heaven" appears 32 times in Matthew and in no other Gospel. It is paralleled only in two other biblical texts: Dan 7:27 and Rev 11:15, which also bear the same explicit theme of all the kingdoms of the world coming under an everlasting heavenly kingdom. Jesus' kingdom contrasts with that of the "exceedingly terrifying" beast (Rome) that Daniel has just described with "teeth of iron and claws of bronze" (Dan 7:19). This beast "shall think to change the times and the law" (Dan 7:25) – such unusual wording suggests an attempt to change what really cannot be changed: the Mosaic Law (cf. Dan 6:5) remains God's unalterable law irrespective of human assault. Where first-century Jewish law aligns with Roman law against the Law (as written) then what should be unthinkable is committed but is not to be followed.

family origins. "Jacob the father of Judah and his brothers" (Matt 1:2) is Matthew's first record of siblings in Jesus' genealogy and brings attention to all twelve tribes of Israel. A Jewish audience, keenly aware of Jacob's marriages, may reflect on his uncensored polygamy in the light of a strict passage on marriage and divorce (Matt 19:1-12). The relationship between Judah and his daughter-in-law, Tamar, would readily come to mind too, especially as Matthew has already named them both in Jesus' genealogy, where Tamar is the first woman mentioned in Matthew's Gospel (Matt 1:3), and highlighted their two sons Perez and Zerah (when only Perez is in Jesus' direct lineage).

The Judah-Tamar union did not necessarily entail incestuous prostitution (cf. "sexual immorality" Matt 19:9) punishable by death, but a cunning legal marital ruse on Tamar's part, with a subsequent separation (not divorce).[21] Matthew's first-mentioned ancestor of Jesus (Matt 1:1), David, cannot escape the charge of "sexual immorality" however, for he specifically commits adultery with "the wife of Uriah" (Matt 1:6). This adultery, and attendant murder, provides the first clear Matthean reference point for understanding the "adultery" of Matthew 19:9, over and against any presumed sexual impropriety of the women listed in Jesus' genealogy.[22] Instead, these women, who might initially be considered sexually immoral or improper, *are all exonerated in their narratives* and therefore serve to *reinforce Mary's propriety* in highly suspicious circumstances. If anything, the list reinforces the sexual impropriety of the related men, some of whom are called evil. Such androcentric judgement may inform our reading of Jesus' teaching on divorce. Nonetheless, David (mentioned six times in Chapter 1) is heralded twice as much as Abraham in Matthew's introduction, undoubtedly because God had mercy on him and messianic hopes centred on a Davidic king.

---

[21] This may entail, unknowingly to Judah, a Levirate wedding. "Levirate marriages were practiced by some ancient peoples prior to the Sinaitic covenant. Tamar's effort to woo her father-in-law, Judah, into marriage (Gen. 38) conformed to provisions of Hittite law. ...Article 193 of the Hittite code provides: 'If a man takes a wife and then the man dies, his brother shall take his wife, (then) his father shall take her'." A. Bloch, *The Biblical and Historical Background of Jewish Customs and Ceremonies* (New York: Ktav, 1980), 41. The Hittite law connection gains extra credibility via the fourth woman Matthew records in Jesus' genealogy: the wife of Uriah the Hittite (Matt 1:6; cf. 2 Sam 12:10). Furthermore, Tamar is charged with "prostitution," but never admits it, nor does the narrative condemn her for it (plus her veiling is unusual for this). She has not committed "adultery" either, for neither are married to another.

[22] "We can rule out the suggestion that the list reinforced Mary's suspected impropriety." L. Cohick, *Women in the World of the Earliest Christians* (Grand Rapids: Baker, 2009), 129.

As Jesus travels towards the Jewish capital, it appears vital to Matthew to maintain a Jewish context. The population of τὰ ὅρια ("the region"),[23] Perea, is mainly Jewish.[24] Significantly, the place where Jesus is tested on a Jewish legal matter is not Samaria, where Second Temple Jews perceived that the Law has been compromised. Jesus skirts Samaria, not necessarily to avoid the Samaritans, but to enter Palestine near Jericho from across the Jordan River. Jesus' public ministry comes full cycle: baptised in the Jordan by John the Baptist at its commencement (Matt 3:13-17), to crossing the Jordan River as it culminates. This passage has John firmly in the background (Matt 14:1-12). Herod even believes Jesus is "John the Baptist risen from the dead" (Matt 14:2), which also intimates that Jesus will share the same views on marriage and divorce that his forerunner did.

John's emphasis on the Law (cf. Matt 11:13; 14:4) should not be seen as "legalism" but in the light of his ministry "beyond the Jordan" preparing the way for Jesus (Matt 3). No new covenant has been inaugurated yet, so the sins repented of here can only relate to violations against the Law, and the water baptism purely a return to the Law. John's heralding of another baptism brings a contrast to his ministry, signalling more effective work and greater judgement. Bolt observes that there "the Israelites came out to confess their sins in preparation for the arrival of the long-awaited time of forgiveness."[25] So beneath the presenting legal issue of divorce, "there also lurked the more serious issue: the human heart" with all kinds of evils that arise out of it that do incalculable harm, including "adultery" and "sexual immorality" (cf. Matt 15:19).[26] In Matthew's scheme, a question of forgiveness from the heart (Matt 18:15-35) – arguably for any offence – underpins a question of the lawfulness of divorce for any offence (Matt 19:1-12).

---

[23] Here is the last of six occurrences of ὅριον in Matthew (others are Matt 2:16; 4:13; 8:34; 15:22; 15:39); Matthew's usage is greater than any other NT writer, suggesting that location is important to him.

[24] Stern, "Herodian Dynasty," 125, 33. "…as distinct from the majority Greek population of the Dekapolis cities." S. Freyne, *Galilee: From Alexander the Great to Hadrian* (Edinburgh: T&T Clark, 1998), 70.

[25] Bolt, *Matthew*, 183.

[26] Ibid., 184.

Verse 2

And large crowds followed him, and he healed them there.

Matthew 4:25 has "great crowds followed him... and from beyond the Jordan" preceding Jesus' first teaching on divorce (Matt 5:31-32). Jesus was popular with the masses; he had impressive authority (Matt 7:28-29) that troubled the Pharisees and Herod. That the crowds "followed him" could suggest discipleship.[27] However, even though the boundaries are not always clear, discipleship involves more than a physical following of Jesus, and the Gospel use of μαθητής ("disciple") is extremely novel.[28] This is extremely important, for just because Jesus teaches large Jewish crowds on a point of Jewish Law, this does not mean that his teaching may be directly translated into Christian law, or the Law may be reinterpreted to suit another situation.

Here, Jesus is not teaching Christian "disciples" under a new covenant, although good application can be made by observing this Jewish legal debate. The only disciples present are ones living under the Law; "new covenant" is absent in this Gospel, and Jesus' teaching is pre-crucifixion. As Matthew 18:23-35 is not labelled a "parable," it can be expected that everyone might understand Jesus' teaching on mercy, and Jesus' subsequent teaching on marriage. True disciples follow Jesus and his teaching.

A little while later, as Jesus left Jericho a "great crowd" still "followed" (ἀκολουθέω) him (Matt 20:29). Then as Jesus entered Jerusalem, the crowds "went before him" and "followed him" (Matt 21:9), which may purely describe a regal welcome, but the narrative change might also signal a change in the crowd. After this point Matthew no longer tells of great crowds following Jesus. Instead, when Pilate gives the crowd an opportunity to "release" (ἀπολύω) "Jesus who is called Christ" (Matt 27:17, 22), whom they have followed

---

[27] D. Hagner, *Matthew 14-28*, WBC 33B (Dallas: Word, 1995), 542.

[28] In the entire LXX, μαθητής is absent. Yet in the Gospels, its presence is massive: 72 times in Matthew, 46 times in Mark, 37 times in Luke, and 78 times in John, almost solely in reference to Jesus' disciples. Then apart from Acts (28 times, but never in reference to the disciples during Jesus' ministry), μαθητής is absent from the rest of the NT. Meier claims, "Prior to the lifetime of the historical Jesus, there is no Jewish author we can point to who speaks of disciples who are at least in some ways similar to the disciples Jesus gathers around himself." It is not until the end of the first century that a use of μαθητής close to that in the Gospels appears in Jewish literature. Meier, *Marginal Jew*, 3, 40-44.

(ἀκολουθέω), they are persuaded "to ask for Barabbas and destroy (ἀπόλλυμι) Jesus" (Matt 27:20).[29]

By the time of Jesus' trial "all the disciples have left him and fled" (Matt 26:56), although Matthew does restore the term ἀκολουθέω to note that Peter temporarily was "following him at a distance" (Matt 26:58). At the crucifixion, "many women" (Matt 27:55) watch "from a distance," and here Matthew has his final use of it ἀκολουθέω to highlight that they "had followed Jesus from Galilee."[30] The temporary separation by death and the physical "distance" of followers is overcome when Matthew concludes his narrative with Jesus' words of eternal togetherness, "I am with you always to the end of the age" (Matt 28:20; cf. Matt 1:23 "Immanuel," "God with us").

The wording καὶ ἐθεράπευσεν αὐτοὺς in Matthew 19:2 is identical to 12:15, but 19:2 substitutes ἐκεῖ ("there") for πᾶς ("all") and thus accentuates the location of Jesus' healing ministry. His miraculous healing of large crowds in this physical setting is of some import, *there* "beyond the Jordan" (Matt 19:1). The parallel draws attention to Jesus' earlier legal conflict with the Pharisees who question the lawfulness of healing on the Sabbath (Matt 12:1-14); Matthew notes that their motive then was "so that they might accuse him." Unsuccessful in establishing guilt, they do not relent but conspire to destroy Jesus (Matt 12:14). So now, against the same backdrop of miraculous healing that the Pharisees fail to appreciate, a deadly plot sits behind their legal challenge.

With an introductory context of mercy (Matt 18:21-35), and an immediate context of healing, the purpose of Jesus' benevolent actions is not to stimulate academic debate, but to care for needy people, to have mercy on crowds (not only "disciples"), and to evidence that he is the Christ (cf. Matt 11:2-5; 16:16-17). Nolland writes,

> Here Jesus performs the same ministry in Judea as he did in Galilee. Jesus' compassion for the needy was a prime characteristic of his messianic ministry.[31]

---

[29] Although the terms ἀπολύω, ἀκολουθέω, and ἀπόλλυμι do not have the same base, a separate phonetic and philological study of Matthew's Gospel may realise thematic links. In countering the local audience thesis, Vine contends that the Gospels were presented by lectors and received orally, and he then devotes two chapters to consider the aural experience. C. Vine, *The Audience of Matthew: An Appraisal of the Local Audience Thesis* (London: Bloomsbury T&T Clark, 2014), 100-201. Cooper agrees that orality is "a neglected area of Matthean studies." Cooper, "Vine. Audience," 101-02.

[30] Meier notes that no women are called "disciples" in any Gospel, but this may simply be a philological problem for there was no feminine form of "disciple" in Hebrew or Aramaic. Meier, *Marginal Jew*, 3, 78.

[31] Nolland, *Matthew*, 703.

Just as the healings were to be readily understood by the crowds (cf. Matt 11:2-5), so too we could expect that Jesus' teaching on marriage and divorce to be readily understood by common people.

Jesus obviously healed *and* taught,[32] but Matthew puts emphasis on his healing ministry being interrupted by the Pharisees with a legal question. This narrative arrangement may serve as a warning not to divert attention away from Jesus' healing power by testing God, or else the antithesis of healing occurs. Matthew has earlier revealed the link between healing and forgiveness (Matt 9:2-5), so his emphasis on *healing* "large crowds"[33] bolsters the link between Matthew 19:1-12 and 18:21-35 – especially the large debt release of 18:27, yet the culpability in not appropriating heavenly mercy (expressed in a story, not a "parable") and the later forsaking of Jesus by the crowds, portends large debt reinstatement (Matt 18:32-35).

Jesus' "woes" against the Jewish religious leaders (Matt 23) *and the Galilean cities* of Chorazin, Bethsaida, and Jesus' "own city" of Capernaum (Matt 4:13; 9:1) – where most of his mighty works had been done but the people did not repent (Matt 11:20-24) – also portends calamity. This is not only for Jerusalem and the Temple system (Matt 24:1-2), but for that generation in general (Matt 23:36; cf. 24:34). The large crowds healed by Jesus, who witness his works and hear his words, are considered more culpable than lawless Gentiles: Tyrians who plundered Jerusalem following the Babylonian Exile (Ezek 26:1-2); Sidonians who exulted themselves (Isa 23:4, 12), took treasure for their own pagan temples, and sold Jews into slavery (Joel 3:5-6); and (stereo)typically "wicked" Sodomites (Gen 19:4-7; Deut 29:23; Isa 3:9, Jer 23:14).

Given the general culpability, any judgement of hard-heartedness and unfaithfulness in Matthew 19:1-12 should not be limited to Jesus' dialogue partners. Nor should judgement be limited to Israel. Anyone who is merciless or within a nation (or crowd) that has had great testimony of Jesus' healing, works and words, and who does not repent, has great culpability.

---

[32] Mark 10:1 has "teaching"; Matthew notes later that the Christ is the one teacher, Matt 23:10.

[33] "Crowds" (often "large crowds") appears 26 times in Matthew (Mark: once; Luke: 12 times; John: zero), exceeding the sum of all other occurrences in the NT.

Verse 3

And Pharisees came up to him and tested him by asking, "Is it lawful to divorce one's wife for any cause?"

Some Pharisees "came to" (προσέρχομαι)[34] Jesus without any hint of following him (cf. the crowds) or therapeutic concern to commend Jesus for his compassion or to obtain healing. Earlier, others "came to" Jesus but sought healing (Matt 17:14) or posed sincere questions about the kingdom (Matt 18:1) and forgiveness (Matt 18:21). Jesus has earlier warned his disciples to beware of "the teaching of the Pharisees" (Matt 16:12). If the Pharisees espouse the teachings of Hillel or Shammai in relation to divorce, then Jesus' words must pertain to their two main understandings of "a matter of indecency" (Deut 24:1). Jesus demands his Jewish audience to practise and observe whatever Moses actually wrote, as spoken by the Pharisees but not necessarily as taught or practised by them (Matt 23:1-3).

The participles, πειράζοντες (literally: *'they are testing'*) and λέγοντες (literally: *'they are asking'*), are in the continuous present, hence several Pharisees could have fielded the same question or variant questions.[35] This allows room for test questions from different angles: Matthew's primary interest lies in the question of divorce "for any matter" (Matt 19:3); Mark's in divorce at all (Mark 10:2).[36] It also allows room for Jesus to tailor his answer to specific concerns, and for hearers to record these different, but not necessarily conflicting,

---

[34] This may indicate a formal approach. Morris, *Matthew*, 479.

[35] "This is a typical Semitic expression in which 'and' is deceptive... the first part of the construction ('tested') is explained by the second part ('saying')." Newman and Stine, *Matthew*, 605-06. As such, a simultaneous sense of "tested him by saying" is most appropriate, but the plurality of testers ("Pharisees," "they tested") may point to a plurality of questions. The Semitic expression again evidences the Jewishness of this Gospel, as against Mark 10:2 with a very different Greek construction: ἐπηρώτων αὐτὸν εἰ ἔξεστιν ("asked him if it is lawful..."). The words προσελθόντες Φαρισαῖοι are absent in the Western MSS, and may well have come into the other witnesses through the influence of Matt 19:3. So Mark's ἐπηρώτων can be read as an indefinite plural ("people asked him"), consistent with his style elsewhere. See W. Lane, *The Gospel According to Mark*, NICNT (Grand Rapids: Eerdmans, 1974), 351. This provides a general question on divorce and puts the indictment of "hardness of heart" (Mark 10:5) broadly on the people or "crowds" (ὄχλοι, Mark 10:1) more so than on the leaders as Matthew does.

[36] It also allows for different translations (by Mark, Matthew, or another) of the Hebrew/Aramaic that the conversation was almost certainly in. E.g. Greek terms for "for a man": ἀνθρώπῳ (here) versus ἀνδρὶ (Mark 10:2), noted later in this section.

perspectives.[37] The ongoing nature of asking echoes John the Baptist's interaction with Herod, "It is not lawful for you to have her" (Matt 14:4), where the context and the continuous past tense of John's criticism "he had been saying" (ἔλεγεν) underscores persistence.[38] However, John was not "testing" God or Herod, but making negative judgement according to the Law. Likewise, Jesus will now bring judgement according to the Law.

In framing the interaction as a test, Matthew is "not concerned with the historical schools of the Pharisees" but suggests the question "was not genuine – indeed, that their motives were malicious."[39] The Pharisees have already judged that Jesus is not from God, deeming "He casts out demons by the prince of demons" (Matt 9:34). Their test is premeditated, for they have held council on how to destroy him (Matt 12:14).

> The most likely reason for questioning Jesus about this topic was due to his association with John… [who] had condemned Antipas… for divorcing his wife and taking up with his sister-in-law Herodias… if Jesus held to the same view, perhaps he could be drawn into making comments that might prompt Antipas to take malevolent interest in him (cf. Luke 13:31, [the Pharisees said] 'Herod wants to kill you').[40]

The Jewish religious authorities side with Rome against Jesus, conspiring with the Herodians earlier (Mark 3:1-6) and subsequently (Matt 22:15-16). In doing so, it is plausible to think that their current divorce laws would comfortably align with Rome.

Pharisees and Sadducees came "to test" Jesus earlier beside the Sea of Galilee by demanding a sign from heaven (Matt 16:1). He responds that they "*cannot* interpret the signs of the times" (Matt 16:3, italics added), and refuses to give a sign "except for the sign of Jonah" (Matt 16:4; cf. 12:39).[41] This exception clause may serve the same purpose as the Matthew 19:9 exception clause: an indictment on the generation of

---

[37] "Jesus probably stated his prohibition a number of times, not necessarily always in the same words." Meier, *Marginal Jew*, 4, 124.

[38] "John had repeatedly told him" (Matt 14:4 NET) comes with a translation note: "The imperfect tense verb is here rendered with an iterative force." Scripture quoted by permission. Quotations designated (NET) are from the NET Bible® copyright ©1996, 2019 by Biblical Studies Press, L.L.C. http://netbible.com All rights reserved.

[39] Luz, *Matthew 8-20*, 488-89.

[40] Evans, *Matthew*, 340.

[41] As with Matt 19:9, the sign of Jonah is also a deadly exception. The "evil" (Jonah 1:2, 7-8; 3:7-10) prevalent in Jonah's generation (Hebrew and pagan) is also comparable with Jesus' generation, so too the judgement of each (cf. Matt 12:41, "The men of Nineveh will rise up at the judgement with this generation and condemn it").

that time that the testers *cannot* interpret, but others surely can – else why speak and record it at all? Significantly, when Matthew provides Jesus' more comprehensive teaching on these topics, as against Mark's account devoid of any exception (on signs: Mark 8:12; on divorce: 10:11-12),[42] **Jesus proclaims an exception that concerns death in both instances, and Matthew highlights both of these as real exceptions by including each of them in Jesus' teachings on two separate occasions (on signs: Matt 12:39 and 16:4; on divorce: Matt 5:32 and 19:9).**

Matthew's narrative presents a certain irony with regard to this question of divorce. Men considered experts of the Law, Pharisees or *"the separated ones"*[43] who were usually married, test whether it is lawful *to separate* for any cause what God has joined together and commanded men[44] *not to separate!*[45] Implicit is that the Pharisees' testing is against God, with major scriptural precedent.

The verb "tested [πειράζω]" can be translated "tempted,"[46] and Matthew has earlier designated Satan as "the tempter [πειράζων]" who "came [προσέρχομαι]"[47] to "test [πειράζω]" Jesus (Matt 4:1-3).[48] Matthew locates the devil's testing of Jesus initially in the "wilderness" (Matt 4:1), echoing Israel's wilderness testing of God (cf. Num 14:22),

---

[42] Luke's "except the sign of Jonah" (11:29) does not impinge on this understanding, for this sign is relevant to Gentiles (for Jonah was sent to a pagan nation), but unlike in Matthew and Mark, it is not set within a framework of Pharisaic testing, and thus is not more narrowly used to indict Israel's leaders.

[43] Danker, Bauer, and Arndt, *BDAG*, 853. Also Mounce, *Expository Dictionary*, 510. Φαρισαῖοι literally means 'the separated ones, separatists'.

[44] The generic may be used here: "humans," but a male perspective (consistent with the question asked) will be examined first to determine whether any insight (positive or negative) can be derived from Matthew's and the Law's predominantly male perspective.

[45] The command to not separate appears in Mal 2:14-16, seen not only in God's strong aversion to divorce, but in the double charge for a man to guard himself and to not be faithless, amidst clear connections to the one-flesh "union" ("make them one") and covenant cleaving ("wife by covenant") of Gen 2:24. Jesus crystallises this command (Matt 19:6), and Paul follows (1 Cor 7:10-11).

[46] It almost always has this sense when evil people are its subject. Blomberg, "Exegesis," 163.

[47] Morris links Matt 19:3 with 4:3 simply via Matthew's first use of προσέρχομαι. Morris, *Matthew*, 479. He notes Matthew has an "overwhelming preponderance" of occurrences of this term: 52 times out of a NT total of 87!

[48] Spadaro notes that Satan's appearance early in Matthew's Gospel "would strengthen the claim that this narrative had something to do with the final conflict foreshadowed by the first divine prophecy (Gen 3:15)." Spadaro, *Matthew*, 56. Longenecker sees that Matthew portrays the Pharisees as the personification of evil (cf. 22:18). "Matthew has highlighted their relatedness to the one who himself is evil and tested Jesus." B. Longenecker, "Evil at Odds with Itself (Matthew 12:22-29): Demonising Rhetoric and Deconstructive Potential in the Matthean Narrative," *Biblical Interpretation* 11, no. 3-4 (2003): 507-08.

although a scene change to the "pinnacle of the temple" (Matt 4:5) suggests testing from the peak rulership of Jerusalem's religious establishment,[49] and with the next scene (Matt 4:8), temptation from the highest authority in the world. Furthermore, Matthew's audacious opening to his narrative, "Book of origins [Βίβλος γενέσεως]" (Matt 1:1; cf. Gen 2:4 LXX), would to the Jewish mind have an unmistakable connection with the Genesis account, one that includes primeval evil. So the activity of the Pharisees also echoes humankind's first temptation, where Satan's crafty test question (Gen 3:1) led to disobedience. This sin brought human separation from God, death, and ruptured relationships. Such undertones imply that this testing of Jesus is evil.

In probing "if it is lawful," the Pharisees set a thoroughly legal context, "a legal issue of the Torah."[50] Contra Loader, the issue *completely concerns* "strict biblical law," even if it was illegal by Roman law at that time to execute its capital demands, not "the common practice of Jewish law in the first century CE."[51] Richard T. France notes,

> There is now widespread agreement with John's statement that at this time the Jews did not have the right to carry out a death sentence (John 18:31), as indeed was the general policy with regard to subject nations in the Roman Empire.[52]

This will not be debated here, but it does highlight the difference between biblical law (the Law as commanded by God and written in Hebrew Scripture) and contemporary Jewish law that may be beholden to imperial law. Within the narrative France references, "It is not lawful for us to put anyone to death" (John 18:31) is technically not "John's statement," but the Jews'. This statement would not be true in Matthew's narrative, for the question of lawfulness concerns every detail of the Law, which for certain offences God provides the right (even demand) to carry out a death sentence, even if secular law opposed implementation.[53]

---

[49] Cf. Spadaro's thesis that *Matthew uniquely portrayed Caiaphas as Jesus' primary opponent*, with vehement opposition also expressed by his colleagues and supporters. Spadaro, *Matthew*, 29.

[50] Osborne, *Matthew*, 703.

[51] W. Loader, "Did Adultery Mandate Divorce? A Reassessment of Jesus' Divorce Logia," *NTS* 61, no. 1 (2015): 71.

[52] France, *Matthew*, 1018.

[53] Cf. Matt 26:59, Matthew writes "they [*the chief priests and the whole Council*] might put him [Jesus] to death," where even under imperial authority, the emphasis centres on Jewish judicial action.

Explicit questions of lawfulness with the same terminology occur elsewhere in Matthew's Gospel: four times relating to the Sabbath (Matt 12:2, 4, 10, 12), once in John the Baptist's judgement of Herod's marriage (Matt 14:4), and once concerning payment of taxes to Caesar (Matt 22:17).[54] These are all dangerous matters. Under the Law, breaking the Sabbath was a capital offence (Exod 31:14), John the Baptist was executed for condemning Herod's marriage as unlawful, and non-payment of Roman taxes was not treated lightly.[55]

Lawful Sabbath-keeping of Jesus has been addressed earlier. John the Baptist's zeal for the Law offers important historical and narrative background to the Matthew 19:1-12 passage, with Jesus completely aware of John's fate (Matt 14:12). Tribute payment requires brief comment here, however, for its lawfulness is not immediately clear, yet the scriptural and historical basis is relevant to the test question on divorce. Nolland notes the challenge:

> The use of ἔξεστιν ('it is permitted/lawful') suggests the possibility that paying the tax might involve disobedience to the law of God and failure to be loyal to him.[56]

To ask the taxation question in such a public way intends to leave Jesus trapped:

> with a choice between being seen to be publicly inciting rebellion against Roman rule or damaging his public support and religious credibility by appearing to be pro-Roman.[57]

By siding with the Herodians, the Pharisees demonstrate their allegiance to Roman rule, "And what symbolises Roman rule better than Roman taxation?"[58] The Pharisees are well-versed in Scripture to test Jesus' Law-allegiance, and with the Herodians (Matt 22:16) to witness any sign of insurrection that could merit a death sentence from the Romans (cf. Barabbas, Matt 27:16; Mark 15:7), this is no innocent "test" (Matt 22:18; cf. 16:1; 19:3). "Either of the choices offered to Jesus would seem to involve a poison chalice."[59] Jesus is aware of their "evil" (Matt

---

[54] Other more implicit questions on lawfulness occur, such as when Jesus is accused of being "a glutton and a drunkard" (Matt 11:19). This seems to allude to Deut 21:17-21 where a rebellious son who has these characteristics ought to be put to death.

[55] The tribute tax was a heavy burden for the Jews in Palestine and a constant reminder of their subjugation. "To seek to avoid payment was from the point of view of the Roman administration a very serious matter indeed!" Nolland, *Matthew*, 896. If Matthew was a tax-collector, he would well know this.

[56] Ibid.

[57] Ibid., 897.

[58] Ibid., 896.

[59] Ibid., 897.

22:18)[60] intent to destroy him, but as with the test topic of divorce, the Law and the Prophets support his taxation stance.

Nolland contrasts lawful submission to pagan rulers with the freedom fighting of the Maccabean uprising. He observes,

> The Babylonian conquest and the Persian restoration offered a biblical pattern of submission to a foreign ruler as acceptance of God's judgment and a restoration based not in resistance to foreign rule but in God's ability to direct the kings of the nations.[61]

The precedent found in the Babylonian Exile is particularly pertinent, for when judgement looms, rebellion against God or God-appointed rulers is no solution (cf. Jer 27-29).[62] Jeremiah knows that it is God who gives the exiles the iron yoke to serve Nebuchadnezzar king of Babylon, so he teaches subservience. The Israelites must seek the "shalom" (welfare, peace, prosperity) of this foreign city, not rebel and destroy it. Yet they were also not to compromise their allegiance to Yahweh by adopting the cultural practices of their imperial rulers. This is evidenced by Daniel's resolution to preserve Israelite food laws (Dan 1:8-9), and by Jewish leaders rejecting idolatry (Dan 3).

After exploring how the question of "is it lawful" is used elsewhere in Matthew, we now return to its use in Matthew 19. Here, not only "the technical, legal sense" of εἰ ἔξεστιν "fits well,"[63] but also the technical, legal sense of πορνεία and μοιχᾶται (Matt 19:9) fits well. Jesus' whole response is to "give his interpretation of Torah,"[64] and in this the concepts of "sexual immorality" and "adultery" should not be lifted out of the Torah and given new meanings, just as 'erwat dabar (עֶרְוַת דָּבָר) "a matter of indecency" (Deut 24:1) should not be given a new meaning. Davies and Allison see that underlying the question of the lawful grounds for divorce is a right interpretation of עֶרְוַת דָּבָר,[65] which was likely the expectation of the Pharisees, but underlying Jesus' response

---

[60] Nolland's "evil" (ibid., 892.) is preferred over "malice" in the ESV here (which Matthew utilises instead of "hypocrisy" in Mark 12:15), for it is in keeping with Matthew's characteristic use of "evil" that Jesus indicts the present generation for and the disciples are to ask for deliverance from (cf. Matt 6:13).

[61] Ibid., 896.

[62] Cf. the false prophet Hananiah, who rebels against God and dies.

[63] Davies and Allison, *Matthew*, III, 9. A distinction between Mark ("is it permitted") and Matthew ("is it lawful") for the same Greek phrase is unnecessary.

[64] Ibid.

[65] Ibid.

appears to be a challenge as to whether עֶרְוַת דָּבָר constitutes grounds for divorce *at all*.[66]

Consistent with Jewish law, the only question concerns a husband divorcing his wife.[67] Hays adds that "The androcentric formula is intentional; for Matthew, only the husband has the possibility of initiating divorce."[68] Jesus does also consider matters from a woman's perspective, for in the parallel passage in Mark he teaches on a wife divorcing her husband (Mark 10:12).[69] However, in Matthew 19:1-12, a man's responsibility is in focus. This should be kept foremost in mind, not to besmirch Matthew or a patriarchal Jewish society, but because

(i) Here only men discuss divorce: Pharisees, Jesus, and Jesus' disciples;

(ii) The male protagonists are not pursuing gender equality but seek to kill a man;

(iii) Much of the Law centres on male accountability, especially for sexual offences; and

(iv) Matthew has another purpose, quite different from that of Mark or Luke.

Jewish men who are typically married ask another unmarried Jewish man an androcentric question, and then a follow-on question exclusively from a male perspective, citing a revered Jewish married man: Moses. Jesus, emphatically male-designated as the 'Son of David', 'Son of Abraham', 'Son of Man' and 'Son of God', responds from a male perspective: "a man shall" (Matt 19:5), "Moses allowed" (Matt 19:8), and "whoever divorce his wife [he] commits" (Matt 19:9).[70] The twelve male apostles, some of whom were married, then comment on the situation between a man and his wife (Matt 19:10), again only reflecting a male perspective. Jesus answers his disciples with a lesson on eunuchs (Matt 19:11-12), men who do not and cannot marry under the Law; he is totally silent on women who do not marry. Overall, the narrow narrative lesson appears to be that it is better *for a man* not to

---

[66] If so, Matthew's version will align more with Mark 10:1-12, although different Gospel purposes remain.

[67] Davies and Allison, *Matthew*, III, 9.

[68] Hays, *Moral Vision*, 357.

[69] Mark uses the more gender-specific ἀνδρί (Mark 10:2) in the test question instead of ἀνθρώπῳ (but the same ἄνθρωπος in Mark 10:7 cf. Matt 19:5), most likely to reinforce his separate rulings for a man and for a woman.

[70] "Let not man separate" (Matt 19:6) is arguably generic but it does match the androcentric question, "Is it lawful to divorce one's wife…? (Matt 19:3), plus the legal nature and male perspective of this passage.

marry than *for a man* to divorce (ἀπολύω), and this is a difficult teaching that *not all men* can receive.[71]

Definition of Ἀπολύω

BDAG defines ἀπολύω in two main ways (there is a third infrequent middle sense of "go away"). Both meanings are summarised here, citing synoptic references only.

> **1. *set free, release, pardon*** a prisoner (Matt 27:15-26; cf. Mark 15:6-15; Luke 23:16-25); *release* a debtor (Matt 18:27); *pardon* (your debtors) *and you will be pardoned* (Luke 6:37); passive: *be freed* of diseases (Luke 13:12).
> 2. let go, send away, dismiss
> a. *divorce, send away* ...one's wife, or betrothed (Matt 1:19; 5:31f; 19:3, 7-9; Mark 10:2, 4, 11; Luke 16:18); *divorce* one's husband (Mark 10:12). This is in accord not with Jewish but with Greco-Roman custom.
> b. *dismiss, send away* ...of a crowd (Matt 14:15, 22; 15:32, 39; Mark 6:36, 45; 8:9); *dismiss* the assembly, also individuals (Matt 15:23; Luke 8:38; 14:4). With the goal indicated (send them away) to their homes (Mark 8:3); passive: be dismissed, take leave, depart; euphemistically: *let die* (Luke 2:29); *discharge* from a long vigil.[72]

BDAG aligns its definition of divorce with Graeco-Roman custom (particularly for Mark 10:12), without noting (as most commentators do) that ἀπολύω accords with a far more ancient Israelite custom, as found in Deuteronomy 24:1-4. Furthermore, BDAG highlights that the ἀπολύω of a crowd comes "with the goal indicated," but surely matters of origin, destination and purpose also apply to other instances of "sending away." Indeed they are weightier concerns, for it is one matter to dismiss crowds from a desolate place so that they may go and buy food in villages (cf. Matt 14:15), but a servant's release from a debtor who intends to sell him into slavery is of crucial import, especially when the release affords freedom to commit a terminal offence that sends him to the tormentors (cf. Matt 18:23-35).

Equally important are matters pertaining to the "sending away" of a wife, especially when the grounds are capital. Given that for non-capital

---

[71] It might also be better *for a woman* not to marry than to divorce, but Matthew makes no point of this, nor does Mark who does mention the possibility of a woman divorcing. Other purposes must be present.

[72] Danker, Bauer, and Arndt, *BDAG*, 96.

grounds the origin, destination and purpose are *indicated in ancient Israelite divorce custom* (cf. Deut 24:1-4),[73] then how much more should such matters be considered for capital grounds (cf. Matt 19:9), and a process followed that accords with what is *commanded in ancient Israelite Law* (cf. Deut 22:13-30)? This should also be done without overinvesting ἀπολύω (and Hebrew equivalents) with meanings that are not found in the Law.

John Woodhouse maintains:

> Heth's argument that in the first century context the meaning of the word 'divorce' included the freedom to remarry is weak. The Greek words used in the New Testament do not necessarily carry a particular technical legal meaning.[74]

Any technical "legal" meaning depends fundamentally on the particular legal framework referenced, otherwise only a cultural or theoretical meaning might be arrived at. Greek verbs like χωρίζω and ἀφίημι only take on the technical meaning of "to divorce" or "to send away" when used in a specific context.[75] In 1 Corinthians 7:10-11, where both these verbs occur, a right to remarry is specifically denied. "The same absence of a distinct technical vocabulary for divorce is true of biblical Hebrew."[76] In the first century, ἀπολύω and other similar Greek terms may have been culturally "synonymous with the right to remarry,"[77] but nothing in the Greek demands this. One caveat is needed: if a Greek term is directly associated with a capital offence in the Law, then it certainly can carry a particular technical legal meaning.

The Pharisees ask about sending away (ἀπολύω) a wife "for any cause," so Jesus is in an environment "in which divorce was widely taken to be permitted by the Torah."[78] Nolland argues that "This moves the starting focus from Mark's 'Is it lawful at all?' to 'Is divorce lawful on any and every ground the husband might see fit to put forward?'"[79] Newman and Stine accept that the legitimacy of divorce is generally assumed, but they also allow for a questioning of this legitimacy. For

---

[73] *Origin:* (life in) first husband's house; *destination:* "out of his house" (perhaps into a second husband's house, but this house does not explicitly concern the first husband); *purpose*: to send a wife away (divorce) from (life in) a husband's house (*without* any destination specified apart from *out of his house*) with written grounds for doing so.

[74] J. Woodhouse, "Divorce and Remarriage," in *The Priscilla & Aquila Centre Conference* (Sydney Moore College, 2014), 7.

[75] Meier, *Marginal Jew*, 4, 100-01.

[76] Ibid., 166.

[77] Heth, "Remarriage for Adultery or Desertion," 67.

[78] Davies and Allison, *Matthew*, III, 8.

[79] Nolland, *Matthew*, 768.

example, they note that the NEB's "on any and every ground" aligns with the usual "for any cause," but if the NEB's alternative wording of "Is there any ground on which it is lawful for a man to divorce his wife?" (cf. Phillips' "on any grounds whatever") is correct, then "Matthew is not considerably different to Mark."[80]

Against Woodhouse, and contrary to viewing Matthew 19:1-12 as a general debate on divorce, concerning any permissible grounds, others see technical legal meanings in ἀπολύω. They make much of purported cultural understandings, such as "the new Hillelite 'Any Cause' divorce" (as Instone-Brewer coins it).[81]

> This new type of divorce was invented by a Rabbi called Hillel (who lived a few decades before Jesus) and was called the 'Any Cause' divorce after the phrase which inspired it in Deuteronomy 24.1 where a man divorced his wife for 'a cause of sexual immorality'. ...Although the 'Any Cause' divorce was theoretically based on some kind of fault, this fault could be such a small thing that it was, in effect, a groundless divorce.[82]

Instone-Brewer holds that 'Any Cause' was well known legal jargon in the first century that was largely forgotten by the second century, similar to phrases today such as "irreconcilable differences," "decree absolute," "joint custody," and "maintenance."[83] Unsurprisingly, it is said that Jesus rejects this common[84] groundless divorce in favour of a Shammaite understanding, which lends support to the Protestant majority view. Instone-Brewer champions a broad understanding of the "sexual immorality" mentioned in Matthew 19:9 to include adultery, sex before marriage, incest and prostitution, as opposed to the Shammaites who might have limited it to "adultery." Yet Instone-Brewer makes a strong assertion about the term πορνεία:

> Jesus (or his translator) used it because it was the best translation of the Hebrew word for general 'sexual immorality' (*ervah*) in the Rabbinic legal phrase 'except "Sexual Immorality"'.[85]

---

[80] Newman and Stine, *Matthew*, 606.

[81] D. Instone-Brewer, *Divorce and Remarriage in the Church* (Carlisle: Paternoster, 2003), 49.

[82] Ibid., 44-45.

[83] Instone-Brewer, *Social and Literary Context*, 134-35.

[84] "The 'any matter' divorce was not only the most common form of divorce, but it was also considered the most righteous form." Ibid., 115.

[85] Instone-Brewer, *In the Church*, 49.

Challenging the idea that "sexual immorality" (πορνεία) is **"the best translation"** for "a matter or indecency" (עֶרְוַת דָּבָר) **forms the crux of this thesis.** This includes showing that עֶרְוָה ('erwah, "indecency" or "nakedness") often has no association with "general 'sexual immorality'" in Scripture, even if it is associated with it in postbiblical Jewish texts and rabbinic literature. Instone-Brewer's divorce view is driven less by the biblical text (which does not mention oral traditions of the Pharisees regarding divorce) than by cultural reconstruction – of a society with views often at odds with Jesus.[86] It is not that Jewish legal jargon such as 'Any Cause' has been obscured for most of history, as Instone-Brewer claims,[87] but the unobscured legal demands of Israel's historic Law as written in Scripture and completely upheld by Jesus in Matthew's Gospel have been neglected, especially understandings of "sexual immorality" and "adultery."

That "any matter" was a technical term for a Hillel-style divorce skews the Pharisees' question in a manner strangely unappreciated for nearly 2000 years of church history. It was more likely an open-ended question designed to test Jesus' absolute position at a time when the Jews accepted that divorce was permitted, if not commanded, under Moses. The test was to see if Jesus would contradict Moses *in any way* – and possibly solicit condemnation of Herod's remarriage, not narrowly to see if Jesus would contradict a Hillel-style or Shammai-style understanding. The "for any cause" of Matthew 19:3 is thus best taken as a general inquiry,[88] devoid of technical terminology that might be found in Hillelite circles, where after Jesus provides an absolute general answer (Matt 19:4-6) he finally specifies one cause (Matt 19:9) that is technically deadly, according to the written Law. The only technical sense of the term αἰτία ("cause") then, which is a rare term in Matthew that will be discussed more when analysing Matthew 19:10, is due to it being connected with a question of lawfulness with respect to Israel's ancient Law, not recent tradition.

---

[86] Refer to exegesis of Matt 19:9 for more discussion.

[87] Instone-Brewer, *Social and Literary Context*, 134-35.

[88] Philo understands from Deut 24:1 that a woman may be divorced "under any pretence whatever." *The Special Laws* III (V. 30-31). Philo, *The Works of Philo: Complete and Unabridged*, trans. C. Yonge (Peabody: Hendrickson, 1993). His opinion agrees with that of Josephus and that ascribed to the House of Hillel. The difference is that Philo sees no separate law that commands the writing of a divorce certificate. "So secondary to his mind is the certificate that it is never mentioned in his summary of Deut 24:1-4." Meier, *Marginal Jew*, 4, 85.

Verse 4

> **He answered, "Have you not read that he who**
> **created from the beginning made them male and**
> **female,**

Jesus takes the Pharisees back to first principles: "the beginning" (Gen 1:1). Creation, not contemporary culture or arbitrary human custom, is the starting point for theology. What is written and read in Scripture trumps what is commonly said and done. Morris writes,

> Jesus is not siding with any of the disputants... Rather, he was
> rejecting them all and calling his hearers to take seriously the
> Scripture that they professed to respect."[89]

Jesus returns a question for a question, with an implied "Surely you know."[90] *What does the Law say on lawfulness and righteousness concerning marriage?*

Rather than avoiding the Pharisees' question of divorce, Jesus' response is best seen as addressing what he considered to be the heart of the matter, namely God's Creational intent – indeed, command (Gen 2:24; cf. Matt 19:5) – for marriage. In this specific matter concerning "male and female," the Law upholds that which was established "from the beginning," without alteration. Jesus completely upholds the Law, so he cannot now be teaching any change to the permanency of marriage with a new divorce rule. One implication is that nothing can sever marriage, *except* (cf. Matt 19:9) – as may be found when Jesus is further tested – only sin equivalent to that which originally severed the God-human relationship, that is, testing of and disobedience to God's clear command.

"Them" is commonly inserted after "created" (κτίσας) to denote the beginning of humankind, but this rather states the obvious. The absence of "them" in the Greek text could instead infer the creation of "marriage" by God "from the beginning" as distinct from the making of individual human entities, male and female (Gen 1:27). Yet God never creates people married; there is a process involved in "what God has joined" (Gen 2:18-25; cf. Matt 19:6). From this it might be inferred that there is also a process by which God – and only God – may unjoin the two.

As in the Greek text of Matthew 19:4, the English "created" is best left without a qualifier. This retains God as the main subject: he is the

---

[89] Morris, *Matthew*, 482.
[90] Newman and Stine, *Matthew*, 606.

one who created (ὁ κτίσας) *everything*, from "the heavens and the earth" (Gen 1:1; 2:4) to humans, "in the beginning" (Gen 1:1). Jesus therefore teaches that the Creator's plan for human male-female marriage was not a late development in an epoch after Creation, dependent on cultural evolution, but instituted from the start of time when all things were made. Pinpointing *the beginning* of "everything that he had made" as "very good" (Gen 1:31) highlights the source and state from which humankind has widely departed, not a destination progressed to. Such a reference implies a call to return to this source: to God the Creator and to his very good Creational intent for marriage. This undeveloped state with a straightforward divine command (which the Pharisees would surely know) points to an uncomplicated ethic that needs no sophisticated human development.

Jesus references a time when divorce was absolutely impossible, not necessarily because marriage was "indissoluble" but purely due to the absence of any sin. In Genesis 2, when God made and brought the sole woman to the sole man to join them in marriage, there was no opportunity or ability to fornicate; and there was no-one else in the Garden with whom to commit adultery, incest, sodomy, or any other form of sexual immorality. Here there were no possible grounds for divorce.

"He made" utilises the same verb (ποιέω) that the Septuagint does to describe when God "created" (בָּרָא) the heavens and the earth (Gen 1:1) and the first humans (Gen 1:27). It is God who has "made them male and female," a biological binary reality, where "them" is Adam and Eve, who demonstrate the ideal for all marriages.[91] Both "male and female" are created in God's image, two equal and complementary persons entirely dependent on their maker for their very lives. As images, they are to reflect the likeness of God, relating to God and each other in all godliness. They exist by God's fiat and from the beginning are to live together entirely on his terms.

---

[91] K. Mathews, *Genesis 1-11:26*, ed. E. R. Clendenen, vol. 1A, NAC (Nashville: B&H, 1996), 221-22.

Verse 5

> **and said, 'Therefore a man shall leave his father
> and his mother and hold fast to his wife, and the two
> shall become one flesh'?**

Jesus' question, "What did Moses command you?" (cf. Mark 10:3) could best be answered with this Matthean command: **"a man shall leave his father and mother and hold fast to his wife"** (Matt 19:5; cf. Mark 10:7; cited from Gen 2:24),[92] not *an allowance* (cf. Mark 10:4).[93] When "Jesus asks his interrogators, 'What did Moses command?'" and they respond with what Moses permitted,

> Jesus then counters by citing texts from the first book of Moses, Genesis 1:27 and 2:24, and implies that they contain Moses' real command as well as the unadulterated will of God for marriage.[94]

It is unlikely that Jesus was merely angling for a Mosaic compromise rather than "Moses' real command," but in knowing his audience, it may remain that "he was soliciting an answer that he would reject."[95]

Alternatively (or alongside this), in the Deuteronomic passage that the Pharisees raise, the sole commandment there may be in view: "…her former husband, who sent her away, may not take her again to be his wife, after she has been defiled,"[96] for this would be an "abomination" and violate God's general prohibition "you shall not bring sin upon the land" (Deut 24:4). If this second view is correct, then Jesus does not reject their "dodge" concerning an "allowance," by teaching, as Meier contends,[97] that Moses did "command" them to write a certificate of divorce and send away a wife (cf. Deut 24:1). Jesus judges that Moses wrote "this commandment" to avoid defilement and sin upon the land because of their hardness of heart (Mark 10:5), and then draws attention back to "Moses' real command" given by God long before Israel's rebellion and hardness of heart (Matt 19:5; Mark 10:7). Therefore, the primary command on marriage, for a man to hold fast to his wife (Gen 2:24), is what Jesus desires that people cherish in their hearts. A Mosaic

---

[92] "Jesus' question was meant to evoke Genesis not Deuteronomy, which the Pharisees cite to avoid doing so." Loader, *Jesus Tradition*, 98 footnote 113, NTS 15 (378).

[93] D. Garland, *Reading Matthew: A Literary and Theological Commentary on the First Gospel*, RNTC (New York: Crossroad, 1993), 198-99.

[94] Ibid., 199.

[95] R. A. Culpepper, *Mark*, ed. R. S. Nash, SHBC (Macon: Smyth & Helwys, 2007), 330.

[96] It is the only piece of legislation in this passage. Craigie, *Deuteronomy*, 304.

[97] Meier, *Marginal Jew*, 4, 36.

"allowance" that mentions the sending away of a wife (cf. Matt 19:9) was only one element of a larger commandment covering the whole of Deuteronomy 24:1-4, to which Jesus directs his challengers. He judges that it is this commandment that Moses wrote for their "hardness of heart," and then refers them to the Creation commandment (Gen 2:24) to serve as the ideal answer to their question.

In Matthew, the concept of a Deuteronomic "commandment" (cf. Mark 10:5) is not even raised by Jesus but only a corrective that Moses merely "allowed" divorce due to hardness of heart (Matt 19:8). The original Creation commandment (Gen 2:24), that righteous people must obey, is central to Matthew and is core to the Law Jesus appeals to in asking "Have you not read...?" (Matt 19:4). When Jesus' "What did Moses command you?" (Mark 10:3) is likewise understood to expect the same original command (Gen 2:24), then it is central to Mark too.[98]

God has declared (εἶπεν) his will for marriage in this command (Gen 2:24); Jesus is not the subject here.[99] The reason is founded in what the Pharisees should have read (Matt 19:4). Cultural views and human laws change, but God's work of creation as recorded in Scripture is unalterable and provides the fixed basis for any command on marriage.

The active verb form of καταλείπω (cf. LXX; for עָזַב, Gen 2:24) means to "leave behind," which in a personal context means to "leave someone (behind) when one leaves a place" (here and Matt 16:4; 21:17) or to leave someone behind at death (Luke 20:31).[100] The same term also occurs impersonally in Matthew 4:13, simply to indicate departure from a place or object (cf. meanings elsewhere of *"abandon," "give up"* in Mark 14:52; and *"neglect"* in Acts 6:2).[101] Its Greek base λείπω differs from λύω (cf. ἀπολύω of Matt 19:3), so the directive is to leave behind parents, not to "divorce," "cut-off," or "loose away" them with any negative connotation. The emphasis is on a man *physically* distancing himself from the one-flesh union he was physically produced from, to be joined in a new one-flesh physical union with his wife. Nolland writes that

---

[98] The original universal command would be most relevant to Gentiles, not a later ruling on Israel's divorce practice described in Jewish Law and a later indictment of "hardness of heart" by a Jewish leader.

[99] Newman and Stine, *Matthew*, 607.

[100] Danker, Bauer, and Arndt, *BDAG*, 413.

[101] Ibid.

In Israelite culture the married couple in fact normally lived in or near the home of the man's parents, not the woman's. So the leaving is not literal.[102]

Wenham expresses surprise at the verb use, as

in traditional societies like Israel where honoring parents is the highest human obligation next to honoring God, this remark about forsaking them is very striking.[103]

A man's priorities change: he now has a higher obligation to his wife.

While not denying the cultural observations, a physical distancing appears to remain associated with the commanded leaving, just as a physical joining is attendant with the commanded cleaving. It is important to recognise that by the Law a marriage union literally involves a man taking a woman into his house, and a divorce literally involves a man sending a woman away from his house. A physical leaving of parents rubs somewhat against the grain of Israelite culture (or any culture); perhaps similarly, a physical sending away of a wife opposes the grain of Scripture.[104]

There are naturally other non-physical unitive elements (e.g. emotional union) nascent in or before marriage or the betrothal period, but σάρξ ("flesh") references a physicality forbidden premaritally and extramaritally. Of course, there is no technical legal meaning inherent to the verb καταλείπω such that the *physical* leaving of parents grants a right to replace them with other parents, which also adds doubt to a purported technical legal meaning in the verb ἀπολύω of a "right to remarry" after the *physical* sending away of a wife. Unlike divorce, in the leaving of parents there is no destructive breaking of family relationships, only the making of new relationships and additional parents to honour.

Heth writes, "*Forsake* (or *leave*) and *cleave* embody covenant terminology," they have "clear covenant significance."[105] Hamilton highlights the firm connection here between human marriage and the Yahweh-Israel relationship,

The verb *forsake* frequently describes Israel's rejection of her covenant relationship with Yahweh (Jer 1:16; 2:13, 17, 19;

---

[102] Nolland, *Matthew*, 772.

[103] G. Wenham, *Genesis 1-15*, WBC (Waco: Word, 1987), 71.

[104] Regarding the Seventh Commandment, Alexander comments: "As a whole the Bible reveals that God desires the establishment of harmonious marital relationships and that neither partner should do anything to undermine this." T. D. Alexander, *From Paradise to the Promised Land: An Introduction to the Pentateuch* (Grand Rapids: Baker, 2012), 213.

[105] Heth, "Divorce, but No Remarriage," 75.

5:7; 16:11; 17:13; 19:4; 22:9; many other examples from the OT could be cited). By contrast, the verb *cling* often designates the maintenance of the covenant relationship (Deut 4:4; 10:20; 11:22; 13:5 [Eng. 4]; 30:20). Thus to leave father and mother and cling to one's wife means to sever one loyalty and commence another. Already Scripture has sounded a note that marriage is a covenant rather than an ad-hoc, makeshift arrangement.[106]

These covenants endure until the death of one party. The important difference is that a man, who leaves his father and mother to marry, has only lived under the authoritative covering of his parents' marriage covenant where, unlike his newly established covenant, he never actively partook of its formation or ratification. Therefore, he can legally exit without covenant violation prior to the death of any party and not attract the death penalty himself for any treason or infidelity.[107] This direction is entirely lawful: a physical and legal move from the jurisdiction of one valid covenant to another. Hamilton confirms that children lie beyond the parental covenanting.[108] A man is directed to forsake ($\varkappa\alpha\tau\alpha\lambda\epsilon\acute{\iota}\pi\omega$) his father and mother – a forsaking that his father and mother in their marriage covenant are never commanded to do – to establish his own legal marriage covenant. This man is never directed to forsake his wife, but commanded to cling to her with the force of the Yahweh-Israel covenant.

"A man" is the protagonist who "will leave," just as *a man's* action is the subject of the Pharisees' divorce question (Matt 19:3). Under this patriarchal system, a man takes the initiative to leave his parents. The command to do this is founded in the Creation ideal (Genesis 2), so it cannot merely reflect a concession to fallen conditions (Genesis 3) and ANE culture. A woman is not given a complementary right to forsake her parents of her own volition, but the man "takes" her from this parental covering (cf. Matt 1:20, 24). Sexual uncovering of this woman by anyone else is a capital offence under the Law. Thus the Law protects marriage, especially the woman and the legitimacy of children, by rigorously upholding, to the extreme penalty of physical death, a physical process of a man taking a wife and taking on primary

---

[106] V. Hamilton, *The Book of Genesis: Chapters 1-17*, NICOT (Grand Rapids: Eerdmans, 1990), 181.

[107] However, capital punishment for children within family settings is not beyond Scripture, for the Law demands death for disobedient sons (Deut 21:18-21) and fornicating daughters (Deut 22:13-21).

[108] Hamilton, *Genesis 1-17*, 181.

responsibility for covenant fidelity. Every Matthean divorce text coheres with this: the man bears the burden for covenant breach.

The use of the passive form (κολληθήσεται) indicates that God does the joining, and this is reinforced in Matthew 19:6, "What therefore God has joined together, let not man separate" (cf. Gen 2:24). Jesus' appeal to Genesis provides the universal basis for all marriages, not exclusively Jewish or Christian marriages. Jesus is not skirting the Pharisees' question; this is his absolute answer concerning divorce. Any one flesh union that deviates from this original one-man and one-woman permanent union created by God is not what God has joined.

There is no oppressive ownership ideology in this text, even if construed elsewhere,[109] but a good sense of belonging and fitting together (cf. Gen 2:23-25) is conveyed. This union is not speculative or conditional; *they will be* (ἔσονται, "become") one flesh. The physical taking of Eve from Adam is in a sense reversed: the "flesh of my flesh" (Gen 2:23) is reunited after God brings the woman to the man. France explains,

> The union is depicted as a vivid metaphor of Genesis as one of "gluing" or "welding" – it would be hard to imagine a more powerful metaphor of permanent attachment. In the context the "one flesh" image derives from the creation of the woman out of the man's side to be "bone of my bone and flesh of my flesh" (Gen 2:21-23); in marriage that original unity is restored.[110]

Craig Blomberg concludes that "the best term to describe this two-fold enterprise is that of covenant."[111] Rather than a metaphysical status which cannot be destroyed, Blomberg sees that "Divorce then becomes breaking a covenant."[112] He uses Proverbs 2:17 to substantiate this (although this proverb does not say anything about "divorce," it does parallel the forsaking of one's companion with the forgetting of one's covenant with God), and its context (2:16-19) sheds important light on understanding Matthew 19:9, for the "house" of the "adulteress" who

---

[109] E.g. "Women are regarded primarily as property and in terms of economic value (Gn 29:20-21; Dt 22:28-29, Ex 21:22-25)." S. Mathew, "Law, Land, and Gender in the Hebrew Bible: A Postcolonial Womanist Reading," *ASJ* 30, no. 2 (2016): 177.

[110] France, *Matthew*, 717. "This is the primary sense of Matthew's Greek κολλάω followed by dative... The Hebrew דָּבַק is widely used metaphorically for 'clinging to' as in the present passage, but its primary sense is of something 'stuck' to another thing (bone to skin, or the joining together of Leviathan's scales, which 'clasp each other and cannot be separated,' Job 19:20; 41:17) and the cognate noun is used of 'soldering' (Isa 41:7)."

[111] Blomberg, "Exegesis," 167.

[112] Ibid.

"forsakes" her spouse "sinks down to death, and her paths to the departed, none who go to her come back, nor do they regain the paths of life."

Breaking a marriage covenant is certainly perilous! However, Blomberg's statement needs revision, for it is "sexual immorality" that breaks a covenant, and divorce is only one possible outcome. *These paths are deadly, but mercy can be shown to the penitent* so that divorce does not occur at all.[113]

---

[113] Proverbs is not Law or prophecy, so warnings given need not imply universal legal inevitability. A proviso must be made: if the forsaking of one's companion and the forgetting of one's covenant with God remain unchanged then this proverb proves absolute.

Verse 6

> **So they are no longer two but one flesh. What therefore God has joined together, let not man separate."**

What God has separated – in making male and female from one man – he rejoins in marriage (Gen 1:26-27; 2:18-24). To separate this unity (again) is not a human prerogative. All authority to create or separate rests with God.[114] Jesus' basic answer to the Pharisees' question on divorce therefore is "No"; the created must not destroy the God-created unity for any cause. Loader notes that Jesus uses the same Genesis passages to forbid divorce absolutely, where "the oneness is no more to be reversed than a body is to be split in two."[115]

The double emphasis on σὰρξ μία ("one flesh," cf. verse 5) drives home the oneness created. The meaning of "one flesh" here is unclear (as in Genesis), but "perhaps the best guess" lies with Wenham.[116] Instead of merely denoting the sexual union, or children of marriage, or even an intimate relationship, though all are involved, "Rather it affirms that just as blood relations are one's flesh and bone ...so marriage creates a similar kinship relation between man and wife."[117] Wenham is not then correct to limit the Matthew 19:9 'exception' to incestuous relationships, but he does make a critical point that new "blood relations" are created by marriage. The covenantal aspect of this will inform the exegesis of Matthew 19:9, and the new kinship may explain the abomination of Deuteronomy 24:4, for this is not terminated by death or divorce.

This union does not simply concern what a man and woman might have on all appearances humanly joined. God has literally "yoked them together" (συζεύγνυμι). Matthew has used the root term ζυγός twice earlier in a very positive context of revelation and rest (Matt 11:25-30), with Jesus' instruction for disciples to shoulder his easy "yoke." This is

---

[114] God also has the prerogative to sever *what he has not joined* – and this includes the separation (or possibly, "divorce") of Israelites *unlawfully married* to certain foreigners "with their abominations" (Ezra 9:1). "Faithlessness" (Ezra 9:4) must be repented of, "We have broken faith with our God and have married foreign women from the peoples of the land" (Ezra 10:2). A lawful solution ensues, "Therefore let us make a covenant with our God to put away all these wives and their children, according to the counsel of my lord and of those who tremble at the commandment of our God, and let it be done according to the Law" (Ezra 10:3). See also Appendix 2.

[115] Loader, *Jesus Tradition*, 101.

[116] Davies and Allison, *Matthew*, III, 12-13.

[117] Wenham, *Genesis 1-15*, 71.

not to suggest that marriage is always easy, but in the light of Jesus' general principle and Matthew's use of ζυγός, marriage is God's yoke, and when both parties follow Jesus, it is restful and never too heavy to bear.

Scripture does not state that a person cannot separate but simply they must not: here is a legal prohibition worded as a warning against removing God's yoke of marriage. No immediate penalty is specified, but the ominous tone – that a mere human creature would dare to separate what God has joined – implies dire consequence for disobedience. Jesus expounds on this in Matthew 19:9, and grave legal penalty comes into view with his judgements of "sexual immorality" and "adultery."

The phrase μὴ χωριζέτω should be translated as "do not separate," where χωρίζω means (actively) to "*divide, separate*" or (passively) "*separate (oneself), be separated of* divorce," "*be taken away.*"[118] A man will actively leave (καταλείπω, Matt 19:5) his father and mother, but he is not to actively separate from (χωρίζω) his wife. Such separation could involve leaving or sending away one's spouse, or dividing a house.

The ἄνθρωπος is not solely Adam, but any married man, as the Pharisees reference (Matt 19:3), as does Jesus (Matt 19:5).[119] The term χωρίζω here is often understood as "divorce," for Jesus uses it directly in response to a question on divorce. In other first-century usage, Paul uses χωρίζω also in a passage explicitly related to marriage, "To the married I give this charge (not I, but the Lord): the wife should not separate (χωρίζω) from her husband" (1 Cor 7:10). However, this separation is not necessarily permanent, even if it may appear complete. The "divorce" rule here for believers is countercultural, for the wife should not χωρίζω ("separate") but if she does, this comes *with no freedom to remarry* ("remain unmarried or else be reconciled"). Paul expressly holds that this charge that he gives is one that Jesus gives, so we can expect conformity with Jesus' divorce teaching in Matthew's Gospel and elsewhere.

A (believing) husband also should not ἀφίημι "divorce" (1 Cor 7:10-11), which is a command by the Lord (via Paul). Paul provides no exceptions of Law (cf. the capital offence of πορνεία in Matt 19:9) which is understandable because he addresses Corinthian Christians who were

---

[118] Danker, Bauer, and Arndt, *BDAG*, 890.

[119] The principle can be generic "human" but the topic here is androcentric. Refer also to verse 3 exegesis.

not Torah observant. As such it is best read as an absolute command in keeping with Jesus' word, "let not man separate" (Matt 19:6). The term ἀφίημι aligns well with the ἀπολύω of Matthew 19:1-12 (where ἀπολύω is used four times) and lessons can be drawn from motifs of forgiving a fellow servant in Matthew 18:21-35 (where ἀφίημι is used four times).

Another similar term ἀφορίζω ("separate") occurs in two verses in Matthew not directly related to marriage (Matt 13:49; 25:32) and twice in Romans (Rom 8:35, 39). These four verses have a more permanent – even eternal – sense of separation. In Matthew 13:49-50, Jesus teaches that the angels will "separate" (ἀφορίζω) the evil from the righteous and throw them into the fiery furnace. In Matthew 25:32, Jesus says that he will "separate" (ἀφορίζω) people as a shepherd "separates" (ἀφορίζω) the sheep from the goats.

Yet there is one New Testament occurrence of ἀφορίζω that could relate to marriage: "Do not be unequally yoked [ἑτεροζυγέω][120] with unbelievers. For what partnership has righteousness have with lawlessness?" (2 Cor 6:14), and it has a permanent sense: "Therefore go out from their midst, and be separate [ἀφορίζω] from them, says the Lord, and touch no unclean thing; then I will welcome you" (2 Cor 6:17). This passage brings righteous separation (ἀφορίζω) *by humans* in touch with the eternal separation (ἀφορίζω) of the righteous and unrighteous (evil) *by all of God's angels and the Son of Man* (Matt 13:49-50; 25:31-46).

This righteous separation (ἀφορίζω) *at the command of God* ("says the Lord") also contrasts with an unrighteous separation (χωρίζω) of existing marriage relationships *against the command of God* ("let not man separate," Matt 19:6). Whether one completely equates "separation" (χωρίζω) with "divorce" (ἀπολύω) or not, the motifs involving both terms (as with ἀφορίζω) are dire.[121] For 2 Corinthians 6:17 to accord with 1 Corinthians 7:10-14, the separation must be effected *before* marital yoking takes place, just as going out from the midst of bad company[122] prior to their lethal action would be prudent in order to uphold the commandment, "You shall not murder" (Deut 5:17). Even if the prohibition on unequal yoking primarily concerns physical

---

[120] The base, ζυγός, is used by Matthew to describe God's joining together in marriage (συζεύγνυμι), just noted earlier for this verse.

[121] As with ἀπολύω, one should be wary of overinvesting the verbs χωρίζω and ἀφορίζω with (cultural) meanings and ideas that are not found in Scripture. In the context of final judgement, certainly none contain a technical sense of "freedom to remarry" and a right to live with another (god).

[122] Cf. 2 Cor 6:17 "from their midst" (plural), as against narrowly forsaking an individual.

participation in idol worship,[123] by obeying this command, marriage covenants with idol worshippers will more likely be avoided. To deter such *"one-flesh"* relationships from ever forming is a sound way to cleanse the Christian community from every defilement of *flesh* and spirit (2 Cor 7:1).

Noting that there are five unity phrases in Matthew 19:5-6, and that God is the one who ultimately brings this unity, France believes

> The "one flesh" metaphor, if it is to be taken seriously, makes marriage indissoluble. To break it is like tearing apart a single body. Moreover, this union is not a matter of human decision or social convention. If it is *God* who has done the "cementing," it is not for a human being to try to undo it. Indeed, it might be argued that it is impossible, that there is something ontological about the "one flesh" union which no human decision can destroy: the man and the woman are no longer two independent beings who may choose to go their own way, but a single indivisible unit.[124]

France acknowledges the objection of pressing the metaphor too far, for as divorces do happen such division cannot be impossible. Nonetheless he is adamant that

> it *should* not happen, that God has created a union which is designed to be permanent, and that human action which purports to dissolve it is not legitimate.[125]

Whether dissolution is legitimate or not, impossible or not, France rightly concludes: "Jesus' argument up to this point is one of total rejection of divorce: it is a violation of what God has created."[126] This provokes the Pharisees' further testing of Jesus, perhaps to find a legal loophole, but most likely to catch him out with an illegal answer (one that contradicts the Law) to prove that Jesus is not (a teacher) from God.[127]

---

[123] "2 Corinthians 6:14 prohibits believers from joining in any activity that forms a covenantlike bond with pagans and their idols (either through literal-physical or metonymical idolatry)." W. Webb, "Unequally Yoked Together with Unbelievers: Part 2," *BSac* 149, no. 594 (1992): 179. Webb assesses the popular view that this verse concerns mixed marriages, noting the strong OT link with idolatry. He finally departs from this view, but his conclusion betrays him, for intermarriage is certainly an activity that forms a covenant (not merely "covenantlike") "bond with pagans and their idols ...and seriously violates the believer's existing covenant with God."

[124] France, *Matthew*, 718. (Italics original.)

[125] Ibid. (Italics original.)

[126] Ibid.

[127] Ibid.

CHAPTER 6 – Divorce Certificate & Hardness of Heart

Exegesis of Matthew 19:7-8

⁷ Λέγουσιν αὐτῷ· τί οὖν Μωϋσῆς ἐνετείλατο δοῦναι βιβλίον ἀποστασίου καὶ ἀπολῦσαι [αὐτήν];
⁸ λέγει αὐτοῖς ὅτι Μωϋσῆς πρὸς τὴν σκληροκαρδίαν ὑμῶν ἐπέτρεψεν ὑμῖν ἀπολῦσαι τὰς γυναῖκας ὑμῶν, ἀπ᾽ ἀρχῆς δὲ οὐ γέγονεν οὕτως.

Textual note:
Verse 7: UBS C-rated variant ἀπολῦσαι [αὐτήν] ("divorce her").

Verse 7

> **They said to him, "Why then did Moses command one to give a certificate of divorce and to send her away?"**

Matthew does not indicate that the Pharisees have contemplated the pre-Law ideal Jesus has just provided. Instead, a legal question extends their test. F. Dale Bruner reasons,

> They may have heard about Jesus' indissoluble-marriage teaching elsewhere (cf. 5:31-32), and so, armed with Deuteronomy's divorce *permission*, they felt they could expose Jesus' antibiblical spirit and so his false claims to ultimacy.[1]

The Pharisees would probably not have regarded Jesus' stance as "indissoluble-marriage teaching," although they no doubt expected a strict position aligning with John the Baptist's, and likely knew of Jesus' earlier teaching on sexual immorality and divorce, where even lustful intent constituted "adultery" (Matt 5:27-32).

Concerning the passage that the Pharisees reference (Deut 24:1-4), Morris sees that

---

[1] F. D. Bruner, *Matthew: A Commentary. The Churchbook Matthew 13-28*, vol. 2 (Dallas: Word, 1990), 675.

They go beyond Scripture, for Moses did not *command* divorce. He pointed to a current custom and did something to regulate it.[2]

The first protasis of the passage simply supposes a case of "if" a man writes his wife "a certificate of divorce and puts it in her hand and sends her out of his house" (Deut 24:1), followed by a second protasis "and if she goes and becomes another man's wife" (Deut 24:2). Not one of these activities is commanded. The only Mosaic command occurs in the apodosis, which prohibits a woman from returning to her "former husband"[3] (Deut 24:4).

Secondary to this main purpose, "Moses permitted the bill of divorce, not because he approved of divorce," but perhaps for reasons raised by Bruner: he wanted to

(i) "avoid *murder*";
(ii) "avoid the *husband's promiscuity*";
(iii) "protect the *wife's reputation*, since by a bill of divorce the husband had to declare the wife's chastity"; or
(iv) "minimize the possibility of hasty or *rash divorce*."[4]

The third option comes closest to recognising the real peril, which is not only to protect the wife's reputation, but to protect her very life!

Instone-Brewer writes,

> This document would be needed by women, not by men, because men could marry more than one woman in any case. It would have been a most valuable document for a woman to possess because it gave her the right to remarry. Without it she would be under constant threat of her former husband, who could claim at a later date that she was still married to him and thus charge her with adultery.[5]

Loader concurs,

> The chief function of the certificate was to declare that the woman was free to marry someone else and could not be

---

[2] Morris, *Matthew*, 482. (Italics original.)

[3] בְּעֻלַּה הָרִאשׁוֹן, also "first owner" or "lord (Baal)," Bibleworks, Holladay 1167. This phrase supports a dissolubility of marriage (cf. "you have had five husbands," John 4:18), as present-tense terms of 'husband' and 'wife' are not applied to any prior marriage post-divorce.

[4] Bruner, *Matthew*, 2, 675. (His own italics added. Here Bruner cites the ideas of others.)

[5] Instone-Brewer, *Social and Literary Context*, 29.

accused of committing adultery against her former husband if she did.[6]

While Instone-Brewer and Loader correctly recognise the threat of a later claim against the woman, why would an accusation of adultery be so great if – in their scheme – adultery simply demanded divorce? By actual fact of the woman's new relationship, she might even welcome extra closure on the old. The threat must involve much more than a fear of being shamed, for the woman's reputation has already been tarnished, because the "matter of indecency" (Deut 24:1) specified on the certificate is generally regarded as something shameful. The real danger is when a woman "goes and becomes another man's wife" (Deut 24:2) and if afterwards a charge of adultery is made by her original husband, then according to the original meaning of the Law, she could be killed (Deut 22:22).

Written evidence to counter this charge, by way of a divorce document noting "some indecency" found in her (Deut 24:1) – obviously apart from a capital offence such as adultery – signed by her former husband and presented to her before she even left his house, would offer invaluable protection. The new husband, even if he then "hates her" (Deut 24:3), also cannot bring a charge of unchastity related to her former marriage, for the woman has been released from the first marriage for only "some indecency," and he certainly cannot condemn her for "misconduct" or loss of virginity, as in another situation where a man "hates" his wife (Deut 22:13). Finally – and more importantly, the documentation produced (though not commanded) offers perspicuity so that "an abomination before the LORD" (Deut 24:4) might be avoided.

Bruner's list above does not justify divorce, but demonstrates several valid reasons for issuing a divorce certificate to mitigate problems in marital breakdown. The cultural emphasis may be on a "right to remarry," but the biblical significance of the divorce certificate (Deut 24:1, 3) centres on distancing the woman from a charge of committing adultery, an offence legislated on just a few passages earlier. Thus "a matter of indecency" (*'erwat dabar*) cannot be equated with "adultery" (*moicheia*) or any other sexual offence of a capital nature (*porneia*) if the chief function of the divorce certificate is to protect a spurned woman from such a charge.

This, however, does not mean that adultery has not been committed in the divorce process itself, but it does imply that any blame for it is

---

[6] Loader, *Sexuality: Key Texts*, 81.

not placed on the woman (cf. Matt 5:32; 19:9), for she has only committed a lesser offence (or no offence at all). Bruner notes a deeper problem:

> The bill of divorce of Deut 24:1 enabled the divorced wife to marry again if she chose, indicating remarriage's *possibility*. But Deut 24:4 says that remarriage somehow "defiled" the divorced wife, indicating remarriage's *problem*.[7]

The problem of defilement is connected with "adultery,"[8] which is condemned in the Law (Exod 20:14; Deut 5:18) as a capital offence (Lev 18:20; Deut 22:22) and features in all of Jesus' prohibitions on remarriage (Matt 5:31-32; 19:9; Mark 10:11; Luke 16:18), so this bill cannot offer any *legal* endorsement to divorce.

A Mosaic description of existing cultural practice[9] does not necessarily provide godly lawful precedent. Preliminary elements of Deuteronomy 24:1-4 may sound gracious, but the only God-given legislation in this passage appears in the apodosis of the final verse:[10] a command *for Israel* to avoid abominable sin on *God-given land*. Whether this can rightly be developed into "God's gracious provision"[11] of lawful divorce for all people, largely in many other lands and not all hard-hearted, is highly doubtful. "The verses do not institute divorce, but treat it as a practice already known," so if the sole command here is in view, in Jesus' response to the Pharisees, he is not changing the Law but "bringing out its true meaning."[12]

The phrase βιβλίον ἀποστασίου is generally taken as *"a certificate or bill of divorce,"* however, ἀποστάσιον is not necessarily a synonym for "divorce," even though the bill obviously does reference marital breakdown. Instead, ἀποστάσιον (literally meaning *"away from the standing of"*)[13] is a substantive in the singular neuter, where the object is unlikely to be "the husband" ("a man": singular masculine) or "the wife" ("a woman": singular feminine) who is left standing away or alone due to a certificate or deed. If Jesus is bringing out the true meaning of Deuteronomy 24:1-4, then by placing the Creation ideal immediately prior, Matthew might have just offered the best referent for

---

[7] Bruner, *Matthew*, 2, 675. (Italics original.)

[8] "The language (*defiled*) suggests adultery (see Lev. 18:20)." Craigie, *Deuteronomy*, 305.

[9] Stassen and Gushee, *Kingdom Ethics*, 278.

[10] Craigie, *Deuteronomy*, 304.

[11] Bolt, *Matthew*, 55-56.

[12] Craigie, Deuteronomy, 305. See also U. Nembach, "Ehescheidung Nach Alttestamentlichem Und Jüdischem Recht," ThZ 26 (1970): 161-71.

[13] From ἀφίστημι ('stand away from'). Bibleworks, Danker 824.

this object: the singular neuter ὅ of "what God has joined together" (Matt 19:6). That is, the unified marriage relationship is stood away from.[14] Charles Cranfield recognises a lawful consideration here: "ἀποστάσιον is a legal term containing the idea of giving up one's right to something."[15] However, a "giving up" of covenant obligations by "giving up" on marriage is the real evil in sight, as against a presumed compulsion "to choose that which is least evil"[16] by divorcing and then seeking God's forgiveness.

Furthermore, a distinction between ἀποστασίου and ἀπολῦσαι should be maintained, for the text does not state: "give a certificate *of divorce* and *divorce*." In questioning Jesus, the Pharisees do correctly differentiate between the *giving* of a deed and the *sending away* of a wife (Matt 19:7). Apart from any practical purposes (raised by Bruner), the giving of a deed created by a man (as against "he who created," Matt 19:4) certifies a state "away from the standing of" (ἀποστασίου) God-created one-flesh marriage.[17] The ἀποστάσιον (deed) then formalises a perilous position of disobedience with an arrogation of God's authority to separate what he has joined. No wonder (in the very next verse) Jesus judges that what Moses allowed the Israelites to do stands against them. The scriptural record attests to this rebellion, as does each divorce deed.

The Hebrew text makes the peril plainer: this certificate סֵפֶר כְּרִיתֻת (Deut 24:1) is literally a "document of cutting off,"[18] comprising a verb base כָּרַת typically used for making or "cutting" a covenant, as applied to the inauguration of the Mosaic Covenant (הַבְּרִית אֲשֶׁר־כָּרַת, Deut 29:1). This "cutting" concept first appears in Genesis 15 in relation to the Abrahamic Covenant, where blood-letting of an animal symbolises the fate of the party who violates the covenant. To be 'cut off' generally infers death.[19]

---

[14] Zodhiates sees that the document entitles a wife "to stand afar off, implying cessation of the marital responsibility." S. Zodhiates, What About Divorce? An Exegetical Study (Chattanooga: AMG, 1992), 91.

[15] C. Cranfield, *The Gospel According to Saint Mark: An Introduction and Commentary*, CGTC (Cambridge: CUP, 1959; repr., 1972), 319.

[16] Ibid., 320.

[17] In Matt 5:31 βιβλίον ("deed") is absent, which may further stress a formal *legal standing (against God)*, with focus removed from a "certificate," although ἀποστάσιον may reference it by metonymy. This could mean that Jesus gives no positive weight in his teaching to the physical *human-made* divorce document.

[18] Davidson, *Flame*, 392.

[19] Another similar OT use of כָּרַת involves body parts: "Any animal that has its testicles bruised or crushed or torn or cut (כָּרַת) you shall not offer to the LORD; you shall not do it within your land" (Lev 22:24); and "No one whose testicles are crushed or whose male organ

With regard to the woman's eviction, a "document of ἀπολύω [sending away]" appears nowhere in Scripture (there is no such nounal state). A "document of cutting off" is given, and a verbal action of "sending away" (ἀπολῦσαι is an infinitive aorist active) follows. To "divorce" (ἀπολῦσαι) is simply *the action* of "sending away" a spouse. The destination is unspecified, but critically worth considering. In Deuteronomy 24:1-4, the woman is not sent to the law courts then off to be executed (destroyed by capital punishment under Mosaic Law for infidelity) but simply *sent away*. The protagonist of this sending is the husband (he also "has found," "writes" and "puts"): it is one man's sole initiative. It is not a judge, a lawyer, or Moses himself who deals with the case, so it cannot involve a matter in the order of a capital offence, for if an innocent woman were privately condemned, there would be an enormous miscarriage of justice in denying her a proper public trial with the Law's requisite witnesses, evidence and procedure.

Alternatively, an enormous miscarriage of justice might occur if the guilty one was only *sent away*. For all kinds of sexual immorality (Deut 22:13-30), the Law demands execution: a sending away to death – not vaguely *away* from the man or "out of his house" (Deut 24:1). This is a death that is physical, not metaphorical.

---

is cut off (בְּרָת) shall enter the assembly of the LORD" (Deut 23:1). These are less bloody but still fearful associations. Other associations include cutting off the head and palms of an idol (1 Sam 5:4), and the destruction of enemies set against ongoing love, "and do not cut off (וְלֹא־ תַכְרִת) your steadfast love from my house forever, when the LORD cuts off (בְּהַכְרִת) every one of the enemies of David from the face of the earth" (1 Sam 20:15).

Verse 8

> **He said to them, "Because of your hardness of heart**
> **Moses allowed you to divorce your wives, but from**
> **the beginning it was not so.**

The Pharisees' opening question that Matthew framed as a test echoed the activity of the tempter in the Garden of Eden. The Pharisees' subsequent question continues this test and elicits a response from Jesus more conspicuously reminiscent of another significant time of evil and downfall in Scripture: "the day of testing" (Heb 3:8; cf. Exod 17:7) at Massah (which means 'testing'), also recorded by Moses. **"Do not harden your hearts" is the stern warning that ensues from that fateful day of "the rebellion"** (Heb 3:8).[20]

Although God had led Israel out of Egypt, he "was provoked with that generation and said 'They always go astray in their heart; and they have not known my ways'" (Heb 3:10). The Lord was so angry at their "hardness of heart" that he swore, "They shall not enter my rest" (Ps 95:11; Heb 3:11). When God's toleration of evil ended, this heart characterisation and terminal verdict followed. Such a judgement is not made for every generation, nor every rebellious and stubborn person. It must be assessed as to whether the "hardness of heart" proclaimed elsewhere in Scripture, especially here in Matthew 19:8, attracts the same wrath of God and final indictment.

In Jesus' response to the Pharisees' next question, the term πρὸς is usually translated "for" (ESV) or "because of" to give a causal sense of why Moses allowed divorce: it was due to "the hardness of heart [*singular*] of you [*plural*]." Spiros Zodhiates remarks on the "interesting" occurrence of *"prós*, 'toward', ...since it is used instead of the more common preposition *diá* which could be naturally used in such an instance indicating cause with the accusative."[21] Rudolf Schnackenburg raises an attractive alternative for the construction πρὸς τὴν σκληροκαρδίαν ὑμῶν,

> it can also mean: "in order that your hearts may become hard,"
> in order that your hardness of heart may become evident.
> Jesus is not attacking Moses' statute here, but is harking back
> to "the beginning," in terms of what is valid according to

---

[20] Even if Matthew had no knowledge of the book of Hebrews, reference to the same rebellious occasion suggests that this historic day was dominant in first-century Jewish (and Jewish Christian) thinking.

[21] Zodhiates, *Divorce*, 282. Cf. *"with reference to* (i.e. *because of*) *your perversity Mt 19:8."* Danker, Bauer, and Arndt, *BDAG*, 710.

God's will. This determination was not impossible for a Jewish understanding of the law (cf. Qumran).[22]

This is not to revive an early church idea that the ritual law was given to Israel "because of their hardness of heart."[23] In another sense Moses' statute stands "against"[24] Israel.

The Markan text parallel to Matthew 19:8, πρὸς τὴν σκληροκαρδίαν ὑμῶν ἔγραψεν ὑμῖν τὴν ἐντολὴν ταύτην, can be interpreted as: "against your hardness of heart he [Moses] wrote you this commandment" (Mark 10:5). A little later Mark uses πρὸς together with γὰρ ὅτι, where πρὸς plus the accusative has a quite separate meaning to γὰρ ὅτι. In Mark 12:12, ἔγνωσαν γὰρ ὅτι πρὸς αὐτοὺς τὴν παραβολὴν εἶπεν ("for they perceived that he had told the parable against them"), γὰρ gives the causal "for" or "because," as perhaps does ὅτι (although it is more nominally "that" preceding a verbatim record, and somewhat redundant in English) but πρὸς is commonly understood as "against." So Mark uses γὰρ (and perhaps ὅτι) to bring the causal or explanatory sense in Mark 12:12, but as γὰρ is absent in Matthew 19:8 it lends support to πρὸς serving a different function (as it does in Mark 12:12): one of condemnation! The parable Jesus told in Mark 12:1-11 stands "against" (πρὸς) the Jewish leaders; it is an indictment for murder with the judgement, "he will come and destroy" them (Mark 12:9). Similarly, it can be understood that what Moses wrote in Deuteronomy 24:1-4 stands "against" (πρὸς) them; what he writes indicts in the same manner as the Markan parable judges the Jewish leaders.[25]

Deuteronomy also indicts a "rebellious and stubborn" people (Deut 31:27) in the same manner.[26] Having finished writing the Book of the Law, Moses commanded the Levites to "put it by the side of the ark of covenant of the LORD your God, that it may be there for a witness

---

[22] R. Schnackenburg, W. Kruppa, and W. J. O'Hara, *The Gospel According to St Mark*, New Testament for Spiritual Reading (London: Sheed and Ward, 1977), 184.

[23] R. Heine, *Reading the Old Testament with the Ancient Church*, Evangelical Ressourcement (Grand Rapids: Baker, 2007), 49-52.

[24] Greeven also takes πρὸς here as condemnatory. H. Greeven, "Zu Den Aussagen Des Neuen Testaments Über Die Ehe," *ZEE* 1 (1957): 114.

[25] Jesus squarely targets his audience with "*your* hardness of heart" here (cf. Mark 10:5). The religious leaders have already been identified as having hearts far from God (Matt 15:8), and Jesus uses the possessive pronoun ("your" wives), but the problem does not centre on "a concession (Moses allowed) for hard-hearted males living in a patriarchal marriage." W. Carter, *Matthew and the Margins: A Socio-Political and Religious Reading*, JSNTS (Sheffield: Sheffield Academic, 2000), 380.

[26] It is not the most direct reference, however; "hard" (קָשֶׁה) is present but "heart" (לֵבָב) is not.

against you [LXX: ἐν σοὶ εἰς μαρτύριον]" (Deut 31:26, italics added). So in this light, when the Pharisees call on Moses for support (Matt 19:7) their case is undermined by God's decree of covenant failure, by a climactic function of the Law that indicts Israel (especially the Levitical leaders), and by the aged Moses himself who with eye undimmed (Deut 34:7) has a dim view of the people's faithfulness, which surely includes the hard-hearted behaviour that he has documented in Deuteronomy 24:1-4.

Judgement is evident not only in the Pharisees' departure from the Creation ideal, "in terms of what is valid according to God's will,"[27] but in the deadly fate of the Israelites under Moses due to the same "hardness of heart" that the Pharisees possess: that generation never reached the Promised Land. If Matthew 19:8-9 is read as one unit, not two unrelated ideas but as the same teaching, then the same indictment remains in view, along with the Law's deadly demands for anyone who commits "sexual immorality" or "adultery" (Matt 19:9). The Mosaic context need not suddenly disappear with Jesus' extended commentary, nor need the Mosaic penalties suddenly change.

With respect to the immediate narrative context, 'The Story of the Unforgiving Servant' (Matt 18:21-35) can be viewed as serving a similar function to 'The Parable of the Tenants' (Mark 12:1-11). Whether or not the Pharisees perceived that Jesus told this saying "against" (πρὸς) them, it still stands *as an indictment against* any unmerciful person. It exposes the Pharisees' heart condition in their reliance on a passage that describes hardness of heart in action (Deut 24:1-4). In contrast, the blessed who are merciful and pure in heart (Matt 5:7-8) honour Moses' command in Genesis 2:24: they cling to a spouse and do not divorce due to any debt, but ask God for forgiveness and forgive one another (cf. Matt 6:12-15; 18:35).

Jesus' response may then be understood as "He said to them (that), 'Moses, against your hardness of heart, allowed you to divorce...'" (Matt 19:8). This now looks less like a "concession"[28] or "gracious gift"[29] and more like a strong indictment that exposes and condemns people for their rebellion against God. The hard-heartedness is not a

---

[27] Schnackenburg, Kruppa, and O'Hara, *Mark*, 184.

[28] "The lesser of two evils... a merciful concession." Lane, *Mark*, 355. Davies and Allison, *Matthew*, III, 14. Also, "God graciously accommodated himself to their rebellious desires." Blomberg, "Exegesis," 171.

[29] "The provision of divorce was a gracious gift of God to meet the pain and difficulty so often found in our world filled with hard-heartedness." Bolt, *Matthew*, 55.

general tendency or distortion due to the Fall.[30] Moses does not legislate a "compromise"[31] to the Creation ideal due to "human weakness"[32] or for ("because of") cultural reasons or hard circumstances. Instead, the legislation serves as a formal written judgement of "hardness of heart" (σκληροκαρδία) "against" stubborn people who divorce. "If God has joined them together, according to the structure of his own creation, divorce is not only 'unnatural' but rebellion against God."[33] Carson's comment aligns with Jesus' charge in Matthew 19:8 that Moses allowed divorce due to "hardness of heart," but *the rebellion specifically in view here* is of an irremediable nature that commentators largely miss. Further support for a terminal meaning of σκληροκαρδία that results in judgement may be found in a closer study of the scriptural concept of 'hardness' as applied to people.

Friberg defines σκληρότης as "literally *hardness*; figuratively, as a resistant attitude denoting unreceptivity *stubbornness, obstinacy*."[34] BDAG has "*hardness* (of heart)" where the heart is purely implied, and "*stubbornness* as a human characteristic."[35] The only New Testament occurrence is in Romans 2:5, where it describes those with "hardness" (σκληρότης) *and* an "impenitent" (ἀμετανόητος) "heart" (καρδία), who store up God's wrath for themselves. The noun σκληρότης ("hardness") describes the person; σκληρός ("hard")[36] is not found here as an adjectival descriptor of the heart. Nonetheless the same subject possesses both "hardness" and an "impenitent heart," where "hardness" characterises the whole person, which must include the heart.

Similarly, if the heart is impenitent, then the whole person is impenitent. A 'person' and 'heart' distinction cannot be made, so "hard, impenitent heart" is equivalent phraseology. Furthermore, "impenitent (ἀμετανόητος) heart" links a refusal to change (μετα) one's *mind* (νοῦς) with an unrepentant *heart* (καρδία). So a 'mind' and 'heart' distinction

---

[30] Contra R. Tasker, *The Gospel According to St Matthew*, Tyndale (Leicester: IVP, 1983), 180. Also B. W. Powers, *Marriage and Divorce: The New Testament Teaching* (Concord: Family Life Movement of Australia, 1987), 63.

[31] Or worse, "The compromise had become the ideal." M. Mullins, *The Gospel of Matthew: A Commentary* (Dublin: Columba, 2007), 417.

[32] B. Witherington III, *The Gospel of Mark: A Socio-Rhetorical Commentary* (Grand Rapids: Eerdmans, 2001), 276. Or "human failure." France, *Matthew*, 719.

[33] Carson, "Matthew," 466.

[34] Bibleworks, Friberg 24577.

[35] Danker, Bauer, and Arndt, *BDAG*, 756. Also cited is Herm. *Mand.* (5, 2, 6), "Of the spirit of *harshness, roughness* w. which the Holy Spirit cannot live," which cannot describe a believer (cf. 1 Cor 2:14; Jas 2:26; Rom 8:9).

[36] "Of persons hard, strict, harsh, cruel, merciless" with only one occurrence in the NT: Matt 25:24. Herm. Mand. (12, 5, 1) uses this term for "Of the devil." Ibid.

is also unwarranted. In heart, mind and soul the person is completely hard and unrepentant. This obstinate unrepentant state is irreversible and God's wrath (cf. Rom 2:8) is inescapable: such people amass it solely *for themselves* (Rom 2:5).

Matthew uses σκληρός adjectivally once in a parable where "the master" (representative of God) is called a "hard man" (Matt 25:24), which is a woeful characterisation by a "worthless," "wicked and slothful" servant who ends up being cast into outer darkness (Matt 25:26-30). This is the sole occurrence in the New Testament where σκληρός is directly applied to an individual. The punishment certainly is harsh but not unrighteous, so there is nothing "hard-hearted" or rebellious about the master.[37] However, the indifference, wickedness, and hypocrisy of the servant (cf. Jesus' indictment of the Pharisees in Matthew 23) could be considered "hard-hearted."

Septuagint usage is also limited; σκληρός describes the men of Korah's rebellion whom God kills, but "wicked" (רָשָׁע) is a better translation as "hard" (קָשֶׁה) is not present in the Hebrew (Num 16:26).[38] Nabal is characterised as "harsh" (1 Sam 25:3), or "hard" is equally suitable (although the Hebrew uses קָשֶׁה adjectivally not directly as a personal description for "the man" but for his "hard" and "evil" (רַע) *practice*). Nabal was a foolish, worthless man,[39] whom God kills after his "heart died within him, and he became as a stone" (1 Sam 25:37-38). If this person is meant to be characterised as "hard-hearted," then it is not done in a straightforward manner (cf. Jesus' use of σκληροκαρδία). Nevertheless, God struck down Nabal in his stone-like hardness; and such judgement for hard-hearted opposition to David may inform us on the hard-hearted (Matt 19:8) opposition to the Son of David in Matthew 19.[40]

---

[37] "Merciless" is appropriate, however, from the perspective of an evil person receiving his master's retribution in a place with "weeping and gnashing of teeth" (Matt 25:30) cf. "eternal fire" (Matt 25:41); "eternal punishment" (Matt 25:46).

[38] The LXX does use the adjective σκληρός and cognates widely, but never as a total characterisation of a godly person. For example, "And the thing was displeasing (σκληρὸν, for רַע) to Abraham… But God said to Abraham, 'Be not displeased (σκληρὸν, for רַע) because of the boy'" (Gen 21:11-12); and when Joseph saw his brothers, he "spoke roughly (σκληρὰ, for קָשֶׁה) to them" (Gen 42:7).

[39] This assessment of "worthless man" is made by a wise servant (1 Sam 25:17) and "worthless fellow" by his wise wife (1 Sam 25:25; cf. the worthless, foolish servant calling his master a "hard man" in Matt 25:14-30).

[40] It may also confirm the authorship of Ps 95 (cf. Heb 4:7), for around this time David is the only person recorded to have been opposed by a man with a heart of stone, and the

In sum, singular terms of "hard" (σκληρός) and "hardness" (σκληρότης) are rare descriptors of individuals in Scripture. This suggests that the characterisation does not equate with the general state of fallen humanity; Scripture is stressing something significant about these evil people and God's dealings with them. This concept of human hardness also occurs in compound terminology, but even then it is limited. 'Hard-hearted' and 'hard-necked' (or 'stiff-necked') are two important concepts that will now be examined, with an assessment as to whether they are synonymous.[41]

The Septuagint uses σκληρότης "stubbornness" (Deut 9:27) [קְשִׁי]; and σκληροτράχηλος "stiff-necked"[42] (Exod 32:9; 33:3, 5; 34:9; Deut 9:6, 13, 27) [קְשֵׁה־עֹרֶף] where "hard" is קָשֶׁה] for people (not merely individuals) in what seems to be the same irredeemable sense. Moses' plea for forgiveness of "a stiff-necked people" (Exod 34:9) could signal that pardon is possible, although it more likely means that a temporary reprieve was obtainable despite the hardness continuing (which it did). Israel *was pardoned* in that the next generation did enter the Promised Land, but *not pardoned* in that the present generation of "stiff-necked people" never entered, for their ongoing stubbornness in testing God ten times (Num 14:22) and quarrelling (Num 20:13) brought them to a terminal point that incurred God's wrath and judgement (Ps 95:8-11). The constant stiffening of Israel's neck, in the face of God's reproof and signs that he did in Egypt and in the wilderness, meant that Israel's heart became hardened (cf. Ps 95:8) and that generation was suddenly broken beyond healing (cf. Prov 29:1).

BDAG defines σκληροκαρδία as "*hardness of heart, coldness, obstinacy, stubbornness*"[43] where καρδία references "the seat of physical, spiritual and mental life."[44] Yet the question remains: for all those in Scripture charged with this particular stubbornness that affects

---

Psalmist warns against "hardness of heart"! (The last-recorded hard-hearted man Scripture records was Pharaoh, about 500 years prior.)

[41] More generally, are they simply "Synonyms for Refusal to 'Hear' or 'See'"? F. Danker, "Hardness of Heart: A Study in Biblical Thematic," CTM 44, no. 2 (1973): 90.

[42] Danker, Bauer, and Arndt, BDAG, 756.

[43] Ibid. Occurrences: Matt 19:8; Mark 10:5; Herm. Vis. 3, 7, 6; Barn. 9:5 Funk (Jer 4:4) [ref. Barn. 9:4 Lightfoot]; and with ἀπιστία Mark 16:14. Usage of σκληροκαρδία in Jer 4:4 (LXX) will be assessed and rejected, as will the longer ending of Mark (although pairing ἀπιστία with σκληροκαρδία is fitting, but only for unbelievers!). Herm. Vis. 3 7[15]:6 rightly links "hardness of heart" with not being saved, but the context is dubiously in a place of torment for those who have participated in the "Righteous Word" and have been rejected, yet will "be relieved from their torments, if the evil deeds, that they have done, come into their heart." Holmes, Apostolic Fathers, 359.

[44] Danker, Bauer, and Arndt, *BDAG*, 403.

the whole of their "physical, spiritual and mental life," have they reached an irredeemable state? In answering this, *very few occasions* are recorded in Israel's history to which σκληροκαρδία relates.

In Scripture, "hardness of heart" is first applied to Pharaoh in his opposition to Moses. The LORD said to Moses, "I will harden (חָזַק) his heart, so that he will not let the people go" (Exod 4:21).[45] While in Egypt, Israel is not referred to as "hard-hearted," although Pharaoh's "hard" (קָשֶׁה) heart (Exod 7:3) can be compared with Israel's "hard" (קָשֶׁה) service as slaves (Exod 1:14). Scripture does record that Israel has always been a "stiff-necked" or "hard-necked" people (Exod 32:9), but is only called "hard-hearted" after testing God in the wilderness (Ps 95:8). This "hardness of heart" is something more than a general stubbornness; it is a terminal verdict that attracts certain judgement. Pharaoh and his firstborn son are killed; one generation of Israel, mercifully released from bondage in Egypt, perishes beyond the Jordan.

Israel's judgement followed constant rebellion.[46] The Lord declared that the dead bodies of "this wicked congregation" (Num 14:35, cf. Matt 12:39; 16:4) would fall in the wilderness over forty years. Korah's rebellion resulted in thousands immediately killed (Numbers 16), and the testing at Meribah and Massah proved that Israel's heart was hardened, a characterisation first found in Scripture hundreds of years later (Ps 95:8) to justify why one whole generation perished beyond the Jordan. Then on the cusp of entering the Promised Land, "beyond the Jordan" (Num 22:1; cf. Matt 19:3), "people began to whore with the daughters of Moab" (Num 25:1) and "Israel yoked himself to Baal" (Num 25:3). The Israelite men were guilty of committing sexual immorality and idolatry; with the "yoke of yokelessness"[47] they were lawless (cf. 2 Cor 6:14). Phil Moore notes that Paul uses this imagery to

---

[45] Wherever the LXX renders חָזַק as σκληρύνω in Exodus (cf. 4:21; 7:22; 8:15; 9:12, 35; 10:20, 27; 11:10; 14:4, 8, 17) God is always the source of the hardening. K. Berger, "Hartherzigkeit Und Gottes Gesetz: Die Vorgeschichte Des Antijüdischen Vorwurfs in Mc 10:5," ZNW 61 (1970): 7.

[46] "You have been rebellious [מָרָה, ἀπειθοῦντες] against the LORD from the day that I knew you" (Deut 9:24). In the NT, this terminology is used for "the most severe form of disobedience, in relation to the gospel message disbelieve, refuse to believe, be an unbeliever (AC 14.2)" Bibleworks, Friberg 2563. It also occurs as a reminder to not be like the hard-hearted Israelites in the wilderness, "And to whom did he swear that they would not enter his rest, but to those who were disobedient [ἀπειθήσασιν]?" (Heb. 3:18).

[47] I.e. lawbreakers have shed the yoke of the Law. For the Corinthians, "If they yoked themselves to men who refused to wear the yoke of Christ, then they were setting their courses for disaster." P. Moore, Straight to the Heart of 1 & 2 Corinthians: 60 Bite-Sized Insights (Oxford: Monarch, 2010), 213.

warn that "The false teachers presented themselves as the true defenders of the Law of Moses,"[48] which is exactly what Jesus contended with (cf. Matt 23:28).

In the wilderness, God's "wrath" and "jealousy" brought a plague that killed twenty-four thousand, and only by an act of atonement did the next generation also not perish beyond the Jordan (Num 25:6-18). Just prior to Israel crossing the Jordan, Moses recounts the Law of God. Thus all legislation, including that on sex and marriage, should be understood in the context of Israel's ongoing national rebellion – before, during and after God gives the Law. The concrete example of the deaths of thousands of people in the present generation for sexual immorality and idolatry, and the perishing of the whole previous generation for rebellion, should make it clear that capital offences are serious and punishments were to be applied literally. Interpretation of Jesus' words on sex and marriage, recounted in his last block of teaching before he crosses the Jordan, should also bear in mind this context of ongoing national rebellion.[49]

The Law should also be understood in the light of Moses' call for Israel to do what God requires, "to serve the LORD your God with all your heart and with all your soul, and to keep the commandments and statutes of the LORD" (Deut 10:12-13). Moses concludes, "Circumcise *therefore* the foreskin of your heart, and be no longer stubborn" (Deut 10:16, italics added). By serving the LORD (keeping his commandments and statues) with *all their heart* (and soul) *the generation of Israel that crosses over the Jordan* to take possession of the Promised Land (Deut 11:31) will avoid the "hardness of heart" (σκληροκαρδία) attributed to the previous generation (Heb 3:8, 15; 4:7). This hardness is a condition of *the whole heart*, not merely the "foreskin" (which, in the sexual analogy, only covers the organ, i.e. it is not a vital part). Simply having a command to "be no longer stubborn" (Deut 10:16) implies that Israel's stubbornness need not be permanent; it may be eliminated by removing a skin-thin layering (עָרְלָה) over the heart (לֵבָב).[50] The recorded occasion of writing is at the end of Israel's forty years in the wilderness, so the "no longer" finds direct historical reference: the previous generation condemned with "hardness of heart"

---

[48] Ibid.

[49] Jesus' first-recorded divorce teaching (Matt 5:31-32) is on a mount (cf. Moses at Mt Sinai, Exod 19); his second (Matt 19:1-12) is "beyond the Jordan" (cf. Moses, Deut 1:1), making it rather Deuteronomic.

[50] Alternatively, the hard part is permanent but it is permanently removed (cf. the foreskin is cut off and dies). Whatever the case, the metaphor calls for wholehearted obedience, devoid of any stubborn element.

has perished and no trace of their stubbornness is to be embodied by the present generation upon entering the Promised Land.

Despite the Septuagint inserting "hardness of heart" (σκληροκαρδία) into Deuteronomy 10:16, the Hebrew (לֹא תַקְשׁוּ עוֹד) does not support it nor do major English translations reflect it. "Stiff-neck" (literally, "hard neck or back") is a better understanding. Instone-Brewer goes so far as to say that σκληροκαρδία is "an invention of the Septuagint"![51] He is right in that for the two main occurrences of σκληροκαρδία under consideration (Deut 10:16 and Jer 4:4) any terminology involving "hardness" of the heart itself is totally absent in the Hebrew. Proverbs 17:20 similarly displays this inventiveness, for עִקֶּשׁ־לֵב best describes a person with a "perverse" (NAB) or "crooked" (ESV) heart rather than with a "hard heart" (σκληροκάρδιος, LXX).[52] Job 41:24 does rightly render the Hebrew (לִבּוֹ יָצוּק כְּמוֹ־אָבֶן, Job 41:16 MT) as "His heart is hard as stone," but this infers nothing necessarily evil or rebellious. Instead, it describes an incredibly strong beast, the Leviathan, with whom no covenant can be made (Job 41:4), let alone can a stubborn disobedience then develop in it against God's commands.[53]

If Israel has any link with the Leviathan, it is that this nation is God's wonderful and powerful creation, but with a "heart of stone" no covenant can be made with it. Just as the Mosaic Covenant was made with Israel before it had σκληροκαρδία or τὴν καρδίαν τὴν λιθίνην, a new covenant will be made with a people without a hard or stony heart. Isaiah also uses the Leviathan as a symbol for Babylon in a prophecy that the Lord will slay this "serpent"[54] (Isa 27:1). To have the same stony heart as the Leviathan implies that Israel is the same as Babylon, the powerful enemy of Israel, and thus an enemy of God (cf. "you are not my people" of Hos 1:9; 2:23) for this time. All those persisting with a stony or hard heart will be slain by God's "hard"[55] sword (Isa 27:1). Even so, a distinction may still be made between "hard" and "stony" hearts, for with redemption a stony heart is miraculously changed,

---

[51] Instone-Brewer, *Social and Literary Context*, 145.

[52] Modern English versions have also read "hardness of heart" into Scripture in places where the Septuagint has not (quite). E.g. Psalm 4:3, "How long, O people, will you be hard of heart" (NAB) builds on the βαρυκάρδιοι ("heavy or slow of heart," LXX), when the Hebrew makes no mention of the "heart" here at all. Instead, עַד־מֶה כְבוֹדִי לִכְלִמָּה is better rendered: "how long shall my honor be turned into shame."

[53] Indeed, the implication of this whole chapter (Job 41) is that this creature is far beyond human control but is certainly under God's authority.

[54] The serpent here echoes the archetype in Gen 3:1.

[55] Yet again the LXX was creative with the idea of hardness, translating קָשֶׁה as ἅγιος!

whereas nowhere in Scripture is it found that a "hard heart" can be changed.

Where the Septuagint could have more justifiably rendered לֵב הָאֶבֶן as σκληροκαρδία it instead uses τὴν καρδίαν τὴν λιθίνην, and the English follows with "the heart of stone" (Ezek 11:19). In not utilising σκληροκαρδία here, the Septuagint may signal that Israel as a whole nation is not terminally indicted and will not be cut off from God forever. The context of this passage is that of the Babylonian Exile and God's judgement for wickedness, where those "whose heart goes after" the "detestable things" and "abominations" of other nations are certainly judged. However, the stubborn rebelliousness of the previous generation will end and Ezekiel's vision provides hope directly to the exiles. This involves a monumental change from "stone" to "flesh" for the nation's heart, with the giving of a "new heart" and a "new spirit" (Ezek 36:26) within a whole "new covenant" (Jer 31:31-33; cf. Heb 8:10). Indeed this is a revival from the dead for the "whole house of Israel' (Ezekiel 37) who have lost hope and are "cut off" from God.

The concept of a hard or stubborn heart is said to occur in only one place in the Hebrew Bible in the context of divorce: Jeremiah 4:4.[56] However, the Septuagint dubiously connects לְבַבְכֶ with σκληροκαρδία ("circumcise your hardness of heart"), for the Hebrew (of the MT) does not have the whole heart in view (only the foreskin). Nor is the same term for circumcision used when referencing the people themselves: הִמֹּלוּ "Circumcise yourselves" (Jer 4:4a) as against וְהָסִרוּ "and cut off" the foreskin of your heart (Jer 4:4b). English translations such as the NIV can also mislead, for "circumcise your hearts" omits עָרְלוֹת "foreskin of" your heart (the ESV correctly retains this, but along with the NIV, does alter the Hebrew singular "heart" to bring an English plural, when only one heart is in focus: Israel's). Explicitly the foreskin is in view, where the command is to "circumcise the foreskin of your heart," not cut out the whole heart. This is not being overly pedantic with the metaphor, for (textually) "hardness of heart" simply does not

---

[56] Instone-Brewer, *In the Church*, 52. See also *Social and Literary Context*, 144 - 45. Instone-Brewer rejects that "hardness of heart" means "sinfulness," as held by Davies and Allison, *Matthew*, III, 14-15. He prefers "human stubbornness," positing that this relates to Israelites "stubbornly refusing to give divorce certificates to their former wives." With only one possible exception noted, Instone-Brewer claims "There is no occurrence of the word or phrase in any context that might suggest it meant 'sinfulness'." However, if the "hardness of heart" involves "adultery that is persistent and unrepentant" (with which Instone-Brewer frames the discussion) – or any unrepentant sexual immorality, then *stubborn capital sin* must be in view. This fits the context of Matt 19:8, for here Jesus brings an indictment, not instruction for stubborn men to give divorce certificates to their former wives.

appear in the Hebrew of Jeremiah 4:4 (in particular, no Hebrew term for "hardness" is found at all, although "heart" לֵבָב is present); and (theologically) to completely cut out a whole hard-heart would leave Israel with no hope.[57]

In both Deuteronomy 10:16 and Jeremiah 4:4, only the excision of an outer part of the organ is in view: the "foreskin of your heart," where the "foreskin" symbolises impurity (uncleanliness). Rectification is possible; God's imperative is that they "remove" or "cut-off" the foreskin. In this only one part of the body dies, though it is *a real death*, symbolic of the whole person being cut-off (set apart *for Yahweh*). The removal of one part avoids full hardness of heart, where the whole body would be cut-off (set apart *from Yahweh*). In the context of Jeremiah 4:4, judgement is pending, but hope remains for Judah; a part (remnant) will survive the destruction and separation God threatens.

The term σκληροκαρδία **occurs only twice in the New Testament, only used by Jesus in the context of divorce**, and primarily in relation to one specific Old Testament occasion.[58] The same concept appears elsewhere, solely in Hebrews, to reference the very same Old Testament occasion: the day of testing in Israel's rebellion. For this rebellion God swore that those people would never enter his rest (Heb 3:8-11). Three times the writer of Hebrews commands, "Do not harden [σκληρύνω] your hearts" (Heb 3:8, 15; 4:7) as Israel did in the wilderness (Ps 95:8 is cited, where the LXX has same term σκληρύνω; MT: קָשָׁה). Such a stern warning to avoid "hardness of heart" shows that it is a terminal evil; the unbelieving heart brings a falling away from the living God (Heb 3:12). Had Israel obeyed God's voice and not tested him, that generation might have entered the Promised Land. "Hardness of heart" was avoidable, but once hardened, the threefold proclamation of judgement confers no hope. In his anger, God does not yield[59] by offering a Mosaic *concession* but swears certain *condemnation* (Heb 3:11).

Hebrew's threefold command assumes that Israel's "hardness of heart" was not present prior to the wilderness testing of God (at least there is no declaration of it, however stubborn they were). Indeed, Israel

---

[57] Following Israel's wilderness time, the next generation was presented with a fresh start, but to cut out Israel's whole heart in Jeremiah's time would kill Israel, leaving no remnant and cutting off all offspring.

[58] A second occasion, the Babylonian Exile, also comes into view (as will be discussed), but the σκληροκαρδία there can be considered reminiscent of the primary occasion, with prophetic reflection on it (cf. Zech 7:12).

[59] Greeven sees that such yielding ("nachgeben") is incompatible with the biblical idea of God. Greeven, "Aussagen," 114.

initially obeyed God and benefitted from Pharaoh's hardness of heart: after Yahweh severely dealt with the Egyptians, they sent the Israelites away. Prior to Moses approaching Pharaoh to let God's people go, it may be reckoned that every Egyptian (and Israelite) was in a general fallen state (since Genesis 3), but hardness only came with direct defiance of God. Pharaoh's heart was not hardened until he heard God's word via Moses and witnessed God's signs (Exod 7:3, 13, 14, 22; etc.). Such hardness is both God-created and human-engineered, for example, "the LORD said to Moses... I will harden Pharaoh's heart" (Exod 7:3) and "when Pharaoh saw that there was a respite, he hardened his heart" (Exod 8:15).[60] The same hardening appears in the New Testament, and ultimately it is the Lord's doing: "So then he [God] has mercy on whomever he wills, and he hardens whomever he wills" (Rom 9:18).[61]

For Jesus to charge the Pharisees with "hardness of heart" (Matt 19:8) was to say that they are the same as Pharaoh: they have heard God's word but they stand in opposition to Moses (and to what God commands through Moses), and they stand in opposition to what Jesus says on marriage. They test Jesus, though they have seen his miraculous work, and they test God, just as Israel tested God in the wilderness, though they had seen God's miraculous work. Frederick Danker's assertion that "stiff-necked" and "hard-hearted" are *"Synonyms for Refusal to 'Hear' or 'See'"* (surprisingly, made without any assessment of the only biblical occurrences of σκληροκαρδία, i.e. Ezek 3:7; Matt 19:8; and Mark 10:5),[62] requires qualification: with repentance the "stiff-necked" may hear and see (turn and be healed, cf. Matt 13:15), whereas the "hard-hearted" will never hear and see. After manifold

---

[60] In the wilderness, the king of Heshbon also opposed Israel, so God hardened (קָשָׁה; σκληρύνω) his spirit (רוּחַ; πνεῦμα), and made his heart (לֵבָב; καρδία) obstinate or strong (אָבָה), or overpowered it (κατισχύω), and gave him over to be killed (Deut 2:30-34). The direct object of the hardening differs, but it echoes Pharaoh's hardening.

[61] For God to do the hardening, and join male and female in marriage, this makes it awkward to claim that "Divorce is necessary because of the male's hardness of heart, that is, because of men's patriarchal mind-set and reality" and simultaneously, "Jesus insists, God did not intend patriarchy." E. Schüssler Fiorenza, In Memory of Her: A Theological Reconstruction of Christian Groups (London: SCM, 1983), 143.

[62] Danker, "Hardness," 89-90. Danker also omits the fact that the only individuals characterised with "hardness of heart" (Pharaoh and Nabal) are killed by God. He cites Prov 28:14, which does address hardness (קָשָׁה) of the heart, but the inevitable calamity is not contrasted with God's promise to those who have hardness (קָשָׁה) of the neck (cf. Deut 9:6). Danker uses Isa 6:9-10 as his "primary source" for the expression "hardness of heart," but the Hebrew here (לֵבָב) describes the heart as "dull" (ESV) or "fat" (KJV), not "hard" (קָשָׁה), and as with Jesus' use of the same prophetic source, "this people's heart has grown dull [παχύνω, not σκληρύνω]" (Matt 13:15), there is a redemptive possibility.

opportunity to obey God's voice and see his work (cf. Ps 95:7-9), God's mercy is revoked (cf. Hos 1:6; 2:4; Zech 1:12; Matt 18:33-4).

As "hardness of heart" is separate from humanity's general fallen state, then although it could be said that "The instructions in Deut 24.1 were given for hardness of heart (= moral and spiritual petrification),"[63] contra Davies and Allison it cannot be so that "they were a 'concession' …to the post-fallen state."[64] This leaves unfounded their earlier argument, where an assumed conflict between marriage as "an indissoluble union" in Genesis 1-2 and the "provisions …made for obtaining a divorce certificate" in Deuteronomy 24:1-4

> is resolved by recognizing that Gen 1-2 refers to a paradisiacal state while Deut 24 applies to a period in which people are hard-hearted; and Jesus, by siding with Gen 1-2 against Deuteronomy, is presupposing the *Urzeit = Endzeit* equation and declaring that eschatological time has entered the arena of history.[65]

An inbreaking of "a new time" has certainly occurred, but "hardness of heart" is not a universal characteristic of "the post-paradisiacal condition," and no-one adjudged hard-hearted will ever partake in the "eschatological restoration of paradise."[66] Therefore it is clear that there can be no "real contradiction with Mk 12.18-27"[67] because all impenitent subjects of this so-called "concession" will be excluded. The considerable impact of Matthew 22:23-33 (teaching of a resurrection without human or angelic marriage) on early Christianity, such that celibacy was "popularly conceived to be an imitation of angels,"[68] also rests on an ill-conceived premise that in this present time all people are hard-hearted.

One place in the Septuagint where "hardness of heart" is not a dubious invention is found when Yahweh says, "all the house of Israel have …a stubborn heart" (Ezek 3:7). Here σκληροκάρδιος suitably translates קָשֶׁה ("hard") and לֵב ("heart").[69] Ezekiel is called to go to the

---

[63] Davies and Allison, *Matthew*, III, 14.

[64] Ibid. Cranfield similarly sees Deut 24:1 not as God's absolute will but as a "divine provision" for human sinfulness, protecting sufferers from divorce's worst effects. Cranfield, *Mark*, 319.

[65] W. Davies and D. Allison, *The Gospel According to Saint Matthew*, vol. I, ICC (Edinburgh: T&T Clark, 1992), 493-94.

[66] Ibid., 494.

[67] Davies and Allison, *Matthew*, III, 14.

[68] Ibid., 229.

[69] Excepting perhaps the substitution of a Greek plural form for a singular Hebrew noun (although the Hebrew adjective is a plural construct).

house of Israel, a rebellious people (Ezek 2:3, 5, 8; 3:9, 26, 27) who "will not be willing to listen" (Ezek 3:7). The occasion is the Babylonian Exile. The Pharisees, whom Jesus charges with "hardness of heart," should be familiar with this last-recorded occasion of Israel's σκληροκάρδιος around five centuries earlier, especially when a Hebrew psalmist (cf. Ps 95) and even Israel's arch-enemy, the Philistines (cf. 1 Sam 6:6),[70] can recall the "hardness of heart" in Israel's history several centuries before their time. This day of rebellion in the wilderness can be no ordinary occasion for it to be remembered so long afterwards! The Pharisees would surely also recall this original time of Israel's hardness of heart. The author of Hebrews certainly does, citing it perhaps a millennium further on than the Psalmist, which only magnifies its gravity. For Ezekiel to connect the hardness of heart *in his day* to this historic judgement day, he too addresses no ordinary occasion.

Mirroring characteristics of the rebellious Israelites, Yahweh grants Ezekiel a "face as hard as their face" and a "forehead as hard as their foreheads" (Ezek 3:8) but *not a heart as hard as their heart*! No prophet in Scripture is ever charged with "hardness of heart" (σκληροκαρδία). Indeed, Ezekiel is commanded to "Be not rebellious like that rebellious house" (Ezek 2:8). He obeys God by eating, going and speaking (or not speaking, as directed) to people who will be judged for their "wickedness" (Ezek 5:6; cf. Num 14:35), "abominations" (Ezek 5:9; cf. Deut 24:4 "for that is an abomination") and "whoring heart" (Ezek 6:9). The prophet certainly does not have a "whoring heart" either, a characteristic of immoral and impenitent Israel which the Septuagint also translates fittingly: לֵב as καρδία "heart"; and זָנָה as ἐκπορνεύω "whoring," where even their eyes are said to go "whoring" (זָנָה as πορνεύω) after idols. Such hard-heartedness and sexual immorality provides strong connection with the σκληροκαρδία and πορνεία of Matthew 19:8-9.

Ezekiel's Babylonian Exile context and his prophetic judgement on Jerusalem also connects with Matthew's emphasis on Babylon and Jerusalem's destruction in his time.[71] The term "Babylon" features

---

[70] The Philistines know that they must not emulate Pharaoh. Their priests and diviners recall the fate of the Egyptians and warn against likewise hardening their own hearts.

[71] Ezekiel 24 holds that Ezekiel's wife died as a prophetic sign of the fall of Jerusalem, "the rebellious house" with "unclean lewdness" (זִמָּה, cf. Lev 18:17 in reference to sexual depravity). This deadly and righteous (not to be mourned openly) termination of a marriage covenant offers a parallel to the judgement awaiting Jesus' rebellious generation. Ezekiel 23 records Israel's "abominations" of "adultery" and "defilement" (cf. Deut 24:4) along with God's resolution, "Thus I will put an end to your lewdness and your whoring begun in the

heavily in Matthew's Gospel, but is found in no other Gospel.[72] "Babylon" occurs twice in Jesus' genealogy (Matt 1:11, 12) and twice in the summary of the genealogy (Matt 1:17), remarkably without any Israelite city mentioned, not even Jerusalem or Bethlehem! Matthew lists fourteen generations from Abraham to David, fourteen from David to the Babylonian Exile, and fourteen from Babylon to Christ (then explicitly highlights this in Matt 1:17). Such intriguing multiples of seven reappear in the context of forgiveness (Matt 18:21-22) preceding Jesus' second teaching on divorce. Later, Jesus proclaims seven merciless woes to the scribes and Pharisees (Matt 23:1-36). This all points to Matthew having a definite purpose in writing, where connections could well be made between evil, adultery, generational judgement, divorce, death, and destruction. In part, Matthew may have consciously written his narrative to fulfil Ezekiel's narrative.[73]

With Jesus' application of σκληροκαρδία in Matthew 19:8 matching the Septuagint's only proper use of it (Ezek 3:7), justification for the same terrible judgement may be central to Matthew's purposes.[74] With "the rebellion" and testing of Moses' time also in view, the Pharisees' "hardness of heart" affords the same sort of punishment as meted out on Israel in the wilderness or during the Babylonian Exile. The judgement is irrevocable for the hard-hearted people of the generation in question (God cuts them off: for they are killed or die outside of their land), but hope remains for future generations. Although primarily aimed at the Pharisees in response to their insistence on a right to divorce, any judgement is not necessarily limited to them. Just as the whole generation under Moses was guilty of rebellion, Jesus' words are spoken in universal terms: "let not man" (Matt 19:6) and "whoever divorces" (Matt 19:9), with judgement on a rebellious, "evil and adulterous generation" (Matt 12:39; 16:4) continuously testing God.[75] The Pharisees stand accountable, and so too the Jewish crowds, for by the end of Matthew's Gospel they follow their religious leaders, not Jesus (Matt 27:15-26).

---

land of Egypt [*a millennium earlier* (cf. verse 8)], so that you shall not lift up your eyes to them or remember Egypt anymore" (Ezek 23:27). Egypt and Babylon are inextricably linked.

[72] 'Babylon' appears only 8 other times in the NT: once in Acts (7:43); once in 1 Peter (5:13); six times in Revelation (14:8; 16:19; 17:5; 18:2, 10, 21).

[73] At least one writer argues this: J. Heil, "Ezekiel 34 and the Narrative Strategy of the Shepherd and Sheep Metaphor in Matthew," *CBQ* 55, no. 4 (1993): 698-708.

[74] More precisely, Jesus likely used the Hebrew here that matched the Hebrew in Ezek 3:7, so Matthew then utilised the same Greek equivalent.

[75] "Hardness of heart" can characterise (Law-less) Gentiles who test God too (cf. Pharaoh).

In the context of national rebellion, the purpose of Deuteronomy 24:1-4 was never to approve divorce and remarriage, nor to categorise divorces as valid or invalid. Its purpose was to rule on disobedient, stubborn and unrighteous behaviour *already occurring*. If Israel was truly no longer stubborn and served God with a clean (circumcised) heart (Deut 10:16) then the legislation of Deuteronomy 24:1-4 would never need applying. Nonetheless, the Law fixes a clear test-threshold: "an abomination before the LORD" (Deut 24:4) that will not be tolerated. Unlike the nebulous idea of "a matter of indecency" (cf. Deut 24:1), abominations and serious sexual crimes are unambiguously defined in the Law.

Return to an original spouse after divorce and remarriage is an unmistakable public act, and unequivocally judged "an abomination" (Deut 24:4). We should expect the same clarity for the 'exception clause' of πορνεία in Matthew 19:9, otherwise Jesus endorses subjective and indeterminant grounds for divorce, and/or supports a change in the Law's rulings on adultery and other sexual offences (contra Matt 5:17-19). So, in introducing the Pharisees' question as a "test," Matthew sets a scene of national rebellion against God that culminates in a terminal charge of "hardness of heart," with a concomitant foreboding of committing the intolerable (cf. Deut 24:4).

It has already been determined that, in the Hebrew Bible, the characterisation of "stiff-necked" is not a terminal judgement, although it can certainly lead to it. Is this consistent with New Testament usage? Acts 7:51 is the only place in the New Testament where σκληροτράχηλος ("stiff-necked") appears. Here Stephen applies it to those in the Jewish council, including the high priest: "You stiff-necked people, uncircumcised in heart and ears, you always resist the Holy Spirit. As your fathers did, so do you." This stubbornness, although grave (for their fathers murdered the prophets, and they will soon murder Stephen), is not irredeemable. The "hardness" metaphor used refers to the neck, not the heart. Specific reference to the "heart" concerns a matter of circumcision (cf. earlier discussion on Deut 10:16 and Jer 4:4), not an excision of a whole hard heart. Stephen's prayer "Lord do not hold this sin against them" (Acts 7:60) is also positively answered, not least in the conversion of Saul recorded immediately after. So although Jesus terminally indicts some Pharisees with "hardness of heart" (Matt 19:8; Mark 10:5) and they face certain judgement, not all are indicted, and this includes one murderer: a Pharisee of Pharisees (Acts 23:6). Some Jewish leaders will believe and follow Jesus; they will circumcise the foreskin of their heart and be no more "stiff-necked" (cf. Deut

10:16); they will circumcise themselves to the Lord and avoid his fiery wrath (cf. Jer 4:4).

The New Testament uses a different Greek term for another "hardness of heart" that is not necessarily terminal. Gentiles, "darkened in their understanding" and "alienated from the life of God," possess a general "ignorance" that is "due to their hardness [πώρωσις] of heart" (Eph 4:18). Friberg defines πώρωσις "literally, as a medical technical term, of covering with a callous or a thick growth of skin *hardening*; of the eyes *dulling, blindness*."[76] Such a medical condition does not infer that the complete organ is petrified and dead, there is only an obstructive outer element where on removal the organ will function properly. The same technical remedial concept does not apply to σκληροκαρδία, a hardness that is a thickening or petrifying of the whole organ, for which Scripture offers no cure.

Such hardness (πώρωσις) of heart, with callousness (ἀπαλγέω, Eph 4:19) and abandonment to sensuality, if unchecked can surely lead to hardness (σκληρότης) of heart (Rom 2:5). However, Paul instructs Christians to no longer walk as the Gentiles do in this futility (Eph 4:17). Life journeying in either direction is possible: ongoing hardening that results in a terminal condition where God gives up people in the lusts of their hearts (Rom 1:24 cf. 26, 28) to see his righteous judgement (Rom 2:5), or liberation that discards the callous dull-hearted old self so that one becomes "tender-hearted" and "forgiving" (Eph 4:17-32).

Ignorant callousness confronts Jesus as he grieves the "hardness [πώρωσις] of heart" of the Pharisees (Mark 3:1-6). Matthew's parallel passage (Matt 12:9-14) makes no mention of this "hardness [πώρωσις] of heart" or Jesus being grieved. Jesus would have known of the Pharisees' "hardness [πώρωσις] of heart" on this occasion, but Matthew saves up his charge of "hardness of heart [σκληροκαρδία]" for the later debate on divorce (Matt 19:8). It might be concluded that πώρωσις and σκληρότης are equivalent, but with the absence of πώρωσις in Matthew 12 (or anywhere in Matthew), it is more likely that there is an increasing callousness of the Pharisees seen in their testing of Jesus, their resolve to kill Jesus and their refusal to understand the works of Jesus (even

---

[76] Bibleworks, Friberg 23890. Also BDAG, "*hardening, dulling*" but in our literature only figuratively "*dullness, insensibility, obstinacy*" (Mark 3:5; Eph 4:18); "*insensibility has come over Israel*" (Rom 11:25). Danker, Bauer, and Arndt, *BDAG*, 732. Cf. πωρόω verbal use: aorist John 12:40; t.r. passive (Job 17:7 [of the eyes = become dim]) "*harden, petrify*" in our literature only figuratively, mostly of hearts "make *dull* or *obtuse* or *blind*," John 12:40; Mark 6:52; cf. 8:17; Herm. *Mand.* 4, 2, 1; 12, 4, 4; of the mind νοήματα (2 Cor 3:14); of persons themselves Rom 11:7. Ibid.

attributing his power to Satan), that reaches a terminal verdict of σκληροκαρδία in connection with a question on divorce.

This progression is evidenced in the increasing hostility of the Jewish leaders towards Jesus. Up until the Sabbath incident of Matthew 12:9-14 (Mark 3:1-6), the scribes, Pharisees and the crowds were simply dull in their understanding of Jesus. This is indicated in a question such as "Why does he eat with tax collectors and sinners?" (Mark 2:16), the watching as to whether Jesus would heal on the Sabbath (Mark 3:2), and the silence in the face of a rational challenge (Mark 3:3). It is this type of hardness (πώρωσις) that Jesus grieves about (Mark 3:5). However, it is only after the Sabbath incident that the Pharisees went out and conspired to kill Jesus (Matt 12:14; cf. Mark 3:6), and only later again that Jesus charges them with "hardness of heart [σκληροκαρδία]" (Matt 19:8; Mark 10:5). In the meantime, Jesus' disciples persist in their "hardness [πώρωσις] of heart" (Mark 6:52). Yet nowhere in Scripture are Jesus' disciples or any righteous people ever attributed with "hardness of heart [σκληροκαρδία],"[77] except dubiously in Mark 16:14.[78]

In Matthew's scheme, Israel's indictment comes after Jewish leaders have conspired to the evil of murdering the "guiltless" (Matt 12:7) "Son of Man" (Matt 12:8) whom they have witnessed healing (Matt 12:9-14, a man with a withered hand; cf. 19:2, large crowds). Their judgement is directly related to the state of their heart in relation to divorce: rebellion that involves testing and infidelity. This precisely aligns with Jesus' judgement of an "evil and adulterous generation" (Matt 12:39; 16:4) where he condemns those who look for a sign but cannot see it.

The direct subject of Jesus' charge of "hardness of heart" is not an abusive, neglectful spouse who callously divorces[79] or warrants 'disciplinary divorce';[80] nor is it vaguely frail humanity; rather, it is the

---

[77] Contra McKnight, "We have to admit the hard-heartedness even of followers of Jesus." McKnight, *Sermon*, 108. Also Richards, "God understands when hardness of heart drives the even the most saintly of his people to divorce." Richards, "Divorce and Remarriage: Variety of Circumstances," 228.

[78] The longer ending, Mark (16:9-20), is not in the earliest and most reliable manuscripts. Aland et al, *Greek New Testament*, 189. Aside from other questionable teachings (on handling serpents and drinking poison), it is uncharacteristically uncompassionate that Jesus would "rebuke" his grieving disciples for "their unbelief and hardness of heart" and theologically impossible if this is a terminal verdict used elsewhere in Scripture only in relation to impenitent unbelievers (Exod 7:3; Rom 2:5), Israel's wilderness rebellion (Ps 95:8; Matt 19:8; Mark 10:5; Heb 3:8, 15; 4:7), and the Babylonian Exile (Ezek 3:7).

[79] Roberts, *Not under Bondage*, 39.

[80] Ibid., 66.

religious men[81] who test Jesus but do not truly hear him.[82] "Their question is exposed as stubborn unbelief; their androcentric marriage moral contradicts God."[83] Judgement is directed at those who have the Law but do not understand it properly. This is reminiscent of Zechariah's[84] prophetic word that Israel was hard of hearing and had "diamond-hard" hearts (Zech 7:12-14; cf. Jer 17:1; Ezek 3:7)! This led to their dispersion among all the nations and their Promised Land being left desolate (Zech 7:14). By rejecting the word of God, and doing the same injustices that their fathers had done, the exiles returning from Babylon would face the same judgement from God. Israel has been long-warned against such obstinacy.[85] This same hardness of heart would be present in Jesus' time (Matt 19:8; Mark 10:5) and the same cataclysmic judgement on a rebellious nation would come again in 70CE.

So, although the God-Israel marriage covenant is broken by diamond-hard hard-heartedness – and Jesus institutes a "new covenant" (cf. Luke 22:20) *unlike the old* (cf. Jer 31:31-33), Jesus in Matthew is most concerned about "the covenant" (Matt 26:28) *that stands in his lifetime*, and this encompasses every iota and dot of the Law, including its bloody demands and curses for disobedience. Yet even after judgement, Israel is not totally rejected and replaced. Just as "Isaiah's prophecies of doom are interspersed with oracles of salvation [cf. Is 4:2-

---

[81] Roberts rightly recognises the gender focus of Deut 24:1, "The callous people in question must have been male... It was principally *male* hardness of heart," whereas some commentators misread it as "Moses permitted divorce because women were hard-heartedly committing sexual sin." Ibid. However, treacherous men in general are not all necessarily "hard-hearted" (and beyond redemption) biblically.

[82] It also applies to Moses' generation who tested God and practised the Deut 24:1-4 divorce customs.

[83] P. Farla, "'The Two Shall Be One Flesh': Gen. 1.27 and 2.24 in the New Testament Marriage Texts," in *Intertextuality in Biblical Writings: Essays in Honour of Bas Van Iersel*, ed. S. Draisma (Kampen: Kok, 1989), 68.

[84] Zechariah is mentioned directly in Matthew (23:35) but in no other Synoptic. "Matthew utilized Zechariah as a significant prophetic template for the life of Jesus." Spadaro, *Matthew*, 44. See also N. T. Wright, *Jesus and the Victory of God* (Minneapolis: Fortress, 1996), 588-600. Keener connects the throwing down of the mountain (Matt 21:21-22) with Zechariah's prophecy (Zech 4:8-9), to be fulfilled with the "reformation of the Jewish religious system." Keener, *Matthew*, 505. Mention of "great anger" and hard hearts (Zech 7:12-14; cf. Matt 19:8) points *first to catastrophic removal* and then reform.

[85] The Lord declared, "I know that you are obstinate" (קָשָׁה "hard") "and your neck is an iron sinew and your forehead brass" (Isa 48:4). This intensification of the more common "hard-neck" ("stiff-neck") and "hard forehead" metaphors tends to imply that when Israel's rebellion climaxes with a verdict of "hardness (of heart)," their stubbornness is as solid as the metal idols that they fashion (Isa 48:5).

6]" a glorious branch of the Lord remains, where "the 'remnant' is *what is left of Israel* after God's punishment."[86]

This eschatological concept appears throughout Matthew's Gospel,[87] such as in Matthew 10:1, where τοὺς δώδεκα μαθητὰς links "the twelve" new leaders of Israel with Matthew's dominant use of "disciples": anyone who is a true follower of Christ – even a tax collector (Matt 9:9) can be a member of this "messianic remnant community."[88] Edgar Johnson finds the concept in the "little ones" and "sheep" (18:1-14) and reproof of an erring brother (18:15-20) *all in the prelude* to Jesus' teaching on forgiveness (Matt 18:21-35) and second teaching on divorce (Matt 19:1-12), and succeeding this teaching (cf. Matt 19:28).[89] It arguably appears within it too, for the unpayable debt along with the Judah-Babylon connection[90] implies judgement and an exilic remnant.

Earlier in Matthew, when the Pharisees and scribes have for the sake of their tradition "made void the word of God" (Matt 15:6), Jesus declares that Isaiah well-prophesied about the vain worship and far-away heart of "this people" – God's people, who are led by "hypocrites" (Matt 15:7-8). The Pharisees judged by Jesus to have "hardness of heart" (Matt 19:8) possess hearts far from God. Their teaching is not from God, but from themselves (and traditions of the elders) to suit themselves. With the "seven woes" pronounced in Matthew 23, Jesus' damning judgement should also be brought to bear on the Pharisees' teaching on marriage.[91]

Following this indictment, Jesus repeats the words of verse 4, ἀπ' ἀρχῆς "from the beginning," producing a doublet to emphasize God's enduring standard from time immemorial. It also consolidates Jesus' response: his answer to the first test question (Matt 19:3) was essentially a "No" with its basis in Creation, and in answer to this subsequent test question, Creation again was his basis to repudiate the Pharisees' line

---

[86] Murphy, *Apocalypticism*, 139. (Italics original.)

[87] E. Johnson, "Aspects of the Remnant Concept in the Gospel of Matthew " (PhD, Andrews University, 1984). E.g. it appears in Matthew's presentation of Jesus, John's message, and the Sermon on the Mount.

[88] Ibid., 179. "Of significance is the fact that he [Matthew] uses the simple title 'the Twelve' only in reference to Judas as εἷς τῶν δώδεκα (Matt 26:14, 26, 47)."

[89] Ibid.

[90] Cf. "hardness of heart" and "sexual immorality" (Matt 19:8-9; Ezek 3:7; 6:9; Zech 7:12-14). See also exegesis of Matt 19:12 regarding "eunuchs."

[91] The Pharisees indict themselves "even though they did not realize it" (Morris, on Matt 23:31). "The prophet killers and the prophet buriers belong together. Their very preoccupation with the tombs shows that their real interest is in the interment of those who spoke from God, not in heeding the messages they gave." Morris, *Matthew*, 587.

of reasoning. The verb γέγονεν lends support – "it was not instituted (not generated, born, or to be)"[92] – where the verb is in the perfect tense, with a sense of "it was not so and it continues to not be so." What was instituted by God is contrasted with what was not instituted by God, in this case: a permanent joining in marriage (Matt 19:6) versus human divorce or separation (Matt 19:7). God's "No" to divorce and remarriage remains unchanged, as from the beginning.

Jesus does not champion a standard contemporary rabbinic platform, but anchors his audience in the much older platform of Creation, "the beginning" (Gen 1:1). As such, he is not appealing to a higher authority, for the written prophetic authority of Moses governs Genesis 1:27; 2:24 *and* Deuteronomy 24:1-4. Jesus does reference the ideal, although not to then grant a concession but to uphold the original standard. Contra Waetjen, in Matthew 19:8 it is not that "Jesus establishes the contradiction between Moses and God" only to abolish an accommodation to human frailties in the ("New") interest of "God's Reign" and justice.[93] Neither does Jesus outlaw divorce and then offer one exception that, in keeping with contemporary Jewish law, perpetuates male privilege such that "men are protected from defiled women."[94] Waetjen recognises that what was said on divorce (cf. Matt 5:31) "appears to be a somewhat distorted paraphrase of Deut 24:1,"[95] so criticism of contemporary Jewish law is called for rather than judgement of Moses and that Jesus "unhesitatingly abolishes those [Law codes] that do not actualize the justice of God."[96] "But [δὲ]..." (here in the last phrase of Matt 19:8 and commencing Matt 19:9) Jesus does justify divorce with one cause that does not conflict with Moses, nor accommodate human weakness. Indeed, Moses specifically ruled on this cause, and it is not just "any cause" (Matt 19:3) but a deadly serious one.

---

[92] Danker, Bauer, and Arndt, *BDAG*, 158.
[93] Waetjen, *Fulfillment*, 77.
[94] Ibid., 78.
[95] Ibid., 76.
[96] Ibid., 71.

CHAPTER 7 – The Exception Clause &
Adultery Charge

Exegesis of Matthew 19:9

⁹ λέγω δὲ ὑμῖν ὅτι ὃς ἂν ἀπολύσῃ τὴν γυναῖκα αὐτοῦ μὴ ἐπὶ πορνείᾳ καὶ γαμήσῃ ἄλλην μοιχᾶται.ᵈ

Textual note: (Byzantine difference)
ᵈ· καὶ ὁ ἀπολελυμένην γαμήσας μοιχᾶται is added more often than not ("and the one marrying a woman who has gained a divorce [for herself] commits adultery"). "The longer reading has had considerable support, but influence from Mt 5:32 remains more likely."[1]

Verse 9

> **And I say to you: whoever divorces his wife, except for sexual immorality, and marries another, commits adultery."**

When Pharisees come to test Jesus (Matt 19:3) their goal is "to destroy him" (Matt 12:14). Presumably this is by capital punishment, so capital implications *within* this discourse cannot be ruled out-of-the-question. With a deadly mission in mind, extra credence is given to Jesus turning the tables on his questioners with a deadly response.

On this occasion of testing Jesus, the Pharisees fail to achieve their goal, but they eventually see Jesus condemned to death on a charge of

---

[1]Nolland, *Matthew*, 765. Holmes argues not only for the longer reading, but sees μὴ ἐπὶ πορνείᾳ as a corruption and παρεκτὸς λόγου πορνείας (of Matt 5:32) as the original exception clause of Matt 19:9. He reasons, "A more comprehensive approach that takes into account simultaneously all the variants in all the parallels results in a more satisfactory and probable decision and explanation of both the text and the subsequent corruption of the passages examined." M. Holmes, "The Text of the Matthean Divorce Passages: A Comment on the Appeal to Harmonization in Textual Decisions " *JBL* 109, no. 4 (1990): 663. However, Holmes' approach of treating all variations simultaneously might not give due weight to the best and earliest manuscripts, and tends to deny the possibility of original oral differences (without doctrinal contradiction) in Jesus' teaching on different occasions. In any case, a reading of παρεκτὸς λόγου πορνείας in Matt 19:9 does not challenge (but may enhance) the main argument of this paper, for "a matter of sexual immorality" could be used for direct contrast with "a matter of indecency" (Deut 24:1).

blasphemy (Matt 26:65-66).[2] This might be lawfully procured by contemporary standards, but unlawfully by the Law.[3] The charge contrasts with Matthew's earlier account of what truly constitutes blasphemy (Matt 12:22-32) and for the Pharisees the same Law perilously applies: "Whoever blasphemes the name of the LORD shall surely be put to death" (Lev 24:16).

Compounding the crime, in their legal proceedings the Jewish leaders "were seeking false testimony against Jesus that they might put him to death" (Matt 26:49), yet the Law commands, "Keep far from a false charge, and do not kill the innocent and righteous, for I will not acquit the wicked" (Exod 23:7 cf. Matthew's emphasis on "evil"). Judgement looms for this generation (cf. Matt 23:36).

Jesus asserts his authority (λέγω …ὑμῖν); this is his word that Matthew closely connects with verse 8. The δὲ can be taken as a mild adversative (cf. ἀπ' ἀρχῆς δὲ immediately preceding) to bring a contrast or simply as "and" to add insight to the Mosaic allowance just mentioned (Matt 19:7-8) and provide deeper teaching. Jesus is no longer quoting Scripture, yet neither does he oppose Moses, just as he did not oppose Moses in the verse prior. In the context of what is lawful (Matt 19:3), Jesus cannot be inventing a new rule that contradicts the Law, else more than an iota or dot is abolished or relaxed (Matt 5:17-19).

This is not a matter of, "What is old has fundamentally a prior claim to truth over what is younger."[4] The truth of Moses in Deuteronomy is no less than the truth in Genesis. Luz notes, "For the rabbis the entire Torah comes from God. Whoever attributes even a single verse only to Moses has despised the word of God."[5] Contra Hays, there is no "substantive contradiction that compels Matthew to regard Moses' commandment as having only relative value," as though Jesus "trumps Scripture with Scripture."[6] Strictly applying the written Law to Matthew 19:9 avoids any truth hierarchy, for no easy concession degrades the

---

[2] W. Loader, *Jesus and the Fundamentalism of His Day: The Gospels, the Bible and Jesus* (Melbourne: Uniting Education, 1998), 28. Other charges of unlawfulness would only have added to, indeed precipitated, this final charge.

[3] "The problem here is that nothing we know of either Old Testament or later Jewish tradition appears to justify the charge. It seems wrong." Ibid. In fact, a large part of Matthew's purpose in writing is to show that *it was wrong*, and that the people condemning Jesus deserve death, not him.

[4] Luz, *Matthew 8-20*, 488-90. Cf. "Jesus' hermeneutics here then assume that the earlier the dictum in Torah, the prior and higher authority it had." Witherington III, *Matthew*. 362.

[5] Luz, *Matthew 8-20*, 490.

[6] Hays, *Moral Vision*, 350.

absolute ethic concerning what God has joined.[7] In no way has "Jesus abolished one part of Scripture, the divorce law, on the authority of another, the creation accounts."[8]

Loader writes that the δὲ ("but," as in Matt 19:8b) "serves to contrast Jesus' teaching with what Moses allowed, corresponding to the contrast in 5.31-32."[9] Yet a contrast itself counts against the view that Jesus was equating πορνεία with "a matter of indecency" in Deuteronomy 24:1, even a "strict" Shammaite interpretation. Contra Loader, to make this equation would not be "upholding Moses' teaching in Deuteronomy 24:1-4 and interpreting it strictly."[10] Instead, it would completely reject Moses' commandment concerning adultery in Deuteronomy 22:22 (cf. Lev 20:10). John Murray likewise rejects Moses' commandment and contradicts Jesus' decree on the indissolubility of the Law (Matt 5:17-19) in claiming, "Our LORD instituted divorce for adultery (Matthew 5:31, 32; 19:9); by implication he abrogated the Mosaic death penalty."[11] Meier asserts, "Once again, Jesus shows himself capable of revoking a major institution of the Torah,"[12] which can hardly be Matthew's vision.

The tone of the whole Matthew 19:3-12 discussion is not one of compromise with cultural norms. Nor need this verse be understood as diluting Jesus' absolute teaching on divorce found in Mark and Luke to bring closer conformity with Moses' teaching.[13] "The contrast just noted makes that unlikely,"[14] but more significantly, when the Law's written punishment for "sexual immorality" is given full weight, Jesus' absolute teaching is not relaxed at all. The teaching certainly contrasts with a Mosaic allowance, but has *absolute conformity with a Mosaic command*.[15]

---

[7] "Jesus demotes Moses' concession in Deuteronomy and subordinates it to Genesis." Heth, "Jesus on Divorce," 9.

[8] Countryman, *Dirt, Greed and Sex*, 174.

[9] Loader, *Sexuality: Key Texts*, 91.

[10] Ibid.

[11] J. Murray, *Principles of Conduct: Aspects of Biblical Ethics* (Grand Rapids: Eerdmans, 1957), 119.

[12] J. Meier, *The Vision of Matthew: Christ, Church, and Morality in the First Gospel*, ed. L. Boadt, Theological Inquiries (New York: Paulist, 1979), 137.

[13] France, *Matthew*, 208-10.

[14] Loader, *Sexuality: Key Texts*, 91.

[15] In the grand scheme, Moses' commands are God's commands, and Jesus is presented as the Son of God (Matt 1:23; 4:3, 14:33, etc.) and God incarnate (John 1). As such, Jesus is the real Lawgiver, so he would hardly contradict himself and alter or abolish original meanings of *his* commands. This does not preclude Jesus from fulfilling the Law, and at the same time inaugurating a new law within a new covenant (while the Law endures *in toto* for all who remain under the old covenant). Yet there would be nothing new about the new law

Rather than making explicit what Instone-Brewer thinks implicit in Jesus' divorce teaching in Mark or Luke,[16] Jesus raises explicit grounds (not strictly an 'exception' to the Law) that can be plainly understood by referencing the Law's explicit legislation on illicit sex. If Luke or Mark had included these grounds, then this could have easily confused their primary readership, because Gentiles would most naturally reference more liberal ways and contemporary Roman law mandating divorce for adultery, not ancient Jewish Scripture demanding death. Blomberg postulates:

> The very natural harmonization which assumes that Mark simply implies the exception which Matthew makes explicit, presupposing the universal acknowledgement in Jewish and Graeco-Roman circles that adultery provides grounds for divorce.[17]

However, *presupposing* is very different to *endorsing*. Jesus' very Jewish teaching may simply not harmonise naturally with universally assumed views, and Mark implicitly acknowledges that Matthew's explicit 'exception clause' confronts Graeco-Roman law. One might theorise that Mark and Luke could have retained (or inserted) a Matthean-type exception clause and then directed their audiences to research the strict demands of Mosaic Law, but (a) this would have been cumbersome,[18] and (b) to indict Israel would not have served – and likely even countered – their own Gospel purposes.

The context of Jesus' first teaching on divorce in Matthew's Gospel informs us here. Meier observes that what was originally a subordinate clause in Deuteronomy 24:1 has been reformulated in Matthew 5:31 as a distinct commandment: "He who divorces his wife *must give* her a certificate of divorce."[19] Meier asserts that Jesus accepts this as a commandment, noting as important a rudimentary pattern that Jesus' *first two 'antitheses'* begin with the phrase "it was said" (Matt 5:21, 27) and they both introduce a commandment from the Decalogue: "You

---

if it were completely the same as the old Law. That the new law, written on hearts, has common moral ground with the Law does not necessitate that the Law as written on stone and in the Hebrew Bible must change.

[16] Instone-Brewer, *Social and Literary Context*, 152-61. Here Instone-Brewer assumes that a more Gentile audience would assume divorce (without death) for adultery as valid.

[17] Blomberg, "Exegesis," 173.

[18] Mark's short evangelistic Gospel (that fitted on one scroll) for Gentile mission would have become larger and costlier to produce, and the Hebrew Bible reference material may then need to accompany it.

[19] Meier, *Marginal Jew*, 4, 37.

shall not kill....you shall not commit adultery."[20] However, the 'antithesis' concerning divorce obviously does not contain a commandment from the Decalogue, plus there is a more significant and sophisticated pattern present that covers *the whole six 'antitheses'*.

It may be more accurate to refer to the teaching of Matthew 5:21-48 as having five main 'antitheses', where the second simply contains an ancillary 'antithesis'.[21] All five are introduced not simply by "it was said," but by "you have heard that it was said" (Matt 5:21, 27, 33, 38, and 43). *Only Matthew 5:31* omits the phrase "you have heard that," adding credence to it being subordinate to one of the five main 'antitheses', along with the "also" (δέ) that also attaches it to the matter of adultery just mentioned. This breaks Meier's truncated introductory "pattern" of the previous two 'antitheses' (**ὅτι ἐρρέθη**), where Matthew's first recorded phrase is significantly longer ('ηκούσατε **ὅτι ἐρρέθη** τοῖς ἀρχαίοις) than the second ('ηκούσατε **ὅτι ἐρρέθη**).[22]

Only the introductory phrase for the 'antithesis' on oaths (Matt 5:33) completely matches the first introductory phrase: "You have heard that it was said *to those of old*" (italics added). It is prefaced by the word "again" (πάλιν) to restore the august formula, which also supports the idea that the 'antithesis' raised immediately prior was somewhat subsidiary, as important as it was. A larger pattern emerges where not only Jesus upholds the Law and goes to the heart of it, but his introductory words signal that there are crucial elements that *have traditionally been left unsaid*, along with elements that *were never said* "to those of old," or if said, then *not in the way that Jesus' hearers have heard* and enacted.

Matthew 5:43 provides an obvious example: "You shall love your neighbour" is certainly a commandment (Lev 19:18), but "you shall hate your enemy" is found nowhere in the Hebrew Bible. It might be implied, however, from God's hatred of evil (Ps 5:5; 11:5) and the Psalmist's hatred of those who hate God (Ps 139:21-22), or from specific ancient occasions when God commanded Israel to destroy enemies and have no mercy (Deut 7:2). Jesus confirms that his audience has "heard" this commandment but in omitting mention of the original recipients, he highlights a misappropriation. The second part of this command was not

---

[20] Ibid. Yet Meier also sees that Deut 24:1-4 does not state that the writing of a divorce certificate is absolutely necessary for the validity of divorce. Ibid., 145.

[21] Cf. F. Filson, "Broken Patterns in the Gospel of Matthew," *JBL* 75, no. 3 (1956): 229. W. Grundmann, *Das Evangelium Nach Matthäus*, Sixth ed., ThHNT, 1 (Berlin: EVA, 1986), 158-59.

[22] Bold has been added to the Greek to highlight Meier's version of the introductions.

a timeless one; Jesus' audience has not heard or really understood that it was *commanded only* "to those of old" and not to them.[23] Indeed, a Mosaic command regarding a few selected enemies, "You shall not seek their peace or prosperity" (Deut 23:6), contrasts with God's later command for Israel to seek the peace and prosperity of another enemy, the Babylonians (Jer 29:7). Jesus, later again, then applies this love principle to everyone, even Roman oppressors and Jewish opponents (Matt 5:44).

For the first sin Jesus addresses (Matt 5:21), the penalty is left unspecified, but for Jews and Romans capital punishment for murder would be the normal expectation. The Law demands it, even if contemporary courts failed to prosecute or a violent insurrectionist was on occasion released (cf. Matt 27:15-26). Likewise, the Law's judgement for committing "adultery" (Matt 5:27-28) would probably be well known, even if commonly relaxed. Morris rejects the idea that Jesus replaces the Law with his own commands, "for in no case does he relax a provision of the law. Rather, he shows that, rightly understood, the law goes much further than his hearers had reckoned."[24]

The Decalogue commandment against adultery was no doubt heard said by Jesus' audience (Matt 5:27), however, unlike the first 'antithesis' on murder, the Law's penalty is conspicuously absent. "You shall not commit adultery" (Exod 20:14; Deut 5:17) leaves *unsaid*: "And whoever commits adultery will be liable to judgement" (as against, "whoever murders will be liable to judgment," Matt 5:21), although judgement was certainly specified for ancient Israel (cf. Lev 20:10; Deut 22:22). It may be that Jesus' audience has not even "heard" that this judgement was *"said to those of old"* (Matthew does not record these introductory words here) because culturally it has been "abolished" or "relaxed" (cf. Matt 5:17-19), such that first-century Jewish leaders did not *teach* 'death for adultery', instead only 'divorce for adultery' (cf. Roman law).

Nonetheless, people no doubt would have known the gravity of adultery.

> No first-century Jew could have spoken of *porneiai* (sexual immoralities) without having in mind the list of forbidden

---

[23] In contrast, the crowds know that prohibitions against murder and false testimony were "said to those of old" (Matt 5:21 and 33) and these ancient addresses always remain applicable.

[24] Morris, *Matthew*, 114.

offences in Leviticus 18 and 20, particularly incest, adultery, same-sex intercourse and bestiality.[25]

They have heard the Decalogue command, but might not have heard that capital punishment for violation *genuinely was – and remains – commanded* by the Law. It appears that contemporary practice diminished or dismissed certain dire judgements of Hebrew Scripture.

Social and legal disparate treatment is perhaps little different today. An inequality endures where grace often surfaces for cases of sexual immorality, such as adultery, but rarely for murder.[26] Indirectly, Wayne House contends this,

> Whenever I speak of capital punishment, I am speaking of it as a universally exacted retribution for murder or complicity in murder, nothing more and nothing less.[27]

House narrows his case for a universal death penalty by appealing to Genesis 9:6, but the Law makes no artificial distinction between the treatment of murder and other capital offences (Deut 5:17, 18; cf. Matt 5:19; Jas 2:10-11). The commands are equal and enduring; the wages of sin identical: death. The "adultery" in Matthew 19:9 (and 5:27-32) is the same as that found in Deuteronomy 5:17, with no lesser legal demand. The absolute prohibitions against both murder and adultery are contiguous in the Decalogue, even with an interchangeable Hebrew-Septuagint verse order (adultery precedes murder in the LXX).

In connection with adultery, when Jesus then teaches on divorce (Matt 5:31-32) there is no scriptural record that "those of old" were ever commanded to write a divorce certificate.[28] This is not how

---

[25] R. Gagnon, "The Bible and Homosexual Practice: Key Issues," in *Homosexuality and the Bible: Two Views*, ed. D. Via and R. Gagnon (Minneapolis: Fortress, 2003), 72.

[26] In modern debates over the validity of the death penalty, the crime of murder is always central, but never is adultery raised as a capital offence, and many would not even consider it a crime at all. When House argues "There are many who would call for the execution of individuals who commit such crimes as treason and rape as well as murder," adultery still does not rate a mention. House, "Death Penalty," 8. It is patent that this would make a modern case too difficult to argue. However, whichever side of the modern debate is taken, it does not negate that the Law did demand death for adultery and as Jesus spoke (in Matt 19:9), the Law remained applicable and indissoluble – in principle, if not in practice.

[27] House in ibid., 184. Yoder, despite his dubious framework that capital punishment arose from "cultural substance" (cf. problematic policies promoting racism, slavery, polygamy) only to end at the cross (ibid., 159-60.), does rightly expose House's narrow view: "some of the pro-death arguments in the mainstream debate, which make more of the Mosaic material than he does, are not represented" ibid., 200.

[28] Likewise, in Scripture, no one was ever commanded to write a marriage certificate. Meier emphasizes that "in ancient Israel, marriage and divorce were basically private matters within a family and between families, not a state-supervised process that had to go through a court procedure. Thus marriage had the nature of a private contract. In the Pentateuch,

Deuteronomy 24:1-4 reads as written and it is doubtful that Jesus rereads it another way. It is possible that Jesus' audience has not "heard" that it was said, "Whoever divorces his wife, let him give her a certificate of divorce," so he has to tell them, "It was also said" (Matt 5:31).[29]

Alternatively, if the "heard" of Matthew 5:27 carries forward and is implied in Matthew 5:31, then the audience has "heard that it was said" but perhaps only by way of common cultural practice or religious rulings based on more recent Shammaite or Hillelite understandings. Carson offers a helpful approach to the 'antitheses': "Jesus is not negating something from the Old Testament, but something from their understanding of it."[30] On Matthew 5:31, Carson observes they have heard that a man "must" give a certificate of divorce, which is "something not quite true."[31] McKnight sees here that Jesus confronts a sense of,

> 'You have heard that it was said that if a man wants to divorce his wife, he must *simply* give her a bill of divorce'. Jesus isn't simply citing Moses; he's using words that were used in his day when it came to a (Torah observant!) man divorcing his wife.[32]

Whatever the case, Jesus does bring a deeper understanding to what was said. Ironically, Jesus may even uphold the notion that Moses commanded the giving of a certificate of divorce, but this is not grounded in any private or trivial matter determined merely *by one man*, as in Deuteronomy 24:1-4. Instead, in determining a matter of "sexual immorality" as the only grounds for divorce, then according to *what was said to those of old* this capital charge must be formally established in a public court *by the testimony of two or more witnesses* (Deut 17:6; 19:15). If a guilty verdict were reckoned, the written sentence serves as a certificate of divorce. Regardless of whether this document was ever culturally labelled a "divorce certificate," legally it did mean that a wife would be cut off and "sent away" to death, and scripturally the Hebrew

---

however, there is no indication that a *written* contract was required for a marriage." Meier, *Marginal Jew*, 4, 77. The only reason a court procedure would originally be needed in relation to marriage, then, is if the grounds for divorce were of a capital nature.

[29] Keener maintains, "Most of Matthew's audience… may have been unfamiliar with the debate between the Hillelites and Shammaites active among the Pharisees of Jesus' day." Keener, *Matthew*, 466. Most of *Jesus' audience* may have been unfamiliar too!

[30] D. Carson, *The Sermon on the Mount: An Evangelical Exposition of Matthew 5-7* (Grand Rapids: Baker, 1992), 39-40.

[31] Ibid., 45.

[32] McKnight, *Sermon*, 99.

prophets did document the grounds (cf. Isa 50:1; Jer 3:8; Hos 2:2) for God's divorce of the Northern Kingdom.

Therefore a divorce certificate *may in a sense be commanded in Scripture*, but only by way of an implied imperative within a judicial process prescribed in the Law for capital offences. This imperative could also be implied from Deuteronomy 24:1-4, in that if a divorce certificate is *customary* for a non-capital offence, then even more so it should be *mandatory* for a capital offence. In this process, it is really God who sends away the wife to death, and thus separates what only he has the prerogative to separate, because the grounds for this divorce are purely found written in God-given commandments of the Hebrew Bible that rule on "sexual immorality." While the husband and the courts do the physical prosecuting, weighing of evidence, judging, document writing and sending away to execution, this must all be in keeping with God's scriptural commands.[33]

If Israel has not been prosecuting cases of adultery in this manner, which is likely true and scholars make much of this to argue that first-century Israelite society has progressed or has yielded to secular restrictions,[34] then Jesus gives a clarion reminder that the Law has not been abolished or altered in the least and extra judgement is heaped on Israel for not obeying God's commandments. Just as murder is strictly judged (cf. Matt 5:21-26), adultery has grave punishments, including hell (γέεννα, Matt 5:27-30). In his first teaching on divorce in Matthew, Jesus is therefore stressing that "sexual immorality" and "adultery" (Matt 5:31-32) attract extremely dire consequences. This must also be so for his second teaching on divorce, especially with its more expansive introductory context of Matthew 18 describing offences with dire, hellish consequences.

Given that the Law, as written, had dire punishments for sexually immoral acts, and if Deuteronomy 24:1-4 functions as a terminal indictment for "hardness of heart" rather than a gracious concession, it cannot be true that "Moses was too lenient."[35] Sanders is correct to say that "Matthew's Sermon on the Mount is not against the law," but there is no implicit criticism that "the law does not go far enough" or reallocation of blame for divorce, as in "it is 'your' fault, not really his

---

[33] "Human courts execute judgment since the Law was given by God. …in all cases, God is understood to be the judge and human beings were seen only as the performers of the necessary rituals." Runesson, *Divine Wrath*, 49.

[34] Hays claims there is considerable evidence that the death penalty prescribed in the Torah for adultery had been replaced by compulsory divorce during Roman times. Hays, *Moral Vision*, 354.

[35] Sanders, *Historical Figure*, 211.

[Moses']."[36] Instead, Jesus draws out existing crucial implications and criticises inadequate conceptions of the Law. Moreover, if "the long form of the prohibition of divorce" (i.e. Matt 19:1-12) that Sanders believes out of all the 'antitheses' "comes closest to explicit criticism" of the Law[37] is found not to be antithetical at all, then all other 'antitheses' cannot be anywhere near antithetical, and contra Meier, Jesus' radical morality upholds the Law.[38]

The phrase, ὃς ἂν ἀπολύσῃ τὴν γυναῖκα αὐτοῦ, in Matthew 19:8 exactly matches that in Matthew 5:31. The dropping of "let him give her a certificate of divorce" supports the above understanding that Jesus counters a reformulation of Deuteronomy 24:1. This reformulated command of what "was also said" (Matt 5:31) is dealt with more comprehensively in Matthew 19:7-8, for here Jesus corrects the Pharisees' "Why then did Moses command [ἐντέλλω]" with "Moses allowed [ἐπιτρέπω]." From this perspective, what follows "whoever divorces his wife" is teaching that replaces "let him give her a certificate of divorce." Alternatively, if the reformulation is taken as affirmed by Jesus, then he expounds on the only type of divorce certificate that may lawfully be given: one with grounds of a capital nature.

Although the legal context is specific, the broad nature of this topic is indicated by this verse's opening terms: ὃς ἂν "whoever" infers any man. Limiting the debate to religiously officiated marriage[39] and then civil or religious divorce does not do justice to the Pharisees' framing of the question: ἀνθρώπῳ ("for a man" in Matt 19:3), and Jesus' immediate response that cites the first marriage – hardly officiated in a church or temple, which serves as a model for all marriages.[40] "Whoever divorces" puts the focus on a general verbal action of ἀπολύω, "to send away," as discussed earlier. "His wife" (τὴν γυναῖκα αὐτοῦ) is general also, for it references "the woman" whomever any man has married.

---

[36] Ibid.

[37] Ibid.

[38] Meier frames Jesus' teaching as "radical morality that annuls the Law," where the antithesis on divorce "is the most hotly disputed of the three antitheses which seem to revoke some command, permission, or institution sanctioned by the written Torah." Meier, *Vision of Matthew*, 248.

[39] Tasker, *Matthew*, 180-82. Limiting πορνεία to betrothal unfaithfulness or pre-marital sex also opposes the general nature of the debate. Edgar, "Divorce & Remarriage for Adultery or Desertion," 173-77.

[40] Marriage "springs from God's character" and the permanent, joyful, intimate connection is to reflect God's image. A. Mathews and M. Hubbard, *Marriage Made in Eden: A Pre-Modern Perspective for a Post-Christian World* (Grand Rapids: Baker, 2004), 175-81. In Matt 19:4-6, Jesus shows that "the frame of reference for men and women in relationship is the creation narrative." Ibid., 193.

The phrase that follows the 'exception clause', "and marries another," where "another woman [γαμήσῃ ἄλλην]" (of the same kind) is implicit, reinforces that marriage is in view: the exiting of one marriage and the entering into of another. One wife is sent away, another wife is taken.

We finally arrive at the crux of the debate: the meaning of μὴ ἐπὶ πορνείᾳ. Stanley Hauerwas provides some initial caution,

> Questions about marriage that begin with trying to specify what "except for unchastity" might mean are too often Pharisaic attempts to separate marriage from its purpose given in creation for the up-building of God's people.[41]

However, in this thesis' determination of the 'exception clause', it can be seen that any attempt, Pharisaic or not, to practise it without showing mercy would certainly separate marriage from its purpose given in Creation.[42] Instead of up-building God's people, a terrible judgement with deadly consequences descends on rebellious people.

Denying that the 'exception clause' provides a real exception defeats Matthew's purpose in writing it. The clause appears in all early manuscripts and efforts to show that μὴ ἐπὶ means "not even for"[43] are unconvincing,[44] for the Greek syntax does not support it.[45] Hagner contends that the μὴ ("not") would need to have been μηδ(έ) ("not even"), and the preteritive meaning is much less natural for παρεκτός in Matthew 5:32.[46]

Powers has an alternate understanding of μὴ ἐπὶ: "Jesus makes an exception in respect of the case where the wife was actually guilty of *porneia*, for the Law of Moses allowed divorce in that case."[47] He argues that μὴ ordinarily means "not" and is never translated "except" in the 1039 New Testament occurrences – except in Matthew 19:9.[48]

---

[41] S. Hauerwas, *Matthew*, BTCB (Ada: Baker, 2007), 305.

[42] God has at times shown "no mercy" (Hos 1:6, 8; 2:4; Zech 1:12), and has sometimes demanded it of Israel in the Law (cf. Deut 7:2), but he certainly does not favour divorce (cf. Mal 2:14-16).

[43] Bruce Vawter followed Augustine in viewing 'except' as preteritive so that the clause read: "setting aside the matter of *porneia* [that is not discussed here]." This meant that the entire proposition was negated. B. Vawter, "Divorce Clauses in Matthew 5:32 and 19:9," *CBQ* 16, no. 2 (1954): 155-67. Vawter later admitted his error. "Divorce and the New Testament," *CBQ* 39, no. 4 (1977): 528-42.

[44] Loader, *Sexuality: Key Texts*, 91.

[45] Janzen, "Porneia," 67.

[46] Hagner, *Matthew 1-13*, 124.

[47] B. W. Powers and J. Wade, *Divorce: The Bible and the Law* (Sydney: AFES, 1978), 17. Powers, *Marriage and Divorce*, 170.

[48] *Divorce and Remarriage: The Bible's Law and Grace Approach* (Preston: Mosaic, 2012), 100.

Powers notes that the Greek text published by Erasmus inserted εἰ in front of μὴ to turn the "not" into "except," but the original manuscripts unanimously have only μὴ ἐπὶ πορνείᾳ.[49] However, Powers does not convincingly account for the parallel παρεκτὸς ("except for")[50] of Matthew 5:32 (there he does call it an "exception"[51] and rightly contends that πορνεία cannot be limited to "adultery"[52]).

Furthermore, Powers' interpretation still suffers a confusion of capital and non-capital crimes, for "if the wife has *put herself* into the category of 'adulteress' by committing 'some indecency' [cf. Deut 24:1],"[53] then the husband might avoid committing adultery in divorcing but only after his wife has been subjected to the law code pertaining to her category of crime, that is, Deuteronomy 22:22. Evading the force of Matthew 5:28 because the sexual offence stops short of "actual intercourse"[54] overlooks the capital extent of the Seventh and Tenth Commandments that Jesus expounds on, and ignores the hellish force of the subsequent two verses. Powers does include adultery, exhibitionism, lesbianism, etc. under the "vague" term "indecency,"[55] but his use of Matthew 5:28 appears to treat the offence there as lesser, and he drastically alters the focus by switching the subject from a lustful man to an indecent woman.

---

[49] Ibid., 100-01.

[50] Collins treats them synonymously, noting that παρεκτὸς ("except") is hapax in Matt 5:32 (elsewhere only in Acts 26:29 and 2 Cor 11:28), while μὴ ἐπὶ ("except") is hapax in Matt 19:9. R. Collins, *Divorce in the New Testament* (Collegeville: Liturgical, 1992), 187-88.

[51] Powers, *Divorce and Remarriage*, 55-56. Powers nonetheless highlights the injustice of any divorce that stigmatises a woman as an adulteress if she has not committed adultery herself, but Deut 24:1-4 offers no guarantee that a husband's judgement of his wife is just.

[52] *Marriage and Divorce*, 173.

[53] Ibid., 170.

[54] Ibid., 166.

[55] Ibid.

Definition of Porneia (Πορνεία)

The Protestant majority view's meaning of *porneia* (πορνεία) accords with BDAG's broad definition:

> **πορνεία** *prostitution, unchastity, fornication,* of every kind of unlawful sexual intercourse
> 1. Literal Rom 1:29; 1 Cor 5:1a, b; 6:13 etc.
> 2. Figurative, in accordance with an OT symbol of apostasy from God, of idolatry; from the time of Hosea the relationship between God and his people was regarded as a marriage bond.[56]

The meaning here is not limited to one kind of sexual offence, such as pre-marital or incestuous sex. It must be highlighted that BDAG's definition centres on sexual *intercourse*, not merely sexual indecency or nudity, and this covers every kind that is *unlawful*. The unlawful activity includes adultery, fornication, homosexual practice, bestiality, incest, etc.[57]

However, the majority view commonly settles on "adultery" as a short-hand summary to describe the main form that would usually violate a marriage, although for some, this is the only form that allows for divorce and remarriage. For the literal meaning, BDAG differentiates πορνεία (*porneia*, "sexual immorality") from μοιχεία (*moicheia*, "adultery") in Matthew 15:19 and Mark 7:21, but aligns the two more closely in Matthew 5:32 and 19:9, where πορνεία pertains to the "sexual unfaithfulness of a married woman."[58] This is without fully equating *porneia* with *moicheia*, for *porneia* reflects a wider taxonomic category and *moicheia* is one sub-type of it along with the other sexual acts prohibited in the Torah.[59]

In pointing to Hosea's marriage, BDAG's meaning of "apostasy" should be kept close to the physical meaning concerning acts of unlawful sexual intercourse, for an absolute "literal" and "figurative" categorisation does not do justice to the complexities, nor does the story of Hosea or the Bible in general have such a clear divide. Those who

---

[56] Danker, Bauer, and Arndt, *BDAG*, 693.

[57] Lev 18:1-23; Deut 22:13-30.

[58] Danker, Bauer, and Arndt, *BDAG*, 693.

[59] Perhaps most sexual unfaithfulness by a married woman would be sexual intercourse with another man. However, questions arise as to whether some sexual acts (e.g. with an animal, or with another woman) could be considered "adultery" or even "sexual intercourse," although by Law they still fall under the broad banner of "sexual immorality."

commit unlawful sexual intercourse can literally commit apostasy by it, as evident in Numbers 25:1-3,

> the people began to whore [ἐκπορνεύω, LXX] with the daughters of Moab... and bowed down to their gods. So Israel yoked himself to Baal.

Conversely, those who commit apostasy can commit sexual immorality simply in their hearts (cf. Matt 5:28). In commenting on Hosea's marriage to a "'wife of whoredom' as a sign of Israel's unfaithfulness and God's unrelenting faithfulness," Hauerwas stresses a crucial connection,

> Jesus, therefore, reminds the Pharisees that marriage is not just about marriage, but it is about the very character of Israel's faithfulness to the one who has been faithful to it. Marriage, and the question of divorce, cannot be abstracted from the purpose of marriage for the people of God.[60]

What is true for the God-Israel union is true for the Hosea-Gomer union and vice versa. Also, what Jesus teaches on marriage, and the question of divorce, which includes what he means by "sexual immorality" and "adultery" in Matthew 19:9, cannot be abstracted from the purpose of marriage for the people of God. A physical or worldly purpose here cannot be divorced from a spiritual purpose, and with such an earthly parallel in Hosea-Gomer, separate special rules for the God-Israel union should not be pleaded.

BDAG's two-fold definition of πορνεία basically coheres with others such as:

> (1) generally, of every kind of extramarital, unlawful, or unnatural sexual intercourse, fornication, sexual immorality, prostitution (1C 5.1); (2) when distinguished from adultery (μοιχεία) in the same context extramarital intercourse, sexual immorality, fornication (MT 15.19); (3) as a synonym for μοιχεία (marital) unfaithfulness, adultery (MT 5.32); (4) metaphorically, as apostasy from God through idolatry (spiritual) immorality, unfaithfulness (RV 19.2).[61]

The third meaning (above) regards πορνεία as a synonym for μοιχεία "(marital) unfaithfulness, adultery," but this is not necessarily the case for the example cited (Matt 5:32) or for Matthew 19:9. Carson comments,

---

[60] Hauerwas, *Matthew*, 303.
[61] Bibleworks, Friberg 22667.

Others hold that *porneia* here means "adultery," no more and no less (e.g., T. V. Fleming, "Christ and Divorce," TS 24 [1963]:109). Certainly the word can include that meaning (Jer 3:8-9 LXX; cf. Sir 23:23). Yet, in Greek the normal word for adultery is *moicheia* (GK 3657). Matthew has already used *moicheia* and *porneia* in the same context (15:19), suggesting some distinction between the word, even if there is considerable overlap.[62]

Kyle Harper also argues against a narrow use of the term, holding that to translate *porneia* as "fornication" (from the Latin *fornicatio*, "derived from *fornix*, literally an arch and figuratively a den of venal sex") is "mere convenience" and "ecclesiastical argot."[63] Even Paul's understanding did not depend on classical Greek heritage, where "*pornos* was the male prostitute" and "*porneia* was the activity of prostituting oneself, not the institution of commercial sex or any class of forbidden acts."[64] This is clearly seen when Paul condemns *porneia* by highlighting an instance totally unrelated to prostitution: "a man has his father's wife" (1 Cor 5:1).[65]

Harper holds that "the Christian understanding of *porneia* was inherited from Hellenistic Judaism... as a calque [loanword] of the Hebrew *zenuth*."[66] The meaning centred on a woman's loss of sexual honour due to extramarital sex: "She became a 'whore'."[67] This meaning later expanded with a metaphorical sense:

> From the time of the prophet Hosea, *zenuth* came to stand as a powerful metaphor for idolatry. Israel's religious promiscuity was compared to the sort of infidelity that was most likely to evoke a visceral reaction in a patriarchal society: feminine unchastity. The rhetoric was jarring, and was meant to be so. The prophets accused Israel of being a 'spiritual slut'.[68]

Harper further believes that the "decisive expansion" of *porneia* "to include male sexual error, occurred extrabiblically,"[69] although the New

---

[62] Carson, "Matthew," 468.

[63] Harper, *Shame*, 88.

[64] Ibid.

[65] This might offer another distinction between πορνεία (broadly: illicit sex; but here narrowly: incest – unlawful sexual intercourse with a close relative) and μοιχεία (adultery; which could be taken narrowly as unlawful sexual intercourse of a woman with *an unrelated man*).

[66] Harper, *Shame*, 88.

[67] Ibid.

[68] Ibid., 88-89.

[69] Ibid., 89.

Testament is replete with condemnation of male sexual sin – and idolatry. A general sexual error rather than a gendered error finally came into focus, and

> By the late Second Temple period, the metaphorical meaning had bled back into the literal meaning, so that spiritual whoring and sexual whoring were irreversibly blurred.[70]

So for a first-century audience, Jesus' use of *porneia* (or *zenuth*) would be extremely jarring; it would not merely evoke female condemnation but **general condemnation for physical and spiritual infidelity** committed individually and nationally.

The term *moicheia* itself can be taken more broadly:

> Sex contributes to adultery. In fact, legalists often apply the term "adultery" only to relationships involving extra-marital sex (and for them "sex" means genital intercourse). Marital fidelity, though, or an adulterous betrayal of intimacy involves much more than sex. As Jesus pointed out to his disciples in the first century, adultery can occur apart from sexual contact.[71]

However, even when Jesus speaks on non-contact adultery (Matt 5:27-28), he does not bring a change to the Law, but he raises the commonly-accepted bar to a level already present in the Decalogue. Although Stanley Grenz discerns that the New Testament does not support "a new Christian legalism,"[72] contra Grenz, in Jesus' efforts to uphold the Law in every detail, it is incorrect that an "antilegalism …is evidenced in Jesus' refusal to become involved in the legalistic debate of his opponents"[73] or "evidenced by the absence of the adultery clause in Mark."[74] Jesus does not shy away from a legal debate; he lives by the Law and correctly expounds it.

Sexual immorality is best interpreted as broadly covering serious sexual sin. Loader confirms that *porneia* cannot be limited to incestuous relations, but then sees it primarily as "extra-marital sexual intercourse" (adultery) mandating divorce as per cultural imperative, not per written

---

[70] Ibid.

[71] C. W. Gaddy, *Adultery and Grace: The Ultimate Scandal* (Grand Rapids: Eerdmans, 1996), 25.

[72] S. Grenz, *Sexual Ethics: An Evangelical Perspective* (Louisville: WJK, 1997), 128-29.

[73] Ibid., 129.

[74] This leads Grenz to question the authenticity of the Matthean 'exception clause'. Ibid.

Law.[75] Contra Janzen,[76] Loader also argues that *porneia* excludes premarital intercourse because this situation is addressed in Deuteronomy 22:13-21, where "the penalty for the woman is stoning, not divorce."[77] He holds that this pre-marital offence is "usually identified with the word, μοιχεία, 'adultery',"[78] but this term can really only be applied if the offence is during the betrothal period.

Adultery" could hardly refer to a woman's loss of virginity to an unmarried man prior to betrothal, for which the death penalty did not usually apply (unless this man did not marry her, and the loss was discovered when she married another man). So Loader rejects equating *porneia* with *moicheia* for premarital sex (of a woman with a man who does not marry her) *because this premarital act is a capital offence* under the Law, but he equates *porneia* with *moicheia* for extramarital sex *despite knowing that this act is also a capital offence* under the Law.[79] This avoidance of analysing and applying, at least in theory, the written capital demands of the Law – not a dot of which Jesus has abolished – overlooks that a **"sending away" to death may itself be a biblical "divorce."**

The prescribed penalty for premarital sex of a woman with a man other than her husband is that she be brought out by the elders to the door of her father's house where she will be stoned to death by the men of the city (Deut 22:21). The initial part of this process echoes the language of a traditional divorce proceeding, where the hated woman (Deut 22:13, 16; cf. 24:3) is sent away from her husband, out of his house and back to her father's house (Deut 22:21; cf. 24:1).[80] The moral also parallels that of the divorce legislation in Deuteronomy 24:1-4, that

---

[75] Loader, *Jesus Tradition*, 76.

[76] Janzen correctly critiques the narrow "incestuous marriage" view, but he solves little by claiming only a slightly wider view of πορνεία than μοιχεία (so that πορνεία includes illicit sex of a wife in the betrothal period *and* in the marriage). Janzen, "Porneia," 66-80. The Law provides clear guidelines for sexual immorality within the betrothal period and marriage; and Janzen could well apply the full ramifications of the Law to these – and many other – matters of πορνεία.

[77] Loader, *Jesus Tradition*, 70.

[78] Ibid.

[79] "Strictly speaking the punishment for adultery was death." Ibid., 69. Loader avoids the full implication of this statement by deferring to Instone-Brewer who cites "the Talmudic tradition according to which the death penalty ceased soon after 30 CE." However, this is not clear even from the sources cited. Earlier records also oppose a cessation of the death penalty. E.g. Josephus asserts it, *Ag. Ap.* 2.199, Josephus, *Works*, 806.

[80] "Widows and divorced women still returned to their father's houses" in the Second Temple period. Collins, "Family," 106. Familial love and honour, clan connection, and blood ties were cultural strengths, so it must not be presumed that divorced women were commonly left destitute and had to resort to prostitution.

is, the "outrageous thing," the "whoring," and the "evil" purged from Israel's midst (Deut 22:21) mirrors the defilement, "an abomination before the LORD," and "sin upon the land" (Deut 24:4).

Contra Loader, rather than the penalty for premarital sex simply being "stoning, not divorce," it could be understood as *divorce by stoning*. After all, Deuteronomy 22:13-21 does not narrowly concern the fornication of an unbetrothed young woman (this is legislated on in Deut 22:28-29), but it concerns the sexual immorality (cf. Matt 19:9) of a wife in a consummated marriage who is certainly sent away. If proven guilty of pre-marital sex ("whoring in her father's house," Deut 22:21), instead of being "sent away" out of her husband's house with safe passage to another man's house (he who had fornicated with her), via perhaps a period of refuge in her own father's house, the woman is brought back to her father's house to face the stern consequences.[81] That the elders must "bring out the young woman" assumes that she has remained in her husband's house until convicted, and it is not the husband who ultimately effects the sending away by a private decision (as in Deut 24:1), but the leaders of Israel who corporately act on God's command.

Mosaic stipulations regarding a false accusation also point in the direction of a divinely instituted divorce ("sending away") being in view here. A guilty man is to be whipped and fined, and God's commandment: "she will be his wife. He may not divorce her all his days" (Deut 22:19) contrasts with a guilty woman's divorce and stoning that immediately follows (Deut 22:20-21). Unlike another crime such as adultery that demands equally the death of both the man and the woman, in this case a husband's malevolence or mistake is seen as a lesser offence than *porneia*. From this perspective, **publicly determined** divorce for *porneia* (judged in a court) is the only divorce that is *prescribed* in the Old Testament, and a major rethink is in order for understanding the **private judgements** of finding "no favour," "a matter of indecency," and the hatred of a wife for lesser offences as *described* in Deuteronomy 24:1-4.[82]

---

[81] The legislation of Deut 22:13-21 seems to assume that the fornicating man cannot be found. Deut 22:22 commands that both the man and the woman who are found committing adultery must be executed.

[82] Richards touches on this, "The fascinating thing here is that the divorce action is taken by the couple with no appeal to an outside tribunal in spite of the fact that a system of courts did exist in Old Testament times." Richards, "Divorce and Remarriage: Variety of Circumstances," 225. One amendment is necessary, for the divorce action here is taken *by the man*, not "the couple." Nonetheless, this private action should alert us to a marked difference between "a matter of indecency" and a capital matter of "sexual immorality."

It is also problematic to use Deuteronomy 24:1-4 to create categories of legitimate and illegitimate divorce. The Protestant majority view depends on this distinction, which Instone-Brewer is at pains to uphold by regularly inserting the word "invalidly" prior to the verb "divorce" in his Gospel texts.[83] This removes the absolute sense of the text and opens the door to multiple other "valid" divorce grounds that are often based on highly subjective exceptions of sexual and non-sexual grounds. It obscures the clear-cut division in the Law between heinous sexual (capital) crimes and other lesser (non-capital) offences – one that is literally a matter of life or death for the accused – where by the Law a capital charge must be objectively established and publicly proven by witnesses and evidence, not subjectively purported and privately judged.

By limiting *porneia* to mean sexual intercourse during betrothal or with someone other than the wife's husband, Janzen rightly avoids the danger of endorsing a multiplicity of other grounds, both sexual and non-sexual.[84] However, his focus on a man's right to divorce without repayment of the dowry, which appears traditionally to be the main concern in judging between a valid or invalid divorce in Israel, overlooks or downplays the much greater concern that Janzen highlights for all ANE cultures: the wife faces a capital offence charge. If proven guilty and the Law is applied in full, then of course there will be no dowry-return, for the wife will be sent away to be executed.

If, however, *porneia* is equated with "a matter of indecency" that entails a lesser offence than adultery, or an offence of adultery that no longer attracts the death penalty of Deuteronomy 22:22, then a very different and less confronting message is taught, one at odds with the Law as originally understood. Instone-Brewer observes,

> A stipulation about **cleanliness in Deuteronomy 24:1** does not have any parallel in the ancient Near East. The teaching of Deuteronomy 24:1-4 has traditionally been understood to mean that one could divorce a wife for adultery. However, it is unlikely that this passage originally referred to adultery because the punishment for adultery was death.[85]

---

[83] Instone-Brewer, *Social and Literary Context*, 150-52. It is also dubious that Deut 24:1-4 recognises "Justifiable and Unjustifiable Divorces" per Heth, "Remarriage for Adultery or Desertion," 63-64.

[84] Janzen, "Porneia," 66-80.

[85] Instone-Brewer, *Social and Literary Context*, 10. (Bold original.)

Given that the stipulation of *'erwat dabar* in Deuteronomy 24:1 had no contemporary parallel, then it is possible that "this strange phrase"[86] covers matters that were not normally seen as grounds for divorce in any other ANE culture. That *'erwat dabar* was "later interpreted as 'adultery'"[87] betrays the original meaning – clearly not "adultery," which had parallels in every ANE culture![88] Not only would divorce for adultery contradict every other ANE law code of the time, but it would contradict the clear legal demands for adultery within Israel's own Law.

For adultery to be included in (or engulf) the meaning of *'erwat dabar* would also create confusion in the Torah over what are matters of cleanliness and what are capital matters. If, by Instone-Brewer's reckoning, we are dealing with a "stipulation about cleanliness in Deuteronomy 24:1" where no other ANE law has any such concern, then surely there must be a clear delineation between this matter, that results in divorce, and more serious matters that demand death, in this and every neighbouring society. Cleanliness may be next to godliness,[89] but uncleanness cannot be avoided by Israel at all times – nor should it always be, else there would be no emission of semen, no menstruation, no sexual intercourse and no children (cf. Lev 15).

Sexual reproductive processes, though "unclean," are not criminal, and ***"any matter of nakedness" oriented around producing the next generation of Israelites cannot automatically be deemed valid grounds for divorce!*** On the other hand, adultery is an "evil" (Deut 22:22), as is the defilement and the abomination of Deuteronomy 24:4, that should certainly be avoided. So, whatever *'erwat dabar* refers to in Deuteronomy 24:1, it must be of a completely different order to that of an evil offence like adultery.

Furthermore, Scripture does not actually stipulate that *'erwat dabar* refers to an "uncleanness" at all. The determination of "a matter of indecency" (*'erwat dabar*) in Deuteronomy 24:1 is based only on one man's judgement ("in his eyes," "he has found," Deut 24:1) that might be totally selfish and wrong. It is not specified that this is an uncleanness found by God (i.e. *in Yahweh's eyes* or *that Yahweh has found*) that might warrant divorce or bring God displeasure, that Yahweh might turn away from Israel (cf. Deut 23:14).

---

[86] Ibid.

[87] Ibid.

[88] "All of the ancient Near Eastern law codes that have rulings about adultery prescribe capital punishment. E.g. Laws of Eshnunna #28; Code of Hammurabi #129; Middle Assyrian laws #13-14; Hittite laws #189-91, 195." Ibid., 9.

[89] Or more precisely, according to Deut 23:14, if Israel's camp stays clean, God will stay next to them!

The whole tenor of Deuteronomy 24:1-4 is that God will turn away from Israel if an abomination is committed by "a man." It completely lacks God's judgement on a woman for "any matter of indecency" found in her by "a man." Therefore, the clear delineation that must be upheld need not be one of cleanliness versus capital matters, as important as this is, but purely between non-capital and capital offences. Not only this, but if the "matter of indecency" of Deuteronomy 24:1 was reckoned out of selfishness, then from a Matthean perspective Jesus cannot be affirming this, for he demands self-denial (Matt 16:24). It would also be absurd for a trivial selfish matter to negate a charge of adultery (Matt 19:9); the freedom granted for divorce and remarriage would effectively legitimise divorce for "any *selfish* cause" (cf. Matt 19:3).

When Instone-Brewer states that "The teaching of Deuteronomy 24:1-4 has traditionally been understood to mean that one could divorce a wife for adultery"[90] it is worth considering the age of this tradition. Shammai, to whom this tradition is credited, is regarded as a Jewish elder of the first century (c.50BCE to c.30CE), a contemporary of another more liberal Jewish elder Hillel (c.110BCE to c.10CE). Moses, credited with authoring Deuteronomy 24:1-4,[91] lived in the second millenium BCE, and even by Josianic (eighth century BCE) or Exilic (sixth century BCE) dating, his legislation was written many centuries before Shammai was even heard of. We cannot be sure Shammai was even a Pharisee, or founded a school, for his opinion was only recorded in the rabbinic literature centuries after his purported lifetime.[92] In Jesus' day, Shammai's tradition was very new, or non-existent.

Jesus is scathing about novel and faulty interpretations of Scripture. When challenged by Jewish leaders, he accuses them of breaking the "commandment of God" in favour of teaching human traditions (Matt 15:1-9). Elsewhere, Jesus warns his disciples to beware of "false prophets" (Matt 7:15), "men" (Matt 10:17), and the "leaven" or "teaching of the Pharisees and Sadducees" (Matt 16:6, 11-12). In general, it would be wise to beware "the tradition of the elders" (Matt 15:2), including that attributed to Shammai, and "the commandments of men" (Matt 15:9), including the reformulated "command" of Matthew 19:7.

---

[90] Instone-Brewer, *Social and Literary Context*, 10.

[91] Moses is credited by the Pharisees in Matt 19:7, "Why then did Moses command"; by Jesus in Matt 19:8, "Moses allowed you"; and is long recognised by Christianity and Judaism.

[92] Meier, *Marginal Jew*, 3, 318-19. Also *Marginal Jew*, 4, 95.

On the matter of divorce, Jesus will immediately take his questioners back to the original meaning of marriage (Matt 19:4-6) as found in Genesis. In keeping with this, a return to the original meaning of Deuteronomy 24:1-4 is profitable. Instone-Brewer signalled this approach, stating that it was "unlikely that this passage originally referred to adultery."[93] For as Instone-Brewer and many others know, and what the Pharisees and Jesus' disciples would no doubt have known, according to the original commandments that God gave to Moses, "the punishment for adultery was death."[94] *Fifty years of possible Shammaite tradition is no reason to abolish up to fifteen hundred years of Scripture, thousands of years of a Creation "one flesh" marriage mandate (Matt 19:4; Gen 2:24), or one marriage at any time.*

Not only is undue weight often given to new tradition, but the meaning of *'erwat dabar* in Deuteronomy 24:1 has regularly been confused with extremely serious – and originally capital – offences, and Instone-Brewer only adds to this confusion in his attempt to explain the Hebrew text:

> The word עֶרְוָה (*'erwah*) occurs frequently and usually includes the connotation of sexual impropriety or sinfulness, but it is certainly not restricted to adultery.[95]

Unfortunately such a statement gives the impression that *'erwah* has a wide semantic range that includes sexual impropriety, sinfulness and adultery, all of which may be read into the *'erwat dabar* of Deuteronomy 24:1. This incredibly glosses over the different contexts in which *'erwah* is found in the Old Testament (to be analysed below) and the fact that "the connotation of sexual impropriety or sinfulness" occurs frequently and usually when the *'erwah* is *unlawfully uncovered* by another party. In the Torah, this is always by a relative and is always a capital offence! A closer study of *'erwat dabar*, and in particular the word *'erwah*, is therefore warranted.

---

[93] France also writes concerning *'erwat dabar* (Deut 24:1), "In the original context the phrase *cannot have meant simply adultery,* since the penalty for that was death, not divorce." (Italics added.) France, *Matthew*, 207. Others, such as Craigie, support this, "It is clear that the meaning [of *'erwat dabar*] *cannot be 'adultery'*, for adultery was punishable by death (22:22)." (Italics added.) Craigie, *Deuteronomy*, 305.

[94] Instone-Brewer, *Social and Literary Context*, 10. Some rituals might change (e.g. Exod 12:8-9; cf. Deut 16:7), but it is unlikely that the gravity of and penalties for sexual offences would change, not least within the same book of Law (e.g. Deut 22:22; cf. 24:1).

[95] Ibid.

Definition of 'Erwah (עֶרְוָה)

The Hebrew noun *'erwah* (עֶרְוָה) itself

> conveys the general sense of being uncovered and exposed
> ...[it is] used to describe *nakedness* in the sense of exposed
> genitals (Gen. 9:22-23); unprotected land (Gen. 42:9),
> indecent activity (Deut. 24:1), and the shame associated with
> covenant infidelity (Deut. 28:48; Mic. 1:11).[96]

The Greek adjective γυμνός has a similar semantic range that is not
essentially negative or immoral: in general it means to be "naked,
without clothes" (from it we derive the term "gymnasium"); in Scripture
it can be used literally e.g. "I was naked and you clothed me" (Matt
25:36); and more figuratively for spiritual poverty (Rev 3:17) or being
exposed before God's judgement (Rev 16:15, cf. Adam and Eve's
shame in knowing they were literally naked after committing a deadly
disobedient act, Gen 2:16-17; 3:7-11).[97]

The standard Hebrew-English Lexicon, HALOT defines *'erwah*
(עֶרְוָה) as "nakedness,"[98] and *dabar* (דָּבָר) as "word," "matter," or
"something."[99] Taken together, *'erwat dabar* is literally "a matter of
nakedness" and in Deuteronomy 24:1 is typically understood
negatively, "what is deprecatory (to a woman),"[100] and similarly in
Deuteronomy 23:15, "what is unseemly, unbecoming"[101] or "anything
indecent."[102] On the other hand, a matter of nakedness of a man with his
wife is not necessarily lawful grounds for divorce, but can be fertile

---

[96] Mounce, *Expository Dictionary*, 462.

[97] Ibid., 462-63. Also BDAG: γυμνός "1. naked, stripped, bare... 2. without an outer
garment, without which a decent person did not appear in public... 3. poorly dressed... 4.
uncovered, bare...; and γυμνότης "1. nakedness... αἰσχύνη τῆς γ disgraceful nakedness... Rv
3:18. – 2. destitution, lack of sufficient clothing... Ro 8:35; 2 Cor 11:27.*" Danker, Bauer,
and Arndt, BDAG, 167-68. "Nakedness" in Rev 3:18 only has a disgraceful sense when
combined with αἰσχύνη ("shame") as BDAG notes; and the γυμνός (being "naked") here is
not even realised (Rev 3:17). In contrast, the γυμνὸς περιπατῇ ("going about naked") in Rev
16:15 is conscious and it is τὴν ἀσχημοσύνην αὐτοῦ – the wilful shameful lifestyle or possibly
"disgraceful deed" (Greek feminine singular) probably with others who live (walk) the same
way (hence the suffix -σύνη cf. Rom 1:27) that is exposed, and not simply "private parts"
(Greek plural) or being γυμνός (Greek masculine) that might be seen.

[98] L. Koehler, W. Baumgartner, and J. Stamm, *The Hebrew and Aramaic Lexicon of the
Old Testament*, vol. 2 (Leiden: Brill, 1994), 882.

[99] *The Hebrew and Aramaic Lexicon of the Old Testament*, vol. 1 (Leiden: Brill, 1994),
211.

[100] *HALOT*, 2, 882. Also, "עֶרְוַת דָּבָר *nakedness of a thing*, i.e. prob. *indecency*, improper
behaviour" Bibleworks, BDB 7411.

[101] Koehler, Baumgartner, and Stamm, *HALOT*, 2, 882.

[102] *HALOT*, 1, 211.

grounds for joyful intimacy! Context is everything: one matter of nakedness may bring "no favour" and be shameful in a man's eyes (Deut 24:1); another matter of nakedness can be "very good" (Gen 1:31) and without shame ("the man and his wife were both naked and were not ashamed," Gen 2:25); yet another matter of nakedness can be quite neutral ("Naked I came from my mother's womb, and naked shall I return," Job 1:21). "Nakedness" per se is not an offence to God.

Even amongst the stern judgements of Leviticus, where the term "naked" or "nakedness" is used thirty-two times,[103] **nakedness itself is not condemned but only illicit sexual relationships**. For example, regarding the command, "You shall not uncover the nakedness of your sister" (Lev 18:9), a sister's nakedness is not in itself immoral (for private bathing, marital sex, etc.), but the action of her brother *uncovering* her nakedness (implicitly for sex) is an offence. Similarly, the pure nakedness of Adam and Eve did not cause sin or offence to God, but the covering of nakedness was required *after sin and guilt* (Gen 3:7-11); Noah's nakedness itself was not a problem – nor is his drunkenness judged within the narrative – but a son *seeing his nakedness, telling others* and *not covering it* brought condemnation (Gen 9:22-27).[104]

So "a matter of nakedness," despite any negative cultural connotation (from Deut 24:1), need not entail a marriage-breaking offence, nor even be offensive to God; a man might simply deem something offensive (shameful or embarrassing) about his wife that negates all that was originally favourable about her ("then she finds no favour in his eyes") and thus he divorces his wife on these grounds. "She finds no favour in his eyes" (Deut 24:1) can be contrasted with "Noah found favour in the eyes of the LORD" (Gen 6:6): a man with fallible judgement rejects his wife over *a matter of indecency* that he finds; God in his infallible judgement favours a man even against *a matter of great evil* that he saw:

> the wickedness of man was great in the earth, and that every intention of the thoughts of this heart was only evil continually (Gen 6:5).

Far beyond any "indecency," a matter of "evil" brings death and destruction: "I will blot out man…" (Gen 6:7).

---

[103] 22 times in Lev 18 alone; cf. OT total: 54 times.

[104] Whereas there would be no shame in Noah's wife privately seeing him naked (especially as she bore to him this son in question, plus two others), she might object to his drunkenness.

Crucial Differences in Offences

As the capital punishment legislated for uncovering the nakedness of a relative is not applied in Deuteronomy 24:1-4, more trivial matters are in view.[105] The fact that the offence is found *merely in a man's eyes* (Deut 24:1) also demonstrates that it cannot be a capital offence, such as adultery, which is *an evil in God's eyes* (cf. Ps 51:4). The husband does not require witnesses to prove "a matter of indecency," in contrast to the explicit legislation of Deuteronomy 19:15 that a single witness is insufficient and the evidence of multiple witnesses is required for any offence against God. If the matter was on par with adultery, then sending a wife away with the freedom to remarry is not called for, but the purging of evil is – which includes the execution of false witnesses in a capital case (Deut 19:19-20).[106]

This does not mean that any matters in Deuteronomy 24:1 cannot be serious, but none demand death as adultery does.

> Though most translators and commentators agree that the phrase refers to sexually indecent behaviour, it is clear that it does not mean adultery, because the biblical punishment for adultery is execution.[107]

Duane Christensen suggests the phrase is analogous to "caught with one's pants down," where the "'naked thing' here is essentially the woman's genitals."[108] He links this "pudenda exposed" interpretation with only one other Scripture, Lamentations 1:8.[109] Yet there it refers to Babylon's conquest of Jerusalem, a city despised because all have "seen [רָאָה] her nakedness [עֶרְוָה]," whereas in Deuteronomy 24:1 there is no mention of anyone having seen the woman's nakedness. The matter in Lamentations 1:8 references a publicly known historical occasion, likely recorded by a godly prophet such as Jeremiah (cf. 2 Chr 35:25), but the matter in Deuteronomy 24:1 references a private, subjective and

---

[105] Although contemporary practice might also include capital matters while neglecting capital legislation.

[106] The maximum penalty is assumed to be deserved, but this does not mean it is always enforced; cf. David's vow, "As the Lord lives, the man who has done this deserves to die" (2 Sam 12:5), and the prophetic response concerning his adultery and murder, "You are the man!" (2 Sam 12:7) but "You shall not die" (2 Sam 12:13). Yet in cases where it is not enforced, attention should be given as to whether God simply overlooks the sin, or is the huge debt (to God) for this evil somehow paid by someone else. The case of Joseph resolving to quietly divorce Mary, ostensibly for adultery, is considered in the next section.

[107] D. Christensen, *Deuteronomy 21:10-34:12*, 6 B WBC (Nashville: Thomas Nelson, 2002), 566.

[108] Ibid.

[109] Ibid., 566-67.

likely ungodly opinion by a hard-hearted man. Jerusalem's exposed grievous sin (חֵטְא חָטְאָה, Lam 1:8) better connects with the capital matters concerning the uncovering of nakedness (cf. Lev 18; Deut 22), along with the idolatry and adultery that Jeremiah condemns Jerusalem for (cf. Jer 5:7-8).

When Jesus speaks on divorce, Deuteronomy 24:1 quickly drops from view because his grounds of "sexual immorality" (Matt 19:9) carries an Old Testament legal demand of capital punishment.[110] In contrast, Nolland believes the relationship to Deuteronomy 24:1 only "drops from sight" because the wording of the Matthew 19:9 'exception clause' is μὴ ἐπὶ πορνείᾳ ("except for sexual impurity") instead of παρεκτὸς λόγου πορνείας in Matthew 5:32 ("except [in relation to] a matter of sexual impurity"), hence "Matthew can suppress the language link with Dt. 24:1, but the very idea of an exception is still a trace of that link."[111] Peterson suggests that the link with Deuteronomy 24:1 may be somewhat suppressed in Matthew 5:31 because "the [divorce certificate] allusion is so vague."[112] Rather than "vague" it might be considered a blatant capital matter if one word (λόγος) concerning sexual immorality (πορνεία) was ever written as grounds on a wife's divorce certificate!

Instone-Brewer, however, confidently reads 'erwat dabar into Matthew 5:32, stating as "fact that porneia is being used to allude to the OT phrase 'indecent matter' (Deut. 24:1)."[113] He then reads 'erwat dabar into Matthew 19:9 – rather than seeing Matthew suppressing this idea as per Nolland – and further reads 'erwat dabar into Mark 10:11 (and assumes it for Luke 16:18). To bolster his case, he asserts that the question "Is it lawful for a man to divorce his wife?" (Mark 10:2) would make no sense without mentally adding "for any matter."[114]

> If the clause ['for any matter'] has been omitted, most intelligent Jews of the day would have mentally added it. …the same is true of the exception clause ['except for sexual immorality'], which is also found only in Matthew.[115]

---

[110] Luz sees that a debate over Deut 24:1-4 quickly disappears, but overlooks the capital sense of porneia. Luz, Matthew 8-20, 488-90.

[111] Nolland, Matthew, 775.

[112] D. Peterson, "Divorce and Remarriage in the New Testament," SMR 115 (1983): 10.

[113] Instone-Brewer, Social and Literary Context, 279. Also stated rather than proven, "The Hebrew for 'unchastity' is in fact identical to 'indecency'." Blomberg, "Exegesis," 164.

[114] Instone-Brewer, Social and Literary Context, 135.

[115] Ibid., 153.

This all reads far too much into Scripture. It ignores the different Gospel purposes, casts aspersions on the intelligence of those who would not follow suit, and his critical phrase *'erwat dabar* is a poor substitute – textually and theologically – for *porneia* in Matthew, Mark and Luke.

Textually, the only occurrence of *'erwat dabar* outside of Deuteronomy 24:1 is in Deuteronomy 23:14 where, as Witherington rightly assesses, "it refers to uncovered excrement and could not possibly be translated λόγου πορνείας which refers to sexual sin."[116] The case of "nocturnal emission" (Deut 23:10-12), which immediately precedes the "matter of indecency" involving excrement (Deut 23:13-15), could more easily be construed as sexual, although even it is not condemned as a matter of sexual immorality (*porneia*), but is simply labelled "unclean" as is a woman's "menstrual uncleanness" in Leviticus 18:19. Peter Craigie further supports a non-sexual meaning in Deuteronomy 23:10-12 by suggesting the nocturnal emission is not semen but urine, especially as the Hebrew here has no explicit mention of semen as found in Leviticus 15:16 (שִׁכְבָה "emission" of זֶרַע "semen"; cf. LXX σπέρμα "seed").[117] This provides a more natural parallel to the concern about human excrement in Deuteronomy 23:13-15.

Additionally, Craigie takes the "evil" of Deuteronomy 23:9 as "anything *unclean*... the adjective *ra'*, depending on its context, may mean 'bad, unpleasant, evil, unclean, etc.'," where the context indicates "the sense is unclean, both hygienically and ritually."[118] However, a man is not "evil" simply due to "what happens [naturally] at night" (Deut 23:10); the "evil" of Deuteronomy 23:9 is more likely to serve as a contrast to the "anything indecent" of Deuteronomy 23:14 and 24:1. "Every evil thing" (Deut 23:9) covers all the evil matters described prior and they are *all capital offences*. Such evil must be purged from Israel, including false prophecy (Deut 13:5); idolatry (Deut 17:2-7); disobeying the verdict of a priest, say in a homicide case (Deut 17:8-12); false witness (Deut 19:18-20); stubborn rebellion of a son (Deut 21:18-21); whoring, no evidence of virginity on marriage, fornication (Deut 22:21);[119] adultery (Deut 22:22); violation of a betrothed virgin (Deut 22:23-24); and rape (Deut 22:25).

The two camp stipulations concerning normal bodily excretions are additional matters of cleanliness that are not labelled "evil," nor are

---

[116] Witherington III, "Exception or Exceptional," 572.
[117] Craigie, *Deuteronomy*, 299.
[118] Ibid.
[119] "Such a law was repeated in Qumran texts and in Josephus." (11QTemple LXV, 7-15; Josephus *Ant.* 246-248.) Collins, "Family," 206.

individual offenders liable to the death penalty. However, it certainly could be considered "evil" for any "man" (Deut 23:10; 24:1) to disobey either law code as a whole, and the nation as a whole would attract deadly judgement, where God forsakes them and no longer delivers them from their enemies (Deut 23:14, an "abomination" will be committed; cf. Deut 24:4). "Evil" again is legislated against with one more miscellaneous law regarding kidnap and enslavement (Deut 24:7), where again this is a capital offence.[120] "Evil" then has five more occurrences in Deuteronomy, each time with a more general, but also deadly, sense (Deut 28:20; 30:15; 31:18; 31:29 (2x)).

Concerning another matter of uncleanliness just mentioned, the term "nakedness" (*'erwah*, not *'erwat dabar*) does appear in Leviticus 18:19, although any sexual immorality or shame *is not found in a woman's "nakedness,"* but only *in a man's action* (the husband's, else it is also adultery) of approaching her for sex – *to uncover her "nakedness"* – during menstruation. At this natural time of a woman's normal bodily discharge (not an "indecent" or "disgraceful" act at all), it is the wilful act by a man that is strongly condemned. Even when consensual, "both of them shall be cut off from among their people" (cf. Lev 20:18). In contrast, the act in Leviticus 15:24 is accidental and is judged much more leniently: "if any man lies with her and her menstrual impurity comes upon him, he shall be unclean for seven days,"[121] just as the woman shall be unclean for seven days whenever she menstruates (Lev 15:19). Obviously, nakedness is a part of this act, but the language of "uncovering nakedness" is completely absent. Instead in Leviticus 15:24, שָׁכַב יִשְׁכַּב (MT) and κοίτῃ τις κοιμηθῇ (LXX) are used: terminology associated with *a man lying down with his wife* (Hebrew) and *sleeping in a (marriage) bed* (Greek) – though sexual intercourse is of course meant.[122] No evil or sexual immorality is in view, only a matter of inadvertent ritual impurity.

---

[120] Cf. *Ant.* 4.271. Josephus, *Works*, 121.

[121] Kiuchi's translation makes the accidental nature clearer: "And if by any chance any man lies with her..." (Lev 15:24). The same construction (אם followed by an infinitive absolute and then a verb) is used in the same way in Lev 13:7, "If by any chance the eruption spreads in the skin..." (also in verses 12, 22, 27). Kiuchi, *Leviticus*, 221-24, 69-72. The spreading of a leprous disease can hardly be due to the man's wilful action. Kiuchi adds that from the context of Lev 13:7 "it probably conveys the notion of least possibility," which likely applies also to the situation of Lev 15:24.

[122] "The protasis means 'but if someone should actually lie with her'; what is meant is 'have sexual intercourse with her'. The cognate structure κοίτῃ κοιμηθῇ represents the Hebrew cognate free infinitive plus verb, which is used to put particular stress on the verbal idea... hence the rendering 'should actually lie with her'." J. Wevers, *Notes on the Greek Text of Leviticus*, Septuagint and Cognate Studies (Atlanta: Scholars, 1997), 234. This stress

Nonetheless, in stark contrast to the vague matter in Deuteronomy 24:1, certain illicit sexual actions involving nakedness are clearly proscribed in the Hebrew Bible, being of the same degree as other capital offences. For example, the offence of Leviticus 18:19 co-occurs with other deadly sins in Ezekiel:

> [a righteous man] does not defile his neighbour's wife [commit adultery] or approach a woman in her time of menstrual impurity (Ezek 18:6);
> In you men uncover their father's nakedness; in you they violate women who are unclean in their menstrual impurity (Ezek 22:10).[123]

Surrounding verses include offences of murder, violence and idolatry, where anyone who has "done all these abominations; he shall surely die" (Ezek 18:13) and be destroyed by God as in a furnace (Ezek 22:17-22).

Leviticus 18:19 is immediately followed by the same offence co-occurring in Ezekiel 18:6, "And you shall not lie sexually with your neighbour's wife [commit adultery], and so make yourself unclean with her" (Lev 18:20). Uncleanness when connected with evil or sexual immorality (here the defilement of a neighbour's wife) is of a totally different order to a matter of impurity (such as the natural bodily discharges of Leviticus 15:1-30) when there is no associated evil or sexual immorality. The more trivial matters, whether they involve nakedness or not, *only become capital matters of defilement* when commandments such as the cleansing laws are disobeyed, as God warns in Leviticus 15:31.

This may help explain why the "defiled" wife in Deuteronomy 24:1-4, divorced on grounds that are vague and possibly not even her fault, and remarried, is not condemned to death in this passage. Indeed, according to Jesus, the condemnation falls on the original husband (cf. "he makes her commit adultery," Matt 5:32a) and on the subsequent husband (cf. "whoever marries a divorced woman commits adultery," Matt 5:32b). By the time Matthew reaches Jesus' second teaching on divorce, Deuteronomy 24:1-4 has already been dealt a comprehensive blow from the perspective of every man involved! The woman's defilement is tolerated in a sense, for she appears powerless and perhaps

---

also supports the "notion of least possibility" (cf. previous note) with its sense of surprise or alarm.

[123] Uncovering a "father's nakedness" may refer to incest (a son violating his father's wife) and/or sodomy. Again, menstruation itself is not a deadly sin, but violating women during this time is.

innocent in a passage that describes what is routinely practised by the culture despite God's command *for a man* to "hold fast to his wife" (Gen 1:24), although corporately the "hardness of heart" (cf. Matt 19:8) will not be without consequence. What will not be tolerated, however, is the breaking of the sole commandment that Deuteronomy 24:1-4 does entail. If the woman's original husband takes her to be his wife again, then the matter of defilement escalates to "an abomination before the LORD" (Deut 24:4).

Deuteronomy 24:1-4 does, therefore, finally legislate on a grievous matter of sexual immorality that would bring "sin upon the land" and jeopardise Israel's very existence, but in describing the vague grounds for the divorce of a woman, and even her defilement, the passage attributes no charge of πορνεία to the woman. Furthermore, the *'erwat dabar* of Deuteronomy 24:1 has zero textual connection with the πορνεία of Matthew 5:32 and 19:9. The Septuagint translates *'erwat dabar* as ἄσχημον πρᾶγμα, not λόγου πορνείας.[124] There is no linguistic resemblance, not even one word (λόγος), which alone should signal alarm about Instone-Brewer's bold claims of allusions and mental additions.

The 'exception clause' in Matthew 5:32 does have a tenuous connection with Deuteronomy 24:1 via the term λόγος (*logos*), that in Matthew is typical of an authoritative "word" or "saying" from Jesus. However (again), λόγος does not appear in the Septuagint of Deuteronomy 24:1, but πρᾶγμα ("matter," also "word"). So rather than parallel terminology, it could well be that Jesus employs λόγος πορνείας "a matter of sexual immorality" (Matt 5:32) in *direct contrast to* ἄσχημον πρᾶγμα "a matter of indecency" (Deut 24:1), such that Jesus' teaching clearly should not be identified with Pharisaic thinking.[125] This is totally contrary to Hays' assertion:

> the unidiomatic Greek of 5:32 is a very literal rendering of the Hebrew of Deuteronomy 24:1 (*'erwat dabar*, "a thing of indecency"), and thus it seems even more clearly than 19:9 to

---

[124] Witherington III, "Exception or Exceptional," 572. Deut 24:4 mentions "an abomination before the LORD," but it is clearly not *'erwat dabar*.

[125] Loader claims λόγος ("matter") here is "legal language," and matches it with Shammai's "shame of a matter." Loader, *Jesus Tradition*, 67. However, if λόγος infers a legal matter, which suggests public court action, then this better supports a contrast with a "matter of indecency," as Deut 24:1 offers no suggestion of public court action (to the contrary, the text describes personal judgement and private action).

identify the teaching of Jesus with the tradition of the school of Shammai.[126]

From another angle, one could argue that since the *dabar* of Deuteronomy 24:1 means "matter" and the Pharisees ask about divorce "for any matter" (κατὰ πᾶσαν αἰτίαν), then despite having no direct textual connection via the Septuagint, there might be a dynamic equivalence between *dabar* and αἰτία. This could be true, but it does raise a question as to why Jesus uses λόγος in Matthew 5:32 (παρεκτὸς λόγου πορνείας) when he could have used his rare term αἰτία to make any extra connection with sexual immorality clear. It raises another question as to why Matthew only uses λόγος in Matthew 19:1-12 in relation to Jesus' sayings (τοὺς λόγους τούτους Matt 19:1, and τὸν λόγον [τοῦτον] Matt 19:11) and not in relation to any grounds for divorce.

Outside of the Pharisees' question in Matthew 19:3, the only time Matthew does use αἰτία in Matthew 19:1-12 is in the disciples' response in Matthew 19:10 (εἰ οὕτως ἐστὶν ἡ αἰτία..., οὐ συμφέρει γαμῆσαι). They do not say, "If such is the '*Matter*' of a man with his wife, it is better not to marry." In the sole passage where the Pharisees ask directly about divorce "for any cause," Jesus gives an answer without the slightest reference to a technical '*Any Matter*' divorce (contra Instone-Brewer) in his words: μὴ ἐπὶ πορνεία (Matt 19:9). Perhaps Matthew left the παρεκτὸς λόγου πορνείας of Matthew 5:32 out of Matthew 19:9 to avoid any matter of such confusion. In all, discourse here on the lawful "cause" or "case" (grounds) for divorce appears to involve a very general question from the Pharisees and a very general response from the disciples, with Jesus specifying not just any cause, but a clear and shocking 'exception' to an absolute rule: *porneia*.

Not only is there no textual link between "any matter" and "sexual immorality," but there is no theological or legal link, for the only two cases of *'erwat dabar* in the Hebrew Bible concern trivial offences, whereas cases of illicit sex in the Hebrew Bible are capital offences. The *porneia* of Matthew 19:9 must also reference Old Testament capital offences, just as *moicheia* is certainly an Old Testament capital offence. This view stands opposed to that of Instone-Brewer who extends his theory to claim that adultery, sexual immorality and "a matter of

---

[126] Hays, *Moral Vision*, 356. Or Gehring, who sees that Jesus' Greek terminology is "even more exactly echoing the Hebrew עֶרְוַת דָּבָר than the ἄσχημον πρᾶγμα in the LXX." R. Gehring, *The Biblical "One Flesh" Theology of Marriage as Constituted in Genesis 2:24* (Eugene: Wipf & Stock, 2013), 218.

indecency" are all the same.[127] His equation of *porneia* with *moicheia* does have more credibility than an equation of *porneia* with *'erwat dabar*, because adultery certainly is a sexual sin whereas failing to bury excrement certainly is not. Yet Scripture is at pains to differentiate illicit sex and indecency, and surely Jesus would not confuse the two.

At this point the Septuagint does add to the confusion: צֵאָה "human excrement" should not be deemed τὴν ἀσχημοσύνην "the disgraceful deed" (Deut 23:13) in the same way the Septuagint has translated *'erwat dabar* as ἀσχημοσύνη "anything indecent" (Deut 23:14). This normal God-given bodily function itself is not "the indecent act," indeed Deuteronomy 23:12-13 describes exactly how to relieve oneself decently! A person must go *outside of the cam*p to a designated place with a trowel, dig a hole and once done, bury the excrement. The act is only indecent if it is *done in the camp* (presumably left uncovered), and the reason provided explicitly emphasizes this:

> because the LORD you God walks *in the midst of your camp*... therefore *your camp must be holy*, so that he may not see anything indecent *among you* and turn away from you. (Deut 23:14, italics added)

When performed properly outside of the camp, defecation is not an "indecent act" or "anything indecent" and the צֵאָה "human excrement" cannot be considered an "evil thing" (Deut 23:9).

The Septuagint translates a phrase with the same term of Deuteronomy 23:13 (צֵאָה) in Ezekiel 4:12 (בְּגֶלְלֵי צֵאַת הָאָדָם) as βολβίτοις κόπρου ἀνθρωπίνης ("human excrement" or "dung"), which could have been done likewise here. The Septuagint would also have done well to translate *'erwat dabar* in Deuteronomy 23:14 precisely as it did for the same phrase in Deuteronomy 24:1, that is: ἄσχημον πρᾶγμα "a matter of indecency." Instead, by translating צֵאָה (*tsa'ah*) and עֶרְוַת דָּבָר (*'erwat dabar*) both as ἀσχημοσύνη (in Deut 23:13 and 14 respectively), the Septuagint has used a term that Scripture reserves for very serious offences. Against cries of "atomistic exegesis,"[128] the plain sense here lays bare a muddling of contexts and a dubious paralleling of texts to suit a highly manipulated interpretation equating trivial and capital offences. However, as plainly found, צֵאָה ("excrement") equals κόπρος

---

[127] "*My Position: Porneia Means Adultery*" Instone-Brewer, *Social and Literary Context*, 278.

[128] *Techniques and Assumptions in Jewish Exegesis before 70 C.E.*, TSAJ (Tübingen: Mohr, 1992), Foreword. Instone-Brewer cites G. F. Moore.

("excrement") in Deuteronomy 23:13, not "an indecent act" or "the disgraceful deed" (τὴν ἀσχημοσύνην).

The Septuagint has not helped by inserting ἀσχημοσύνη into Deuteronomy 23:13 and 14, because ἀσχημοσύνη is used elsewhere to reference capital offences. This is particularly evident in Leviticus 18, where the nineteen occurrences of ἀσχημοσύνη all relate to sexual crimes. The only two occurrences of ἀσχημοσύνη in the New Testament reference comparable offences (Rom 1:27, ἀσχημοσύνη "indecent acts"; and Rev 16:15, ἀσχημοσύνη "naked, shameful") that jeopardise entry into God's kingdom.

A similar term to the ἄσχημον ("indecency") of the Septuagint is απρέπεια (also "indecency"), but this occurs nowhere in Scripture. Its antonym πρέπω[129] is found however, but only once in Matthew and unrelated to divorce: "it is fitting [πρέπον] to fulfil all righteousness" (Matt 3:15), and once directly in relation to a wife: "is it proper [πρέπον] for a wife to pray to God with her head uncovered?" (1 Cor 11:13). It logically follows that it would be "improper" – a matter of απρέπεια – for a wife to pray without her head covered, but this hardly constitutes "sexual immorality" and hardly constitutes the grounds for divorce that Jesus stipulates in Matthew.

The closest connection of πρέπω to the Matthean 'exception clause' comes in Paul's instruction,

> "But sexual immorality [πορνεία] and all impurity or covetousness must not even be named among you, as is proper [πρέπει] among the saints" (Eph 5:3).

However, it is not the "sexual immorality" that is proper or improper, but it "is proper" not to "name" (ὀνομάζω[130]) such sin, as with Ephesians 5:12, "For it is shameful to even speak of the things that they do in secret." Sexually immoral people have not simply committed "a matter of indecency" or are even labelled "indecent" or "improper" here, but (much stronger) they are judged "sons of disobedience" with "no inheritance in the kingdom of Christ and God" (Eph 5:5-6).[131] Paul's

---

[129] Danker, Bauer, and Arndt, *BDAG*, 699.

[130] "*Sexual vice... is not even to be mentioned among you* (much less is it actually to be practiced)" ibid., 574.

[131] Conversely, those who improperly or indecently speak about the sexual immorality (and all impurity or covetousness) that others do in secret are not necessarily to be labelled "sexually immoral" themselves.

"Therefore do not become partners [συμμέτοχοι[132]] with them" is not a command to divorce, but to not share or partake in what these people are doing, upon whom "the wrath of God comes" (Eph 5:6-7).

The more trivial indecencies Paul does speak about in a little detail: see 1 Timothy 2:8-10 with his call for "proper" (πρέπει) adornment; and Ephesians 5:4, "Let there be no filthiness, nor silly talk, nor levity, which are not fitting [οὐκ ἀνῆκεν]."[133] Vulgarity, rudeness, uncouthness, silly speech and crude joking are thus all indecent, out of place, improper and not fitting among saints, but they are no grounds for divorce. The bar would be exceedingly low if that were the case, such that divorce would be permitted "for any cause" (Matt 19:3), precisely what Jesus counters. However, from Ephesians 5:3 we find that sins in the order of "sexual immorality" are so severe that saints are

> not only to avoid their indulgence, but also to avoid thinking
> and talking about them, so completely are they to be banished
> from the Christian community.[134]

The term (or any cognate of) ἀσχήμων ("indecency," from the LXX of Deut 24:1) is found nowhere in Matthew. As an adjective it appears only once in the New Testament, where it refers to "unseemly, shameful, unpresentable" body parts (1 Cor 12:23). There is no negative judgement or connection with illicit sexual intercourse here, only a positive statement of fact that these body parts εὐσχημοσύνην περισσοτέραν ἔχει "are treated with greater modesty." Indeed, εὐσχημοσύνη functions in an antonymous sense for ἀσχήμων, and thus the "indecent" members are treated with excessive "decency" –

---

[132] The prefix συμ- means "with," which lends some weight to the suffix of ἀσχημοσύνη giving a sense of nakedness "with" others. Paul might have otherwise used ἀσχημοσύνη here for it is in the context of πᾶς πόρνος "everyone who is sexually immoral" (Eph 5:5), but he needs a broader term because he also covers everyone who is ἀκάθαρτος "impure" and πλεονέκτης "covetous (that is, εἰδωλολάτρης an idolater)." The term ἀκάθαρτος "impure" or "unclean" is used here separately to πόρνος "sexually immoral" (Eph 5:5), as too just prior: πορνεία δὲ καὶ ἀκαθαρσία πᾶσα "But sexual immorality and all impurity" (Eph 5:3). This characterises the same people, all "sons of disobedience" (Eph 5:6), but it appears that different sins are warned against. So, although πορνεία (Matt 19:9) references capital grounds for divorce (where the *"sexual immorality" is the disobedience, not the divorce*), it is *those who divorce* for what might be a matter of uncleanness (Deut 24:1) who act in disobedience (with "hardness of heart," Matt 19:8; cf. Israel's wilderness rebellion, Heb 3:8). The LXX does not use ἀκάθαρτος in Deut 24:1 but ἄσχημον, so an entirely different (more trivial or non-purity) matter is likely in view.

[133] Stott treats ἀνῆκεν in this verse as a synonym for πρέπει in the previous one: "as is *fitting* among the saints" (Eph 5:3); "which are not *fitting*" (Eph 5:4). J. Stott, *God's New Society: The Message of Ephesians*, BST (Leicester: IVP, 1979), 191. (Italics added.)

[134] Ibid., 192.

something unfathomable if this matter has any connection with a capital offence of ἀσχημοσύνη!

Another variant of ἀσχήμων found in the New Testament is a verbal form in 1 Corinthians 7:36 (ἀσχημονέω "[behave] disgracefully, improper or rude").[135] It is highly unlikely that ἀσχημονέω is of a capital nature here because of how Paul uses the same verb later (the only other occurrence in the New Testament) to teach that love is not ἀσχημονεῖ (1 Cor 13:5).[136] Surely he would condemn a capital offence with a far stronger term than what is commonly translated as "rude."

These rare New Testament instances of ἀσχήμων and ἀσχημονέω refer to shameful acts that *a man* might do, never an indecent act or an act of adultery on the part of a woman (or wife). The same appears so for the New Testament use of ἀσχημοσύνη.[137] Direct *textual* connection of ἀσχήμων, ἀσχημονέω, or ἀσχημοσύνη with πορνεία (or μοιχεία) *committed by a woman* is completely absent in the New Testament. Where ἀσχήμων, ἀσχημονέω, and ἀσχημοσύνη have any *conceptual* connection with πορνεία (or μοιχεία) in the New Testament (nowhere in Matthew, apart from the common assumption for Matt 5:32 and 19:9),

---

[135] A similar term αἰσχρότης (Eph 5:4) does appear once, but it literally means 'ugliness', and only 'indecency' figuratively; Bibleworks, Friberg 700. From the context, BDAG sees the concrete sense as equivalent to the αἰσχρολογία ("obscene or abusive speech") of Col 3:8; Danker, Bauer, and Arndt, *BDAG*, 25. The LXX uses the root αἰσχρός "ugly, shameful, base" to describe the "ugly" thin cows of Pharaoh's dream in Genesis 41. 'Αἰσχρότης is thus a rather different term from ἀσχήμων, but if it could be equated with πορνεία, Jesus would then be advocating ugliness or unattractiveness as grounds for divorce (or filthy speech along with "foolish talk" and "coarse joking" which are of the same order in Eph 5:4); cf. Rabbi Akiba's grounds, "Even if he found someone else prettier than she, since it is said, *And it shall be if she find no favor in his eyes* (Deut 24:1)" (*m.Git.* 9:10). Neusner, *Mishnah*, 487. Out-of-character radical liberalism could then explain the disciples' strong reaction (Matt 19:10).

[136] Even if this 1 Corinthians' term referred to a matter of the same magnitude as an OT capital offence, Corinthian believers are not under the OT Law, so execution is hardly in view (although self-control certainly is, as evident in subsequent verses). This term could of course be applied to women too, but the context is that of a letter from a man, Paul, firstly to church leaders, his "brothers," and Paul's soliloquy here is inherently from his male perspective (e.g. "If I …have not love," When I became a man…").

[137] Rom 1:24-27 shows that God has given up certain men *and* women "in the lusts of their hearts to impurity," where both sexes have "dishonourable passions" and have exchanged natural relations for those that are contrary to nature. However, only men are specifically said to be "committing shameless acts with men and receiving in themselves the due penalty for their error." Hence, according to Scripture, there is a gender equality of dishonourable passions but not of shameless (biological) acts and (physical) consequences. That this term (ἀσχημοσύνη) only occurs elsewhere in Rev 16:15 suggests understanding it likewise there (especially as the suffix -σύνη "with, together with" tends to indicate joint action, and the phrasing is identical: τὴν ἀσχημοσύνην "the indecent act"), or at least as male public nudity.

the offence is always on the part of a man towards another man (Rom 1:27), a man towards his betrothed (1 Cor 7:36), a man's behaviour as a man (1 Cor 13:5, in contrast to his behaviour as a child cf. 1 Cor 13:11), and a man not being seen exposed by other men (Rev 16:15).[138] Hence, **textually and conceptually there is no "matter of indecency" (ἄσχημον πρᾶγμα) committed** *by a woman* **in relation to "sexual immorality" (πορνεία) or "adultery" (μοιχεία) found anywhere in the New Testament.**

In Matthew, however, Jesus does have a distinct focus on "sexual immorality" (the *porneia* of the Matthean 'exception clause') that generally involves *a woman* and *a man* who is not her husband and "adultery" committed *by a man* in divorcing when the 'exception clause' is not satisfied (Matt 5:32; 19:9), or "adultery" *by a man* in marrying a divorced woman (Matt 5:32). Matthew also specifies "adultery" committed *by a woman* but *caused by a man* divorcing when the exception clause is not satisfied (Matt 5:32), but he does not rule on divorce by a woman.[139] Therefore, in relation to divorce, the "sexual immorality" (including "adultery") in Matthew is highly androcentric, whereas the "matter of indecency" in Deuteronomy initially appears gynocentric, judging by the long interpretative history that centres on determining the offence of a woman who is unfavoured, hated and divorced. Yet Deuteronomy 24:1-4 is actually androcentric too, for although the indecency concerns a wife, the judgement is made subjectively only from a male perspective ("in his eyes"; "he has found"; and "he hates her"). Marcus Borg defines "androcentrism" as "seeing from a man's point of view," which he attributes to Jewish tradition as a whole: "texts, laws, and customs reflected how women looked through the eyes of men."[140] Thus Deuteronomy 24:1-4 is androcentric to the core, but such androcentrism is not endorsed by Jesus, indeed he condemns hard-hearted men for it (Matt 19:8).

This is not all part of a "subversion of patriarchy,"[141] for Jesus challenges *cultural norms* that judge a woman from a male point of view, not *laws written* from a male point of view. Such blame-passing of male to female and ultimately to God harks back to that of the

---

[138] 1 Cor 13:5 (ἀσχημονέω "ill-mannered or rude") may be more general (non-gender specific), but there is still no connection with illicit sexual intercourse.

[139] Mark specifies adultery committed by a woman, caused by herself (when she divorces her husband and marries another) with no explicit exception. Exact reciprocity is absent, for Mark does not say that the wife then makes her husband commit adultery, nor rules it adultery if a woman marries the divorced man.

[140] M. Borg, *Jesus in Contemporary Scholarship* (Valley Forge: Trinity, 1994), 105-06.

[141] Ibid., 107.

archetypal marriage from the beginning (Gen 3:12; cf. Matt 19:4), where devilish testing and disobedience led to divorce, that is, a deadly separation between God and humankind. The Garden of Eden's parallel with the Jerusalem Temple[142] infers that the first people were "sent out" of God's house (Gen 3:23 cf. "out of his house" Deut 24:1); and thus Genesis as a book may serve as a divorce certificate, giving just cause of infidelity (disobedience to God's clear command) with deadly judgement: "You shall surely die" (Gen 2:17; cf. 3:3, 19; 5:5). It is significant that although both the man and the woman suffer punishment from this disobedience, it is only Adam who has heard the command from God (Gen 2:16-17) and is held responsible for violating it (Gen 3:17). The New Testament fully supports this male culpability (cf. Rom 5:12-19; 1 Cor 15:21-22).

When it comes to the question of divorce in Matthew's Gospel, instead of judgement falling on females, Jesus accuses his male interlocutors of forcing women to commit adultery when they divorce them (except on capital grounds of sexual immorality) and of committing adultery when they marry a divorced woman. His 'exception clause', whereby a case of "sexual immorality" exempts them from this charge of adultery, does not necessarily relieve men from responsibility either. In citing a capital matter, this is not to 'up the ante' of a woman's guilt, such that the "matter of indecency" of Deuteronomy 24:1 must after all be a very serious offence (as with the Protestant majority view). Rather, it serves to expose men's hearts that are often guilty of serious offences (cf. Matt 5:21-30). With such hearts, men are ill-qualified to pursue the deadly avenue of the Matthean 'exception clause' to divorce their wives, and if they do divorce for any other reason, they commit another serious offence: adultery. All are in need of mercy, but only the merciful shall receive mercy, only the pure in heart shall see God (Matt 5:7-8).

Murray provides six convincing reasons to support why "indecent exposure" in Deuteronomy 24:1 cannot refer to "adultery."[143] After covering Pentateuchal provisions for adultery, suspected adultery, tokens of virginity, defilement of a betrothed virgin, rape and fornication, he summates:

> the law provides for all sorts of contingencies in the matter of sexual uncleanness. *But in none of the cases ... does the phrase*

---

[142] "The parallels between the Garden of Eden, the desert Tabernacle and the later Holy Temple in Jerusalem and other Near Eastern sanctuaries are striking." L. Schachter, "The Garden of Eden as God's First Sanctuary," *JBQ* 41, no. 2 (2013): 74.

[143] Murray, *Divorce*, 10-11.

עֶרְוַת דָּבָר *or even the word* עֶרְוָה *occur.* In every case the remedy or redress is entirely different from recourse to divorce. In none of these contingencies could the prescriptions of Deuteronomy 24:1-4 apply. We must conclude, therefore, that there is no evidence to show that עֶרְוַת דְּבָר refers to adultery or to an act of sexual uncleanness. Indeed the evidence is preponderantly against any such interpretation.[144]

Davidson overreaches to assert that *'erwat dabar* must refer to "a serious sexual indiscretion nonetheless."[145] If the *porneia* of Matthew 19:9 references only capital offences, then *'erwat dabar* remains too trivial to warrant divorce, no matter how serious an indiscretion (short of capital).

For the *'erwat dabar* of Deuteronomy 24:1 to include "adultery" a critical problem in the Law presents, especially conflict with Deuteronomy 22:22. Two rather arbitrary options arise to deal with adultery: either as a capital or a trivial offence.[146] Otherwise, a change in the Law is sought (such as completely dismissing the capital demand), contra Jesus' teaching in Matthew 5:17-19. A "new way" to read the Law is favoured by Loader:

> The shift to mandating divorce for adultery provided the basis for reading Deut 24.1 in a new way. The ground for divorce ('shame of a matter') / ('a shameful matter') would now include adultery, *whereas it had not before...*[147]

A novel *cultural demand* (and political reality, if the Romans did not allow the Jews to enforce capital punishment) drives Loader's reading, despite his recognition of the clear original *scriptural demand*: "It [adultery] mandated death (Lev 20.10; Deut 22.22). This sentence is widely assumed (Prov 2.16-19; 7:25-27)."[148]

Jesus would surely not confuse trivial offences (such as a wife spoiling a dish or becoming less attractive) with capital offences (adultery, bestiality, incest, etc.) in a conglomeration of special new grounds for divorce. In Matthew 19:9 there would be an incredible lack of legal category equivalence: for a trivial offence a husband could remarry and avoid committing a capital offence. The Law was never so reckless. Rigorous legislation covering sexual immorality is recorded in

---

[144] Ibid., 11-12. (Italics added.)

[145] Davidson, *Flame*, 391-92.

[146] If in practice *'erwat dabar* included capital offences, then it further exposes Israel's Law-breaking.

[147] Loader, "Adultery," 69. (Italics added.)

[148] Ibid., 68.

places such as Deuteronomy 22:12-30. There could hardly be a development by Deuteronomy 24:1-4 that would legally absolve or ignore all the evil just described (or confuse any of it with an unspecified matter of indecency) and allow remarriage as an alternative to purging by capital punishment.

The Pharisees, who test Jesus, claim reliance on Moses (cf. Matt 19:7) but they dilute and distort the Law.[149] Distinctions in capital and non-capital offences should not be blurred. Even Josephus, who condones divorce, reinforces the severity of sexual offences,

> A husband, therefore, is to lie only with his wife whom he hath married; but to have to do with another man's wife is a wicked thing; which, if any one venture upon, death is inevitably his punishment: no more can he avoid the same who forces a virgin betrothed to another man, or entices another man's wife...[150]

> Now the greatest part of offenses with us are capital, as if any one be guilty of adultery; if any one force a virgin...[151]

Jesus' meaning of *porneia* can hardly be nebulous like that of *'erwat dabar*. Under the Law, all sexual offenses are carefully determined – fornication, sodomy, rape (in town or in the country), adultery, bestiality and so forth – for the stakes are high: life or death. For example,

> In his exposition of Mosaic law (*Spec.* 3.37–3.42), Philo not only cites the sentence of death mandated in Leviticus 20:13, but insists it should be immediate (*Spec.* 3.38).[152]

It would be surprising if Jesus were to advocate less distinct causes for divorce, let alone leave them indeterminable. This would relax the Law, lower the stakes and, in the final analysis, not clearly answer the Pharisees' test question on lawful cause (whereas Jesus' initial response provided a clear absolute decree).

The major relaxation at stake here is a change from divorce *with the death penalty* for sexual immorality such as adultery, according to the Law, to divorce *without the death penalty* for the same offence, according to culture. A right to remarry is consistent with both types of divorce but for vastly different reasons. Obviously under the Law only

---

[149] Powers and Wade, *Divorce: Bible and Law*, 18.
[150] *Ag. Ap.* 2.201. Josephus, *Works*, 806.
[151] *Ag. Ap.* 2.215. Ibid., 807.
[152] W. Loader, "Same-Sex Relationships: A 1st-Century Perspective," *HTS* 70, no. 1 (2014): 2.

one party would be able to exercise this right; whereas by cultural practice it is uncertain whether the "guilty party" could also remarry, let alone was it right that the "innocent party" may remarry while the original spouse remained alive?

For capital matters, such as adultery, the Law provides definitive judgements on guilt and innocence via strict juridical process. However, in Scripture there is no sure basis to determine "matters of indecency," so "innocent" and "guilty" become hazy and subjective judgements, and so too any categorisation of divorces as "valid" or "legitimate." Valid by culture does not necessarily mean "righteous." Mainstream positions are on shaky ground when they divide divorces into "valid" and "invalid" without reckoning what is righteous. Heth proposes,

> Thus when it comes to the core form of Jesus' divorce saying, "Whoever divorces his wife and marries another commits adultery" (Matt. 5:31-32; 19:9; Mark 10:10-12; Luke 16:18), the only assumption that the first-century readers would bring to make sense of it is the assumption that the divorce was not valid.[153]

However, first-century readers could easily *bring* the assumption that the divorce was "valid" by culture (and for adultery, divorce was both valid and mandated by Graeco-Roman law) and hence "valid" by God, but then *come away* shocked by Jesus that it was "invalid" by God. They may also *bring* this same assumption to the text of Deuteronomy 24:1-4, only to find that this culturally "valid" practice of divorce for "a matter of indecency" was, according to Jesus, hard-hearted practice. The divorce is only "valid" in that it works – it happens, it is permitted by Moses, it is mentioned in legislation to warn of an "abomination" – but it is not "validated" by God at all, and so it cannot have been undertaken for righteousness' sake.

In the context of *what is Lawful*, if one may mentally add any cultural exception, then where is the limit? Why restrict the grounds for divorce only to "sexual immorality"? Why focus on the worst of crimes with the most extreme penalty? **Yet the further one strays from the most serious sexual offences with their capital demands in the Law, the closer one gets to permitting divorce** *for any culturally valid cause.* When questioned on "Is it lawful to divorce one's wife for any cause?" (Matt 19:3), Jesus would have saved much deliberation had he not mentioned μὴ ἐπὶ πορνείᾳ, and simply replied with nothing more than, "Yes, for any valid cause."

---

[153] Heth, "Remarriage for Adultery or Desertion," 74.

As μὴ ἐπὶ πορνείᾳ is a textually strong reading, it begs why Mark and Luke omit it and solely have Jesus' absolute teaching. In a footnote, Davidson offers a key insight,

> It is also possible that Matthew preserves the original complete wording of Jesus (in translation of course) and that Mark and Luke simply left out the reference to *porneia* in the Greek translation because Jesus' original intent is clear without it (since *porneia* called for death or being "cut-off," which implies a de facto dissolution of the marriage in those cases). In other words, one does not have to decide on the question of the Synoptic problem... to reconcile this apparent contradiction.[154]

Naturally, "death" is not a "de facto dissolution" of marriage, but a real dissolution, a complete termination! To the Israelites, being "cut-off" was little less grievous than the extreme penalty of physical death, for it meant being God-forsaken and ejected from the whole community. It could even be viewed as worse than death, for the convicted criminal would suffer lifelong rejection without love and hope.[155]

> The greatest punishment for the sinner in Israel was that he be *kārēt*, 'cut-off' (a divine curse of extinction not only for himself but especially for his progeny).[156]

In another effort to resolve an apparent contradiction between Jesus' absolute teaching on divorce and that of Matthew 19:9, Christensen posits a metaphorical understanding of the 'exception clause':

> Divorce is a form of death, the only difference being the simple fact that the corpses are still walking around! ...Divorce provides an ending, without the possibility of returning to what may have been, at least within the limitations of this present world.[157]

However, this odd understanding of death is not necessary to resolve the matter, nor would it likely be immediately obvious to Jesus' hearers or Matthew's readers. In some agreement with Christensen, divorce *is a form of death*, but only when the grounds for divorce are "sexual

---

[154] Davidson, *Flame*, 656.

[155] This resonates with the belief that *divorce is worse than death*. (E.g. see C. Martin, "Why Is Divorce Considered Worse Than Death?," Quora, https://www.quora.com/Why-is-divorce-considered-worse-than-death.) A crucial difference is that the spouse who experiences this by being unwillingly divorced may not be the one who has committed sexual immorality, and is thus undeserving of such dire punishment.

[156] Davidson, *Flame*, 466-67.

[157] Christensen, *Deuteronomy 21:10-34:12*, 568.

immorality" (Matt 19:9) and the guilty party is, contra Christensen, definitely not "still walking around."

Under the Law, the guilty party is given a death sentence, sent away from the spouse, from society, from life and from God. Craigie writes of those who flaunt the Law: the one "who cursed God would be accursed of God" and in incurring the penalty of death (cf. Deut 21:22-23),

> was to die the worst possible kind of death, for the means of death was a formal and terminal separation from the community of God's people.[158]

While commentators do not explicitly read "death" as "divorce" from such texts, "a formal and terminal separation" from God's people, and ultimately from God, sounds very divorce-like. There is no possibility of return from this divorce, unless one is shown mercy or rises from the dead.[159] If, however, mercy is not shown or desired and the guilty party is sent away, yet is not destroyed and *does not remarry*, then the abomination of Deuteronomy 24:4 has not been committed (even if adultery has), and there remains the possibility of returning to the original marriage. God definitely desires this over divorce and destruction.

If the (cultural) assumption is granted that the term "divorce" normally carries the meaning of a "right to remarry," then even more so another (scriptural) assumption should be granted: when speaking in the context of the Law, the term *porneia* bears the weight of a capital crime, as does the term *moicheia*. This would be basic knowledge for all those in the immediate audience who are under the Law (even if penalties were not applied), those who test Jesus on the Law (the Pharisees), and anyone who holds that not the least part of the Law has passed away. It naturally raises the bar to powerfully protect marriage from every kind of sexual infidelity. On the other hand, as Wenham correctly observes, remarriage readings "lead to an illogicality" that even offer "a perverse incentive to sexual immorality."[160] Keener recognises this too,

---

[158] Craigie, *Deuteronomy*, 285-86.

[159] This is within the limits of thinking and prophecy. Cf. Ezekiel 37, the dry bones of those from the divorced Northern Kingdom, along with those from the separated Southern Kingdom, will live again. Furthermore, if the act of God forsaking Jesus on the cross (Matt 27:46) entails a divorce for all the evil and adultery of his people, then reconciliation post-death is also possible with the same evil and adulterous people (who repent).

[160] Wenham, "No Remarriage," 29.

> Often 'exceptions' can become excuses – one spouse urging the other spouse to commit adultery so he or she can have the excuse to file (this has happened).[161]

In all, Wenham's (now Protestant minority) view does not require a strained syntactical argument to align with the strict early (and historical majority) church view against divorce and remarriage. Heth, after earlier defending the historical view of divorce with no remarriage, at the same time was right to make his re-assessment of Matthew 19:9 to conclude: "Valid divorces always included the right to remarry."[162] The Greek grammar does favour Heth's new position, for there is no better place to locate a real 'exception' to the rule. Majority interpretations rest on a "right to remarry," but it remains that "valid divorces" should not be determined by cultural standard, but by the immense scriptural legal gravitas of "sexual immorality."

It is this straightforward understanding that has really "opened the door to harmonizing Matthew with an absolute reading of Mark, Luke, and Paul."[163] It also opens a window onto what may have been the church's original reason – a thoroughly Jewish *and* biblical one – for firmly holding onto such a strict view on divorce and remarriage that persisted for so many centuries. Furthermore, it may open hearts to reassess the state of one's house to ensure it embodies mercy, purity and faithfulness, especially when the revocability of mercy is frightful and historical (cf. Matt 18:23-35). For the Lord not only "had the legal right to disown his people due to their infidelity (cf. Hos 2:2a/ /1:9),"[164] but fearfully the legal right to disown and destroy them by sending them away, in a separation or divorce, as per the covenant curses of the Law (Deut 28:15-68).

Contra Heth, it is doubtful that Yahweh "only threatened Israel with divorce,"[165] for it was neither "only" a threat nor "only" divorce, for this "sending away" originally meant destruction at the hands of the Assyrian army.[166] So too one cannot merely say "only" adultery, for in Scripture this is "a heinous wrong" that courts death (Gen 20:7) and a "great wickedness and sin against God."[167] The 'exception clause' of

---

[161] Keener, *And Marries Another*, 108.

[162] Heth, "Jesus on Divorce," 10.

[163] Ibid., 16.

[164] Ibid., 20.

[165] Ibid.

[166] Given the promises to restore all Israel, it may be noted that God's act of delivering the death sentence to the Northern Kingdom could ultimately be reversed through the miracle of resurrection.

[167] Heth, "Jesus on Divorce," 19.

Matthew 19:9 has already played out at least once in Israel's history to deadly effect. With respect to Matthew's purpose in writing, Jesus' lesson here is not only that God "had" the legal right to disown, destroy and send away his people due to their marital infidelity, but he still has.[168]

Should the 'exception clause' of Matthew 19:9 not be satisfied, then Jesus' judgement is that the man has "committed adultery" (μοιχᾶται). BDAG defines the verb μοιχάω as "cause to commit adultery" (the man who divorces his wife *"causes her to commit adultery"* cf. Matt 5:32a) or passively "be caused to commit adultery, be an adulterer or adulteress, commit adultery" (for the man who marries a divorced woman cf. Matt 5:32b; 19:9; or marries again after divorcing his wife cf. 19:9).[169] This definition covers all uses of μοιχάω in Matthew's Gospel. The related verb, μοιχεύω, is also found in Matthew (5:27, 28, 32a; 19:18) and most frequently occurs in the New Testament (cf. Matt 5:27, 19:18; Mark 10:19; Luke 18:20; Rom 13:9; Jas 2:11) – and is always present – in a direct citation of the Seventh Commandment, "Do not commit adultery" (Exod 20:14; Deut 5:18). This connection is so strong that "Do not commit divorce" could be read as an ancillary command to the Seventh Commandment.

"Adultery" itself, *moicheia* (μοιχεία, also μοιχαλία) may be narrowly defined as "an act of sexual intercourse with someone not one's own spouse."[170] With Jesus' mention of "adultery," the Seventh Commandment would have immediately come to mind for any Jewish audience. Somewhat surprisingly, Jesus' divorce teaching in both Matthean passages puts the responsibility or "cause" (cf. Matt 19:3) for adultery completely on the man, for he is the one guilty of causing his wife to commit adultery (Matt 5:32a) or he commits adultery himself (Matt 5:32b; Matt 19:9). Here Jesus in Matthew does not contradict any biblical legislation, for every man who commits adultery or any other sexual sin must bear full responsibility for his willfulness.

---

[168] The Roman Siege of Jerusalem (70CE) may entail the next occasion of divine divorce or separation.

[169] Danker, Bauer, and Arndt, *BDAG*, 526.

[170] Bibleworks, Friberg 18669.

The Exceptional Case of a Righteous Man Resolving to Divorce

Lawful precedent is set for not holding a woman responsible for adultery, as legislated in the case of a man who has illicit sexual intercourse with a betrothed woman against her will (Deut 22:25-27). The *absolute male responsibility* for adultery in all of the Matthean divorce sayings of Jesus, and the direct textual connection of shameful acts (of ἀσχήμων, ἀσχημονέω, and ἀσχημοσύνη) with primarily (if not solely) male sexual immorality in the whole New Testament, lends support to an explanation that Joseph resolved to righteously divorce Mary (recorded only by Matthew, in 1:19) not because he regarded her as having committed a "matter of indecency" or worse, a matter of "sexual immorality,"[171] but because he believed her to be *absolutely innocent* of committing any sexual immorality, including adultery.[172] He may not have known how – perhaps he simply trusted Mary, and her innocence was later proven true.

This aligns with the narrative function of all the women recorded just prior in Jesus' genealogy. Each might appear to set the stage for Mary's alleged sexual immorality, but all are vindicated by a closer reading of Scripture. All may also have married under peculiar circumstances, including Tamar as discussed earlier, which signals that the women are "more righteous" (cf. Gen 38:26) than expected. It further signals that all five women (not only Mary) have a bearing on understanding Jesus' teaching on marriage.

Alternatively, it could be said that what made Joseph "righteous" was that, in suspecting Mary's guilt before the angelic revelation of her innocence, he chose to be merciful by resolving to privately send his betrothed away rather than to charge her in court, which might put her life at risk.[173] This is possible, but has significant problems. A private sending away usually assumes a Hillel-style divorce for any "matter of indecency" (cf. Deut 24:1), a practice that Jesus condemned (cf. Matt 19:8). It could assume a private sending away for a matter of "sexual immorality" (cf. Matt 19:9), but if Joseph did suspect *any guilt* on Mary's part in this capital offence, then to send her away privately,

---

[171] E.g. "When Joseph learns that Mary is pregnant, he assumes that she had committed adultery with someone." Loader, *Sexuality: Key Texts*, 62.

[172] Matthew's text may have another hint of this in recording that Joseph was "unwilling to put her to shame" (Matt 1:19), for he trusted that Mary had done nothing *herself* to deserve any shame. Also, for Joseph to be called "righteous" it is highly likely that he was betrothed to a righteous woman.

[173] Mary may receive a guilty verdict of sexual immorality, and with her testimony, potentially a more dangerous one: blasphemy.

without heavenly revelation as can be found recorded in the Law, he would take the Law into his own hands and risk breaking it himself.

A righteous person is bound to do all of God's statutes and obey all of God's commandments (cf. Deut 6:24-25), and this includes following every piece of legislation for dealing with capital offences, unless otherwise commanded by God. In any case, why would Joseph risk breaking the Law (or at least relaxing it) if it is true that by contemporary standards there was no risk to Mary's life – even by the stricter Shammai-style rulings on adultery? A small "mercy" might be shown at the high cost of Law-breaking.

Moreover, biblically, mercy is appropriately shown to those who are guilty, who acknowledge their hopeless state, and who plead for mercy (cf. Ps 51; cf. Matt 18:21-35). Yet there is no indication in Matthew's text that Mary is guilty of any offence, acknowledges any sexual sin to Joseph, or pleads with him or God for mercy. For Matthew or Jesus to teach or to even hint that it is "righteous" to grant mercy to people who do not need it (or who reject their need for it), and to grant it on good intentions but in violation of clear commands of God, runs contrary to Scripture. Given that only Matthew's Gospel records Joseph's resolution to divorce Mary, a spurious concept of "mercy" that forgives the innocent does not aid our understanding of the Matthean 'exception clause', where "sexual immorality" is a serious offence *that someone must be guilty of* – if it is to be applied as grounds for divorce. Such "mercy" undermines true mercy, which fully pardons debt and entails no divorce at all.

If Joseph overlooks a suspected case of "sexual immorality" with a private divorce, he not only breaks the Law as written, but pardons in pretense. In the light of Jesus' teaching in Matthew 18:21-35, it would be like proffering forgiveness on a fellow servant's one hundred denarii debt *and* putting the fellow servant away.[174] There can be no compromise to the debt (or to the Law); a binary decision must be made: what is legally owed stands in full, or wholehearted forgiveness is wrought from God and within human relationships (cf. Matt 18:35) such that no one is ever sent away.

Joseph's intent to divorce Mary is often heralded as proof that adultery mandated divorce, where Matthew has modified Jesus' absolute teaching

---

[174] All the while, suspecting an unresolved 10,000 talent debt of his betrothed and ignoring his own debt.

in the interests of at least bringing the saying into closer conformity with what was the all but universally assumed view and practice in the cultures of his setting.[175]

Loader elaborates that it implied Joseph

> was committed to keeping God's Law as set out in Scripture relating to women who fell pregnant out of wedlock to someone other than their fiancé. But it also meant that in applying the options Joseph chose the more compassionate alternative. He chose not to take her to court, but to deal with the matter in privacy.[176]

Joseph certainly "was committed to keeping God's Law," but the Law did not necessarily align with the "universally assumed view and practice in the cultures of his setting." The Law as written establishes guilt or innocence, but a public court (of any day) would struggle to believe Mary's account. She would face great shame, not a presumption of innocence.

Hays surmises,

> Under such circumstances, Deuteronomy prescribes capital punishment, but actual practice may have been for the man simply to dismiss the woman.[177]

Does this moral vision really do justice to Matthew's vision of Joseph acting as a "just man" (Matt 1:19)? For Joseph to be righteous means that he does what is right and obeys the Law.[178] To show compassion, does this mean that Joseph had to skirt, disobey, or relax the just requirements of God's good and perfect Law (Ps 19:7)? Joseph's resolve to not take Mary to court may point completely away from a suspected offence of adultery on her part, toward a moral vision and legislation concerning *guiltless* or *righteous* "women who fell pregnant out of wedlock to someone other than their fiancé."

The Law had very specific legislation concerning sexual matters inside and outside of marriage. For example, Instone-Brewer contends that prior to 70CE the Rite of Bitter Waters was still performed, so there

---

[175] Loader, "Adultery," 73.

[176] *Fundamentalism*, 80.

[177] Hays, *Moral Vision*, 354.

[178] Commenting on Matt 5:45, Newman and Stine note "**Evil**...**unjust** are synonyms, as are **good**...**just**" and "the adjective **just** is first used in 1:19" to describe Joseph. The contrast between good and evil, the just and the unjust, persists throughout Matthew, where "**the just** and **the unjust** are 'people who do right' and 'people who do evil,' or 'people who obey God's law' and 'people who disobey God's law'." Newman and Stine, *Matthew*, 158. (Bold and underscore original.)

was no need for a man to divorce a woman in suspicious immoral circumstances, because it was assumed that a guilty woman would die.[179] This rite was applied to a wife when there were no witnesses to the suspected adultery. If the woman died, then it would be a deadly separation or "divorce" by God's direct act, according to God-prescribed legislation (Num 5:11-31). However, this rite is inapplicable to Mary's situation, for it was not given to pregnant women.[180]

Instone-Brewer purports that Joseph "considered using an 'Any Cause' divorce" and although Instone-Brewer considers this unrighteous grounds,[181] he sees that Joseph "chose this type of divorce for the best of reasons – he wanted to avoid putting Mary to shame in a public court."[182] Loader knows the danger, "An option open to Joseph, according to Deut 22:13-21, was to haul Mary before the courts and have her stoned,"[183] but similarly believes that Joseph chose a more compassionate avenue. He asserts that "It is certainly possible to read Deut 22:13-21 as optional," and he presupposes that the private divorce of Deuteronomy 24:1 was a lawful alternative.[184] However, had Joseph divorced Mary for "a matter of indecency," he could not be "righteous"[185] (Matt 1:19) but would stand condemned by Jesus as having "hardness of heart" (Matt 19:8). Loader does admit,

> The implication is that anyone seeking true obedience to God's will should not be availing themselves of Moses' allowance for hard hearted people.[186]

Trivialising the offence with 'Any Cause' grounds – when any pregnancy is a serious matter from familial, societal and legal standpoints – simply to avoid public court cannot be righteous behaviour either. A righteous person would treat this matter seriously and seek a lawful legitimate course. Yet surprisingly, the course that

---

[179] Instone-Brewer, *Social and Literary Context*, 96.

[180] Ibid., 97.

[181] Ibid., 115.

[182] Instone-Brewer, *In the Church*, 108. This compassionate reading still masks the fact that the real risk of a trial for infidelity is, by the Law's written demand (unabolished in any detail by Jesus), not simply public embarrassment but public execution – with great personal and family shame.

[183] Loader, *Jesus Tradition*, 75.

[184] Ibid.

[185] Contra Loader, righteousness and purity of heart must not solely "be understood in terms of mercy, gentleness and peacemaking." Loader, *Fundamentalism*, 80. Right judgement is fundamental to "righteousness," and Matthew's placement of this characterisation means that Joseph's decision to divorce was not unrighteous, even though a better direction was forthcoming (cf. Matt 1:20-21).

[186] *Jesus Tradition*, 98.

Instone-Brewer advocates would not even result in a proper divorce: "Jesus taught that the 'Any Cause' divorce was invalid and so the first nativity story almost started and ended with an invalid divorce!"[187] Surely Mary's husband Joseph, "being a just man and unwilling to put her to shame, resolved to divorce her quietly" (Matt 1:17) *and validly.*

There is no suggestion in Matthew's Gospel that Joseph "*should*" divorce Mary because he believed "she had committed adultery" (contra Heth), even if everyone else "agreed that a Jewish wife could be justifiably divorced, *and should be* (cf. Mat. 1:19), if she had committed adultery."[188] Joseph never charges Mary with "adultery"! As much as the pre-marital pregnancy must have shocked and perplexed him, Joseph would have been presumptuous and unrighteous to charge her so, especially if he had ignored any of Mary's pleadings of innocence. Mary never admits to committing adultery, just as Tamar (Matt 1:3) never admitted to committing adultery. There is really only one cause in the Law for which he could have divorced Mary justly and quietly without relaxing any commandments. It is for a case of "sexual immorality" (*porneia*, cf. Matt 19:9), but one where the woman is considered *completely innocent*. This is the only offence in the Law that does not demand the death of both parties involved in illicit sexual intercourse.

Before Joseph understood the situation, as a "righteous man" (Matt 1:19) he might have hoped for divine revelation, via the visitation of a prophet or an angel, or a vision from God, as found within narrative sections of the Hebrew Bible (cf. Nathan's prophetic word to David in 2 Sam 11-12; and Hosea's redemption of his adulterous wife as an example of God's mercy on unfaithful Israel). Pending this direct revelation from God (which finally eventuates), Joseph must adhere to Scripture's written commandments. With no doubt arduous consideration of the Law, it is likely that Joseph can really only believe that Mary has been raped out in the countryside (cf. Deut 22:25-27).[189] He cannot ignore the pregnancy, but in his estimation, Mary cannot have committed adultery. He trusts that she would have cried out for help, but no-one was there to rescue her. He might assume Mary is so traumatised that she cannot remember the ordeal, or is delusional, as

---

[187] Instone-Brewer, *In the Church*, 108.

[188] Heth, "Remarriage for Adultery or Desertion," 67.

[189] A Jewish polemic that Mary was raped by a Roman soldier named Pantera (cf. Origen, *Contra Celsus* 1.69; Tosefta *Chullin* 2:22-24) may reflect a false rumour that genuinely circulated at the time of Mary's pregnancy. It was likely written in response to Matthew's account of Jesus' birth from a "virgin." See J. Schaberg, *The Illegitimacy of Jesus: A Feminist Theological Interpretation of the Infancy Narratives* (Sheffield: Sheffield Phoenix, 2006).

demonstrated by her fabulous story about the divine origin of the child in utero. Whatever the case, Joseph demonstrates a loving, tenderhearted response to his betrothed, with no sign of "hardness of heart" that Jesus condemns others for (cf. Matt 19:8) in relation to divorce.

If this view is correct, then the rapist would obviously be guilty of "sexual immorality" (cf. Matt 19:9) and Mary totally innocent. Even so, grounds for divorce remain, for "sexual immorality" has occurred, and here again, in full keeping with Jesus' teaching on sexual immorality in Matthew, the responsibility falls completely on the male. The rationale from the Old Testament as to why Joseph would divorce in these tragic circumstances, however, is less clear, but may have much to do with a righteous requirement for legitimate children and godly offspring (cf. Mal 2:15), the strict expectation of a wife's virginity (cf. Deut 22:13-21), and perhaps even a defilement that bars him from taking Mary as his wife (cf. Deut 24:1-4). Mercy can still triumph nonetheless, and divorce is finally avoided post-revelation, but in this view at least there is certain transgression of the Law and guilt that mercy can triumph over.

Jesus' later teaching in Matthew 19:9 would have permitted Joseph to divorce Mary and to marry another woman without being condemned for committing "adultery." This proves, firstly, to be a peculiar example of where the law concomitantly permits the betrothed woman to remain alive and the "husband" to marry another woman, on the grounds that his betrothed is held guiltless in the asserted sexual immorality (cf. Deut 22:26a). Indeed, it serves as an 'exception' to the deadly exception! Yet this is not the end of the matter, for just as King David received a personal revelation, and Joseph received a personal revelation, so Jesus brings a personal revelation full of mercy and forgiveness that intends reconciliation, not separation.

Secondly, as there was never a consummated marriage with a "one flesh" union and any solemn wedding vows of permanency, there is also a distinction between terminating a betrothal period (which by definition is impermanent) and terminating the final form of marriage, even though semantics overlap, such as the use of "husband," "wife," and "divorce." David Gushee and Glen Stassen note that "betrothal – though a serious commitment to marriage – is not yet marriage"[190] to suggest that the only proper word Jesus can use in his exception clause is *porneia* because *moicheia* does not apply to betrothal. Even if this

---

[190] D. Gushee and G. Stassen, *Kingdom Ethics: Following Jesus in Contemporary Context* (Grand Rapids: Eerdmans, 2016), 276.

were so, it does not account for why other instances of "sexual immorality" (including "adultery") cannot be grounds for divorce within marriage.

There are even significant practical differences in terminating a betrothal as against a full marriage. Unlike divorce post-wedlock, the betrothed woman would not physically be "sent away" and this is simply because the husband has not yet "taken" her into his house (Matt 1:20, "do not fear to take Mary as your wife"; cf. Matt 1:24, "he took his wife"). The spurned woman would remain in her own father's house, presumably with any illegitimate children cared for there too.

Thirdly, Joseph would not make Mary "commit adultery" by this divorce, which then serves as a peculiar 'exception' to Matthew 5:32. Broadly-speaking, Mary could not be unfaithful to a marital covenant because it had not been socially established (with vows, witnesses, etc.) and physically inaugurated (consummated). Narrowly-speaking, "adultery" is only committed when there is sexual intercourse with someone other than one's spouse, but this assumes that sexual intercourse has first taken place with one's spouse. Any woman's pre-marital illicit sex is biblically described not as "adultery" but as prostitution (Deut 22:21) or violation (Deut 22:24, cf. Deut 22:28-29 where, significantly, the same term "violated" is used for sexual intercourse with "a virgin who is not betrothed").

Of course, an angel of the Lord finally assured Joseph, "do not fear to take Mary as your wife, for that which is conceived in her is from the Holy Spirit" (Matt 1:20) and not from prostitution or violation. Thus there was no sexual immorality and no divorce. Against a cultural zeal of divorce "for any cause" (Matt 19:3) with a right to remarry, understood as a man's right to sex and guaranteed progeny of his own, Joseph with "rightful zeal"[191] defied culture: "he took his wife, but knew her not until she had given birth to a son" (Matt 1:25) – God's son, not his!

Furthermore, the lawful divorce that Joseph resolved to undertake was surely not motivated by a right that he could lawfully marry someone else, and it would be perplexing if Joseph *must* divorce Mary and yet another man may lawfully marry her. Keener acknowledges that Mary's

---

[191] A husband's "jealousy" (cf. Num 5:1-31) is a godly trait when it is a "rightful zeal to protect the exclusively intimate covenant of marriage as God had instituted it." Davidson, *Flame*, 350-51.

premarital pregnancy had likely ruined any chance of her ever marrying, a horrible fate in an economically male-centred society."[192]

If Joseph did write Mary a divorce certificate – and this is far from clear, for there is no mention of it – then a divorce certificate would help protect Mary from capital punishment, *but not automatically provide her with a right to remarry.* (Any perceived unfairness in this for the woman could be counter-balanced with a man's fate in being born or forcibly made a eunuch; cf. Matt 19:12). Even if the death penalty was not enforced at that time, a divorce certificate that does not charge her with committing *porneia* could also help protect her from much shame in being judged immoral for having a child without a husband. This sharply contrasts with the shameful and potentially unjust divorce certificate charge of Deuteronomy 24:1.

Adultery and Judgement

Jesus does not necessarily posit "a fundamental redefinition of adultery,"[193] whether in Mark 10:11-12 or Matthew 5:27-28, but makes explicit what was already implicit in the Law. His teaching "leads us to a different level of understanding adultery" where what happens in the heart or mind "can lead to attitudes and behaviours which are equally destructive."[194] Here is no "stunning element of a new ethic" such that "lust is equivalent to adultery,"[195] for this old ethic is contained within the Tenth Commandment. It is also found in Israel's history, for Stephen judges that "*in their hearts* they turned to Egypt" (Acts 7:39, italics added) during the wilderness time. Their covetous hearts were also hard hearts (cf. Matt 19:8), resulting not only in unrighteous divorce practices that Jesus judges adulterous, but in idol-making and the craving of a return to Egypt, purportedly "a land flowing with milk and honey" (Num 16:13) where they "sat by the meat pots and ate bread to the full" (Exod 16:3). To worship other gods and to desire foreign land was to commit adultery against God. This covetousness, behind Israel's complaining and testing of God, brought grave judgement. God eventually turned away from his people, gave them over to worshipping other gods, and sent them away to another pagan land (Acts 7:40-43).

---

[192] Keener, *Matthew*, 93.
[193] Hays, *Moral Vision*, 352.
[194] Loader, *Jesus Tradition*, 242.
[195] McKnight, *Sermon*, 88.

A traditional definition that adultery "always involved illegal sex with a married person"[196] stands challenged by the Hebrew narrative of Israel's relationship with God. It is also challenged by Jesus' words on lustful intent (Matt 5:27-28), and by the Tenth Commandment, which not only forbids an unmarried man from coveting his "neighbour's wife" but also "his female servant," who may be unmarried, and "anything" else of his neighbour's, which may include unmarried daughters. So lustful intent or coveting did not always involve actual sexual intercourse, nor did it necessarily involve at least one married person. The core problem of adultery must still concern a breach of covenantal fidelity, but if no married persons are involved in the adulterous intent or action, then the only covenantal reference we have is the God-Israel one in which all of the commandments on murder, adultery, lust, etc. are couched. Therefore anyone, including a eunuch, could be indicted for adultery; indeed, a whole generation of Israelites could be indicted (cf. Matt 12:39; 16:4).

Lewis Smedes sees that the Seventh Commandment serves, "in its narrowest sense, as a warning to Israel's males to keep away from their neighbour's wives."[197] He continues,

> The concern ...is not merely with sex; its real business is with marriage and its wholeness... Adultery, defined Christianly, is anything that violates a marriage – including divorce... total fidelity... human respect for the covenant of marriage is what is at stake.[198]

The general concern then is not for men's or women's rights but for *our neighbour's rights* (cf. "love your neighbor," Lev 19:18; Matt 19:19). This provides a certain balance in a patriarchal society, as it intends to control the sexual behaviour of a man and also protect the "integrity of his marriage and certitude about his descendants."[199] What is at stake is so precious that it is protected by threat of death.

Although Barbara Roberts holds the opinion that not only adultery, but also abuse and desertion, are grounds for divorce, she is one of the few scholars to recognise that "**Moses made it clear that adultery was a serious crime by requiring** *divorce by execution* **for proven adultery**."[200] Some others touch on this capital understanding of divorce:

---

[196] Instone-Brewer, *Social and Literary Context*, 149.
[197] Smedes, *Mere Morality*, 158.
[198] Ibid., 157.
[199] Ibid., 158.
[200] Roberts, *Not under Bondage*, 108. (Italics added.)

...adultery violates the 'one-flesh' principle underlying marriage, which may be why at least in Old Testament times sexual marital unfaithfulness was punishable by death (Lev. 20:10; Deut. 22:22). After all, it would be difficult to continue a marriage if the partner guilty of adultery had been stoned to death![201]

Now a "right" to send away a wife to real death on the grounds of *porneia* (or *moicheia*) of Matthew 19:9 remains a "right" for those strictly under the Law, as written and unabolished in any detail, but this jars with a "responsibility" to continually love, and Jesus' teaching immediately prior. The story of Matthew 18:21-35

> Intones that mercy requires mercy. If one has received mercy, how can one still insist on coldly asserting one's rights and claims over others?[202]

Here Garland calls the unforgiving servant of this passage "hard-boiled."[203] Thomas Manson claims, "The wrath of God is kindled against the hard and relentless more than against the weak and foolish."[204] (Although, "hard" and "foolish" can be synonymous in Scripture; cf. Nabal.) As such, "hard-hearted" (cf. Matt 19:8) would well describe this "evil [πονηρός] servant" (Matt 18:32; cf. "evil [πονηρός] unbelieving heart," Heb 3:12), further tying this story to Matthew 19:1-12. The Law "allowed" (Matt 19:8) for such men to divorce their wives "for any cause" (cf. Matt 19:3; Deut 24:1-4) but this is not what righteous or merciful people do. The rejection or "hate" (cf. Deut 24:3, and Mal 2:16) and "hardness of heart" (Matt 19:8) of those who do not forgive from their "heart" (Matt 18:35) so infuriates God ("in his anger," Matt 18:34; cf. "in my wrath," Heb 3:11; 4:3) that he swears they shall not enter the "kingdom of heaven" (Matt 18:23; or God's "rest" cf. Heb 3:11, 18; 4:3).

Nonetheless, mercy does not imply minimising sin or ignoring solemn commitments. Heth emphasizes that

> the most important covenant obligations were not normally written down. This is because everyone already understood what they were.[205]

---

[201] Köstenberger and Jones, *Foundation*, 219.

[202] Garland, *Matthew*, 195.

[203] Ibid.

[204] T. Manson, *The Sayings of Jesus as Recorded in the Gospels According to St Matthew and St Luke* (London: SCM, 1949), 213.

[205] Heth, "Remarriage for Adultery or Desertion," 62.

He notes that "sexual faithfulness" was one of the most important obligations, assumed yet not actually written into a Jewish marriage contract, but

> confirmed by the fact that the death penalty for adultery *is* recorded throughout the ancient Near East and in the Old Testament itself (Lev 20:10; Deut 22:23-24; cf. Jer 29:23).[206]

While this is completely true, it is strangely used to support the Protestant majority view which replaces death for adultery with divorce and a right to remarry, instead of supporting an understanding of divorce with a right to remarry that fully applies the known penalties for sexual unfaithfulness as *is* recorded in the Old Testament and throughout the ANE. Heth's premise on "covenant obligations" explains why for Jesus' original Jewish hearers and Matthew's original readers, the terminal implications for "sexual immorality" and "adultery" of Matthew 19:9 were not specified, for "everyone already understood what they were" – even if all were reluctant or unable to apply them.

Andrew Macintosh provides another insight into how adultery was viewed in the Old Testament in commenting on Ezekiel 16:39, "Stripping and humiliation of an adulteress was the prelude to her execution by stoning or by the sword."[207] Macintosh then applies this to the God-Israel covenant,

> If unrepentant, Israel and her land will become like a waterless desert just as a divorced adulterous is reduced to nakedness.[208]

To be totally consistent with Macintosh's observation just prior, one need add "…in the prelude to her execution." Aversion to mentioning such drastic judgement should not obscure the fact that this dire consequence was commanded both for infidelity in human marriages and for the nation's marriage relationship with God. The two concepts cannot be easily separated, for in Scripture,

> adultery is defined not primarily as a private matter, a sin against a spouse, but was regarded as an absolute wrong, a sin against God.[209]

David's adultery with Bathsheba is a classic example of this: "I have sinned against the LORD" (2 Sam 12:13), "Against you, you only, have

---

[206] Ibid. (Italics original.)

[207] A. Macintosh, *A Critical and Exegetical Commentary on Hosea*, ICC (Edinburgh: T&T Clark, 1997), 43.

[208] Ibid.

[209] Rosner, *Paul, Scripture and Ethics*, 126.

I sinned" (Ps 51:3; cf. Gen 39:9). This sin, as with all sexual immorality, is conceived in Scripture as "fundamentally one of religious allegiance" where disloyalty to God is tantamount to apostasy.[210]

So "sexual immorality" and "adultery" (Matt 19:9) are not only specific matters accountable to a public court according to the Law, but matters that affect Israel as a nation in relation to God. On the other hand, "something indecent [cf. Deut 24:1] is nonspecific"[211] and is personally determined by one man outside of court, where

> divorce is basically a matter of internal family law that does not require the involvement of the civil authorities (the elders) to examine the causes or grounds of the divorce.[212]

To be more precise, a *private (non-capital) divorce* procedure is basically a matter of internal family law, or even hard-hearted (cf. Matt 19:8) lawlessness (cf. Matt 23:28), in contrast to a *public (capital) divorce* procedure. Thus within the Law itself a human divorce tradition (Deut 24:1-4) is described that flaunts the only divinely prescribed grounds for sending away a spouse (found just two chapters earlier), that is, "sexual immorality." Moses records this tradition as a testimony against Israel and to warn against an associated abomination that imperils their national existence.

Matthew's Use of Apolyo ('Απολύω)

Wenham, in his effort to justify that *for the Pharisees* ἀπολύω means "to divorce" with remarriage permitted whereas *for Jesus* it means "to separate" without the right to remarry, points to the principle of linguistics that the sense of a word exists not in the word alone but also in the utterances in which it is embedded.[213] Wenham also notes that the linguistic situation is more complicated than this.

> Clearly Jesus and the Pharisees were debating not in Greek but in Aramaic or possibly Hebrew. So they probably used the term *šālaḥ* [שׁלח], not *apolyō* [ἀπολύω]. What is important to notice is that by themselves these terms are quite general: *šālaḥ* means to send, and *apolyō* to loose, or undo.[214]

This gives good reason to examine every case of where Matthew uses this general term ἀπολύω, whether embedded in dialogue that

[210] Ibid., 126-27.
[211] C. Wright, *Deuteronomy*, NIBC (Peabody: Hendrickson, 2007), 255.
[212] Ibid.
[213] Wenham, "No Remarriage," 34.
[214] Ibid., 55.

might translate the term *šālaḥ* constitutive of his own Greek narrative, or derived from a Greek source. Such an approach is not taken to force connections between disparate passages, but primarily to determine if a technical legal meaning ever arises. The term (or cognates of) ἀπολύω appears nineteen times in Matthew: eight times directly in the context of marriage and divorce (Matt 19:3, 7, 8, 9; also 1:19; 5:31, and twice in 5:32). How Matthew uses ἀπολύω in places outside of this context could well inform the meaning within.

Jewish "crowds" (Matt 19:2) are present as Jesus deals with this matter of "divorce" (ἀπολύω) and we know from earlier events how Jesus dealt with a matter of "sending away" (ἀπολύω) "crowds" (Matt 14:15, 22, 23; 15:32). This includes a Gentile woman whom Jesus' disciples beg to "send away" (ἀπολύω) as she pleads for mercy (Matt 15:22-23), when Matthew has twice already recorded Jesus' appeal for people to learn the meaning of "I desire mercy, and not sacrifice" (Matt 9:13; 12:7). Obviously, these men do not plead to "divorce" (ἀπολύω) this woman so that they will have the freedom to cleave to another less demanding woman, nor is Jesus reluctant to "divorce" (ἀπολύω) the crowds or this Gentile woman in any marital sense. However, in general terms and in the particular, Matthew's usage of ἀπολύω shows that Jesus is averse to sending away needy people who seek and follow him.

Jesus has compassion, heals, feeds the hungry, and shows mercy (Matt 14:13-21; 15:32-39) to those who come to him. Even a woman who does not belong to "the house of Israel" (Matt 15:24), Jesus does not send away (ἀπολύω) "out of his house" (cf. Deut 24:1, 3), but on listening to her heartfelt plea, he fulfils her "desire" (Matt 15:28) for "mercy" (Matt 15:22) – reflecting God's desire for mercy (Matt 9:13; 12:7; Hos 6:6). Jesus mercifully heals the woman's daughter from demonic oppression and commends her great faith (Matt 15:28). The only time Jesus does send away (ἀπολύω) anyone is when they have eaten of his provision and they are "satisfied" (Matt 14:20; 15:37), where the separation is undoubtedly amicable.

The common verb ἀπολύω, for at least eleven out of nineteen times that Matthew uses it, has no technical legal meaning invested in it that demands a formal written certificate, court action, or a freedom to do anything other than to simply "send away" the narrative object in question. Only by narrative implication, ἀπολύω can infer to not have compassion, to not heal, to not provide, and to not show mercy. By narrative implication, ἀπολύω can also mean temporary separation for a time of devotion to prayer or for testing by opponents as occurs immediately after Jesus sends away the satisfied crowds (Matt 14:23; Matt 16:1; cf. 1 Cor 7:5).

The narrative object may be sent away from a subject such as a spouse, a prison term, a financial debt, or a sinful habit, so the context in which the term is found is critical in determining whether the ἀπολύω constitutes an act of mercy. So too it is vital to know whether the protagonist is good and righteous (cf. the "master," Matt 18:27; 34), or evil and unrighteous (cf. the "wicked servant," Matt 18:32), in carrying out this act. Jesus' words about a king settling accounts, placed immediately prior to Matthew 19:1-12, provides perfect opportunity to consider this, especially with its unmistakable link between ἀπολύω and motifs of mercy and forgiveness.

In this lesson about the kingdom of heaven (Matt 18:23-35), a master initially "released" (ἀπολύω) his servant from dire consequences and "forgave" (ἀφίημι) him his tremendously large unpaid debt (Matt 18:27). When this released servant then refuses forgiveness to another with a much smaller debt, he stands condemned and is delivered to the jailers with the master's judgement: "you should have shown mercy on your fellow servant, as I have shown mercy on you" (Matt 18:33-34). In the narrative context, the original ἀπολύω "sending away" from bondage entails an act of mercy, whereas in earlier contexts of Matthew 14:13-21; 15:32-39, the ἀπολύω "sending away" from Jesus prior to being satisfied would have lacked mercy. For the master to reinstate the jail sentence and debt payment (Matt 18:34), he is not suddenly unrighteous in doing this to the "wicked servant" (Matt 18:32). Mercy is desirable but cannot be demanded – that is its nature, one receives what one does not deserve.

When we come to the Matthean divorce texts, the narrative subject and the protagonist are the same: a man who might "send away" his wife from himself. The above lines of inquiry apply: first, is it an act of mercy for a wife *to be sent away* from her husband, or is *to not be sent away* an act of mercy? Second, is any man who does "send away" his wife good and righteous in doing this? At the same time, the needs of the narrative object should be borne in mind. Does the wife seek and receive the sort of compassion, healing, satisfaction of hunger, and mercy of Matthew's previously recorded narrative objects, witnessed in the prime example of Jesus in his dealings with those who follow him? Even if the narrative object has what may be an exceptionally heavy and seemingly unforgivable debt, such as a crime of πορνεία ("sexual immorality," Matt 19:9; cf. "ten thousand talents," Matt 18:24), the lines of inquiry remain unchanged.

A pattern presents in Matthew's narrative. Within a setting of large crowds (Matt 19:2), Matthew uses ἀπολύω four times (Matt 19:3, 7, 8, 9) on the question of divorce. Earlier, Matthew used ἀπολύω four times concerning divorce (Matt 1:19; 5:31, and twice in 5:32) and four times (Matt 14:15, 22, 23; 15:32) with respect to sending away crowds.[215] Matthew later records another question[216] regarding Jesus' imprisonment, where the Roman authority is accustomed "to release" from capital punishment one prisoner "for the crowd" (Matt 27:15-17). To describe this "release," Matthew again uses ἀπολύω four times (Matt 27:15, 17, 21, and 26). Are these crowded quaternaries coincidental or can commonality be found?

The usage of ἀπολύω after Matthew 19:1-12 is clearly in keeping with an authorial indictment purpose. Spurred by Jewish leaders to "ask for Barabbas and destroy Jesus" (Matt 27:20), the crowd condemns a "righteous man" (Matt 27:19) and a "notorious prisoner" (Matt 27:16) is released. By the Law, there is no righteous cause for the release of Barabbas. The only cause given for Jesus' death sentence is "envy" (Matt 27:18) – a completely unrighteous cause. Confronted with Jesus' innocence, "all the people" give a chillingly hard-hearted answer, "Let his blood be upon us and on our children!" (Matt 27:24). Therefore, those who call for this "release" (ἀπολύω) and wrongful destruction (ἀπόλλυμι, Matt 27:20) indict themselves and they deserve destruction for the injustice. Capital punishment, blood, death and destruction are all motifs related to Matthew's use of ἀπολύω. Simply from a thematic point of view, the Jewish religious leaders and the general populace get it wrong on "divorce."

Matthew's usage of a "binding" and "loosing" motif[217] may also connect with both discipleship and marriage. In the prelude to the discussion on divorce (ἀπολύω), Jesus' disciples are bestowed an authority to bind and loose (λύω), which Matthew records with *positive double emphasis* (Matt 16:19; 18:18). If binding and loosing has any link with divorce,[218] it is in no cavalier manner, but is contingent on

---

[215] Refer to the exegesis of verse 3 to see an analysis of how ἀπολύω has already been used by Matthew.

[216] In keeping with his characteristic use of doublets (including two instances of the 'exception clause' for divorce), Matthew records this question twice: "Whom do you want me to release for you: Barabbas, or Jesus who is called the Christ?" (Matt 27:17) and "Which of the two do you want me to release?" (Matt 27:21).

[217] Space does not permit a close study here, but it does appear to be a dominant Matthean motif.

[218] E.g. "The Roman pontiff's authority to dissolve nonsacramental marriages in "favor of the faith" (as an extrapolation of the 'Pauline Privilege') ...is frequently attributed to the

whatever is (already) bound and loosed in heaven, collegially asked and done in Jesus' name by his heavenly Father (Matt 18:19-20). Thus no other divorce teaching conflicts with Jesus'.

Beyond Matthew, the usual connection made between the ἀπολύω of the Matthean divorce passages and Deuteronomy 24:1-4 is not the strongest textual link with the Hebrew Bible. Technically, ἀπολύω does not even appear in Deuteronomy 24:1-4; the Septuagint uses βιβλίον ἀποστασίου twice (Deut 24:1, 3) to translate the noun "bill of divorcement" (סֵפֶר כְּרִיתֻת), but this is not in the place of any supposedly special technical term ἀπολύω for "divorce."[219] It is the simple verbal action ἐξαποστέλλω (LXX for שָׁלַח) "send away" that aligns with the verb ἀπολύω of Matt 19:3, 7, 8 and 9, plainly seen when paralleled:

> he writes her **a certificate of divorce** (βιβλίον ἀποστασίου) and puts it in her hand and **sends** (ἐξαποστελεῖ) her out of his house (Deut 24:1)

> Why then did Moses command one to give **a certificate of divorce** (βιβλίον ἀποστασίου) and **to send** (ἀπολῦσαι) her away? (Matt 19:7) [Bold added.]

It would have been even clearer if the Septuagint had utilised ἀπολύω instead of ἐξαποστέλλω!

It remains, however, that the Pharisees (or commentators) read far too much into ἀπολύω, giving their question a sense of "Why then did Moses command one to give *a certificate of divorce* and *(command one) to divorce [her]*?"[220] Jesus not only shows that it was not a command to divorce (Matt 19:8) but also offers no hint of approval for a man to specifically write a certificate of divorce and to send (ἐξαποστέλλω) his wife away "out of his house" (Deut 24:1). Jesus does not accept the whole cultural divorce process; only the verbal action of ἀπολύω, *the sending away* (of a wife), is in view if Deuteronomy 24:1 is referenced.[221]

'power of the keys' to bind and to loose (Matthew 16:19)." Himes and Coriden, "Indissolubility," 461.

[219] This is not to say that divorce is not in view, but ἀπολύω is simply not in the LXX text of Deut 24:1-4.

[220] Matt 19:7 (brackets and italics added) where "her" is an uncertain, C-rated variant. Aland et al, *Greek New Testament*, 71.

[221] "The AV [KJV] is generally recognised to be wrong to translate Deut 24:1 '…then let him write her a bill of divorcement'" (prescribing how a man should send his wife away; a sense also followed in the ERV). Woodhouse, "Divorce and Remarriage," 11. Even if ἀπολύω culturally became a word to designate a standard practice of divorce, the focus here

Like the Greek ἀπολύω, the Hebrew here, שָׁלַח, relates to other non-technical verbal actions in the Old Testament. For example, Jeremiah 3:1 uses שָׁלַח in the context of divorce, and the Septuagint translates it in the same way as in Deuteronomy 24:1 (ἐξαποστέλλω "to send forth"), but the same term also occurs in Genesis 42:4, "Jacob did not send Benjamin," and in Exodus 5:22, "Moses turned to the LORD... Why did you ever send me?" where שָׁלַח simply means "send." This plain verbal action is found for other synonymous Hebrew terms, for example, in Ezra 10:11 בָּדַל is usually taken to mean "to separate" or "to divorce" (cf. LXX: διαστέλλω "set apart" or "distinguish"), but the same term occurs in Genesis 1:6, "separate the waters," and in Genesis 1:14, "Let there be lights... to separate the day from the night," where בָּדַל simply means "separate."

Sure, context is determinative, but too much may also be read in from surrounding or later cultural ideas. This is not to deny that even within a common context such as marriage, synonymous terms like שָׁלַח and בָּדַל can have different connotations. The divorce in Jeremiah 3:1 implies a corporate "sending away" to destruction, whereas the separation in Ezra 10:11 forebodes no such peril,[222] but implies a "sending away" of unlawfully married wives, perhaps out of the Israelite community. Nonetheless, there remains a plain verbal action of "sending away" that is central to both meanings.

The verb ἀπολύω has a much older referent in another book of Moses, textually stronger than the indirect one found in Deuteronomy 24:1-4, where ἀπολύω is absent. It appears in the Septuagint when Abraham says, "Sovereign LORD, what will you give me, since I continue [ἀπολύομαι] childless and my heir is Eliezer from Damascus?" (Gen 15:2). Within a context of Abraham's concern for an heir and God's revelation of the fate of Abraham's descendants more than four hundred years later (Gen 15:1-21), ἀπολύομαι is best understood as referring to Abraham's death. Wenham translates this idea of "sending away" (to death) without offspring as "since I depart childless," noting

---

for Jesus is on the "sending away" and not on any of the other actions in a whole *marriage and divorce* process as found (but not prescribed or recommended) in Deut 24:1. The verbal actions there are: "he takes" (a wife/woman), "he marries" (so that they live together in a house, συνοικήσῃ), "he has found" (some indecency), "he writes" (a bill of divorce), "he puts" (the bill in her hand), and "he sends (away)," that is, the man sends the woman out of his house (οἰκίας).

[222] Indeed the opposite is true: it is perilous if the Israelites do not separate, for God may "consume" them (Ezra 9:14) in his "fierce wrath" (Ezra 10:14).

that here הָלַךְ is "used figuratively either meaning 'live' or 'pass away, die' (BDB, 234),"[223] and in Psalm 39:13 (WTT Ps 39:14) הָלַךְ also means "die" or "depart."[224]

Luke's Gospel also uses ἀπολύω in the same sense as Genesis 15:2 for the death of a righteous man. Simeon, after "waiting for the consolation of Israel," took the baby Jesus in his arms and blessed God and said "Lord, now you are letting your servant depart (ἀπολύω) in peace" (Luke 2:28-29).[225] This clearly refers to Simeon dying, for the narrative context is "he would not see death before he had seen the Lord's Christ" (Luke 2:26).

The contrast could hardly be greater: Luke, traditionally a Gentile, records the peaceful ἀπολύω "release" of a righteous man after Jesus is presented at the Temple according to the Jewish "custom of the Law" (Luke 2:27); whereas Matthew, traditionally a Jew, records the unjust ἀπολύω "release" of a notorious criminal according to Gentile custom (Matt 27:15) instead of a righteous man Jesus, "the son of Abraham" (Matt 1:1; cf. Gen 15:2), all at the instigation of Jewish leaders seeking to "destroy" Jesus (Matt 12:14, 27:20). The indictment in Matthew against an "evil and adulterous generation" (Matt 12:39; 16:4) only grows, while Jewish custom of the Law outshines worldly customs and injustice. *With or without a lawful cause of "sexual immorality"* (πορνεία, Matt 5:32, 19:9; cf. Luke 16:18) a "release" (ἀπολύω) from marriage, from life, or even from the Law, has deathly overtones.

Irrespective of whether or not Matthew knew Paul's writings, death is also associated with release from marriage in Romans 7:1-6. Paul speaks of dying to the Law ("written code") so as to belong to another (to serve in "the new way of the Spirit"), and this he compares with a woman's "release" (καταργέω) from marriage by the death of her husband. Remarriage (only) in this case does not attract a charge of adultery (cf. Matt 5:32; 19:9). Release from the *Law* and *marriage* are paralleled, but neither of these die, only the subjects are freed by death. To insert any exception clause that does not involve death completely ruins the principle taught here.

---

[223] G. Wenham, *Genesis 16-50*, WBC (Dallas: Word, 1994), 323-24.

[224] The LXX renders the Hebrew in Ps 39:14 ἀπελθεῖν (ESV Ps 39:13) which offers it equivalence to the ἀπολύω of Gen 15:2, despite a different base: ἀπέρχομαι ("to go away, depart") cf. Matt 16:4, perhaps adding deadly undertones of Jesus departing towards the cross (Matt 16:21-28) to fulfil the "sign of Jonah" in the exception clause just given (providing another link to the deadly exception clause in Matt 19:9).

[225] Also Gen 15:15, the Lord said to Abraham "you shall go (ἀπελεύσῃ) to your fathers in peace" (as in Ps 39:14 LXX, from the same base ἀπέρχομαι).

Jesus does not "abolish" or "destroy" (καταλύω) the Law (cf. Matt 5:17, twice); but for Christians it is rendered unemployed, useless or idle, where their "release" from the Law is expressed by the passive form of καταργέω (*"be discharged from, be freed from,"*[226] Rom 7:2 cf. ἀργός, Matt 20:3, 6). The term καταργέω "always denotes a nonphysical destruction by means of a superior force coming in to replace the force previously in effect."[227] For example, "light destroys darkness; ...as release by removal from a former sphere of control *free from.*"[228] More precisely, it is Christians who have been rendered unemployable (passive subjects of καταργέω) in relation to the Law, for *they have died* and not the Law (Rom 7:4, 6). Ephesians 2:15 similarly uses the same term to show that the Law's power to divide Jew and Gentile Christians has been overcome or "abolished" (καταργέω) by Christ, but Christ has not destroyed or "abolished" (καταλύω) the Law in the least detail for anyone under it.

In Matthew 19:1-12, Jesus' immediate Jewish audience is under the Law; Jesus has just been asked a question on a matter of Law; and Jesus' next words are loaded with explosive lawful consequences according to details of the Law that he has not abolished in the least. Jesus has already rejected divorce on the grounds found in Deuteronomy 24:1, connecting it with "hardness of heart" (Matt 19:8), so the culturally-legitimate practice described there could not have been righteous. Other culturally-legitimate grounds to divorce a wife, that are recorded extrabiblically, involve all sorts of offences such as a wife giving a husband untithed food, uttering a vow and not fulfilling it, going out in public with hair unbound, and speaking with any man in public.[229] Matthew gives not the slightest indication that such grounds were endorsed by Jesus.

The 'exception clause' of Matthew 19:9, however, does provide one legitimate *and* righteous cause for divorce, plus it does include a right to remarry – for the one left alive. Via a strict reading of the Law, "home plate"[230] *can be found* for Heth's old exegetical problem:

> The major criticism of the minority view that Jesus did not permit remarriage after divorce, even divorce for sexual immorality, has always been that in the first-century world a legitimate divorce included the right to remarry. ...I tried

---

[226] Bibleworks, Friberg 15296.

[227] Ibid.

[228] Ibid.

[229] Heth cites *m. Ketub.* 7:6 as legitimate grounds. Heth, "Remarriage for Adultery or Desertion," 67.

[230] "Jesus on Divorce," 7.

several times to argue that Jesus *had* made it sufficiently clear that he was investing *apolyo* ("I divorce") with a different semantic content, but my arguments have not proved convincing.[231]

Instead of investing the word "divorce" with new meanings, such as '*divorce a mensa et thoro*' (a de facto separation, where a couple remain legally married),[232] it is contended that Jesus' idea of a "legitimate divorce" is one solely based on the grounds of "sexual immorality" which by *very old meanings* involves capital punishment. This does not divest from divorce "the right to remarry," but this right – and it is a legal right (cf. Deut 25:5; Ezek 44:22; Rom 7:1-3) – can only come at an extremely high cost, as prescribed by very specific biblical legislation for sexual immorality. It is a deadly direction that is not ultimately desired by God, but the righteous demand is plainly found written in his Law, upheld in every detail by Jesus (Matt 5:17-19). To change or ignore the capital meanings in the Law would mean Jesus was investing *porneia* ("sexual immorality," and not "*apolyo*," contra Heth) with "a different semantic content."

---

[231] Ibid., 16.

[232] Although this 'separation from bed-and-board' is a much later idea, Luz maintains that "the Catholic practice of refusing divorce while allowing the partners to have separate living arrangements comes the closest to Matthew's intention." Luz, *Matthew 8-20*, 494. Luz here favours a Catholic interpretation over the Protestant, but then concludes that ancient laws are basically no longer useful for a modern ethic.

CHAPTER 8 – Jesus' Disciples &
Teaching on Eunuchs

Exegesis of Matthew 19:10-12

[10] Λέγουσιν αὐτῷ οἱ μαθηταὶ [αὐτοῦ]· εἰ οὕτως ἐστὶν ἡ αἰτία τοῦ ἀνθρώπου μετὰ τῆς γυναικός, οὐ συμφέρει γαμῆσαι.
[11] ὁ δὲ εἶπεν αὐτοῖς· οὐ πάντες χωροῦσιν τὸν λόγον [τοῦτον] ἀλλ᾽ οἷς δέδοται.
[12] εἰσὶν γὰρ εὐνοῦχοι οἵτινες ἐκ κοιλίας μητρὸς ἐγεννήθησαν οὕτως, καὶ εἰσὶν εὐνοῦχοι οἵτινες εὐνουχίσθησαν ὑπὸ τῶν ἀνθρώπων, καὶ εἰσὶν εὐνοῦχοι οἵτινες εὐνούχισαν ἑαυτοὺς διὰ τὴν βασιλείαν τῶν οὐρανῶν. ὁ δυνάμενος χωρεῖν χωρείτω.

Textual Notes:
Verse 10: UBS C-rated variant οἱ μαθηταὶ [αὐτοῦ] "his disciples"
Verse 11: UBS C-rated variant τὸν λόγον [τοῦτον] "these words"

Verse 10

The disciples said to him, "If such is the case of a man with his wife, it is better not to marry."

A combined, presumably spontaneous, reaction to forsake even entering into marriage indicates an immediately clear lesson. That the disciples see the *gravity of divorce*, and the *horrific type of divorcing* that Jesus speaks of in Matthew 19:9, is evidenced by the fact that Jesus does not clarify the 'exception clause'. There is no extended lecture on what πορνεία and μοιχᾶται culturally or lawfully really mean.

David Hill notes that the disciples "are virtually making the attractiveness of marriage contingent upon the possibility of easy divorce!"[1] Even if this were true, to give them some credit, it may actually be a merciful response. In anticipation of testing times within

---

[1] D. Hill, *The Gospel of Matthew*, NCBC (London: Oliphants, 1972), 281.

marriage, such as temptation and conflict (cf. Matt 18:7-9, 15-22), and from without marriage, such as persecution and flight (cf. Matt 5:10; 10:16-25), they might see that a single life *is better* than potentially destroying a wife's life or being destroyed by one's own failure to be faithful.

Most viewpoints, including that of the Protestant majority, do not properly account for the disciples' strong response.[2] To elicit anything like this sort of exclamation, the reasons are generally too reasonable, such as Jerome's idea of an amicable separation without divorce.[3] The disciples' *purported* "incredulity" and "horrified reaction" could hardly be from the thought that a marriage "*may* still be kept together" against a Jewish practice of "divorce for *porneia*"[4] – without death.[5] Nor could it be "unexpected"[6] that God would desire the restitution of marriage and the redemption of a spouse after a matter of "sexual immorality," especially as Hosea sets biblical precedent, as Heth appreciates:

> Jesus' goal would parallel Yahweh's relentless pursuit of unfaithful Israel throughout the OT and that he would try to save a marriage at all costs.[7]

A straightforward understanding of how Jesus fulfils the Law and the Prophets (Matt 5:17-19), without relaxing the Law, provides a better reading that may shock more than ever.[8]

In keeping with Jesus' radical discipleship demand, as found in Matthew 16:24, where one must "deny self" in renouncing common

---

[2] "It is better not to marry" are blunt words, especially for a married disciple (cf. Peter; Matt 8:14-15).

[3] Jerome, himself unmarried, appears to have regarded marriage as an inferior state and sex as unclean, even for the original marriage. In *Ag. Jov.* I he writes, "And as regards Adam and Eve we must maintain that before the fall they were virgins in Paradise: but after they sinned, and were cast out of Paradise, they were immediately married." Jerome, *Letters and Select Works*, vol. 6, Nicene and Post-Nicene Fathers: Second Series (New York: Cosimo, 2007), 359.

[4] Heth, "Jesus on Divorce," 16.

[5] Stott asserts that Jesus "abrogated the [Mosaic] death penalty for sexual infidelity and made this the only legitimate grounds for dissolving the marriage bond." J. Stott, *Issues Facing Christians Today*, 2nd ed. (London: Marshall Pickering, 1984; repr., 1990), 295. Cornes counters that this would cause no surprise for the disciples, whom he regards as "flabbergasted," because "no influential Jewish school was advocating the death penalty for adultery in Jesus' day, and the dissolution of the marriage bond in cases of infidelity was precisely Shammai's widely known position." Cornes, *Divorce and Remarriage*, 221.

[6] Heth, "Jesus on Divorce," 16.

[7] Ibid.

[8] Similarly, today's Protestant majority view would likewise shock the early church. "The modern notion of divorce as a 'dissolution' of the marital relationship with the possibility of remarriage afterwards was unheard of in the early Christian centuries." Heth, "Divorce, but No Remarriage," 95.

rights (cf. a "right to remarry"), "take up his cross" which means to take on suffering and shame – and not put shame on another (cf. Joseph in Matt 1:19), and to "follow" Jesus, who did not follow the crowds or worldly ways,

> the call to renounce the option of divorce would have been understood in the first century as an extraordinary call to costly discipleship.[9]

It is so costly that the extraordinary call is literally to "lose" (ἀπόλλυμι) or destroy one's own life (Matt 16:25), not the life of a spouse (cf. ἀπολύω for a capital offence).[10] Forsaking marriage altogether is not necessarily a better way, however Jesus does embrace and expound on non-marriage, and perhaps in sympathy with his disciples' sentiment, does confirm that it is a difficult but not impossible matter.

At this point in Matthew's narrative, the Pharisees disappear. It is not so much that their response "is irrelevant,"[11] but it is eye-catching that *Matthew does not record any celebration or complaint of Jesus aligning with a Shammaite or Hillelite position*. Their question (Matt 19:3) has led to a lawful response from Jesus where he has not added or subtracted one dot from the Law, bringing eye-opening revelation of the Law to uphold God's firm view on marriage. The pure in heart (Matt 5:8), and this includes Jesus' disciples, have blessed eyes that do see (Matt 13:16-17). A sincere desire for truth is fulfilled: "Open my eyes, that I may behold wonderful things out of your law" (Ps 119:18), whereas hard-hearted people may see but "never perceive" (Matt 13:14).

In the face of legal-minded opponents who test for lawful loopholes, Jesus has presented a lawful case in defence of permanent marriage. When pressed, Jesus has provided one stunning lawful 'exception' to the rule, but there is some ambiguity as to whether his disciples respond more specifically to this deadly case, or to his overall teaching. In either case, they attempt to summate his case.

The term αἰτία ("case") is found also in Matthew 19:3 where it is rendered "cause" (κατὰ πᾶσαν αἰτίαν, "for any cause"). Commentators tend to differentiate the meanings, but Nolland sees, "Matthew's use of αἰτία here is likely to be influenced by the use in v.3."[12] Morris observes

---

[9] Hays, *Moral Vision*, 377.

[10] The suggestion here is not that the Greek root is the same, but that Jesus' discipleship demand is an even more extraordinary call than the Law's capital demand to divorce a spouse for "sexual immorality."

[11] Davies and Allison, *Matthew*, III, 19.

[12] Nolland, *Matthew*, 775.

that for Matthew's very limited use of this term (three times), in the only use outside of this passage (τὴν αἰτίαν αὐτοῦ, "the charge against him," Matt 27:37), it has the "technical sense of an accusation, a reason for a judicial verdict."[13] This adds weight to αἰτία having a legal technical sense here too, where Jesus did not provide any *lawful human cause or case* (cf. Matt 19:3) for a man to divorce his wife (Matt 19:4-6; cf. Mark 10:3-12; Luke 16:18), but finally specified one *divinely legislated cause or case* (Matt 19:9).

Even then, this does not need to be construed only as a divine cause to divorce, it could also be taken as a divine cause to remain married. The same sort of double entendre occurs in Matthew 27:37, where against Morris, Nolland is adamant that "αἰτία is not a technical term for a legal charge" but τὴν αἰτίαν αὐτοῦ simply means "his cause" (cf. "cause" in Matt 19:3, and "situation / state of affairs" in Matt 19:10).[14] Both scholarly positions reveal the truth, however, for it is perfectly reasonable that the Romans would write the charge of a condemned man on his cross (even if in a mocking way), but it also truly heralded the general situation, or the state of affairs, or the cause of his death, or even the cause of his life: "This is Jesus, the King of the Jews." Additionally, all three Matthean uses of αἰτία occur in passages directly related to life and death: a couple's life allegiance to the marriage covenant that is to be terminated only by natural death or capital punishment, and Jesus' life allegiance to the Mosaic covenant that in fulfilment of the Law is terminated by capital punishment.

The disciples' exclamation concerns the lawful state of marriage, where the focus is on "the man *with* (μετὰ) the woman" and not narrowly on "a man *divorcing* (ἀπολύω) his woman" (italics added, and "wife" is naturally implied). The language nuance is nounal (the noun *with* the noun); it no longer centres verbally on a man's action of "sending away" (ἀπολύω) a woman. Similarly, the emphasis now is not on "any cause" or even "a cause" for divorce. The definite article with αἰτία is significant: "the case" or "the cause" allows for no other reason for a judicial verdict to alter the permanent state of "the man with the woman" or "one flesh"[15] union (cf. Matt 19:5, 6). By God's command to "hold fast" (Gen 2:24; Matt 19:5), "such" (οὕτως) a covenantal state is permanent: 'unto death do us part'. The lawful prerogative to

---

[13] Morris, *Matthew*, 484.

[14] Nolland, *Matthew*, 1194.

[15] Matthew's doublet may (again) reflect a fixed determination by God, where such lawful oneness cannot be humanly separated, even if humans separate by unlawful means.

terminate marriage does not rest with "the man"[16] but only with God himself.

In combining apparently conflicting scholarly ideas on αἰτία, this "such" (οὕτως) case then refers to the whole legal situation that Jesus has just taught (cf. "the word," Matt 19:11) on marriage, and not just narrowly to a spontaneous reaction based on the last sentence that Jesus has uttered. The focus is not so much on the extreme and deadly import of the 'exception clause', but on the extreme and deadly import of the absolute permanency of marriage. "Concerning this [matter]" (περὶ τούτου) – which in the Mark 10:10 parallel does not explicitly concern an exception – or a case "like this" (οὕτως) here, Jesus highlights what is so important about "the man with the woman."

The disciples have been judged here as sympathising with the views of Hillel,[17] and as being defeatist, believing "a lifetime of commitment to one woman is more burdensome than no involvement at all."[18] However, "The correct inference from Jesus' exaltation of monogamy is hardly the exaltation of celibacy."[19] Lifetime celibacy in church thinking might be traced to this conclusion by the disciples, but if the 'exception clause' is original to Jesus, along with the eunuch sayings, then it could not be in reaction to later asceticism. One might argue that Jesus prophetically *anticipated* this trend, where the church would also follow certain Essenes and Greek and Roman philosophers,[20] but it is better to interpret this word as Jesus adhering to and fulfilling *what has gone before* according to the Law and the Prophets.

The term συμφέρει ("it is better") parallels other frightful courses of action taken to avoid more fearful outcomes. This includes, with double emphasis, "it is better that you lose one of your members than that your whole body be thrown into hell" (Matt 5:29, cf. 30), spoken in relation to "adultery" and in the immediate context of Jesus' first teaching on divorce. The identical idea occurs again just prior to Jesus' second teaching on divorce, "It is better for you to enter life crippled or lame than with two hands or two feet to be thrown into the eternal fire" (Matt 18:8), and "It is better for you to enter life with one eye than with two eyes to be thrown into the hell of fire" (Matt 18:9).[21] If the thematic

---

[16] Or "the woman," but this is not Matthew's traditional concern.

[17] A. T. Robertson, *Commentary on the Gospel According to Matthew* (New York: MacMillan, 1911), 208.

[18] Davies and Allison, *Matthew*, III, 19.

[19] Ibid.

[20] Ibid.

[21] The "it would be better" of Matt 18:6 may link too, with the same outcome of hell (this time only implied).

paralleling continues into Matthew 19, which is likely, given "it is better" is a striking doublet in Matthew 18, as it is in Matthew 5 where the same doublet is *within the same speech* as Jesus' first divorce teaching (Matt 5:27-32), then the disciples find that the frightful course of non-marriage "is better" than the fearful inescapability of marriage. "Gehenna" has a narrative equivalence with marriage, but only insofar as the sin that sends anyone to a permanent place of fire and torture for debt payment is the same sin that violates the permanent state of marriage.

This is not to say that marriage is hell, but *the absolute permanency* expressed by this literary technique helps the reader to understand the disciples' strong reaction, and intensifies the reader's shock! An alternate understanding might be that Matthew wants to show that the disciples simply got it wrong: there should be no connection between marriage and hell, and therefore celibacy is not to be preferred. Or they got it right, and celibacy is to be preferred. However, the fact that Jesus supports both marriage and non-marriage counts against this. Instead, everything points to permanency, with a call to be faithful and merciful. It may also point to a deeper biblical principle, where whoever is unfaithful in marriage and disobeys God is "yoked" to another god, as seen in the ancient connection of sexual immorality with idolatry,[22] and the prohibition against marrying a foreigner (cf. Exod 34:15-16; Deut 7:2-4) to prevent adulteration of Israel's religion. Such rebellion equates with apostasy and attracts dire judgement.

In all, "it is better" to see that the disciples actually understood this "case" of "the man with the woman," and did not "go ballistic"[23] with a "foolish objection."[24] During their time with Jesus, the disciples have progressed to learn the meaning of God's mercy (cf. Matt 9:13) for they are blessed with understanding (Matt 13:16) – demonstrated in their comprehension of Jesus' parables (Matt 13:51), corporate worship of Jesus as "the Son of God" (Matt 14:33), final insight about false teaching (Matt 16:12), recognition of "Elijah" (Matt 17:13), and in Peter's testimony, "You are the Christ" (Matt 16:16). This understanding is also evident when marrying the disciples' response

---

[22] In the context of divorce, Jeremiah speaks of the "whoredom" of Judah that "polluted the land" in "committing adultery with stone and tree" (Jer 3:9), Israel's "detestable things" that must be removed (Jer 4:1), and Jerusalem's children who "have sworn by those who are no gods" and have "committed adultery and trooped to the houses of whores" (Jer 5:7).

[23] Witherington III, *Matthew*. 363.

[24] Also, "macho objection." U. Ranke-Heinemann, *Eunuchs for Heaven: The Catholic Church & Sexuality* (Hamburg: Hoffmann und Campe Verlag, 1990), 23.

with Matthew's "speech-narrative" pattern.[25] In comparing Matthew 18 with Matthew 19, we can figure that they have figured out Jesus' figure of speech. The disciples provide the perfect punchline to their Teacher's case, but one that is no laughing matter.

In Matthew 19:9, the sin to be resolutely avoided is "sexual immorality" (of the woman[26]) that could serve as capital grounds for divorce, or "adultery" (of the man) which is the capital offence committed for divorce without capital grounds. "If such is the case of the man with the woman," rather than ever committing this sin, then in exactly the same way as "it is better" not to have a hand, a foot, or an eye – which are all good and healthy body parts – if they cause temptations to sin that will result in being thrown into the eternal fire of hell (Matt 18:8-9), "it is better" for a man not to have a wife – who would otherwise be a good and healthy part of his "flesh" (cf. "one flesh," Gen 2:24; with double emphasis in Matt 19:5-6). However, cutting off this avenue to sin without committing "sexual immorality" or "adultery" in the process *is only possible outside of marriage*, which best explains why Jesus then expounds on eunuchs following the disciples' seemingly shocking but fitting response. Yet the disciples themselves are not necessarily shocked in any sense that they are upset, surprised or against this teaching. What they say may shock the reader with its firmness or simplicity, but Matthew attributes no fear or astonishment to them (as recorded elsewhere, in Matt 8:26; 19:25; cf. 7:28; 9:8).

Permanency is therefore central to Jesus' firm teaching and to the disciples' firm response, but the 'exception clause' remains firmly in view. The only lawful way to separate what God has joined in a "one flesh" union (Matt 19:6) involves action that is more drastic than tearing out one's own eye or cutting off one's own hand or foot (Matt 18:8-9), and this is the sending away of one's wife to be executed for a lawful charge of "sexual immorality." If one cannot take this extreme action – and it is not being recommended – then no marriage is to be terminated, otherwise the man who divorces his wife for any other "cause" (cf. Matt 19:3) risks being thrown into the eternal fire of hell (Matt 18:8-9) for committing "adultery" himself (Matt 19:9; cf. Rev 21:8).

The point is not facilely that "it is better" to cut off a wife just as "it is better" to cut off a limb to avoid hell, but if a man does resolve to

---

[25] Bolt, *Matthew*, 6.

[26] This may include matters where the woman is innocent, such as rape in the open country (cf. Deut 22:25-27) and unwanted or unwarranted divorce (cf. Deut 24:1-4), yet she is still defiled.

divorce his wife, then the only way for a man to avoid *adultery and hell* is that she be cut off only in the way that the Law specifies. At the same time, the man must never have had – and must do everything possible to avoid – even one lustful look at any other woman, otherwise he would be guilty of adultery too and deserve hell (cf. Matt 5:27-30). Even taken metaphorically, this means doing everything possible to avoid sin and to obey God's command to "hold fast" to a wife, with the same effort one would have to avoid self-dismemberment. It does not mean to divorce a wife for any cause, even for sexual immorality, and to treat her "as if dead."[27] This would be analogous to forever treating a healthy arm or good eye "as if dead" because it caused a person to sin. From this perspective, the disciples *rightly desire not to do any cutting off at all*, but to avoid marital union completely is not the only solution, nor necessarily their solution.

---

[27] Cf. the Reformed view, cited earlier.

Verse 11

> **But he said to them, "Not everyone can receive this saying (or [this] the word), but only those to whom it is given.**

The abandonment of marriage, simply because there is no easy exit, and a call to celibacy is far from the intended moral.

> Jesus' response should not be read as a concession to the disciples, as it would be if verses 10-12 were simply a call to celibacy... Such a reading would be totally out of character in Matthew's gospel.[28]

Such a reading would also overlook the function of Matthew's "narrative-speech-narrative pattern" that is useful to see this narrative section in a new light.[29] Rather than abandoning or severing marriage, mercy and forgiveness should be found within and without it. It is also highly unlikely that the disciples act as a kind of Pharisaic foil of lax divorce practices or give voice to a common low view of marriage, especially as the Pharisees have disappeared from the narrative scene and there is no rebuke or even sense of disappointment recorded on Jesus' part.

Jesus does not soften his message or offer any other grounds for divorce. Nor does he condemn celibacy as shameful. It is a difficult matter by whoever's λόγος (*logos*, "word"). Two main options have widely been "fiercely defended and also opposed"[30] on the main reference point for this word: Jesus' teaching on marriage, or the disciples' view that it is better not to marry. Nolland prefers the latter position, but even then, the disciples' word is given completely in reaction to Jesus' word, and Jesus may completely confirm their word, or simply extend his word to temper their word or correct it (just like in verse 9, the δὲ is not a strong adversative). So there need not be a definite distinction, but it would be unusual for Jesus to reference "the word" of his disciples, especially if it were inadequate.

"These words," located at the end of each of the five major teaching blocks in Matthew, always references Jesus' words there, but this does not preclude references to his words elsewhere (e.g. "these words of mine," Matt 7:24, 26). The only time Matthew uses "a word" for anyone else is in the negative ("a word against the Son of Man," Matt 12:32).

---

[28] Wenham, "No Remarriage," 32.
[29] Bolt, *Matthew*, 6.
[30] Nolland, *Matthew*, 776.

He uses "words" only once to refer to the disciples' speech ("hear your words," Matt 10:14) but what they say (and are rejected by others for) is precisely what Jesus has told them, "proclaim as you go, saying, 'The kingdom of heaven is at hand'" (Matt 10:7).

Jesus' original teaching upheld permanent marital faithfulness, and now further words will buttress and complement it with teaching that upholds permanent non-marital faithfulness. In the opening verse of Matthew 19:1-12, Jesus' previous teaching was referenced as "these words" (Matt 19:1).[31] If this or "the word" recorded in Matthew 19:1-12 is an extension of Jesus' prior teaching, "these words" in Matthew 18:21-35, then it can best be understood as providing the prime example of a relationship that requires forgiveness from the heart. "The word" reflects on Jesus' teaching that can only be received by some, whereas others will follow their own hard hearts (cf. Matt 19:8).

Nolland footnotes two more ways on how to take "this word" and it seems, especially from the fourth option, that the degree of difficulty seen in Jesus' teaching influences the reference point.[32] For instance, if Matthew 19:9 is understood "as allowing the man to divorce but not remarry in the case of marital infidelity on the part of his wife," then this might be viewed as "eunuch-like behaviour" that not all men would find easy.[33] It makes it even more apparent that if Jesus has taught a 'deadly exception' in Matthew 19:9, as proposed here, then not all can receive this truly difficult teaching, for it would mean that the "eunuch-like behaviour" permitted frightfully does pertain to the flesh.

Yet the εὐνουχίζω ("to make a eunuch of") is not to be achieved by self-castration, but by *physically cutting off the woman* to whom a man is joined to in a one-flesh union. Such language pre-dates Jesus by centuries (even if not with a capital sense):

> 'If she go not as you would have her go, cut her off and give her a bill of divorce' (literally 'cut her off from your flesh,' a reflection of the phrase 'they shall be one flesh' in Gen 2:24) (Ecclus. 25:26).[34]

---

[31] Cf. a later reference to Jesus' words, "the Pharisees went and plotted how to entangle him in his words" (Matt 22:15).

[32] Nolland, *Matthew*, 776.

[33] It is doubtful this would fit into one of Jesus' eunuch categories, for this man is not born that way, he is not made that way by another for he has instigated the divorce, and it is unlikely that Jesus advocates divorce for the sake of the kingdom. Also, "It is arbitrary to think that divorced people are universally gifted with celibacy." D. Turner, *Matthew*, BECNT (Grand Rapids: Baker, 2008), 462.

[34] Lane cites Joshua ben Sira (c.200BCE). Lane, *Mark*, 355.

This of course would also neuter the man's prospects for descendants with her (eunuchs forgo *marriage and children*), but it is not a practice that Jesus − or the Law − ever demands (cf. the metaphor of self-mutilation in Matt 18:7-9). Sin is to be avoided at all costs, not bodies abused or lives voided.

The perspective from which the judgement is made that "not everyone can receive ...but only to whom it is given" confirms that "the word" is Jesus', for he has the sovereign authority to give this word, the omnipotence to determine those "to whom it is given," and the omniscience to know that it will only be received by these people. The phrase ἀλλ' οἷς δέδοται is a "Greek idiom, dative case of relation and perfect passive indicative,"[35] where the perfect tense references a completed action with continuing results. The action or "gift from God" here is "not celibacy itself" or lifelong "eunuch-hood" as Ciampa and Rosner note.[36] Rather, it concerns Jesus' teaching that can be received only by those, *eunuch or not*, to whom the gift of receiving it has been given. From the time of receiving Jesus' word, these people have an ongoing ability to receive it, which implies empowered conviction, irrespective of any amount of innate ability to *remain celibate* or to *remain married*. Ciampa and Rosner frame it as contented service;[37] Jesus counts his disciples "blessed" (Matt 5:2-11) in their extraordinary call.

Heth writes that Matthew 13:11 is "the closest conceptual and linguistic parallel to Matthew 19:11" and explains this aspect of Matthean theology,

> To you [faithful disciples] it has been given to know the secrets of the kingdom of heaven, but to them [that is, unbelieving outsiders] it has not been given.[38]

So there are not two classes of disciples, one with a gift of celibacy and one without, but true disciples with insight as opposed to the Pharisees and unbelievers without, who will not accept Jesus' high standards for marriage.[39] Jesus' opponents, whilst fixated on a "right to remarry," will never know the secrets that would not only enable them to understand

---

[35] Robertson notes the connection with verse 12, but even there any "spiritual intelligence" granted does not *only involve voluntary* renunciation of marriage. W. Perschbacher, *Word Pictures of the New Testament*, vol. 1, The Updated Classic Work by A. T. Robertson (Grand Rapids: Kregel, 2004), 163.

[36] R. Ciampa and B. Rosner, *The First Letter to the Corinthians*, PNTC (Grand Rapids: Eerdmans, 2010), 285-86.

[37] Ibid., 286.

[38] Heth, "Divorce, but No Remarriage," 105-06.

[39] Ibid., 106.

(cf. the purpose of the parables in Matt 13:10-17) his teaching on marriage, but to obtain a righteousness based on mercy and the non-assertion of rights – including any right to marry at all – in order to enter the kingdom of heaven, where there is no marriage (Matt 22:30).

Verse 12

> **For there are eunuchs who have been so from birth,
> and there are eunuchs who have been made
> eunuchs by men, and there are eunuchs who have
> made themselves eunuchs for the sake of the
> kingdom of heaven. Let the one who is able to
> receive this receive it. "**

Without understanding the legal and prophetic implications of Jesus'
words about eunuchs, one should hesitate before applying this teaching
to pastoral situations. The Law remains in view here, and by it eunuchs
could not participate in Temple worship or marry.[40] Today, the Temple
no longer functions (and is inessential for Christian faith), and by
secular law, there are no barriers to a eunuch marrying (for example,
nothing in the Australian Marriage Act prevents this).[41]

Just as "hardness of heart" was a terminal judgement for Moses'
generation and for Jesus' generation (Matt 19:8), as were "sexual
immorality" and "adultery" (Matt 19:9) terminal judgements by the
Law, so too the term "eunuch" has terminal meanings in the Law,
although not in so deadly a sense. "Eunuch" (εὐνοῦχος), derived from
εὐνή ("bed") and ἔχω ("to hold"),[42] means

> (1) strictly *one in charge of the bed chamber*; hence *eunuch,
> castrated male* (MT 19.12b); often a trusted official in Middle
> Eastern courts (cf. AC 8.27-39);
> (2) of a male born without ability to reproduce (MT 19.12a);
> (3) figuratively, of one who imposes sexual abstinence on
> himself, *celibate* (MT 19.12c).[43]

The term could also be used as an insult (literally: "half-man").[44] By the
Law, eunuchs could not enter the assembly of Israel, so to be a eunuch
meant to be cut-off from the people (cf. Deut 23:1). As with the physical

---

[40] Scripture contains no explicit prohibition, but it appears implicit because the Hebrews
saw marriage as a social institution that demanded procreation. "A dry tree" without sons or
daughters (cf. Isa 56:3-5), cut-off from mainstream society (cf. Deut 23:1), implies celibacy,
as Jesus assumes in Matt 19:12.

[41] A eunuch may not be able to physically consummate the marriage, but it would still
be a valid marriage nonetheless, just as Joseph's unconsummated union prior to the birth of
Jesus was considered marriage (cf. Matt 1:20-25).

[42] Matthew uses this common term in relation to another question of Law to mean "be
married to another" ("It is not lawful for you to have [ἔχω] her," Matt 14:4), so in Matt 19:12
εὐνοῦχος could infer "(by Law) one (solely) married to a bed," or simply "a bed holder"!

[43] Bibleworks, Friberg 12123.

[44] Keener, *Matthew*, 471.

act of castration or a physical genital birth defect, once cut-off meant always cut-off from society. Without the ability to marry, eunuchs were thus forbidden from sexual intercourse, and therefore their name would also be cut-off, for they would have no descendants.[45] Only men were called eunuchs, which Jesus' teaching here reflects, and there was much shame in being considered one.

"For there are eunuchs…" is a phrase repeated three times, once for each type of eunuch, that connects this teaching with Jesus' prior statement to justify why "Not everyone can receive this saying" (Matt 19:11). Jesus does not say that "*not every eunuch* can receive this saying" nor "only those *eunuchs* to whom it is given;" instead, "not everyone" (Matt 19:11) has a general sense, just as the "for any cause" (Matt 19:3) and the "whoever divorces" (Matt 19:9) occur with the general sense. "Let the one [*anyone, not narrowly a eunuch*] who is able to receive this receive it" (Matt 19:12).

Those born without ability or disposition to marry could be accounted as "eunuchs," which could be taken positively as "made that way by God" for his special purposes, or negatively as "cursed by God" and never able to obey what was traditionally seen as a Creation mandate to procreate (Gen 1:28). "Made eunuchs by men" principally refers to castrated men, made that way by others. In the context of literally cutting off people by the Law's demand for execution for sexual offences (Matt 19:9), those divorced and who remain single (against a cultural "right to remarry") could also be accounted as "eunuchs," made that way by another.

As castration was forbidden by the Law,[46] the forcible making of another to be a "eunuch," including by divorce, cannot be condoned by Jesus. This also connects with the forceful act in Matthew 5:32, where a man *makes a woman* "commit adultery" if he divorces her – apart from divorcing her on the capital grounds of "sexual immorality." The man cuts off his wife in an unfaithful way that makes both of them break their covenant vows, *and* he cuts off his own flesh as forbidden for a one-flesh union (cf. Gen 2:24; Matt 19:4-5) in a painful and rebellious way as comparable with castration, resulting in grave permanent harm to himself and his family.

---

[45] However, a married man may become a eunuch by castration, separation or divorce.

[46] Davidson, *Flame*, 488. This Jewish understanding was based on Lev 21:20, 22:17-25, and Deut 23:1, such that no one with a blemish could offer sacrifices or enter the assembly, nor could any animal be given as a peace offering that was not whole.

Yet one eunuch, forcibly made that way, may have made his way into Jesus' genealogy. Matthew records Jechoniah[47] as "the father of Shealtiel" (Matt 1:12), but Luke lists Shealtiel as the "son of Neri" (Luke 3:27). If Shealtiel is the same person in both accounts, then one explanation is that Jechoniah adopted him from Neri, his biological father, because Jechoniah was made a eunuch in Babylon (Jer 22:30; Isa 39:7). Another explanation by Raymond Brown is that,

> *Luke makes* Shealtiel the son of the otherwise unknown Neri rather than of the last king Jeconiah; but his motivation may have been theological, namely, to avoid having in Jesus' ancestry a figure whom Jeremiah cursed thus: 'Write this man down as childless... for none of his offspring shall succeed in sitting on the throne of David and ruling again in Judah' (Jer 22:30).[48]

Brown also believes that "In the list from Zerubbabel to Jesus there are signs of confusion."[49] However, this still does not preclude the historical adoption of Shealtiel, and confusion surrounding the '*descendant of Babel*'[50] cannot be unexpected.

If Shealtiel were adopted, then he possessed the full legal standing as that of a biological son, gaining kingly inheritance rights (through Jechoniah, Hezekiah, Solomon, and David). This aligns with Matthew's goal in demonstrating that Jesus has a legitimate claim to Davidic kingship. It also squares with the Hebrew meaning of Shealtiel: '*I asked El (for this child)*',[51] suggestive of a difficult child-producing predicament (perhaps castration) that God overcame. It may not be a virgin birth (cf. Matt 1:18), but parallels of a "fatherless" child resonate, and it is astonishing that the Davidic line continues out of Babylon, let alone via a eunuch![52] So, rather than Luke creating or confusing vital

---

[47] Carson refutes Schweizer's suggestion that Jehoiakim and his son have been fused into a single character "since Matthew betrays deep knowledge of the OT not likely to be confused by one versional mistranslation [of 2 Kgs 24:6]." Carson, "Matthew," 95.

[48] R. E. Brown, *The Birth of the Messiah: A Commentary on the Infancy Narratives in the Gospels of Matthew and Luke*, ABRL (New York: Doubleday, 1993), 93. (Italics added.) Concerning whether Shealtiel or his brother Pedaiah (1 Chr 3:19) fathered Zerrubbabel, Turner suggests that Shealtiel died and Pedaiah entered a levirate marriage with his widow. Turner, *Matthew*, 60.

[49] Brown, *Birth*, 93.

[50] Zerubbabel: "זְרֻבָּבֶל begotten in Babylon," Bibleworks, BDB 2715. Literally: in 'Babel', which means confused (cf. Gen 11:9), ibid., BDB 1004. Hence, Zerubbabel may infer being born in confusion.

[51] Shealtiel: "שְׁאַלְתִּיאֵל *I have asked* (him) *of God*." Ibid., BDB 9597.

[52] Marriage is not essential to God's purposes; not only is God able to raise up children for Abraham from stones (Matt 3:9), he is able to raise up the long-promised Davidic king from a eunuch and a virgin! It may also be significant (and an area for further research) that

procreative events, Brown's best explanation for the inclusion of the women in Matthew's record of Jesus' genealogy might in principle solve any confusion: "It is the combination of the scandalous or irregular union and of divine intervention."[53] This also fulfills God's word to Hezekiah:

> And some of your own sons, who will come from you, whom you will father, shall be taken away, and they shall be eunuchs in the palace of the king of Babylon. (Isa 39:7)

Isaiah's prophecy of an eternal ruler on the "throne of David" (Isa 9:7) is significant too, although there is great mystery about how this will occur. Something incredible – outside of normal marriage relations – is foreseen: "the virgin shall conceive and bear a son" (Isa 7:14; cf. Matt 1:23). So, just as there was a question under Roman rule of Jesus' authority involving his birth and lineage, a similar question existed on how the Israelite kingly line could survive Babylonian rule. Matthew, with his strong motif of scriptural fulfillment, not only opens his Gospel with direct reference to a miraculous birth and a matter of divorce (Joseph and Mary), but he includes a eunuch (Jechoniah) to provide an intriguing Judah-Babylon connection with Jesus' teaching on divorce. Extraordinarily, the son of David (Matt 1:1), a ruler from Judah (Matt 2:6), a eunuch king of Israel, will be cut-off from his people, and Judah will again be sent away from God's house in a Babylonian exile, on the grounds of a dire matter of infidelity (cf. Matt 5:32; 19:9), but the Davidic throne will continue forever (2 Sam 7:13).

Earthly norms of marriage and child-bearing are not essential for the sake of the kingdom of heaven; eunuchs and adopted people have royal significance. God works in unexpected ways, sometimes through people least considered (cf. Matt 20:16) and lowly servants (cf. Matt 12:18; 20:26). Jesus, conceived "from the Holy Spirit" (Matt 1:18, 20), is essentially presented by Matthew as an adopted son himself, for it is Mary "of whom Jesus was born" (Matt 1:16) and it was prophesied "She will bear a son" – not Joseph. However, in naming Jesus (Matt 1:21, 25), Joseph accepts him as a legal son and firstborn male heir of God's promises to David and Abraham (Matt 1:1).[54] Matthew also presents Jesus as the "Son of God," an identity tested by Satan (Matt 4:3-6) and

---

this baby is born within marriage and yet not conceived within a blood covenant of a man-woman sexual union, that is, consummated marriage.

[53] Brown, *Birth*, 74.

[54] Kingsbury, *Matthew as Story*, 45.

the Jewish high priest (Matt 26:63), yet confessed by his Jewish disciples (Matt 14:33; 16:16) and a Roman centurion (Matt 27:54).[55]

Jesus' final category deals with those who have chosen not to marry for the sake of the kingdom. They could be designated "eunuchs," without physically being castrated or born that way. Obvious candidates associated with Matthew's Gospel include John the Baptist – who was killed for his views on divorce and remarriage, and Jeremiah – who was hugely unpopular in speaking of the divorce of the Northern Kingdom, and of Judah's evil and adultery (Matthew has the only occurrence of Jeremiah's name in the New Testament, implying important direct connections).[56]

Daniel is a possibility too.[57] Hauerwas writes,

> We must not forget that Jesus is a 'eunuch'. Accordingly, not all called to be his disciples will find it necessary to be married or have children. Jesus's commendation of those who for the sake of the kingdom have become eunuchs is a direct affront to Israel.[58]

Yet there is hope for these eunuchs,

> God promises the eunuch who feels like a 'dry tree' that he will be specially honored in God's house with a 'monument and a name better than sons and daughters' and with 'an everlasting name that shall not be cut-off' (Isa 56:3-5).[59]

After a "brief moment" of forsaking Israel "like a wife deserted," God will gather in his people as their "maker" and "husband" with great compassion (Isa 54:5-7), and his salvation will include Gentiles and eunuchs. The foreigner joined to Yahweh will enjoy God's house "for all peoples," no longer fearing that "The LORD will surely separate me from his people" (Isa 56:1-8). Isaiah contrasts these honoured ones with Israel's blind leaders, "offspring of the adulterer," who have deserted God and have made a covenant with worthless idols (Isa 56:9-12; 57:1-13).

---

[55] This positive testimony by Jew and Roman indicates that not all Jews face indictment, nor all Gentiles.

[56] God commanded Jeremiah, 'You shall not take a wife'" (Jer 16:1). "Jeremiah" occurs three times in Matthew (2:17; 16:14; 27:9), implying a highly intentional association. He was "a man of strife and contention to the whole land" and cursed by all (Jer 15:10), who "sat alone" because God's hand was on him (Jer 15:17). The person and words of Jesus, particularly on marriage, could be equally unpopular.

[57] "Daniel's chastity led to his being viewed as a eunuch (Josephus, *Ant.* 10.186; Liv. Pro. 4.2; *b.Sanh* 93b)." Turner, *Matthew*, 463.

[58] Hauerwas, *Matthew*, 306.

[59] Davidson, *Flame*, 489.

"Let the one who is able to receive this receive it" largely repeats the thought in verse 11. This doubling may indicate God's fixed determination: this is an ability that he will not revoke. The success in receiving is guaranteed, even though the receivers will not be perfect in following Jesus, whether as eunuchs or not. The teaching applies to everyone, meeting the greatest fear with the greatest hope. The greatest punishment for a man in Israel was to be "cut-off," which was a divine curse of extinction not only for himself but especially for his progeny.[60] It is the same fear that the eunuch faced every day, "The LORD will surely separate me from his people" (Isa 56:3), but the prophets assured that this would not be forever. In God's kingdom, "The cut-off were no longer cut-off."[61]

Jesus' teaching on marriage in Matthew is bounded by teaching on "children" (Matt 18:1-6; 19:13-15) and "eunuchs" (Matt 19:12). Both these unmarried social groups are often neglected or rejected. An implication for their inclusion is that these people have great value in the kingdom of heaven. Marriage, at least in the usual earthly sense, is not ultimate.

Many who are closest to the cultic centre – in tradition, power and proximity – are furthest from God's kingdom; and the furthest, the closest. Thus, a reversal is apparent: the cultural 'insiders' closest to the Jerusalem Temple system, many who are first, they will be last (Matt 19:30), cut-off or divorced from God as 'outsiders' destined for "outer darkness" (Matt 8:12; 22:13; 25:30). Yet the last, the distant – Galileans, Jews from lost tribes, plus Gentiles beyond the Jordan – and the socio-religiously cut-off, they will be first. This pericope that encompasses Jesus' most comprehensive teaching on divorce (Matt 19:3-12) begins with separatist leaders of society who test God and hold to a right to separate and remarry, yet will be forever separated from God for their hardness of heart. It ends with those cut-off from society who are tempted to fear that they will be cut-off forever, who hold no right to marry, who choose the things that please God, and who hold fast to God's covenant (Isa 56:4); such "blessed" people (Isa 56:2; cf. Matt 5:2-11) will be shown mercy and gathered in to God's house to forever belong.

---

[60] Ibid.
[61] Witherington III, *Matthew*. 365.

CHAPTER 9 – Marriage as Covenant

In keeping with the current Protestant majority view, the Matthean 'exception clause' ("except for [except on the ground of] sexual immorality") is taken as original and provides valid grounds for divorce, but the lawful ramifications of key words (as contended in this thesis), especially πορνεία and μοιχᾶται, bring vastly different conclusions. Heth, an influential supporter of the Protestant majority view, once humbly pondered,

> It may sound odd for me to say this, but my switch to the majority view could be wrong. Nevertheless, I have tried to enumerate the conceptual, theological, and exegetical reasons for my shift this time in my life, and the reader will have to decide for himself or herself whether or not I have made the right decision.[1]

Two crucial details led Heth to accept this current majority view:

> (i) That biblical covenants can be violated and dissolved; and
> (ii) That the 'one flesh' marital-kinship union (cf. Gen 2:24) is not a literal flesh and blood relationship.[2]

The first point is true, but does not necessitate a shift away from Heth's earlier view. It actually offers better grounds for it. All covenants can certainly be violated, but they do not then automatically dissolve. Covenant stipulations are enacted, which may be bloody.

The "first covenant" was inaugurated with blood (Heb 9:18; cf. Exod 24:6-8), and by its Law "almost everything is purified with blood" (Heb 9:22). So too it climaxes with blood, evidenced in Jesus' declaration, "this is my blood of the covenant, which is poured out for many for the forgiveness of sins" (Matt 26:28). **Matthew's sole use of the word "covenant" (διαθήκης) clearly refers to a blood covenant. His lack of "new" prefacing "covenant" puts Matthew's focus on the existing (Mosaic) covenant**, although this need not contradict Luke's focus on

---

[1] Heth, "Jesus on Divorce," 22.
[2] Ibid., 17.

"the new covenant in my blood" (Luke 22:20). Jesus' blood serves both to fulfil one covenant and inaugurate another.

Heth's second point is intimately related to his first, for the 'one flesh' marital-kinship union can truly be considered a blood covenant, where "literal flesh and blood" are integral. Physician Donald Downing explicates that after wedding vows are taken, "the covenant is sealed on the bed of copulation" where

> blood touches blood coming from the husband's semen and the wife's broken hymen. Marriage is a blood covenant …never to be broken.[3]

Likewise Bruce Malina writes, "The blood on both conjugal partners symbols that their marriage is a type of blood relationship."[4] **A key feature of blood covenants is that they terminate only upon death, which coheres with Jesus' teaching on the permanency of marriage, and his deadly Matthean 'exception clause'.**[5]

This helps to explain why the Law prizes virginity (Deut 22:13-21), and the high priest was to marry only a virgin (plus priests were not to marry women defiled by divorce or prostitution, Lev 21:7-14). The ruptured hymen offers the archetypal sign of a life-long blood covenant. The "one flesh" union of Adam and Eve was also a physical re-joining of the one same flesh that God separated to make Eve from Adam (Gen 2:18-24), possessing universal import (cf. Matt 19:4-6).[6] Even in non-virginal marriage, modern science shows that "blood touches blood" remains the case, despite increased risk of sexually-transmitted 'BBVs' (blood-borne viruses). **When one party dies, the blood covenant of marriage dissolves (cf. Rom 7:1-6; 1 Cor 7:39).**

Likewise, God's covenant with Israel is a blood covenant that only terminates with death. Israel cannot simply opt out and marry another (god), not without consequences. Instone-Brewer rightly stresses that marriage is a "mutually binding" covenant agreement with sanctions that come into force when a stipulation is broken,[7] but he neglects the deadly terms. From a human stance, any covenant or contract may be dissolved, perhaps with minimal loss or penalties ignored, but for the breach of a marriage covenant that God is party to, solemn vows are not

---

[3] D. Downing, *Marriage from the Heart* (Maitland: Xulon, 2012), 126.
[4] B. Malina, *The New Testament World: Insights from Cultural Anthropology*, Third ed. (Louisville: WJK, 2001), 149.
[5] Exegesis of Matt 19:1-12 was undertaken in this thesis independent of this blood covenant premise.
[6] Loader, *Jesus Tradition*, 243.
[7] Instone-Brewer, *Social and Literary Context*.

to be lightly dismissed, nor the "treachery"[8] of separating what God has joined considered inconsequential. While Israel lives, blessings for fidelity (Deut 28:1-14) and curses for infidelity (Deut 28:15-68) remain operative and the God-Israel marriage covenant stands *undissolved*.

With all ANE covenants, when violated, inviolable covenant stipulations are enacted. The vassal in a suzerain-vassal treaty cannot flaunt bonded demands with impunity. In marriage, God is the sovereign, *the* ANE suzerain or "king" of "the kingdom of heaven" (Matt 18:23, cf. Matt 19:10), who inaugurates the covenant with a binding stipulation that no human is to separate what he has joined together. In keeping with the Protestant minority view,

> Covenant-breaking on the part of Israel (unilateral withdrawal) calls for severe punishment... Punishment is not an expression of a broken relationship; punishment maintains the covenant.[9]

This needs only one proviso: punishment maintains the covenant unless it brings death.

Fidelity in marriage is so fundamental that it hardly needs stipulating, but in the Law the penalty for infidelity *is clearly stipulated*. Heth writes,

> Sexual faithfulness is one of the stipulations that is rarely listed in these ancient Near East marriage covenants, and thus one of the most important. This is confirmed by the fact that the death penalty for adultery *is* recorded throughout the ancient Near East and in the Old Testament itself (Lev. 20:10; Deut. 22:23-24; cf. Jer. 29:23).[10]

"Sexual immorality" (Matt 19:9) features as the only lawful grounds for termination of the marriage covenant, and when dealt with precisely according to what is written in Scripture, it is *a deadly divine divorce by God's prerogative*, for the separation is grounded in God-commanded Law. Jesus also teaches that divorce and remarriage on any other grounds is unlawful and attracts a deadly divine decree of "adultery," as grounded in God-commanded Law, unrelaxed in any detail. This applies to all who are party to the Mosaic Covenant. Despite the Law's sanguinity and perpetuity, it "does not preclude the

---

[8] In a marriage context, God decrees, "do not be faithless" (ESV) or "ye deal not treacherously" (KJV), and here divorce is connected with violence (Mal 2:16). Scripture also links violence to treachery (cf. Prov 13:2), and links both to evil and judgement (cf. Gen 6:11; Neh 13:27; Jer 3:8, 20; 5:11; Ezek 39:23).

[9] Heth, "Jesus on Divorce," 6.

[10] "Remarriage for Adultery or Desertion," 62. (Italics original.)

completely unexpected and infinitely gracious possibility that God may yet establish a new covenant"[11] – with the same marriage partner (cf. Jer 31:31-33).

The question of "what is the outcome if we take Jesus' sayings about divorce and remarriage in their most literal sense?"[12] is best answered not by wondering whether marriages are "indissoluble," or if "remarried couples are living in adultery,"[13] but by contemplating: who would be alive if Jesus' sayings were taken in their most literal sense? While it is true that "Divorce wreaks havoc in the lives of all concerned,"[14] a metaphorical notion of "Divorce is a form of death" where the "corpses are still walking around"[15] is far outside the Mosaic notion of death. The Law "does not merely define what is illegal; it also prescribes the sentence"[16] – a real corporal sentence – and marriage covenants must only be terminated by real death: natural or capital.

McKnight recognises the covenantal significance of marriage:

> The Bible's Story grounds all love in God's covenant love (Gen 12; 15). This covenant understanding of love means marital love reflects God's love, which means divorce destroys the reflection of the God who is utterly faithful.[17]

However, it is not "divorce" that destroys the reflection of God, but "sexual immorality" (cf. Matt 19:9). Indeed, God himself historically divorced a rebellious generation, so divorce can reflect God's utter faithfulness to promises made in covenant love. Just cause for this divorce is identical to that of Matthew 19:9: "sexual immorality," which biblically equates with unfaithfulness.[18] McKnight sees that the grounding of "all love" is exemplified in the Abrahamic Covenant (Genesis 12; 15), but overlooks that this grounding includes blood and death for the violator, as signified by the severed animals on covenant inauguration.

The Mosaic Covenant, *which also grounds all love* and is a reflection of marital love, likewise has bloody consequences for the covenant

---

[11] "Jesus on Divorce," 6.
[12] "Remarriage for Adultery or Desertion," 128.
[13] Ibid.
[14] Christensen, *Deuteronomy 21:10-34:12*, 568.
[15] Ibid.
[16] Harvey, *Promise*, 21.
[17] McKnight, *Sermon*, 95.
[18] Cf. "For all the adulteries of that faithless one, Israel, I had sent her away with a decree of divorce. Yet her treacherous sister Judah did not fear, but she too went and played the whore" (Jer 3:8). "For they are all adulterers, a company of treacherous men" (Jer 9:2).

breaker.[19] Concerning another covenant that Judah made, mirroring the emancipation of slaves in the Mosaic Covenant, God declared (by Jeremiah) that the transgressors would be like

> the calf that they cut in two and passed between its parts – the officials of Judah, the officials of Jerusalem, the eunuchs, the priests, and all the people of the land who passed between the parts of the calf. (Jer 34:18-20)

Jeremiah's prophecy only strengthens the Judah-Babylon connection with Jesus' teaching on divorce, portending deadly judgement for covenant violators.

---

[19] A major difference is that in Abraham's case, *only God* (as symbolised by a smoking pot and a flaming torch) passed between the severed animals (Gen 15:17), indicating that this covenant will not be broken.

CHAPTER 10 – Conclusion

This thesis set out to determine whether Matthew 19:9 contains a deadly exception that permits divorce and remarriage. Permanency of the Mosaic Law serves as the primary hermeneutic for understanding a deliberation on lawfulness. Given that Matthew's Gospel is steeped in the Hebrew Bible, and has a dominant scriptural fulfilment motif, it quickly became apparent that legal and prophetic considerations cannot be simply separated. The fierce intramural Jewish conflict, central to the plot, also signalled that the conflict within Matthew 19:1-12 was core to Jesus' indictment against "an evil and adulterous generation" (Matt 12:39; 16:4). Hence the Yahweh-Israel marriage covenant could not be ignored, although the divine judgement for this generation's infidelity does not mean God totally forsook his people.

In treating Matthew's Gospel as a bios of Jesus, and in examining Matthew 19:1-12 particularly within its narrative setting, it is found that Jesus' teaching on marriage and divorce has grave implications. Jesus proves himself to be a fully Torah-observant Jew, clearly demonstrating that he has not come to abolish the Law or to relax it in the least (Matt 5:17-19). If Jesus is taken at his word, and reference is made to what he references in Scripture, then "sexual immorality" and "adultery" are deadly matters for all who pose a question on lawfulness and appeal to Moses. Thus, when grounds of "sexual immorality" (Matt 19:9) are employed in accordance with biblical commandments as found written in the Law (e.g. Lev 20:10; Deut 22:22-24),

(i) A wife may be executed for this capital crime and then (and only then) can the husband remarry (if his wife is dead, he does not commit adultery in remarrying); or

(ii) A husband who does not have his wife executed for this (and only for this) capital crime and yet divorces her and remarries another woman, then he commits adultery and deserves execution himself.

Hence, one should pause before appealing to Moses and relying on the Matthean 'exception clause', for it is deadly.

No wonder Jesus' disciples provide a shocking moral (Matt 19:10). If a man has to resort to legal execution to terminate a marriage, and only then may he remarry without committing adultery, then it is better not to marry! This is far stricter than even Shammai's stance.

When critical terms are examined, a clear distinction can be made between "sexual immorality" (*porneia*, Matt 19:9) and "a matter of indecency" (*'erwat dabar*, Deut 24:1). The Protestant majority view errs in obscuring or denying a difference between these capital and non-capital offences under the Law. The legal text that the Pharisees reference, Deuteronomy 24:1-4, is not prescriptive but merely descriptive of cultural practice indicative of Israel's "hardness of heart," which includes religious defilement. Its sole legislation involves a warning against committing the abominable; it does not legislate grounds for divorce. Moses permitted divorce for "a matter of indecency" to expose those who test God and break his command for marriage, but Moses never permitted divorce for "sexual immorality" – not without the God-commanded penalty!

Study of the term עֶרְוָה (*'erwah*) shows that "nakedness" is not sinful in itself, but can be viewed negatively, positively or neutrally according to its context. In Deuteronomy 24:1, עֶרְוַת דָּבָר (*'erwat dabar*) is commonly understood as a negative characteristic of the woman that provides grounds for divorce, but the matter is never objectively substantiated. Nor does the text designate it as ritual uncleanness. Instead, the matter is anything unfavourable about a wife as found in the eyes of a hard-hearted husband. This matter originally could not have inferred "adultery" or any other kind of "sexual immorality," for this would conflict with other Mosaic legislation just prior. In upholding the Law, Jesus did not confuse "a matter of indecency" with "sexual immorality" (or "adultery"), even if capital punishment was no longer enforced, or was never enforced (highly unlikely, as it was widespread ANE law and practice for centuries). Neither did Jesus follow Jewish traditions (such as Shammaite and Hillelite) that conflated these matters.

Study of the term ἀπολύω (*apolyo*, to "divorce" or "separate") reveals that this verb is simply a non-technical term used for the act of "sending away" a narrative object; it never carries an implied nounal state granting a culturally assumed "right to remarry." **Indeed Matthew 19:9 speaks powerfully against any such right, labelling remarriage "adultery" in all cases apart from one deadly 'exception'.** Different contexts can of course afford different meanings, but too often far too much has been read into this basic verb, particularly via cultural practice that Scripture does not endorse. In the context of divorce, ἀπολύω raises critical questions, routinely overlooked, regarding the origin and the destination of the one sent away, and whether the sender acts righteously. To be sent away from a house – especially God's house – for "sexual immorality" is a fearful judgement, as is the judgement for unrighteous or unmerciful eviction. To be reconciled in a house is a hallmark of mercy.

Other relevant terms certainly have legal, technical and deadly meanings. In particular, σκληροκαρδία ("hardness of heart") does not refer to general human fallenness, but is a rare characterisation that functions specifically as a terminal indictment. The term is used twice in the New Testament, solely by Jesus in relation to divorce. It only properly occurs once in the Septuagint and this is in a prophetic context concerning the Babylonian Exile. On that grim occasion, Israel's hard-heartedness that resulted in expulsion from the Promised Land finds primal meaning in the hard-heartedness that prevented an earlier generation from entering the Promised Land. Opposed to God's word, Israel's stubborn rebellion matches that of their pagan slavemaster back in Egypt.

The concept of a hard heart does occur elsewhere in Scripture, but similarly only in relation to stubborn rebellion with deadly consequences. This implies that the divorce practice in Deuteronomy 24:1-4 is not to be followed, for it involves testing God and violating his clear command, via Moses, to permanently cleave to one's wife (Gen 2:24). Therefore, interpreting Matthew 19:8 as an indictment, and not as a concession, facilitates understanding Matthew 19:9, where this one sentence develops the one argument.

"Hardness of heart" (σκληροκαρδία) could signal "irreconcilability,"[1] but this does not mean that "the subsequent remarriage is no sin for the released partner – whatever the reason for divorce may have been."[2] The remarriage *is no sin* only if a former spouse has died directly due to the irreconcilability – purely for a capital matter (cf. *porneia*, Matt 19:9), and not for Gehring's "whatever the reason" (cf. Matt 19:3). Even so, today's legal language of "irreconcilable differences" should make us shudder, for God will not forgive those who do not forgive each other (cf. Matt 6:15; 18:35).

The terms πορνεία and μοιχᾶται also have legal, technical and deadly meanings. In Matthew 19:9 (and 5:32), Jesus provides *real and lawful* grounds to exit *real and lawful* marriage. Nonetheless, the church's

---

[1] Gehring, *Marriage*, 228.
[2] Ibid.

ancient position against divorce can be upheld without resorting to exegetical gymnastics.[3] The death of a spouse, by natural or capital means, is of course valid grounds for remarriage. Paul – a former "Pharisee of Pharisees" (Phil 3:5) knows this (cf. Rom 7:3; 1 Cor 7:39), and Jesus' Jewish audience – including Pharisees who test him – would surely know this. The early church, aware of their Jewish roots, would also have known this.

There is a common understanding that marriage ends with death, as reflected even to this day in the marriage vow: "*until death do us part*," where the term "part" derives from "separate"[4] in Matthew 19:6. Death can be considered 'The Great Divorce'.[5] This straightforward interpretation explains why other biblical writers need not mention the deadly 'exception clause' at all. Indeed, for those with a more Gentile audience in mind, it would likely cause confusion, especially with Roman law at the time mandating divorce for adultery.

The application of a Hebrew Scripture such as Deuteronomy 22:22 to the "sexual immorality" of Matthew 19:9 produces a clear-cut, lawful and awful conclusion. Unlike the current Protestant majority view, with its lack of clear grounds and enormous boundary pressure to include other offences, the only boundary problem for this 'deadly divorce' view concerns what constitutes a capital offence *within* the Law's category of sexual immorality? The adultery of Matthew 5:27-30 informs us here, especially as it forms the introductory context for Jesus' first teaching on divorce (Matt 5:31-32). The boundary includes not merely physical immorality, but even lustful intent or coveting, as already covered in the Decalogue.

Jesus never offers a more relaxed divorce provision than the Law. His teaching is not antithetical to the Law, especially when we take his word for it (Matt 5:17-19). Nor is it even an intensification, because the

---

[3] "If, however, one can find a view that satisfies the usual objections to the traditional view without resorting to exegetical gymnastics, then it is certainly worth close scrutiny." Witherington III, "Exception or Exceptional," 571.

[4] E.g. an early Quaker Marriage Certificate reads, "'Friends, in the fear of the Lord, and before this assembly, I take this my Friend A. B. to be my wife, promising through divine assistance to be unto her a loving and faithful husband, until it shall please the Lord **by death to separate us:**'…and the like *mutatis mutandis* for the woman; *who was also now required to sign by her maiden or widow name*." (Italics original. Bold added.) L. Howard, "Quaker Marriage Ceremony and Records," *The Yorkshireman: A Religious and Literary Journal by A Friend* 3, no. 50 (1834): 23. Note the woman is to sign in anticipation of the decease of her husband!

[5] C. S. Lewis, *The Great Divorce: A Dream* (London: Geoffrey Bles, 1946). A thematic connection here does not mean that Lewis had the same understandings on divorce as this thesis.

Tenth Commandment already legislates on heart-matters,[6] the other nine commandments are equally intense (all contain elements of capital punishment[7]), and "most of the sentiments found in the Sermon [on the Mount] already appear… in old Jewish sources."[8] That adultery must be avoided at all costs (cf. Matt 5:27-30) is not "something startlingly new"[9] either (cf. Gen 39:7-20).

Calvin gives an obvious objection to a strict legal reading, "For if the adulteress was punished by death, what is the point of talking about divorce?"[10] This is countered by realising that a "sending away" to death *is divorce* in the most strict and terminal sense. Yet rather than rueing that adultery largely goes unpunished due to the "perverted indulgence of magistrates" who refuse to execute,[11] the full lawful implications for covenant infidelity must be seen in the light of the unpayable debt of Matthew 18:21-35. Hearers and readers are to obey Jesus' words, but those under a new covenant – unmentioned in Matthew's Gospel – are not commanded to obey the capital codes of the Mosaic Covenant or enforce these codes as they make disciples of all nations. Instead, they must observe the lessons: sexual immorality and adultery (and even the rebellion of a son) are offences against God that attract the death penalty by the Law (as written and originally understood), but without changing the Law – and with precedent in the Hebrew Bible, they are to desire mercy (cf. Hos 6:6) and champion forgiveness.

Marriage is a perfect place to practice the merciful love that God desires and models. Divorce ultimately reveals an unwillingness to show mercy, to forgive, and to love as promised. With respect to solemn vows to love in sickness and in health (and similar sentiments) 'until death do us part', mercy is forever apt for any two sinners whom God has joined together, so that when trouble occurs – even adultery – resolve is made to always cleave to one's first love, and to never send them away. Unforgiveness and a refusal to cancel debts jars with the

---

[6] Guelich notes that πρὸς τὸ ἐπιθυμῆσαι αὐτὴν (Matt 5:28) "means literally 'in order to desire having her (sexually)'. The very same desire to have her (ἐπιθυμέω) appears in the tenth commandment." Oddly, Guelich then concludes that Jesus' demand "completely transcends the Law's demands." R. Guelich, *The Sermon on the Mount: A Foundation for Understanding* (Waco: Word, 1982), 193-94. On Matt 19:9 he then claims, "Jesus' teaching on divorce, according to Matthew, actually countered the Law." Ibid., 209.

[7] Although not expressed in the (summary) Decalogue form, these commandments are expounded on elsewhere in the Law, with capital legislation. Hamilton, *Pentateuch*, 196-98.

[8] Allison, *Sermon*, xi.

[9] Ibid.

[10] Calvin, *Harmony*, II, 247.

[11] Ibid.

typical depiction of Jesus' compassion (cf. Matt 6:12; 9:2; 18:21-35), and there are terrifying consequences for those who do not forgive.

The disciples' response to Jesus' teaching (Matt 19:10) draws attention away from those who demand a "right to remarry" to those who are cut-off from any "right to marry." No further questions are then recorded on the topic, which suggests that the disciples understood, or Matthew's readers should now understand, a straightforward lesson. As the two questions (Matt 19:3, 7) were from hard-hearted opponents with a crafty agenda, this may also mean that when God's voice is heard (cf. Heb 3:7, 15; 4:7) and he is not tested on "any matter," including the command to permanently "cleave" (Gen 2:24), but is simply obeyed, then hearts will not be hardened (Matt 19:8). Furthermore, Jesus' teaching on eunuchs offers hope even for those who can never marry, have been cut off from marriage, or have chosen not to marry for the sake of his kingdom. Mercy abounds for all who can receive Jesus' word.

A prohibition against divorce appears to be closest to the early church's position, but in questioning the (more recent) doctrine of the 'indissolubility of the bond',[12] the permanent 'indissolubility of the Law' offers a better original basis. However, perpetual separation (from life, or from bed and board) should not occur at all if mercy is granted. Scripture's only positively stipulated separation is that for a mutually agreed time of prayer (cf. 1 Cor 7:5), but never for unlimited detachment in a divided house. Houses are important for security, fellowship, and belonging; Matthew associates godly houses with wisdom and mercy, as against divided ones with foolishness and destruction.

Those who advocate divorce "for any cause" (Matt 19:3) prove just cause for their own destruction, for "hardness of heart" (Matt 19:8) is a terminal charge grounded in dire offences against God (Matt 19:9). This coheres with Spadaro's proposal that Matthew intentionally wrote to "demonstrate 'just cause' for the termination of the Levitical constitution and its house/temple."[13] Essentially Matthew can be read as "the story of two houses: one of these houses would survive the cataclysmic events of AD 70, while the other would become desolate."[14]

---

[12] Cf. Himes and Coriden, "Indissolubility."

[13] Spadaro, *Matthew*, 280.

[14] Ibid., 283. One house will bear God's name with a son of King David ruling it forever (2 Sam 7:12-16).

> For any post-70 reader, the words 'your house is forsaken'
> [Matt 23:38] would naturally evoke thoughts about the
> destruction of the Temple.[15]

However, Matthew's knowledge of this event need not imply "clearly a post-70" publication date.[16] As Matthew's core interest lies in the fulfilment of the Law and the Prophets, justification for this destruction is given not only in Jesus' words a generation prior to the event (cf. Matt 23:36) but centuries earlier in the Hebrew narrative of the God-Israel marriage covenant.

Bauckham and others have brought good direction in seeing Matthew as historical biography, but Spadaro discerns that

> the use of this bios genre may not satisfactorily explain the
> interest of Matthew's author in connecting his document to
> the existing Hebrew story with its specific emphasis on
> fulfillment.[17]

Something greater is here than an attempt to relate the life of Jesus. The striking polemical rhetoric presents as a unified feature and central to Matthew's purpose. En route to Jerusalem, where "the house of God" (Matt 12:4; cf. "my house," Matt 21:13) stands, Matthew 19:1-12 is situated as the first clash between the two "house-keepers" (Jesus and the Jewish religious leaders), suggesting a deeper significance than merely a difference on household marital affairs. The marriage relationship between God and his people is ultimate, and fidelity is vital.

It is better not to marry (cf. Matt 19:10) than to send away a spouse – or to be a spouse sent away – in the manner God has ordained for the grounds of sexual immorality, or to remarry without sending away a spouse in such a manner – which would be to commit adultery (cf. Matt 19:9) that warrants death according to the Law as written. Jesus offers other reasons for not marrying – likely better reasons than the fear of divine judgement (although Jesus is not recorded as saying "It is *even* better") or at least more common. One reason stems from birth, which Jesus himself might claim because his life mission did not involve sex. A second reason is prevention; *physically* this may include Daniel (overseen by "the chief of eunuchs," Dan 1:7) and Jeconiah (Jer 22:30) in Babylon, and *legally* those divorced for any (non-capital) cause without divine sanction to remarry while their former spouse lives (otherwise, adultery is committed). A third reason is for the sake of the

---

[15] M. Goodacre, *The Case against Q: Studies in Markan Priority and the Synoptic Problem* (Harrisburg: Trinity, 2002), 23-24.

[16] Ibid.

[17] Spadaro, *Matthew*, 5.

kingdom of heaven; Jeremiah exemplifies this (Jer 16:1), and Jesus is the exemplar par excellence. These reasons are not actually 'exceptions' to an absolute law, for although marriage is the norm *it is lawful* to not marry.[18]

For those who do marry, it is perilous to lightly use the Matthean 'exception clause' as an 'escape clause'. This completely relaxes Jesus' lawful answer in the Pharisaic test and misreads Matthew's purpose. Neither does it square with Israel's history and ancient wisdom. For covenant infidelity, God brings destruction on a hard-hearted generation, and a grave warning from the wilderness long resounds. Notwithstanding due judgement, "should you not have had mercy…" (Matt 18:33) reveals God's utmost desire, and offers wisdom for fellow servants who have solemnly vowed to love and to hold 'until death do us part'. That Jesus taught both "no divorce, yet one allowable exception" does not involve him in "hopeless contradiction."[19] Taking Jesus at his word on the Law's indissolubility (Matt 5:17-19) avoids a hopeless contradiction in equating a capital offence of πορνεία (*porneia*, "sexual immorality") with a non-capital offence of עֶרְוַת דָּבָר (*'erwat dabar*, "a matter of indecency"), and provides consistent biblical teaching *for any case* concerning marriage or non-marriage.

---

[18] Likewise, Mary's case is exceptional but not an 'exception' to the Law (for had she been raped in the countryside, it is *perfectly lawful* to not execute the innocent), and also the men of Ezra's time did something rather exceptional when they finally *obeyed the Law* and put away their unlawful wives. Cf. *lawful* cases of the poor taking *peah*, or Temple work, *comprise (and do not break) Sabbath law.*

[19] Contra J. Reumann, *Jesus in the Church's Gospels: Modern Scholarship and the Earliest Sources* (Philadelphia: Fortress, 1968), 240.

APPENDICES

APPENDIX 1. Extra Notes on Methodology

Reading Matthew's Gospel as a Biography

Matthew's Gospel centres on Jesus' life, death and resurrection. Richard Bauckham notes a strong current trend of treating the Gospels as ancient biography, each "written with the intention that they circulate around all the churches (and thence even outside the churches)."[1] Graham Stanton considers it undeniable that the Gospels come under the broad literary genre of 'lives', that is, biographies.[2] While recognising the uniqueness of the Gospels, David Aune has done much to locate them in this genre amongst the wider literary landscape of antiquity, where

> Biography may be defined as *a discrete prose narrative devoted exclusively to the portrayal of the whole life of a particular individual perceived as historical.*[3]

For Richard Burridge, the similarities between the Gospels and Graeco-Roman biography are clear from structural affinities and shared topics such as personal history, sayings, and deeds.[4] This leads Michael Bird to surmise that Matthew and Luke are even more like the biographical genre,

> given their exploration of Jesus' ancestry, birth, childhood, and early life, than are Mark and John, which have no account of Jesus' birth and upbringing.[5]

---

[1] Bauckham, *Gospels*, 1-2.

[2] G. Stanton, "Foreword," to R. Burridge, *What Are the Gospels?: A Comparison with Graeco-Roman Biography* (New York: Cambridge University, 1992), ix. Stanton adds, "Even if the evangelists were largely ignorant of the tradition of Greek and Roman 'lives', that is how the Gospels were received and listened to in the first decades after their composition."

[3] D. Aune, *The New Testament in its Literary Environment* (Philadelphia: Westminster, 1987), 29. (Italics original.)

[4] Burridge, *Gospels*, 111-26.

[5] M. Bird, *The Gospel of the Lord: How the Early Church Wrote the Story of Jesus* (Grand Rapids: Eerdmans, 2014), 238.

With an opening genealogy reminiscent of the "scroll of origins" (Gen 2:4 and 5:1) and littered with heroes from Israel's sacred history, Bird sees that

> Matthew has thus performed an intensification of Mark's biographical form and brought together Greco-Roman and Jewish literary patterns in the process.[6]

Irrespective of early or late publication, Matthew's Gospel presents a pre-70CE perspective, so Matthew 19:1-12 is viewed in this context, not an unspecified later one. All New Testament books offer this perspective; none record the fall of Jerusalem as past tense. Matthew depicts the divorce question as one asked by *Pharisees who approach Jesus*, not a Matthean exchange with rabbis post-70CE.[7] Assertions of a post-70CE situation spread doubt on the historicity of an original situation, and Matthew's integrity in recording it as original. Even if other ancient writers put their own words into the mouths of other figures, this gives no reason to believe that Christian writers did the same, especially when their revered subject was so committed to the truth and so against false witness.

For this text, the author's location is unknown, but Jesus' location is provided by the author ("the region of Judea beyond the Jordan," Matt 19:1), along with prior ("he went away from Galilee," Matt 19:1) and later movements ("we are going up to Jerusalem," Matt 20:18). The date of publication is also unknown, whereas Jesus' historical setting is reasonably determinable ("At that time, Herod the Tetrarch..." Matt 14:1). Matthew's church politics is a matter of wide conjecture, but Jesus' geo-political setting can be sufficiently understood from the text and other contemporary sources. Matthew intends his readers to understand Jesus' situation rather than his own.

The tendency "to read the Gospels as though they were Pauline letters"[8] falters due to no sense of occasion being provided by Matthew. Even when a scholar "looks for the Evangelist's beliefs as they are embedded in the First Gospel and considers what his beliefs meant in their cultural and religious contexts,"[9] determining "the Evangelist's beliefs" is difficult given the wide-ranging beliefs of scholars, many of

---

[6] Ibid., 242.

[7] For example, Meier writes, "The Pharisees of Matthew and John are largely the post-70 Pharisees and their allies who are swiftly on their way to becoming the early rabbis of tannaitic Judaism." Meier, *Marginal Jew*, 3, 335.

[8] Bauckham, *Gospels*, 2.

[9] McKnight, "Gospel of Matthew," 532.

whom are uncertain about the identity of any evangelist, let alone where and why they write! For example, Mark Powell speaks about

> An author (in this case, the person we call 'Matthew' – though we do not actually know who he was or what his name might have been) composes a text.[10]

Naturally "cultural and religious contexts"[11] are important, but *conjectures* on them should not be considered more important than the contexts (cultural, religious, historical, and narrative) provided by Scripture.

Issues persist on whether the 'exception clause' of Matthew 19:9 is original (Jesus' *ipsissima verba*)[12] or a late insertion by a Matthean community (Jesus' *ipsissima vox*),[13] but this clause and the "any cause" of the Pharisees' test question (Matt 19:3) will not be treated in this thesis as fictional where "their removal eliminates difficulties."[14] Although some commonality in conclusions is reached, Luz's methodology is rejected:

> *I suggest* that the fictitious elements in Matthew's story can be understood only from the perspective of the transparency of his Jesus story for the situation of the post-Easter Matthean community. ...The starting point for *my reflections* is *the assumption* that historical developments lie behind Matthew's compilation of sources and traditions.[15]

For Luz, the meaning of the text is not found primarily in the ancient text but in modern theories about "historical developments." Rather than seeing the gospel as a true historical account, Matthew is presumed to be a "bold composer" who "creates sequences of the Jesus story and

---

[10] M. Powell, *Methods for Matthew*, Methods in Biblical Interpretation (Cambridge: CUP, 2009), 15.

[11] McKnight, "Dictionary: Matthew," (1992) 532.

[12] Even Streeter believes that the Matthean dialogue (at least in part) is "more original" than the Markan, "Matthew's section on Divorce (Mt. xix. 3-12) is both more naturally told and more closely related to the Jewish usage than the parallel in Mark (Mk. x. 2-12). The words 'for every cause' in the question put by the Pharisees look more original..." B. H. Streeter, *The Four Gospels: A Study of Origins* (London: Macmillan, 1936), 259.

[13] Reumann sees that Matthew likely adds the 'exception' due to Christian community experience over the ensuing decades. Reumann, *Jesus in the Church's Gospels*, 240. Similarly, Instone-Brewer, *Social and Literary Context*, 135-36. However, late insertion challenges Matthew's integrity for he presents these words as Jesus': Matt 19:9 "And I [Jesus] say to you..." cf. Matt 19:4 "He [Jesus] answered..."; Matt 19:8 "He [Jesus] said to them..."; and Matt 19:11 "But he [Jesus] said to them..."

[14] Davies and Allison, *Matthew*, III, 5.

[15] U. Luz, *Studies in Matthew* (Grand Rapids: Eerdmans, 2005), 7. (Italics added.)

of Jesus' preaching which are fictional in character, and he knows this."[16] Such fabrication is purportedly justified by

> Matthew's openness to rabbinic influences, his desire to lessen apparent conflict with the Torah, and his tendency to tack on qualifying phrases.[17]

The resultant surgery takes the text back to look something very like Mark 10:1-12. However, it does not adequately explain the difficulties but explains them away, especially when a judicial reading of the Torah can well suffice.

A literary-critical study of Matthew's Gospel forms the main approach of this thesis, largely bracketing out source-critical issues. Matthew is treated as an "open" text with a relatively open implied readership, as against implied readers in a specific Christian community as many scholars have assumed.[18] Stephen Barton has a healthy scepticism of "such a slippery, ideologically 'loaded' word as *community*"[19] and he questions using the text as a mirror of it,

> Has sociological inquiry replaced theological inquiry, even to the point of being (implicitly or explicitly) antitheological: God is out, community is in?[20]

Barton bemoans that too often the meaning of the text lies

> sociologically speaking, less in what the author meant than in how the text functions to legitimate the interests of the community. Thus, for example, the emphasis on rigorous observance of the law in Matthew betokens a community in competition with Pharisees and at risk from Gentile antinomians...[21]

Authorial intent is respected by striving to find meaning from a straightforward reading of the author's account that those who oppose Jesus, and test him on matters of Law, really did oppose Jesus. As Donald Carson writes,

> To argue that Matthew's chief opponents are not really the "Pharisees" of A.D. 30 but the rabbis of A.D. 85 ...presupposes a known and agreed set of disjunctions

---

[16] Ibid.

[17] Davies and Allison, *Matthew*, III, 5.

[18] Bauckham, *Gospels*, 2.

[19] S. Barton, "Can We Identify the Gospel Audiences?," in *The Gospels for All Christians: Rethinking the Gospel Audiences* (Grand Rapids: Eerdmans, 1998), 176. (Italics original.)

[20] Ibid.

[21] Ibid., 177.

between the two. In reality there is an enormous amount of scholarly disagreement about who the Pharisees of Jesus' day were, the authority they enjoyed, the influence they wielded, their relationships with the Sadducees, and much more.[22]

Rather than a strongly reductionist reading focussed on concerns of a community reconstructed behind Matthew's Gospel, this thesis focusses on reading the Gospel as a narrative about Jesus. In doing so, Matthew's "emphasis on rigorous observance of the law" then finds relevance not simply for an ancient local situation, but for anyone (without demanding universal Law-observance).[23]

The historical-cultural background certainly offers "a rich treasure of material that will usually aid the exegetical task immeasurably."[24] However, as Gordon Fee cautions,

> much of our background literature has come down to us by chance circumstances, and that much of our information is pieced together from a wide variety of extant sources that reflect but a small percentage of what was written in antiquity. While it is proper to draw conclusions from what we have, such conclusions often need to be presented a bit more tentatively than NT scholarship is wont to do.[25]

Carson reminds us that "we have almost no access to the history of the early church during its first five or six decades *apart* from the New Testament documents."[26] Some historical speculation is welcome, but "it is methodologically indefensible to use those speculations to undermine large parts of the only evidence we have."[27] This impacts much study of Matthew 19:1-12 and intensifies the need to find meanings within the framework of given texts, rather than where "New

---

[22] D. Carson, "The Jewish Leaders in Matthew's Gospel: A Reappraisal," *JETS* 25, no. 2 (1982): 163.

[23] See Vine, *Audience*. Runesson provides a positive review of Cedric Vine's argument, with a conclusion that "local audience reconstructions are nonviable, the only options remaining being general: either 'Jewish-Christian' or 'all Christian' audiences." A. Runesson, "The Audience of Matthew: An Appraisal of the Local Audience Thesis," *RSR* 41, no. 1 (2015): 24-25.

[24] G. Fee, *New Testament Exegesis: A Handbook for Students and Pastors* (Louisville: WJK, 2002), 111.

[25] Ibid. Blomberg echoes this concerning "the confidence with which various scholars compound speculative hypotheses to create elaborate reconstructions of the history of the formation of Q, the nature of the supposed itinerant preachers who created it, and the makeup of the Q community to which this document was addressed." D. Black and D. Beck, *Rethinking the Synoptic Problem* (Grand Rapids: Baker, 2001), 27.

[26] D. Carson, *Exegetical Fallacies* (Grand Rapids: Baker, 1996), 132.

[27] Ibid.

Testament documents are squeezed into… reconstructed history."[28] Even when historical reconstruction of early tradition is trustworthy, including that of Jewish culture preserved *within* Matthew's Gospel, care must be taken to determine whether this is upheld or challenged by Jesus.

In his landmark social and literary study, Instone-Brewer warns: "All readers come to the text with their own presuppositions. This was true in NT times as now."[29] This statement follows his own presupposition: "The background knowledge and assumptions of a first-century reader were already forgotten by the second century."[30] Seeking "to understand the New Testament through the eyes of a first-century reader," Instone-Brewer makes a further claim,

> The first-century readers of the New Testament were not particularly interested in the meaning of the Old Testament.
> …The original intent of the words to the original audience of the Old Testament was of little interest to them.[31]

Instone-Brewer footnotes, "This does not mean that they were not interested in the context or the plain meaning of the text," which tends to contradict what he has just proposed. He seems to mean that the early church was "not particularly interested" in the first-century meanings found in rabbinic Judaism.

However, it would be more accurate to say that the early church was extremely interested in the Jewish scriptural epic (cf. Acts 7), but not particularly interested in rabbinic teaching that did not align with their Christological reading of the Law and Prophets. Instone-Brewer's own "'plain' meaning of the text"[32] is rooted in early rabbinic Judaism, but methodologically this does not mean that he has arrived at a better Christian understanding, simply a rabbinic one. This itself has problems, for the rabbinic literature greatly postdates the New Testament (e.g. the Mishnah was recorded around 200CE), so there is a danger of anachronistically reading later rabbinic views back into Jesus' teachings.

Furthermore, we can all be guilty of "confusing our own world-views"[33] with Jesus' view. Less distance in time or place from Jesus' own social location need not guarantee more enlightenment, perhaps

---

[28] Ibid.

[29] Instone-Brewer, *Social and Literary Context*, ix.

[30] Ibid.

[31] Ibid., x. Instone-Brewer's support for this is found in his own study of *rabbinic traditions* that could be arguably dated back to the pre-70CE period.

[32] Ibid., 304.

[33] Carson, *Fallacies*, 105.

only more shock (cf. Matt 19:10) at teachings that challenge cultural norms. There is a definite "need for distanciation on the part of the interpreter" or else "we will read our mental baggage into the text,"[34] but also "it is possible to overemphasize the historical 'gap'."[35] We cannot assume that the original audiences, whether the direct hearers of Jesus or the initial readers of Matthew's text, did not have their own unscriptural cultural practices and mental baggage. On such a personal topic as divorce, ingrained biases are natural and powerful. It is better to "recognize them and, in dialogue with the text, seek to make allowances for them."[36]

Synoptic Matters

Since Burnett Streeter's work, the Four Source Hypothesis (4SH) that posits Markan Priority and the existence of a sayings source underlying the double tradition in the Gospels of Matthew and Luke has been the general consensus of New Testament scholars. Streeter famously asserted,

> only a lunatic would leave out Matthew's account of the Infancy, the Sermon on the Mount, and practically all the parables, in order to get room for purely verbal expansion of what was retained.[37]

The consensus position that Matthew's Gospel is a Greek text that was dependent on the Greek text of Mark has led many scholars to doubt the older Patristic tradition that the author was the Apostle Matthew. However, John Robinson has observed,

> The consensus frozen by the success of the 'fundamental solution' propounded by Streeter has begun to show signs of cracking.[38]

Flaws in the 4SH (refined 2SH) continue to surface and Ward Powers guards Mark from Streeter's charge of lunacy for any dependency on Matthew.[39] One argument stems from assessing the situation in the early church and the way Jesus' teachings were disseminated in the Christian communities. Powers contends,

---

[34] Ibid., 104.

[35] J. Green, *Hearing the New Testament: Strategies for Interpretation* (Grand Rapids: Eerdmans, 2010), 37.

[36] Carson, *Fallacies*, 104.

[37] Streeter, *Four Gospels*, 158.

[38] J. A. T. Robinson, *Redating the New Testament* (London: SCM Press, 1976), 93.

[39] B. W. Powers, *The Progressive Publication of Matthew: An Explanation of the Writing of the Synoptic Gospels* (Nashville: B&H, 2010), 257-345.

It is impossible to believe that Mark would not have known any of the Sermon on the Mount and other teachings until and unless he read it in Matthew and/or Luke.[40]

This turns Streeter's argument on its head, for if Mark wrote first,

> Why then did he omit all this teaching from his Gospel? …However, if Mark was the last Synoptist… it is quite simple to account for his omission… *it was already available to those for whom it was intended, the church, in the Gospels of Matthew and Luke* – and he had a different purpose in writing.[41]

Space does not permit examination of this direction in scholarship,[42] but it does signal that Matthew's 'exception clause' *need not be* a late insertion. It could further be held that a late insertion would put the original audiences of other Gospels at a disadvantage, for they have only known absolute prohibitions against divorce and remarriage. That they took for granted Matthew's 'exception' (without explicit text) is problematic, especially when the early church leaders unanimously did not have this understanding.

Jesus and Sabbath Law

If the narrative parallels of the Sabbath and divorce accounts are sustained, Jesus' personal word has immense shock value in both accounts because it jars those who know the deadly written demands of the Law. Even if first-century Jews did not normally apply the death penalty, the Law was still sought (and misused) to eventually warrant Jesus' death (cf. Matt 26:65-66). Yet the Hebrew Bible also testifies to mercy on those who live under the Law, as shown to David and his famished followers in 1 Samuel 21:1-9. (Whether David was guilty or not, God shows his mercy by making the Bread of Presence available.) In this case, Matthew uses "hunger [πεινάω]" for strong desire (Matt 12:3; cf. 4:2) – which is linked to Law-giving (Deut 9:9, 18), righteousness (Matt 5:6), and the alleviation of physical need (Matt 12:1; 15:32; 21:18; 25:35, 37, 42, 44). These three elements are not necessarily in conflict. On the Sabbath, Jesus shows mercy by healing a man with a withered hand (Matt 12:9-14); and he teaches that mercy

---

[40] Ibid., 260.
[41] Ibid. (Italics original.)
[42] See e.g. W. Farmer, *The Synoptic Problem: A Critical Analysis* (New York: Macmillan, 1964). B. Orchard and H. Riley, *The Order of the Synoptics: Why Three Synoptic Gospels?* (Macon: Mercer, 1987). D. Peabody, *One Gospel from Two: Mark's Use of Matthew and Luke* (Harrisburg: Trinity, 2002).

must be shown to one another, notably in marriage (Matt 18:21-19:9). This is completely righteous and lawful.

Yet something greater[43] is here than the Temple system that demands death and sacrifice for human sin, and it contrasts sharply with the Pharisees' merciless desire to destroy Jesus (Matt 12:14), the son of David. Nonetheless, Jesus still honours the Temple (Matt 21:12-14), as against the Jewish leaders who denigrate it and the altar (Matt 23:16-22), and the chief priests and the scribes who are indignant about "the wonderful things that he did, and the children crying out in the temple, 'Hosanna to the Son of David!'" (Matt 21:15). Spadaro highlights the Gospel's priestly subtext, "Matthew makes his account an ultimate contest between two high priests; only one would survive Matthew's theodicy."[44] This contest may be nascent with David and the Levitical priesthood. David is from Judah, but he appears to be a priest (2 Sam 6:12-19) in the order of Melchizedek (Ps 110:4).[45]

So, any sanction given to David and his followers in 1 Samuel 21:1-9 need not be read as a change in Sabbath law, because even from Genesis, within the written Law a different law of a different priesthood is at work that surpasses the Law (cf. Hebrews 5-7). The Christ-event further reveals this deeper law available for those under the Law, before the Law, and without the Law. *The love command summarises both laws (Matt 22:40).* In the event of Christ being tested on a point of Law (on the Sabbath, or divorce), he does not change the Law for his own sake, the sake of his immediate followers, or the sake of the church within a new covenant (unmentioned by Matthew) after the Christ-event. Instead he points to God's steadfast love (mercy) from of old. Mercy cannot be demanded, but in the light of a priesthood greater than that of the Temple, it can certainly be asked for.

Nevertheless, is it valid to reinterpret Sabbath law not for *the sake of any human need* but for *the sake of human life* in a time such as the Maccabean Revolt? This might be compared with assisting a sheep that has fallen into a ditch on the Sabbath (Matt 12:11); how much more is it right to protect human life? Beyond the major difference in a planned rebellion versus a spontaneous act of compassion, the following matters

---

[43] "Mercy" could be "something" greater than the Temple, for μεῖζόν here is neuter, but this is unlikely to be the direct referent. Even if so, mercy stems from Jesus, thus he is ultimately the greater one in view. See Yang, *Sabbath*, 181. Also McIver, "Sabbath," 238.

[44] Spadaro, *Matthew*, 29.

[45] Melchizedek was *king and priest* of Salem – the old name for Jerusalem (Gen 14:18), so David may be Jerusalem's king and priest too. Psalm 110 is clearly in view with respect to Jesus' identity as the Son of David (Matt 22:41-45).

raise much doubt that the Maccabean Revolt provides a godly precedent for a change in Law.

Was there any scriptural precedent or prophetic word that gave the Maccabeans God's sovereign sanction? If so, resounding success for this revolt would be expected, with foreign enemies vanquished and the Hellenising influence removed. Even if no express scriptural support were found, victory might validate a special exception in Sabbath law. The author of 1 Maccabees obviously believed that a change was lawful to protect human life, and the revolt was righteous (2 Maccabees makes this even clearer as the revolt happens after God reportedly sees the righteousness of the martyrs who died in chapter 7). Prior to this historical account, there was no clear biblical ruling on the subject.

Other Jews may have well-disagreed with the Maccabeans and considered that the revolt was not righteous at all, perhaps believing that oppression under the Seleucids was divine judgement on Israel (analogous to the Babylonian Exile) or that God would apocalyptically intervene to liberate them (cf. Daniel). God has long-used other nations to punish or discipline Israel for her unfaithfulness. Revolt against divine judgement is tantamount to rebellion against God. Therefore, to interpret or bend the Law to suit any effort to counter God's discipline is to disobey God.

A good precedent can be found in the book of Jeremiah, where (against false prophets such as Hananiah and Shemaiah) one godly prophet urges the Israelite king to surrender to the foreign power, and tells the Israelites to seek the "shalom" (welfare, peace, prosperity) of Babylon (Jer 28-29). Resistance, including any fighting or flight on the Sabbath, is unwarranted and futile. Concerning another later attack on Israel with "the abomination of desolation," Jesus does not counsel revolt or suggest a change in Sabbath law, but instead urges people to pray that their flight *will not be on a Sabbath* (Matt 24:15-20).

There is also contention as to whether the "*so-called* Maccabean revolt"[46] was primarily an act of war against a foreign power – was it really a revolt or a civil war between traditionalist (Hebrew) Jews and Hellenised Jews; infighting that recalls Jesus' words about a divided house (Matt 12:25). Historically, this hostility did not usher in an era of "shalom" in the land – at least in the longer term. It led to more Jewish infighting and (against the original ideals) increasing Hellenisation of the Jews (with less strict observance of Torah).[47] The military and

---

[46] "The most important literary sources for the *so-called* Maccabean revolt are Daniel, 1 Maccabees, and 2 Maccabees." (Italics added.) D. Harrington, *The Maccabean Revolt: Anatomy of a Biblical Revolution*, Old Testament Studies (Eugene: Wipf & Stock, 1988), 14.

[47] Ibid., 87-108.

political power wielded by the Hasmoneans stands in direct contrast to the type of power (in meekness) displayed by Jesus. It might be said that such faith in human power betrayed a faithlessness in the power of God, whom Israel was meant to trust to fight their battles for them, even on a Sabbath, even against the goliath of a Roman army.

Despite all good intentions, the Maccabean Revolt did not offer Israel lasting peace and security, it ultimately failed to stop foreign rule, and it resulted in even greater foreign influence (meaning compromise of the Law due to the imposition of foreign law). Rabbi Ken Spiro summates,

> The history of the Hasmonean Dynasty is a classic case of one of the great tragic families starting off so illustriously and ending so disastrously, bringing the Jewish people to ruin.[48]

Some general principles can be gleaned from this. Lawful exceptions did allow for Temple workers to profane the Sabbath for the purpose of fulfilling their Temple duties, while Sabbath-keeping remained the norm (working on it could still attract the death penalty for non-Temple duties, at least in theory). It might be reasonable to extend the lawful exceptions in Sabbath rest to all Jewish people at a time of war or revolt – *if any Jewish fighting is not ultimately against God*, while maintaining the Sabbath strictness at other times. However, to change the meaning of "adultery" or "incest" or "rape" or any other sexual offence – *sins with very clear biblical rulings* – based on a change in circumstances, such as war or a change in government, is not reasonable at all.

In times of foreign rule, it could be deemed necessary for Israel to alter punishments for sexual offences, such as mandating divorce (without death) for adultery. Even then, it must not be assumed that the gravity of these offences changes – adultery still deserves death under the Law, even if another (lesser) punishment is meted out. However, if offences of the Law can be altered according to secular law, it can be assumed that when the state ruler assumes Judeo-Christian beliefs and (rightly or wrongly) attempts to uphold the Law, then any capital demands may be reinstated.

---

[48] K. Spiro, "History Crash Course #29: Revolt of the Maccabees," Aish HaTorah, www.aish.com/h/c/t/h/48942121.html. Spiro footnotes, "Perhaps the greatest irony of the legacy of the Maccabees is what is named after them today: The Maccabiah Games (the Jewish Olympic Games, started in 1932 and held every four years in Israel). There is virtually no cultural institution that more typifies ancient Greek culture than their athletic competitions. That the Maccabees, who gave their lives to save Judaism from Greek influence, should have Greek-style sporting events named after is the most ironic of endings to this tragic story." See also, www.maccabiah.com/2017/

This fearfully was the case with Emperor Constantine – indeed the demands of the Law in the realm of sexual offences were taken in an even more strict direction.[49] Also, sixteenth-century Protestant reformers championed a strict return to the Law:

> Luther vehemently rejected adultery, appealing to Scripture (death sentence for adulterers in Lev 20:10; Deut 22:22) and demanding that the government authorities put adulterers to death.[50]

Calvin too

> appealed to Scripture to demand the death of the adulterer... This was put into practice to a certain extent in Geneva after his death, where a number of adulterers were actually executed.[51]

Faulty Interpretative Roots

In considering the topic of marriage and divorce, Origen interpreted the "release" (ἀπολύω) of Barabbas in Matthew 27:16 as an act of adultery, where the people

> went out from the dwelling of her husband, and, going away, has become joined to another man, to whom she has subjected herself, whether we should call the husband Barabbas the robber, who is figuratively the devil, or some evil power.[52]

Unfortunately, Origen tried to align this schema of events with Deuteronomy 24:1-4, which he also reformulated, somewhat like Meier believes Jesus did (discussed earlier):

> God neither commanded nor willed divorce. But Moses wrote that a bill of divorce should be given 'on account of the hardness of the heart' of the Jews.[53]

With Isaiah's passage concerning a divorce certificate (Isa 50:1) in mind, Origen thought that the "mother of the people" (Judah) initially

---

[49] E.g. Edict 9.24.1 in Pharr, *The Theodosian Code and Novels and the Sirmondian Constitutions*, 245.

[50] S. Müller, "Adultery: IV. Christianity," in *Encyclopedia of the Bible and its Reception, Vol 1* (Berlin: de Gruyter, 2009), 466.

[51] Ibid.

[52] Origen, *Matthew*, 2.14.19. Origen, "Commentary on the Gospel of Matthew," in *The Ante-Nicene Fathers*, ed. A. Menzies (New York: Cosimo, 2007), 508.

[53] Origen, *Hom. Num.* 16.4.4. *Ancient Christian Texts: Homilies on Numbers* (Downers Grove: IVP, 2009), 94.

separated herself from Christ, her husband, but afterwards
when there was found in her an unseemly thing, and she did
not find favour in his sight, the bill of divorcement was written
out for her.[54]

Although "a sign that she has received the bill of divorcement is this,
that Jerusalem was destroyed"[55] proves insightful – and coheres with
this thesis, there are serious problems with Origen's overall
understanding.

Firstly, there is no indication in Matthew's text that God's people
left "the dwelling of her husband," and in "going away" became "joined
to another man" (Barabbas) in marriage.[56] This leaving of the husband's
dwelling can easily be construed for the dispersive event of 70CE, when
the Jerusalem Temple or "house of God" is destroyed, but not for Jesus'
crucifixion. Choosing Barabbas over "Jesus who is called Christ" (Matt
27:17, 22) can be viewed as "adultery" (cf. Matt 5:32; 19:9), that is, a
breach of faith with the Messiah in a treacherous unrighteous act that
sees him killed, but this does not mean that Israel as a nation
metaphorically married the devil, or an evil power, in the guise of
Barabbas.

Secondly, there is no hint that the nation of Israel "subjected
herself"[57] to Barabbas, who quickly disappears from the scene.
However, it could be said that "an evil and adulterous generation" (cf.
Matt 12:39; 16:4) subjected herself to *evil leadership at that time*, to
religious "blind guides" (Matt 15:14; 23:24; cf. Isa 9:16), who sided
with pagan Rome. In doing so, she ultimately subjected herself to the
devil, where Barabbas is simply an alternate "Son of the Father"[58]
favoured by "sons of serpents" (Matt 3:7; 12:34; 23:33). This charge by
Jesus might be a Matthean way of saying "You are of your father the
devil" (cf. John 8:44). From a positive perspective, the old tradition that
identifies the criminal as *Joshua Barabbas* could be understood as
"Yahweh saves" Israel by having another *Joshua* (Jesus, the true Son of
the Father) take his place.

Thirdly, as an archaic antecedent to the Protestant majority view,
Origen confuses an "unseemly thing" (cf. "a matter of indecency," Deut
24:1) with "adultery" (Matt 19:9; cf. Deut 22:22):

---

[54] Origen, *Matthew*, 2.14.19. "Matthew," 508.

[55] Ibid.

[56] Ibid.

[57] Ibid.

[58] Danker sees this as a common Aramaic name: 'son of Abbas' [where Abba means
"father"]; and according to old tradition, his full name was Ἰησοῦς Βαραββᾶς Joshua [Jesus]
Barabbas. Bibleworks, Danker 1144.

for what was more unseemly than the circumstance that, when it was proposed to them to release one at the feast, they asked for the release of Barabbas the robber, and the condemnation of Jesus?[59]

This was not "unseemly," but criminal! So too, "the first wife, accordingly, not having found favour before her husband"[60] understates the offence. God's *first and only wife* is found to be guilty of adultery, treachery, sexual immorality, and idolatry, as Isaiah, Jeremiah, Hosea and Ezekiel all prophesy, and these offences all deserve death. The divorce of an ill-favoured wife, with a right for her to remarry, finds no parallel with Israel's perilous state. It is true that a third-century Alexandrian scholar such as Origen, renowned for allegorising his sources, may not be the best guide to what Matthew meant in his original historical context, yet the Protestant majority view has some alarming connection with these deep interpretative roots.

---

[59] Origen, "Matthew," 508.
[60] Ibid.

APPENDIX 2. Engaging Other Relevant
Biblical Accounts

A Woman Caught in Adultery

Even if John 8:5 reflects commonly knowledge,[1] this still does not mean that first-century Jews applied capital punishment, or in any way favoured it. Likewise, most Christians reject applying any capital code of Moses, including taking life for life. 'The Woman Taken in Adultery' (John 7:53-8:11) "reflects the dilemma: the Jewish Law required execution but Roman law forbad it,"[2] although this rather oversimplifies the matter, for as already noted, Roman law did provide scope for execution (for example, killing by fathers). This episode has largely developed into a classic case of Jesus superseding the Law to bring grace, in the context of an unlawful mob-lynching. Grace certainly prevails, but even in assuming the integrity of the account,[3] did Jesus really change the Law here, and were those testing Jesus intentionally flouting the Law?

J. Duncan Derret offers good insight into the way in which the Law was traditionally interpreted to avoid a capital conviction of adultery, and shows how the testing of Jesus in John 8:1-11 actually indicts the testers (cf. Matt 23:28) without relaxing the Law.[4] In this way it parallels the test of Matthew 19:1-12. Israel was not to test God but to diligently keep God's commandments and follow all of his statutes (Deut 6:16-25). They were to be a holy people (Lev 19:2; Deut 7:6), with even a holy camp (Deut 23:14) and holy vessels (1 Sam 21:5). Thus if no one was ever condemned for adultery as per the written Law code, Israel might claim to be very holy. Jesus fundamentally challenges any such notion, for he condemns his generation as evil and adulterous.

---

[1] The Mishnah distinguishes two cases for adultery: *Sanh* 7.4 specifies stoning for sex with a woman betrothed to another man. Neusner, *Mishnah*, 596-97.; *Sanh* 11.1 specifies strangulation for sex with another man's wife. Ibid., 607.

[2] Loader, *Making Sense*, 64.

[3] "The pericope …is missing from significant early manuscripts of the Gospel." M. Thompson, *John: A Commentary* (Louisville: WJK, 2015), 178. Also, Aland et al, *Greek New Testament*, 347. For this account to be considered canonical centuries after Christ, it must have remained reasonable to claim that in the first century the known Mosaic penalty for adultery was death by stoning.

[4] Derret, *Law*, 156-88.

Derret explains why it was practically impossible for the Jews to convict anyone for adultery, and this had nothing to do with whether Roman law prevented Jewish trials of capital cases. In John 8:1-11, Jesus is clearly asked to rule on a woman caught in the very act of adultery, and "since stoning was in question there can be no doubt that two or more persons had seen her in the act."[5] According to "common semitic customs" the witnesses "saw this woman and man actually *in coitu*" with "absolutely no question of their having seen them merely in a 'compromising situation'."[6]

> Failure to agree in all details would be fatal to the criminal case they themselves would promote (for the witnesses were the accusers), and might bring penalties upon their own heads.[7]

This accords with Deuteronomy 19:18-19 (cf. Exod 23:1),

> The judges shall inquire diligently, and if the witness is a false witness and has accused his brother falsely, then you shall do to him as he had meant to do to his brother. So you shall purge the evil from your midst.

Derret believes that the woman was almost certainly caught in a trap:

> People are hardly ever caught in adultery, but to require that they shall be seen *in coitu* by two or three persons is to make convictions for adultery rare indeed.[8]

He then questions the whereabouts of the adulterer, not simply to posit gender equality, but (with some conjecture based on known Jewish custom) to highlight a deeper socio-economic reality:

> The woman had no free property of her own with which to redeem herself from her husband's wrath. Her paramour was in a better position: at least he had his labour to pledge. *He* could arrange matters. The witnesses, as 'respectable' and righteous men, would surely not allow this? The law requires that both the culprits be put to death, But the witnesses can be 'squared', especially, as we suspect, they have been planted by previous arrangement...[9]

---

[5] Ibid., 160.

[6] Ibid., 160-61.

[7] Ibid.

[8] Ibid.

[9] Derret notes, "The husband had the usufruct of all the wife's property acquired before or after the marriage, and owned all her earnings and chance acquisitions." Ibid. The Law did not demand this, but it was a cultural outcome of demanding a dowry and retaining a (promissory) *ketubah*.

In the economic relations of marriage, the scales of Jewish law in Jesus' cultural setting (as opposed to the Law as written) were further tilted in favour of the male. A further factor presents against the woman in John 8:1-11, assuming she has been warned:

> If the trial had been before a regular court the witnesses might have had to establish that the woman had been warned. In Talmudic law it is settled that they must depose that they *themselves* had warned the woman and received her acknowledgement of the warning... From the rule that they must prove that she acknowledged the warning and persisted in the crime notwithstanding the warning we can be sure that the rabbis intended to make death sentences of adultery impossible.[10]

When the length of time required for intercourse is considered (not only a woman's seclusion), all witnesses must have passively and quietly observed the couple for quite a long period. This adds doubt to the situation (*Why were they there? How were they not seen?*), and indicts the witnesses for doing nothing to prevent evil from occurring.

These witnesses may hope that Phineas' example (Num 25:5-15) will spur Jesus to order rapid execution, but they do not imitate Phineas, for on the sight of evil, he acted without warning (which undermines the Talmudic understanding just cited). Misreading of the Law is writ large. Yet at every stage of this episode Jesus upholds the Law. Derret asserts that although Jesus "avoids a direct interpretation of the Law, he merely reminds his questioners of its requirements."[11] The witnesses are tainted simply by watching a crime that they did nothing about, and likely by

> watching human beings in sexual intercourse, which oriental peoples regard as an inevitable prelude to jealous, lustful, sinful, and possibly harmful thoughts: "Whoever witnesses a suspected woman in her disgrace should withhold himself from wine" is a typical comment.[12]

Derret goes so far as to say that had the woman been warned, and had the accusers been sinless, her stoning could have taken place with Jesus' approval.[13] This can hardly be the main point, for if sinless witnesses were requisite, then no court (formal or informal) could ever convict anyone for anything in the Law. It was a lawful outcome for Jesus to simply show mercy, just as God had mercy on King David for

---

[10] Ibid., 171. (Italics original.)
[11] Ibid., 187.
[12] Ibid., 182-83. Cf. Deut 5:21; Matt 5:27-30
[13] Ibid., 187.

his adultery, and a sinless Son of David can righteously shoulder the sin of any guilty person, and provide another warning in doing so.

The episode concludes with Jesus refusing to condemn the woman for a charge that the witnesses have failed to convict her for. This is in keeping with the Law, for Jesus has not been a direct witness to the claimed adultery, and he does not support the dubious process and witnesses. Yet there can be no doubt that this woman is a sinner, perhaps no less than those who have departed the scene. Although Jesus does not condemn the woman, she is not necessarily innocent.[14] Being "caught in the act of adultery" (John 8:4) and "sin no more" (John 8:11) imply guilt.[15] Furthermore, and contrary to popular understanding, there is no mention or guarantee of forgiveness, just as there is no guarantee that this woman will sin no more (according to the Law in this Jewish setting). It is an open-ended story, and final (positive or negative) judgement awaits.

Overall, it is not difficult to see why Israel does not have a solid history of capital convictions for adultery. Yet convictions for adultery that attract economic penalties are not lacking, particularly in divorce cases. This exposes a double-standard, for if a definite verdict of adultery can be obtained for economic purposes in the Jewish cultural setting, then why cannot the same verdict be obtained for the purpose of strictly obeying God's commandments as written in the Law? Even if Roman law prevented or suppressed Jewish executions (for quick zealous lynching could hardly be *prevented*), then there is still nothing to prevent reading Jesus' divorce teachings in light of the Law's capital meanings that remain unabolished – at least in God's sight. After all, these involve violations of *God's commands*, not Jewish or Roman commands, and these are high offences *against God*. Derret discerns, "Jesus requires the whole Law to be applied even in contexts where the usual formalities would be relaxed."[16] So surely the whole Law must be applied to a formal question of Law (cf. Matt 19:1-12).

Derret acknowledges that the traditional punishment for adultery was stoning, and in the story of Susanna, he finds support that "death by mangling on or by rocks" was a penalty for adultery not so long before the incident of John 8:1-11.[17] Similarly Loader notes that had Susanna not been found innocent, "she would have faced death" for

---

[14] "Jesus does not sanction the stoning of the woman, but neither does he condone or excuse her actions." Thompson, *John: A Commentary*, 179.

[15] If the woman was innocent, she should clearly be declared not guilty, and by the Law the false witnesses should then suffer the same penalty that they had demanded.

[16] Derret, *Law*, 187.

[17] LXX Sus. 60-2. Ibid., 168-69.

adultery, although he postulates that the "shame" to describe Susanna's charge

> may reflect a context where the death penalty could not be carried out for adultery… and instead was included under ערות דבר as grounds for divorce… Divorce was the next best thing to execution.[18]

Firstly, death for adultery was certainly the original biblical demand,[19] but before any revision of this, the term "divorce" needs revising to align with its original biblical verbal use (as contended in this paper). Then it can easily be maintained: "divorce" (sending away) to a father's house is immeasurably the next best thing to "divorce" (sending away) to execution (of a wife). "Adulterers were seen as destroyers of households (Pss. Sol. 4:9-10, 20; 15:11)."[20] Therefore, rather than returning this woman to her father's house, and potentially destroy another household, the Law required that an adulterous wife be sent away ("divorced") from her husband's house to be destroyed. So too the adulterer, who has grievously infringed the rights of another man and sowed destruction, reaps destruction.

Secondly, in Deuteronomy 24:1, adultery could have been wrongly included under *'erwat dabar*. This may have happened originally, but factually – because Moses wrote in relation to divorces that occurred for all sorts of causes, which might have mixed trivial and capital grounds from the start. Or it may have happened finally, which was an unlawful development, because adultery had a separate law code.

Thirdly, some caution is needed regarding a text like Susanna 63 (Theodotian), for it may confuse terminology and rulings for capital and non-capital offences. The text might accurately reflect respective cultural settings, but not accurately reflect Jesus' teaching and first-century Christian practice. In general, Derret prudently questions whether Jewish rulings made after 70CE reliably reflect earlier understandings:

> Jesus himself narrowly escaped lynch-justice, the followers of Jesus including Paul himself, actually experienced it. Notwithstanding the procedural developments in Jewish law until the coming of the Romans, the positive obligation to stone, for example for blasphemy, was taken for granted. Stoning was the traditional penalty from remote antiquity, to

---

[18] Loader, *On Sexuality*, 59.

[19] "Originally ערות דבר in Deut 24:1 would not have included adultery, for which the penalty was not divorce but death." Ibid., 58.

[20] Ibid., 4.

be resorted to wherever the law said 'he shall certainly die' or words to that effect without prescribing a different penalty. The provisions of the Talmud on this subject might mislead us, for they embody the speculations of Pharisees who believed that the mildest penalty possible should always be chosen, and who wanted not to disrupt the skeleton, and who, from the Fall of Jerusalem, had few opportunities to test their theories in practice.[21]

To always choose "the mildest penalty possible" (including financial instead of corporal punishment) aligns with popular progressive cultural ideas, but completely contradicts God's choice – indeed command, as written in the Law – of the harshest penalty possible: death.

"Both Philo and Josephus boasted of the Law's strictness in imposing such a sentence."[22] Loader speculates:

> when Jews lost the right to execute capital punishment, the woman had at least to become effectively dead for the man through divorce and he must never receive her back, not even in the far off future.[23]

He dismisses as "atypical executions performed under regal prerogative" the execution of Salome (the first husband of Herod's sister) for adultery (*B.J.* 1.486) and Herod's execution of Mariamme and his uncle for adultery (*B.J.* 1.443), despite just noting Josephus' and Philo's boast, and that the death penalty is also assumed for both parties in Sir 9:9 and Sus 22.[24] Nonetheless, whenever the Jews lost the right to execute capital punishment, God remained above and beyond human legal jurisdiction. That humans even have a right to decide what penalties can "be chosen" for offences ultimately against God reeks of hubris. Yet to be chosen by God to not suffer the harshest penalty possible *as written in the Law – and as deserved by the Law*, reeks of mercy.

---

[21] Derret, *Law*, 169.
[22] Loader, *Making Sense*, 64. (Philo: *Spec.* 3.11; *Hypoth.* 7.1; Josephus: *Ag. Jov.* 3.274-275; 7.130-131; *Ag. Ap.* 2.15)
[23] Ibid.
[24] Ibid.

Ezra and Unlawful Marriage

It might be construed that there was a progression in divorce law in Ezra-Nehemiah's time, but this is not necessarily so. Israelite men who had married non-Israelite women, against God's command in the Law (Deut 7:3; cf. Ezra 9:12), "put away" their wives according to the Law (Ezra 10:3; cf. 7:10). The Israelites had "broken faith" with God (Ezra 10:2), but in repentance the "fierce wrath" of God was turned away (Ezra 10:14).

This wrath has a strong antecedent when "Israel yoked himself to Baal of Peor" by "whoring with the daughters of Moab"; and God killed twenty-four thousand with a plague (Num 25). Psalm 106:28 also stresses the unlawful nature of the unions with marriage terminology, "they yoked themselves to the Baal of Peor"; in their sexual immorality the Israelites had essentially married another god. Hosea recalls the same occasion, "But they came to Baal-peor and consecrated themselves to the thing of shame, and became detestable like the thing they loved"[25] (Hos 9:10). He uses it to justify God's divorce of Israel due to their comparable behaviour: "Because of the wickedness of their deeds I will drive them out of my house" (where "divorce" literally means "to send away" from a house); "I will love them no more" (Hos 9:15). Judgement falls, yet hope remains, for when God's anger turns his steadfast love (mercy) continues (Hos 14:4; Ps 106:45).

Due to Israel's repentance, God mercifully did not apply the Law's death penalty for the infidelity in Ezra's time. The unfaithfulness *of the men* deserved but did not mandate divorce from God. With respect to Matthew 19:9, the men stood condemned for "sexual immorality," not their wives (there is no hint of say adultery by the women). Scripture does not condemn the wives, presumably because they were not members of God's covenant people, so they had no allegiance to Moses and thus could not violate the Law. This is implicit in the fact that they are regarded as "foreign" or non-Israelites, without any indication that they have converted (unlike say Rahab or Ruth). The women are "from the peoples of the land" (Ezra 10:2) who retain "their abominations" (Ezra 9:1) and have filled the land "from end to end with their uncleanness" (Ezra 9:11). The Israelites have broken a command of God

---

[25] This "shame" [בֹּשֶׁת] differs from the "shame" [עֶרְוָה] in Deut 24:1, for here it involves idol worship (cf. Jer 3:24; 11:13) and directly results in becoming "detestable" [שִׁקּוּץ] to God, whereas other conditions must be satisfied before an "abomination" [תּוֹעֵבָה] before the Lord is declared in Deut 24:1-4. Therefore, the "sexual immorality" (cf. Matt 19:9) at Baal-peor and the intermarriage of Ezra's time, is of a very different order to the "matter of indecency [/shame]" used as grounds for divorce in Deut 24:1.

that is directly premised on the abominations and uncleanness of these peoples: "*Therefore* do not give your daughters to their sons, neither take their daughters for your sons, and never seek their peace or prosperity" (Ezra 9:12; italics added). Unlawful one-flesh unions – what God has not joined together – must be severed.

In order to avoid God's fierce wrath again, the Law was rewritten in a stricter direction:

> The fear of mingling the Jewish race with others continues in the Second Temple period even after the time of Ezra-Nehemiah. This is quite evident in rewritings of biblical law where additions are made forbidding intermarriage with other races, even to the point of death.[26]

Thus, the death penalty did not entirely fall out of favour with the Jews, and even if never applied to this type of unfaithfulness to God, the judicial threat ("to the point of death") would have fostered great cultural aversion to intermarriage. In contrast, if in Jesus' time the death penalty for adultery (unfaithfulness not only to a wife but to God) was no longer enforced, we should expect the opposite trend: rewritings of biblical law in a more liberal direction. With not even a dire judicial threat, an increased acceptance and ease of divorce could be expected. Nonetheless, for Jesus to support "rewritings of biblical law" in either direction (stricter or more liberal) on intermarriage or adultery (or anything else) to mirror fluid cultural trends contradicts his decree in Matthew 5:17-19.

---

[26] Chapman, "Second Temple Judaism," 201.

APPENDIX 3. Theological & Pastoral Application

Importance of the Problem

An ancient theological problem addressed in this thesis concerns how Christians view the Law, and this (still) greatly affects how Christians understand Jesus' teaching on marriage and divorce, and particularly how the Matthean 'exception clause' is read. Far too often, interpreters have rushed to 'Christian Application' and personal situational ethics without sufficiently grappling with Matthew's authorial purpose and the original context of Jesus' very Jewish teaching. Many have denigrated considerations of the Law (as "legalistic") and reinterpreted Mosaic legal codes to suit new covenant ideals. This can display an insensitivity to the enduring ideals, purpose and people of the Law. The Law, including divorce law, has also been relaxed or voided to conform with cultural traditions and political pressures in ways that might not accord with the word of God.

Another theological problem is background to a very large – and largely recent – social problem. Until a generation ago, divorce remained greatly stigmatised, but with increasing individualism (especially in Western society), the ethical landscape for Christians has trended in a direction widely supportive of divorce and remarriage. Simultaneously, new understandings of marriage have emerged and divorce rates have soared.[1] Undoubtedly, this generation has more divorce than any other generation in history! Furthermore, the biblical gravity of sexual immorality has largely vanished.

With elevated divorce rates, destructive consequences mount for spouses, families and nations. Recent dips are negligible, for divorce is nowhere near the rarity it once was; it has levelled at a high rate.[2] Children of divorce are more prone to illness, accidents and suicide,

---

[1] Divorce in Australia was relatively rare before World War II. Following the introduction of the Family Law Act in 1975, the rate of divorce increased substantially. It more than doubled, levelling to about one in three marriages failing: 1.0 divorces in 1970, 2.1 in 2013 (per 1000 population). "Divorce in Australia," Australian Institute of Family Studies, https://aifs.gov.au/facts-and-figures/divorce-australia.

[2] "The divorce rate has declined to 1.9 per 1000 people, the lowest level since the introduction of the Family Law Act." N. Berkovic and E. Visontay, "Divorce Rate Drops, for Better or Worse," *The Australian*, 21 April 2018.

along with other social "evils" (disadvantage).[3] Although divorce is largely a matter of private law, the massive cost of family breakdown and unmarried parenthood corrodes national economies.[4] While taxes and death are inevitable, divorce is not, yet it has often been described as deathly – even for children involved,[5] and worse than death.[6] It needs to be asked whether Jesus would have sanctioned divorce by providing even a single exception when divorce leads to destruction (of individuals, families, and nations) and death (or something regarded worse)? Moreover, with such evils and unfaithfulness, does God's judgement mount for this generation, as it did for Jesus' generation?

Poor theology, buoyed by modern secular 'no-fault' divorce laws, surely fuels divorce and generates poor outcomes, for in painful times the easiest route endorsed by both church and state is well-trodden. Hence, theological and pastoral matters are seen as inextricable. Civil laws may drastically differ from scriptural mandates regarding what is lawful, but a better understanding of the biblical legal framing of Matthew 19:1-12 and its narrative function may curb a myriad of long-assumed grounds for divorce.

---

[3] C. Colson and N. Pearcey, *How Now Shall We Live?* (Wheaton: Tyndale, 1999), 323-24. See also K. Sandvig, *Adult Children of Divorce: Haunting Problems and Healthy Solutions* (Dallas: Word, 1990). E. Beal and G. Hochman, *Adult Children of Divorce: How to Achieve Happier Relationships* (London: Piatkus, 1991).

[4] The cost of divorce to the Australian economy in 2014 alone was $14 billion, or $1,100 for every taxpayer, calculated from government assistance payments and court costs (excluding increased costs of health care, aged care, childcare, housing, etc.). L. Wilson and L. Cornish, "Divorce Is Costing the Australian Economy $14 Billion a Year," News Corp, http://www.news.com.au/lifestyle/relationships/marriage/divorce-is-costing-the-australian-economy-14-billion-a-year/news-story/e5a101ea76351d4ba145279011b934ac. The annual cost of divorce in the US was $112 billion (2008); Britain £41.74 billion, or £1,364 for every taxpayer (2011); and Canada $7 billion (2009). P. Parkinson, "Another Inconvenient Truth: Fragile Families and the Looming Financial Crisis for the Welfare State," *Sydney Law School Research Paper*, no. 12/05, January (2012): 4.

[5] In destroying the "ontological security" of children, "divorce is a death borne within the young person." A. Root, *The Children of Divorce : The Loss of Family as the Loss of Being*, ed. C. Clark, Youth, Family, and Culture Series (Grand Rapids: Baker, 2010), 55-56.

[6] E.g. "If my ex-husband had died, I would have grieved bitterly, but I would have known, he loved me until the end. But when my husband of over 20 years suddenly fell in love with a much younger woman, and just tossed me aside, it was a betrayal of the most intimate and destructive kind." Martin, "Why Is Divorce Considered Worse Than Death?".

"Sexual Immorality" as Sole Grounds for Divorce

Matthew's very Jewish Gospel provides one clear and objective cause, in an 'exception clause', for the divorce or "sending away" to death of a spouse, based on a reading of the Law as originally written. Matthew did not supply any other exceptions. Mark and Luke gave no exceptions at all. Loader writes,

> The fact remains that nowhere in the New Testament do we find any hint that breach of obligations (except that of sexual fidelity) is ground for divorce.[7]

If Jesus only permits divorce for a capital offence by the Law, then could anyone else really permit divorce for any lesser reason?

The Protestant majority view holds that divorce with a right to remarry is justified not only on the grounds of adultery, but also on the grounds of abandonment – which Paul purportedly championed. However, any offence that is more trivial than a capital one would certainly undermine Paul's argument in Romans 7:1-6, where he compares being released from the law of marriage with being released from the Law (of Moses). It would also contradict what he writes in 1 Corinthians 7:39, which gives the legal perspective of being bound (δέω)[8] in marriage until death. Here the same Greek term is used as in Romans 7:1 to describe the binding unto death nature of the Law, and Romans 7:2 that states, "For a married woman is bound [δέω] by law to her husband while he lives, but if her husband dies she is released from the law of marriage."

The term δέω both in 1 Corinthians 7:39 and Romans 7:2 occurs in the perfect passive sense, which points to an enduring nature of the relationship that the person is put into (by God) – not something that is actively and independently chosen (even though it may feel that way). Nor is it to be actively opted out from, independent of God. The term is an antonym of λύω ("to loose") which serves as the base for ἀπολύω ("to divorce," "to send away," or "to separate"), that has already been closely studied in this thesis. What can be concluded is that this binding

---

[7] Loader, *Jesus Tradition*, 120.

[8] Bibleworks, Friberg 6114. "**δέω** 1aor. ἔδησα; pf. δέδεκα; pf. pass. δέδεμαι; 1aor. pass. ἐδέθην; (1) *bind (together), tie (up)* (MT 13.30), opposite λύω (*loose, untie*); (2) of burial procedures *wrap up* (JN 19.40); (3) of arrest and imprisonment *bind, tie up* (MK 6.17); (4) figuratively, of mutual commitment to the marriage vow *be restricted* (RO 7.2); (5) of physical incapacity *cause to be ill* (LU 13.16); (6) the binding and loosing (λύω) in MT 16.19 and 18.18 may be interpreted (a) according to Jewish rabbinic custom: to declare what is forbidden and permitted or (b) according to the understanding of early church fathers: to impose or remove the ban of excommunication; cf. JN 20.23."

(δέω) clearly matches Jesus' words on the permanent God-binding nature of marriage, where what God has joined together, no one must separate (χωρίζω). No one is "to loose" or send away (ἀπολύω) their spouse for any cause (cf. Matt 19:3), unless it be capital (cf. Matt 19:9).

So the interpretation provided in this thesis, that in Matthew 19:9 Jesus gives a deadly exception, completely aligns with what Paul writes on marriage and divorce. In 1 Corinthians 7:10-11, Paul gives the same sort of charge to believers as the Lord does in Matthew 19:4-6,

> To the married I give this charge (not I, but the Lord): the wife should not separate from her husband (but if she does, she should remain unmarried or else be reconciled to her husband), and the husband should not divorce his wife.

This legal domain of binding (δέω) is to be differentiated from the more social domain of a believer not being bound or enslaved (δουλόω)[9] to an unbelieving partner if that spouse chooses to separate (1 Cor 7:15). What Paul discusses (without Jesus' direct word, but nonetheless with godly wisdom) is not an entirely new or unforeseen circumstance. Space does not permit in-depth examination of Pauline theology, for primary attention has been on Matthean theology. However, just as Jesus distinguishes between those who obey God's commands and the hard-hearted who do not (cf. Matt 19:8), Paul makes a similar distinction. Any unbeliever with a "hard and impenitent heart" (cf. Rom 2:5) can do whatever they want to do in the realm of marriage and divorce (though not without consequence of course); they are a law unto themselves.

This echoes the situation in Israel's wilderness experience, where the ones divorcing acted as unbelievers. In characterising those who follow this practice as hard-hearted, Jesus implicitly labels them as unbelievers, and the writer of the book of Hebrews (in relation to the same wilderness experience) explicitly condemns their evil and unbelief (Heb 3:7 to 4:13). "So we see that they were unable to enter God's rest because of unbelief" (Heb 3:19) is juxtaposed with a warning, "Take care, brothers, lest there be in any of you an evil, unbelieving heart, leading you to fall away from the living God" (Heb 3:12).

At the same time, not every unbeliever who separates from their spouse is necessarily "hard of heart" – for they may yet repent and follow Jesus. Hence the New Testament teaching on hardness of heart

---

[9] Ibid., Friberg 7180. "**δουλόω** fut. δουλώσω; 1aor. ἐδούλωσα; pf. pass. δεδούλωμαι; 1aor. pass. δεδουλώθην; literally, as requiring absolute obedience *enslave, make* someone *a slave* (AC 7.6); figuratively *gain control over* someone; with ἑαυτόν as the object of one who gives up personal rights for the sake of others *make oneself a slave, submit oneself to* (1C 9.19); passive *be enslaved, be subject to* (GA 4.3); *be under obligation, be bound to* (1C 7.15)."

is useful: it warns against a terminable state, but not an inevitable one. This uncertainty helps to account for why Paul, unlike Jesus in Matthew 19:8, withholds judgement in 1 Corinthians 7:16, "For how do you know, wife, whether you will save your husband? Or how do you know, husband, whether you will save your wife?" A Christian cannot expect an unbeliever to follow Christian marriage ethics (or any Christian ethics), but neither can the Christian be expected to follow an unbeliever who separates (cf. 1 Cor 7:15).

Salvation for the unbeliever remains a central concern for any true believer, but if the unbeliever remains in their sin and leaves the believer, then the believing "brother or sister is not enslaved" (1 Cor 7:15). While together in this unequally yoked marriage there is some hope and holiness for the family (1 Cor 7:14); but when an unbeliever leaves, this is nothing to celebrate. God offers peace in it for the believer, but not in the arms of another marriage partner (at least while the original remains alive). Yet God offers no peace for the unbeliever, because if they remain unrepentant, they incur God's wrath, and they never enter his rest.

When an unbeliever leaves a believing spouse, this "separation" might still be considered a "divorce." However, it may bear little or no resemblance to the Mosaic process described in Deuteronomy 24:1-4. Paul makes no mention of an unbelieving husband writing a divorce certificate, putting it in his wife's hand (before she exits), and sending her away from his house. (To the contrary, today the husband could lose his house if he looses his wife away!) The unbelieving husband in 1 Corinthians 7 may be a Gentile who is under no obligation to follow Jewish custom. (The believing wife under a new covenant, is under no obligation to follow Jewish custom either, or the Law.) Neither does he feel bound by the Creation command to cleave to his wife (cf. Gen 3:24), nor bound to Jesus' command to do the same (Matt 19:4-6). Although he still stands accountable to his Creator in this, and he has no excuse (Rom 1:18-20), the unbeliever simply separates from his wife in whatever way he wants,

The word "separate" ($\chi\omega\rho\iota\zeta\omega$, 1 Cor 7:10, 15; cf. Matt 19:6) appears to have a much more general meaning than "divorce" ($\dot{\alpha}\pi o\lambda\dot{\upsilon}\omega$, cf. Matt 19:3, 7, 8, 9), especially if "divorce" has a basic verbal meaning of "to send away." In 1 Corinthians 7:15 the husband might not send his wife away at all, but simply leaves, and deserts the house (and any children) as well. This all-too-common occurrence does not mimic the divorce process of Deuteronomy 24:1-4 in the slightest. (Furthermore the "abomination" there may be regularly committed in complete ignorance.) Yet even when the behaviour of an unbeliever does mimic the Mosaic divorce practice of hard-hearted Israelites, Paul shows no hint of endorsing it.

The unbeliever may, however, stand less accountable than those divorcing "for a matter of indecency" (cf. Deut 24:1) or "for any cause" (cf. Matt 19:3). This is because Paul does not record any judgement that is made by the husband in 1 Corinthians 7:15, unlike the husband in Deuteronomy 24:1-4 who makes a negative judgement that "she finds no favour in his eyes" because "he has found some indecency in her," or he "hates her." Paul is very strict on those who judge (Rom 2:1), as is God (Rom 2:2), and Jesus, "Judge not, that you be not judged" (Matt 7:1). In all, it seems extremely unlikely that in 1 Corinthians 7 Paul takes the "matter of indecency" (of Deut 24:1) for granted as a background concession to permit divorce. The grounds for divorce claimed in Deuteronomy 24:1-4 could even be seen as abuse (of power, and of the Law), and it would be difficult for a wife to cope with such subjective, hard-hearted (Matt 19:8) condemnation by a husband. To avoid abuse, a woman might separate, but is to remain single or be reconciled (cf. 1 Cor 7:10); here the wife does not "send away" ("divorce") a husband, but may feel forced *to leave* an unsafe situation (at least for a time).

Neither would Paul confuse "a matter of indecency" (Deut 24:1) with the "sexual immorality" (and its penalty in the Law he well knows!) that he has just commanded believers to flee from (cf. 1 Cor 6:18). This does not mean that a wife or husband may simply flee from a sexually immoral spouse, in the sense of divorcing them. However, it does mean that they are to avoid their spouse's sexually immoral practice. In a key passage background to Paul's command to flee from sexual immorality, we find that Joseph fled from Potiphar's wife (Genesis 39), not his own wife; there is no moral precedent here to flee from one's own wife. Hosea certainly did not flee from his sexually immoral wife Gomer, but demonstrated steadfast love and great mercy, even as his own wife had abandoned him.

A general principle is that a spouse is to flee from evil acts (of sexual immorality, or other evils such as violence), but not from the covenant relationship of marriage.[10] This is in keeping with how Jesus taught his disciples to seek not only forgiveness for their own sins (or "debts," cf. Matt 18:23-35), but to seek deliverance from the evil of others, or ultimately from the evil one himself (Matt 6:12-13). The evil could even

---

[10] This is only a "general" principle, for it must be balanced with Jesus' call to deny self, take up one's cross, and follow him (Matt 16:24) – which for Jesus involved taking a route of suffering evil and persecution. This need not be contradictory, for Christians might flee certain evil acts and yet still suffer the evil of this world – including evil in their immediate (marital or non-marital) situation. Spiritual wisdom, not strict law, is invaluable here.

come in the form of one who appears to be very religious, be it a nominal Christian spouse, a religious false teacher, or as Spadaro sees in the original context, the highest earthly religious leader: the Jewish high priest – who leads "an evil and adulterous generation"[11] (with their hard-hearted ways, which includes ungodly divorce doctrine).

When the evil is unrelenting, the rule does not become any less relevant, but prayer and pastoral care are vital. In 1 Corinthians 7, Paul also forces a decision, not about whether a believer should divorce (he gives a clear command against this), but whether a spouse who commits such evil is a believer at all. Final judgement belongs only to God, but discernment is called for that heeds Jesus' words: "You will recognize them by their fruits" (Matt 7:16-20). This applies even to the nominal Christian, and Jesus' judgement is terrifying for those who claim allegiance to God but do not do his will: "I never knew you; depart from me you workers of lawlessness" (Matt 7:21-23). Jesus prefaces this section with a warning against hypocritical judgement (Matt 7:1-5), so self-examination in any marital conflict is paramount. 'The Golden Rule' naturally applies (Matt 7:12), but it naturally remains too that one's spouse will not always do what one wishes them to do, and Jesus' way that leads to life is hard, and those who find it are few (Matt 7:13). It could be said that it is the exceptional few who find and follow Jesus' hard way, and they do not use the Matthew 19:9 'exception clause' to go their own easier way.

Paul provides good guidance for anyone who might be married to an unbeliever, or for anyone associated with a professed believer who acts as an unbeliever (or worse than one), but to interpret his words to the Corinthians as offering licence to remarry while one's spouse remains alive runs contrary to everything that he says elsewhere, and to everything Jesus teaches. To remarry would be to commit adultery (Matt 5:32; 19:9; Rom 7:3), an offence that Paul (as a former Pharisee of Pharisees) knows is a capital matter by a strict reading of the Law. It might be countered that Christians are not under the Law (cf. Rom 6:14-15; Gal 3), but this is the case in point. It is not legalistic to point out that Matthew 19:9 must be interpreted within the framework of the unabolished Law (cf. Matt 5:17-19), but one could certainly be judged legalistic in strictly applying the Law to execute a spouse without considering one's own guilt by the same Law.

---

[11] Spadaro, *Matthew*, 29. Caiaphas is considered Christ's "true and final antagonist" in Matthew's Gospel. Ibid., 188. Spadaro adds, "The book of Revelation, interestingly, describes the adversary of God adorned in garments that strongly resemble the garments of the high priest (Exod 28:6-21; Rev 17:3-6)." Ibid., 264.

Some, including Instone-Brewer, argue for valid grounds for divorce based on Exodus 21:10-11, that is, failure to provide material and emotional support ("neglect"), but this argument fails to justify why all the Gospel writers neglect to mention this, or explain how a Jewish court would verify what could involve highly subjective grounds. The early church was much more objective and informed. Loader rightly questions Instone-Brewer's poor estimation of the early church:

> As Instone-Brewer shows, the early writers beyond the New Testament interpreted the prohibition of divorce strictly, allowing an exception only in cases of adultery, and although they, too, would have affirmed the vows of material and emotional support, they did not see a breach of these as grounds for divorce. One can argue, as Instone-Brewer does, that this was because the early church "lost touch with its Jewish roots in or before 70 CE." ...Is such discontinuity credible? On balance, it seems to me more likely that the silence about the breach of material and emotional support in the context of determining grounds for divorce in the New Testament stems not from the assumption that they are still valid, but from the assumption that they are not.[12]

In any case, Exodus 21:10-11 hardly applies to freely engaged monogamy. At most, Exodus 21:10-11 concerns the breakdown in a polygamous relationship with a Hebrew slave girl, sold by her father to a slave master.[13] Davidson notes that this passage is one of *case law* that does not legitimise the activity of the case described but only prescribes what should be done.[14] Here is a one-sided arranged relationship where the master "takes another wife to himself" (Exod 21:10), echoing Lamech who "took two wives" (Gen 4:19). That which a slave master has bought and abandoned is categorically different to what God has "brought" (cf. Gen 2:22), "joined together" and commands people to "not separate" (cf. Matt 19:6).

---

[12] Loader, *Jesus Tradition*, 120.

[13] Meier is "surprised" by Instone-Brewer's "claim on very slender grounds (scattered testimony to women's power of divorce in other cultures in the ancient Near East and the law concerning slave women taken as wives in Exod 21:10-11) that Israelite women had the power to divorce their husbands under certain circumstances of neglect. Instone-Brewer's claim involves more than one major leap in logic, not to say evidence." Manumission of a female slave, without monetary obligations on her part, is "a far cry from free Israelite women having the power to divorce their husbands." Meier, *Marginal Jew*, 4, 139-40.

[14] "Thus this case legitimates polygamy no more than the case law in Exod 21:37 (ET 22:1; 'When someone steals an ox or a sheep...') legitimizes theft." Davidson further argues that Exodus 21:10-11 "does not even deal with polygamy, let alone support or legitimize it." Davidson, *Flame*, 191-93.

Alternatively, if for Exodus 21:8 the Septuagint errs in using the prepositional phrase: "for himself" (that most English versions follow) instead of the word "not" – and textual evidence for such substitution is not strong, then "The best translation of this passage is, 'If she does not please her master so that he does not betroth her…' (cf. NIV margin, 'master so that he does not choose her')."[15] It is therefore a case where the master might give the slave girl to his son (Exod 21:9); or he might take "another wife to himself" (Exod 21:10), but not as a bigamist, as Davidson further reasons:

> 'another instead of, different' rather than 'another in addition to' – the former a well attested meaning for this word in the MT. The contingency clause of v. 10 thus details the treatment that should be given to the slave girl if her master takes another wife instead of (not in addition to) her. In other words, if v. 8 makes clear that the man does not marry the slave girl, then v. 10 cannot refer to her (sexual) marital rights.[16]

This is another case where the Masoretic Text should be followed, and not the Septuagint, and it best explains why the early church did not use the case law of Exodus 21:7-11 in relation to divorce. It was not because the church had "lost touch with its Jewish roots,"[17] but because this law concerning an unwanted Jewish slave girl was irrelevant to the topic of divorce.[18] In any case, to be "*sent away*" (שׁלח; ἐξαποστέλλω; or more precisely: ἀπολύω) for anything considered "indecent" (cf. Deut 24:1) is very different from possessing a right to "*go out*" (יצא; ἐξέρχομαι)[19] for nothing (Exod 21:11) and for committing nothing indecent.

Were the principles of Exodus 21:7-11 somehow applicable to the breakdown of a monogamous marriage and a freedom to remarry assumed, then it would conflict with Jesus' declaration that remarriage apart from the (sole) grounds of "sexual immorality" constitutes "adultery" (Matt 19:9). If an innocent versus guilty party distinction is made, then a multiplicity of 'exception clauses' could easily ensue, with a quagmire of court cases to rule on what constitutes a valid divorce and

---

[15] Ibid., 192.

[16] Ibid.

[17] Instone-Brewer, *Social and Literary Context*, 238.

[18] Not only is polygamy unlikely to be in view here, but Exod 21:10-11 "probably does not deal with a situation of divorce at all, and thus no comparison of this passage with the ANE laws should be drawn." Davidson, *Flame*, 387.

[19] Cf. Matt 11:7, "Why did you *go out* [ἐξέρχομαι]…" (italics added); the crowds were not "*sent away*" into the wilderness to see John.

remarriage. Unlike the Law's capital and non-capital distinction, these cases would not be clear-cut, for example, "If she does not please her master" (Exod 21:8) could even mean the woman is not entirely innocent herself. Such complexity is not naturally expected in the straightforward word from Jesus on divorce; and it begs why Jesus did not explicitly include this "breach of material and emotional support" in his exception clause of Matthew 19:9. Would such strange case law really be assumed as (unwritten) grounds for divorce? Surely its absence does not mean that Matthew or Matthew's (Jewish Christian) community had "lost touch with its Jewish roots," let alone that Jesus himself had lost touch.

Some valid exceptions to the rule prove obvious. In the related matter of committing adultery by lustful intent (cf. Matt 5:28), looking at one's own lawful spouse naturally makes an acceptable exception.[20] Nonetheless, Jesus' teaching still demands a wholehearted effort to avoid committing adultery, just as one would avoid being thrown into hell (Matt 5:29-30). The same wholehearted effort to avoid committing "sexual immorality" and "adultery" in Matthew 5:32 and 19:9 also applies, along with the same commonsense regarding any 'exception' to the rule.

Yet the only 'exception' that is explicit regarding divorce (in Matt 5:32 and 19:9) concerns an obvious and a deadly matter as found written in the Hebrew Bible. Similarly, when Jesus refuses a sign for the crowds, the only exception he gives is a deadly one cited from Scripture, "but no sign will be given to it except the sign of Jonah" (Matt 12:39; 16:4; Luke 11:29), meaning Jesus will be dead for three days and nights (Matt 12:40).[21] It is also a sign to urge people to repent of sin, not to condone hard-heartedness, nor to tout other mental assumptions of exceptions to justify the non-forgiveness and divorce of a spouse.

No "process of adaptation"[22] is required when the "sexual immorality" Jesus mentions bears the full penalty of the Law. The foreboding judgement here offers no compromise in the "interest of practicability."[23] Legality not practicability is in question (Matt 19:3), and when the old Law is fully applied, no new door is opened to a great range of offences as grounds for divorce, nor is Jesus' vision of marriage bent "in the interest of creating a workable rule for the community's

---

[20] Heth, "Remarriage for Adultery or Desertion," 74.
[21] Blomberg compares the harmonisation of the divorce passages with that of Matt 16:4 and Mark 8:12. Blomberg, "Exegesis," 174. Likewise, a deadly exception is explicit or implicit.
[22] Contra Hays. Hays, *Moral Vision*, 355.
[23] Ibid.

life."[24] Instead it upholds God's absolute rule for a man to cleave to his wife (Gen 2:24), and honours Jesus' word that not one dot of the Law is abolished (Matt 5:17-19).

The deadliness of sexual offences is evident in the New Testament judgement that those who practise sexual immorality will not inherit the kingdom of God (Eph 5:5; 1 Cor 6:9) but will end up in the lake of fire, "which is the second death" (Rev 21:8). This is supported by Matthew 5:27-30, where

> Jesus is saying that lust, as a form of adultery, merits a capital sentence before the heavenly court: eternal damnation. Thus it is better to tear out one's eye than to keep lusting.[25]

Trivial offences of "*unspecified* sexual immodesty or misconduct"[26] can hardly be in view for this capital sentence, nor should a wife tear out her own eye to keep her from spoiling a dish. The Law is highly specific on capital matters, and they should not be confused with any other (lesser) matter.

Marriage in the Context of Mercy

John Stott holds that

> only sexual infidelity breaks the marriage covenant, and that even this does not lead automatically or necessarily to divorce, but may be an occasion for forgiveness.[27]

Against a strong background of death for adultery in ANE culture for over one thousand years,[28] this merciful idea can even be found in Old Babylonian law: "the husband may spare his wife's life if he so desires, allowing the king opportunity to pardon her paramour."[29] This compares well with the king in Matthew 18:23-35 who pardons an unpayable debt. In the light of Jesus' teaching immediately prior to Matthew 19:1-12, "sexual immorality" and "adultery" are unpayable debts, comparable to a servant owing his master 10,000 talents. Such infidelity is a sin against God (cf. Ps 51:4). If married, an aggrieved

---

[24] Ibid., 355-56.

[25] Keener, *Matthew*, 188.

[26] Hays, *Moral Vision*, 354. (Italics added.)

[27] J. Stott, *Divorce: The Biblical Teaching* (London: CPAS, 1972).

[28] For the neo-Babylonians, the means of execution *was even commonly specified within a marriage contract!* E.g., "If PN is found with another man, she will die by the razor." Not all marriage contracts carried such a stipulation, but Janzen assumes that this was because the culture simply took it for granted. Janzen, "Porneia," 76-77.

[29] Ibid., 77.

spouse has grounds for (a deadly) divorce (cf. Matt 19:9), but with repentance and forgiveness, divorce is never necessary. If Matthew has located this story of a king settling accounts to show that "the marriage relationship is the most intense example"[30] of the need for forgiveness, and he is the only writer who mentions Joseph's resolve to divorce his betrothed, then let us imagine for a moment that Mary was actually guilty of "sexual immorality" (*porneia*). When we monetarise the relationship, as per Matthew 18:23-35, Mary's sin against God would be in the order of a μύριοι ("myriad" or "ten thousand," which itself could mean "beyond number") talents (cf. Matt 18:24), a debt that in today's economy, "ran into billions of dollars."[31] This is clearly unpayable. The dowry, had Mary brought one into the relationship, was likely to have been small, for another record suggests that this family was poor (cf. Luke 2:22-24). Let us further suppose that Mary's dowry was worth one hundred denarii (cf. Matt 18:28), which is not an insignificant amount (a denarius was the average daily wage of a labourer, and there were six thousand denarii to a single talent[32]). From this perspective, Keener's proposition can be weighed:

> Joseph might have profited from divorcing her [Mary] publicly. By taking her to court Joseph could have impounded her dowry – the total assets she brought into the marriage – and perhaps the bride price if he had paid one at the betrothal.[33]

One concern here is that "a righteous man" would have accepted, even demanded, a dowry according to tradition (an unscriptural practice), but he might not have paid the bride price (a scriptural practice). Dowry repayment and a "right to remarry," which are crafty human appendages to the Law that principally favour the husband, cannot be Joseph's concern. Shame and potentially the death penalty – or at least a guilty verdict in a Jewish court that could not or would not execute – is his fear for his betrothed.

The bigger concern, however, is whether Matthew recorded Joseph's resolve to divorce Mary for his readers to wrestle with financial considerations, which if not about dowry, may involve property settlement. Even if there was a dowry in relation to Joseph's case, it is ludicrous to imagine that a penalty of non-dowry return that amounted

---

[30] Osborne, *Matthew*, 699-700.

[31] Hagner, *Matthew 14-28*, 538. Josephus records that in 4BCE, 600 talents in taxes were collected from all of Judea, Idumea, and Samaria, plus a further 200 talents from Galilee and Perea. *Ant.* 17.317-320. Josephus, *Works*, 473.

[32] Hagner, *Matthew 14-28*, 539.

[33] Keener, *Matthew*, 93.

to say one hundred denarii was in any way equivalent to the penalty that *porneia* merited in the sight of God, which monetarily is 600,000 times greater, and metaphorically, was a "practically incalculable" debt![34] Yet this reflects the problem with the Protestant majority view in equating "sexual immorality" (*porneia*) in the 'exception clause' of Matthew 19:9 (a dire offence against God that no sacrifice in the Law covered, which was totally unpayable and attracted the death penalty) with a lesser "matter of indecency" (*'erwat dabar*) found in Deuteronomy 24:1 (based on one man's opinion, that was commonly used as easy grounds for divorce). All sins here are certainly forgivable, but to say that a small and payable debt is the same as an incalculably massive and unpayable debt is not only financially reckless and untrue to normal experience, but misses the gravity of the debt and the depth of mercy that thunders from Jesus' story.

The Protestant majority view also confuses the debtors. The smaller debt is payable to a fellow servant, and this might include "any matter of indecency" as found in a woman, or any matter of indecent allegation or hatred as might be found in a man (cf. Deut 24:1-3). Technically this smaller debt does not include any matter of "sexual immorality" (cf. the defilement in Deut 24:4; and the *porneia* and *moicheia* of Matt 19:9) for that debt is owed only to God, although the heartache and trouble flowing from it that both parties are responsible for can account for the much smaller, though still not insignificant, debts that can accrue between married couples. This sort of debt or personal offence matches the one hundred denarii debt of Matthew 18:28 far better than a dowry amount, because the giving of a dowry (or *ketubah*, or *mohar* for that matter) should hardly be reckoned as an "offence" that might be forgiven within a marriage union. Irrespective of the true or imagined magnitude of the marital offence, no person should refuse to forgive such a debt that is miniscule in comparison to their own debt that is (or was) owed to God.

Taking seriously that "sexual immorality" and "adultery" are ultimately sins against God, then if a guilty spouse pleads with God for forgiveness, God can release that person from any bondage that has led to or has resulted from this sin. He will forgive them *completely* for their unpayable debt (owed to God, not the spouse), as in Matthew 18:21-35, where verses 21-22 are embraced, in case this happens more than once! Yet where mercy has not been sought from a spouse or has been sought but rejected, the consequences are deadly and the marriage may be

---

[34] Ibid., 538-39.

terminated along with one of the covenant partners (by God – directly or by his Law for those under the Law).

However, once mercy is sought and received from God, and the sin is completely forgiven, could this "sexual immorality" remain attached as a personal charge and be held as grounds for the man to divorce his wife? Or in the "new world,"[35] with values of the kingdom of heaven, would it purely be a case of "such were some of you": "the sexually immoral" and "adulterers" who are washed, sanctified, justified, and called again to "flee from sexual immorality" (1 Cor 6:9-11, 18)? If God has removed this person's transgression of the Law, as far as the east is from the west (cf. Ps 103:12), and has been "merciful toward their iniquities" and has "remembered their sins no more" (Heb 8:12; cf. Isa 43:25), then could a husband nonetheless remember the sin and hold it against his wife as grounds for divorce? Surely a righteous husband would not cling to this legal "right" with a cultural "right to remarry," but would "cling" (Gen 2:24) to his wife instead! He would also cling to God's mercy in having had his own sins forgiven.

Any "matter of indecency" (Deut 24:1) pales as valid grounds for divorce when the capital grounds of "sexual immorality" can be invalidated by mercy. After God has forgiven so much, only a hard-hearted person, who does not know or appreciate the immense forgiveness of God, could then divorce for any matter, whether of a trivial or capital nature. Whoever does not forgive from the heart (cf. Matt 18:35) will not have their sins far "removed" (רָחַק, cf. Ps 103:12), but will be in the same spiritual state as Israel when facing the Babylonian Exile. Here the people "removed" (רָחַק) themselves far from God (cf. Jer 2:5), so God judged: "you will be removed (רָחַק) far from your land, and I will drive you out, and you will perish" (Jer 27:10).

With sexual sins being ultimately against God, the means of forgiveness must come from outside of Israel's Temple system, for there are no ritual sacrifices specified in the Law that can atone for them, and in any case, within a generation of Jesus bringing an indictment on Israel, the Jerusalem Temple is destroyed. The Matthean motif where God desires mercy and not sacrifice, points to a greater way of righteousness, a righteousness that exceeds that of the scribes and Pharisees (Matt 5:20). To claim that this can be achieved by self-effort is discordant with being "meek"[36] (Matt 5:5), "humble" (Matt 11:29),

---

[35] de Boer, "Ten Thousand," 231.
[36] Cf. "Moses was very meek, more than all people who were on the face of the earth" (Num 12:3).

and "poor in spirit" (Matt 5:3). The standard Jesus demands is perfection, which cannot be reached by normal human Law-allegiance.

Jesus' teaching on prayer and forgiveness assumes a (daily) failure to keep the Law (Matt 6:9-15). Everyone, whether married or not, amasses an unpayable debt to God; God has grounds to send away or divorce all. Righteousness is obtainable however, but this is purely by God's mercy. God cancels the unpayable debt when the pure in heart plead for forgiveness. Conversely, the hard-hearted act as unforgiving servants who continue to hold sins against others. They divorce for any cause: these separatists separate others from themselves. God, in his wrath, will separate these people from himself; he will not forgive those who do not forgive.

As a shepherd separates the sheep from the goats, God will finally separate people from one another (Matt 25:32). *It is only God's prerogative to separate, and he does so with just cause and on terminal grounds.* Those who disobey God's commands will be separated from God forever, they – with their sins – will be irrevocably "sent away" ("divorced") to destruction. The earthly truism that "divorce is worse than death"[37] captures only a terrible glimpse of divorce in its most terminal eternal sense. On the other hand, those who obey God will have their sins separated from them forever, their sins will be irrevocably "sent away" ("divorced") and these righteous forgiven people will not face destruction. All those who do not or cannot marry, and those who cannot remarry, can still possess great hope in the ultimate marriage between God and his people. What God has joined to himself he will never separate, for any cause.

What about those who do not forgive? The shocking point about Matthew 18:21-35 is not so much that a huge debt can be cancelled, but that such mercy is revocable. Mercy requires mercy.[38] The one who was released from bondage and a debt of 10,000 talents, when he did not have mercy on a fellow servant who owed him only 100 denarii – a

---

[37] "Few things are more painful than divorce. It cuts to the depths of personhood unlike any other relational gash. It is emotionally more heart-wrenching than the death of a spouse." J. Piper, *This Momentary Marriage: A Parable of Permanence* (Illinois: Crossway, 2009), 158. See also, Martin, "Why Is Divorce Considered Worse Than Death?".

[38] The point is shocking, but the concept is not new. E.g. David testifies of the Lord, "With the merciful you show yourself merciful" (Ps 18:25), whereas "with the crooked" God makes himself "seem tortuous" (Ps 18:26) – which could also include tortuous divorce law with nebulous grounds, as against straightforward readings of all the rules and statutes that God has set before us (cf. Ps 18:22). Furthermore, the righteousness and cleanness of people *in God's sight* (Ps 18:24) contrasts with the "haughty eyes" God will bring down (Ps 18:27), and the wicked who has "no fear of God before his eyes" and "flatters himself in his own eyes" (Ps 36:1-2) – *ungodly human sight* (cf. Deut 24:1, "she finds no favour in his eyes).

much more trivial amount – his bondage and huge debt were reinstated and he was handed over to the tormentors forever! The unforgiving servant presents as having "hardness of heart" for not forgiving from his heart. Jesus indicts the Pharisees as having "hardness of heart" for following a merciless cultural divorce practice that God did not command. Such divorce meant holding "a matter of indecency" against a woman as grounds for divorce, and this matter could be anything a man found unfavourable in a woman. The concept of forgiving or overlooking the matter does not appear in Deuteronomy 24:1. This trivial matter can be equated with the 100 denarii debt that a fellow servant owed to another in Jesus' story. Such debts must be forgiven from the heart (cf. Matt 18:35), otherwise a greater forgiveness will be revoked by God. As marriage is instituted by God, then a larger spiritual test – of hearts – underlies Matthew 19:1-12.

Hays sees Matthew as the consummate "ecclesiastical politician" and "reconciler of differences" who adapted "Jesus' unconditional teaching against divorce" in order that it might function as a rigorous yet *merciful rule* for his community.[39] However, this raises greater questions than any problem it seeks to solve. For example, when Jesus taught his original audiences, was he not as merciful as Matthew? If mercy is the ultimate rule, then would not the greater penalties prescribed in Scripture call for greater mercy, and greater motivation in avoiding sexual immorality, such as adultery (Matt 5:27-30), in the first place? If the sin committed is not as serious as *porneia* or *moicheia*, and it does not deserve capital punishment, then it begs the question: *Is it really able to break a marriage?* Surely for more trivial sins Jesus would advocate forgiveness and reconciliation? Or to simply overlook them (cf. Prov 19:11)? Yet even for grave sins, if the offender seeks forgiveness, then Jesus teaches to "loose away" (forgive) the sin "seventy times seven" (Matt 18:22), not to "loose away" (divorce) the person.

Given that "everyone who looks at a woman with lustful intent has already committed adultery with her in his heart" (Matt 5:28), then every married person might have grounds for divorce! Has Jesus opened the field to easy divorce for any number of sexually immoral thoughts? By this logic, even a split-second look of lust would be valid grounds for divorce. Rather, this serves as grounds for indictment, not to mandate divorce or terminate a spouse, but to drive offenders to seek mercy from God and others. Certainly the death penalty is not to be applied for every lustful thought – and the Law does not support this (in

---

[39] Hays, *Moral Vision*, 355-56. (Italics added.)

any case, two witnesses are required to sustain a charge). However, radical action to avoid death remains in view (cf. Matt 5:29-30).

Adultery may be a once-off act[40] but not without enduring consequences. If it were, say, a matter of uncleanness, then purity rituals could be observed and the person pronounced clean again. In the Law, judgement for adultery did not simply evaporate over time, nor was there any ritual or sacrifice specified that could absolve this sin. That a state of adultery exists, from even a single act, finds support in the case of the woman of Deuteronomy 24:4 who is forever prohibited from returning to her original husband due to her defilement. Davidson perceives,

> Already in Deut 24:4 it is indicated that breaking the marriage bond on grounds less than illicit sexual intercourse causes the woman to defile herself, that is, commit what is tantamount to adultery, and Jesus, the master exegete, restores the true meaning of the text [in Matt 5:32].[41]

Proverbs supports this enduring nature of adultery,

> He who commits adultery lacks sense;
> he who does it destroys himself.
> He will get wounds and dishonor,
> and his disgrace will not be wiped away. (Prov 6:32-33)

While adultery can form of way of life, Heth knows it takes only a single act:

> I find it utterly arbitrary to argue… that the term *unchastity* in Matthew 19:9 refers to a lifestyle of immoral sexual behavior, then claim that Matthew 19:9 supports the permission for the spouse to remarry… For Jesus' Jewish hearers *one* instance of *porneia* was enough to put an end to the marriage.[42]

To continue the Jewish contextualisation, the full ramification of a strict reading of the Law is that *one* instance of *porneia* was enough to put *an end to the person*, not just "the marriage." One instance of extramarital sex (Deut 22:22) meant execution; premarital loss of virginity – and there can only be one instance of this (Deut 22:20-21) – meant loss of life. There is nothing metaphorical about these deaths. When we recognise that one instance of *porneia* was truly "enough to put an end to the marriage" decisively and permanently, we can best appreciate the

---

[40] C. Osburn, "The Present Indicative in Matthew 19:9," *Restoration Quarterly* 24 (1981): 193-203.

[41] Davidson, *Flame*, 656.

[42] Heth, "Divorce, but No Remarriage," 101. (Italics original.)

strong reaction of Jesus' closest Jewish hearers (Matt 19:10). They –
along with the now silenced Pharisees – knew what Jesus meant. It was
a very Jewish way of saying what all people know: death terminates a
marriage.

Grounds for Personal Judgement

According to Blomberg,

> Infidelity does not by itself dissolve a marriage; it does so
> only if it is accompanied by a refusal to continue to honor the
> commitment to 'leave and cleave'.[43]

Even then, infidelity with such stubborn refusal does not inevitably
break a marriage, but whoever violates their covenant – even once –
stands accountable to God. In Jesus' teaching on divorce there is one
clear guilty party who is judged by the Law: either the woman who
commits "sexual immorality" (in the 'exception clause' of Matt 19:9)
or the man who commits "adultery" (in the apodosis of Matt 19:9). One
clearly stands condemned for sins that are ultimately against God, not
against each other. Yet Jesus adds another dimension, for his divorce
teaching is in the context of the forgiveness and release (divorce) of an
unpayable debt[44] (Matt 18:21-35), and these sexual offences certainly
amount to unpayable debts. Under Law, a man's very life is owed.
Naturally, "his wife and children and all that he had" (cf. Matt 18:25)
would also be forfeited, but this would still not pay the debt. Note that
his wife, does not "pay" with her life for this man's debt, but of course
she pays in other ways with the loss of her husband and father to her
children.

A spouse who commits sexual sin cannot do anything to atone for it,
but if true repentance is made, the other spouse who refuses to show
mercy, to forgive, and "to continue to honor the commitment to 'leave
and cleave'" then faces God's wrath. The marriage is not automatically
broken, nor is it dissolved by infidelity, but unrepentant infidelity and
refusal to forgive the penitent are both perilous. God will not forgive
those who do not repent (cf. Matt 3:2-12) or forgive (cf. Matt 6:15;
18:35); they will be "sent away" from God's presence and forfeit all
rights. "Divorce" (ἀπολύω) is therefore best understood in relation to
Matthew's meta-narrative, as against conforming to cultural practice
that majors on a presumed right to remarry.

---

[43] Blomberg, "Exegesis," 168.
[44] "The magnitude of the debt was simply unpayable by any means, and the man would
never escape the torturers." Keener, *Matthew*, 461.

A settling of accounts of the king of "the kingdom of heaven" (Matt 18:23) sheds much light on Jesus' teaching on marriage and divorce. Instead of enjoying unearned freedom from being released – or "sent away" (ἀπολύω) – from judgement and being forgiven (Matt 18:27), the unmerciful and unforgiving shall be "delivered [παραδίδωμι]" to the "jailers [βασανιστής]" (Matt 18:34). Friberg defines βασανιστής "as a legal technical term, one who examines by using torture *judicial examiner, tormentor*; in the NT *jailer, torturer, prison guard.*"[45] This term recalls the account of the demons earlier who feared Jesus came "to torment [βασανίζω]" them (Matt 8:29).

Soon Jesus will face immense torment himself, he will be "scourged" and "delivered [παραδίδωμι]" to be crucified, while a real criminal is "released [ἀπολύω]" for the people (Matt 27:26; cf. "divorce" [ἀπολύω] in Matt 19:3, 9). Clearly the verbs παραδίδωμι[46] and ἀπολύω, both in the same verse here, carry no legal technical meaning, but βασανιστής certainly does. Why are Greek terms with real legal technical meaning sometimes so minimised (e.g. for βασανιστής the ESV has "jailers" versus the KJV: "tormentors" and NASB: "torturers"), whereas others without are sometimes so inflated? *'Context is everything'* can mean *'everything a reader wants'*.

Nolland writes,

> Though Jewish justice involved corporal punishment, it did
> not use torture. But in wider circles, torture was frequently
> used in Jesus' day and has a long history.[47]

However, the Law's stipulation of death by stoning (cf. Deut 22:20-22) could qualify as "torture," and God's eschatological judgement of wicked people is not only portrayed by Jesus as deliverance to the "torturers" (Matt 18:34), but his teaching on being "thrown into the hell of fire" (Matt 18:9) also shrieks of torment. Moreover, Jesus' use of ἀπολύω in Matthew 18:27 signals that only God has the sovereign

---

[45] Bibleworks, Friberg 4598.

[46] Other uses of this term in Matthew include: a man who "delivered" or "entrusted" (παραδίδωμι) his property to his servants (Matt 25:14), with one "delivered [παραδίδωμι]" five talents (Matt 25:20) and another "delivered [παραδίδωμι]" two talents (Matt 25:22). Jesus also applied the term to himself to say he will be "delivered [παραδίδωμι] into the hands of men to be killed" (Matt 17:22-23), "delivered [παραδίδωμι] over to the chief priests and scribes, and they will condemn him to death," (Matt 20:18), and "delivered [παραδίδωμι] up to be crucified" (Matt 26:2; cf. 27:2, 18).

[47] Nolland, *Matthew*, 760. Nolland cites "countless references to standard whipping instruments like *virgae* (rods) and *stimuli* (goads)" of the Romans, plus "iron chains, hot tar, burning clothes, the rack, the pillory, and the mill."

prerogative *to send anyone away*, and here it is in a thoroughly good and merciful sense, whereas unrighteous people send others away in an evil and merciless sense (cf. Matt 27:26). God can also send away the evil and adulterous in an unmerciful sense, on the righteous grounds that they are unfaithful or commit "sexual immorality" (*porneia*, Matt 19:9).

Commentators have little problem in saying that torture was common in Jesus' day, with torture used on Jesus himself, and that the Jewish justice system – however constrained by the Roman justice system – involved corporal punishment, which Jesus suffered too. However, they baulk at applying, even if only hypothetically, any physical punishment for sexual offences as prescribed in the Law. A prime assertion of the Protestant majority view is that "divorce" (ἀπολύω) carries a technical legal meaning that assumes "a right to remarry," while any technical legal meanings of "sexual immorality" and "adultery" (cf. Matt 19:9), with physical capital demands as found written in the Law, are virtually ignored or 'virtuously' condemned as "legalistic."

So with little or no threat of physical punishment, either temporal or eternal, the majority position can in practice even *reward* those who behave immorally and who favour another relationship. Smedes writes of the straying wife: "at first she was to be stoned, but later, following the Talmud, she was to be divorced without the privilege of marrying her lover."[48] The Protestant majority view has largely morphed this further into an entitlement of remarriage for both parties, without question or condemnation (even if "adultery" or "desertion" is given as grounds by one party), aligning with secular 'no-fault' divorce views. In contrast to the aforementioned torture and corporal punishment, and Jesus' words on drowning, self-mutilation and hell-fire (Matt 18:5-9), this divorce with "a right to remarry" emphasis hardly serves as a strong deterrent against sexual offences that have destructive temporal and eternal consequences.

With or without the temporal punishment of the Law, adultery has destructive temporal consequences. Likewise, "Divorce destroys relationships, or presupposes the destruction of relationships."[49] By comparison, polygamy, although never God's ideal and often very destructive, was generally culturally accepted and biblically treated less

---

[48] Smedes, *Mere Morality*, 158.
[49] Heth, "Divorce, but No Remarriage," 91. Also Garland, "God hates divorce because, like all sin, it destroys. Divorce in particular is like an atomic bomb that leaves deep emotional craters and strikes all kinds of innocent bystanders with the fallout." Garland, "Divorce," 427.

sternly because it "multiplied relationships,"[50] and within covenants (especially of the rich) a man usually provided for his wives without harming other men or women. So it should be of little surprise "When Nathan condemned David for his disastrous affair with Bathsheba, the prophet did not say a word on behalf of David's own wives (2 Sam 11, 12)"[51] for David's coveting of his neighbour's wife (against The Tenth Commandment), the adultery he commits (against The Seventh Commandment) and the murder he is responsible for (against The Sixth Commandment) are grave offences that cause much more harm to those outside of his familial covenant relationships than to those within.

Jesus lists adultery among the evils that come out of a person's heart, including murder, sexual immorality, theft, false witness, and slander, and these are what "defile" a person (Matt 15:19-20). Here the "heart" is "less the seat of feeling than the seat of thinking and intent."[52] This connects with Pharisees, who with evil intent to kill Jesus, test him on a matter of divorce, only to be charged with "hardness of heart" (Matt 19:8) in relation to a Mosaic stipulation that indicts a man for a woman's defilement (Deut 24:1-4). Therefore the Pharisees, who might never have had "illegal sex with a married person," are still guilty in their "thinking and intent" and represent what Jesus twice in Matthew judges "an evil and adulterous generation" (Matt 12:39; 16:4).

Smedes notes that adultery, seen in the Old Testament foremost as an offence against God (Gen 39:7), is linked with murderers (Job 24:14-15) and treacherous men (Jer 9:2) who misuse God's name (Jer 29:23) and oppress widows (Mal 3:5).[53] "God will judge the sexually immoral and adulterous" (Heb 13:4) and

> a sexual sin like adultery – one that could receive the death penalty throughout the Old Testament world – is viewed as a major violation of the faithfulness vow.[54]

This violation is a treachery that can occur without sexual contact, and has temporal and eternal consequences (cf. Matt 5:27-30).

---

[50] Heth, "Divorce, but No Remarriage," 91. Wright notes divine disapproval nonetheless, for God intended a single relationship. C. Wright, *Old Testament Ethics for the People of God* (Leicester: IVP, 2004), 332.

[51] Smedes, Mere Morality, 158.

[52] Loader, *Jesus Tradition*, 17.

[53] Smedes, *Mere Morality*, 62.

[54] Ibid., 63.

Grounds for National Judgement

With Matthew being the only New Testament author to mention Jeremiah, and he does this three times (Matt 2:17; 16:14; 27:9), Babylonian-like removal and destruction is set to revisit Judah. Such judgement is all in the context of Israel "as a bride" (Jer 2:1) of God who has "played the whore (הָנָה, cf. πορνεία of Matt 19:9a) with many lovers" (Jer 3:1), has been "committing adultery (נָאַף, cf. μοιχᾶται of Matt 19:9b)" (Jer 3:9) and is "treacherous" (Jer 3:11). For "all the adulteries" of the "faithless" Northern Kingdom, God has already "sent her away with a decree of divorce" (Jer 3:8), and Judah's imminent removal from her land, on the same grounds, appears remarkably similar to this earlier divorce.

Instone-Brewer sees that the absence of a divorce certificate in Jeremiah 3:1 means that there was no divorce: "There was therefore no legal problem if Judah and God were reunited, because this would not be a remarriage but a reconciliation."[55] Another way to see this is that Judah was divorced (after all, she was literally "sent away" from the Promised Land, and God's "house" / Temple), but as there was no divorce certificate that specified sexual immorality (cf. Israel), she was not sent away to be executed (even though Judah was exceedingly guilty of the same capital offence).[56] Mercy is foreshadowed. The separation or divorce (sending away) is only temporary. In either case, contra Instone-Brewer, a cultural "right to remarry" is not of any importance here. The emphasis is on the fact that God had a right to execute Judah (cf. Israel), but instead chose to show mercy. The extreme penalty highlights God's immense mercy.

A real legal problem only arises if Israel or Judah had been divorced and had married another; for according to Deuteronomy 24:1-4 it would then be an abomination to return to God (her original husband). The problem can be resolved by:

(i) denying a divorce (cf. Instone-Brewer),
(ii) acknowledging divorce but denying marriage to another – and "whoredom" (Jer 3:9) tends to suggest this (as does "committing adultery" in the same verse), or
(iii) acknowledging divorce and marriage with another (at least for Israel, if not Judah) but allowing for a resurrection from the dead (cf.

---

[55] D. Instone-Brewer, "Three Weddings and a Divorce: God's Covenant with Israel, Judah and the Church," *TB* 47.1 (1996): 14.

[56] Alternatively, the sexual immorality (that would otherwise be recorded as just cause on a divorce certificate) will not be held against Judah forever.

Ezek 37) – for Deuteronomy 24:1-4 does not rule against a wife returning to her original husband *after she has been sent away to be executed.* Indeed, Deuteronomy 24:1-4 is premised on sending a woman away alive, in a divorce process where the full legal weight of "sexual immorality" is not applied (cf. Deut 22:22) and trivial offences are not forgiven by the hard-hearted (cf. Matt 19:8).

Matthew 18:21-35 has a deeper level beyond fresh responsibilities to personally forgive "from your heart" (Matt 18:35). The initial "release" or "divorce" (ἀπολύω) of the unforgiving servant, with the forgiveness of his unpayable debt, and then finally the reinstatement of his debt after he has shown another no mercy, teaches us that "the release may be revocable."[57] For a story that exposes "hardness of heart" (cf. the Pharisees in Matt 19:8), its world-shattering moral relates not simply to "a necessary consequence for [bad] community behaviour"[58] (the intransigence of, say, a Pharisee in a Christian community hardly respects the principal point), but heralds a whole 'new world' where the unmerciful have no place, so are sent away by God to the worst imaginable place to pay their unpayable debt.

Yet this is no antinomian story, for what is lawful is fully and awfully applied: debts must be paid. What should not be missed, however, is that this unpayable debt has been fully cancelled once before, and for the nation of Israel this is true. In fact the story may better fit this corporate interpretation, for an individualistic "lost" then "saved" and "lost again" can be theologically challenging, whereas it is not for Israel's corporate history (cf. the Hosea-Gomer marriage metaphor for God-Israel, along with the naming of their children, brothers and sisters e.g. "she has not received mercy" and "she has received mercy" etc.). All the sexual immorality, evil and idolatry of Israel was forgiven by God in releasing Israel from Babylonian bondage. An unpayable debt that Israel owed to God, comparable to 10,000 talents, had been cancelled. Yet Babylon beckons again for what Jesus calls "an evil and adulterous generation" (Matt 12:39; 16:4).[59] The debt and bondage will be restored. Judgement will come upon *this generation* – not every generation, but this hard-hearted one. Even so, salvation from sins and

---

[57] Nolland, *Matthew*, 761.
[58] Ibid.
[59] This portends exile, and it may be said that Jerusalem is now Babylon (or has become Babylonian) with her "sexual immorality" (Matt 19:9; cf. Rev 14:8, 16:19; 17:5; 18:2, 10, 21) as grounds for divorce.

deliverance from evil will also come for God's people within this generation.[60]

Due to covenant infidelity, Israel had earlier been sent by God into bondage in Babylon: Israel was evicted from her land and the house of God was destroyed. By the Law, the nation had an unpayable debt for all the sexual immorality, idolatry and other evil. By God's awesome mercy, he forgave Israel and released her from Babylon; after seventy years, God restored his bride to the Promised Land and to his house. Solemn remembrance of this is worthy, but a Jewish custom such as the Tashlich ceremony,[61] where sins are ceremonially cast into water (with some parallel to John's baptism in Matt 3:11), does not account for how an unpayable debt *is actually paid.*

Jesus' story in Matthew 18:23-35 illustrates how the kingdom of heaven does thoroughly deal with debt, however it also provides another shock: why in Jesus' comparison is a debt that equals (or exceeds) all the money currently in Israel placed on one man? Keener quips, "the poor man owes the king more money than existed in circulation in the whole country at the time!"[62] This debt would be totally unpayable for any normal person, and yet it provides a fascinating parallel with Jesus' own life story of being delivered up for crucifixion in the place of a rebellious man, or an adulterous people. Sanders helps us to appreciate the massive sum here:

> Crassus (an ambitious and avaricious Roman general), intending to attack the Parthenians (c. 54BCE), raided the temple in Jerusalem on his way. …he took 10,000 talents in cash and valuables [2,000 talents in gold or silver coins, 8,000 talents in golden vessels].[63]

Crassus' raid was within living memory in Jesus' time. If Matthew 18:23-35 informs Matthew 19:9, then it could be significant that all the (lost) treasure of the Temple (however exaggerated) might have only sufficed to cover one person's debt to God for sin that was equivalent to only one act – *or thought* (cf. Matt 5:28) – of adultery.

Israel's historic return from the Babylonian Exile meant release from bondage by God's mercy, but the prominence of "Babylon" in Matthew's Gospel portends national debt reinstatement. The last word

---

[60] This aligns with Matthew's concomitant salvation and judgement motifs, and Jesus' pre-crucifixion mission "only to the lost sheep of the house of Israel" (Matt 10:5-6; 15:24).

[61] Keener finds a parallel "royal release of a city's debt serves as an early third-century parable of God's forgiveness of Israel on Rosh ha-Shanah (Pesiq. R. 51.8)." Keener, *Matthew*, 459.

[62] Ibid., 458-59.

[63] Sanders, *Judaism*, 83-84.

of the Hebrew Bible (in the Christian canon), which serves as the immediate introductory context for Matthew's Gospel, also forebodes national destruction: חֵרֶם (*cherem*)! David Jeffrey highlights that Jesus is introduced "over the page from the last words of Malachi," so to understand the impact of Jesus upon the literary consciousness of his world, he must be understood as "a living, breathing Jewish workman, a man with a Jewish family tree and Jewish textual tradition."[64]

In this tradition, Malachi 4 warns Israel that they will be devoted to God for destruction, like the Canaanites, if they do not remember the Law of Moses and turn their hearts in the great and awesome day of Yahweh, when all the arrogant and all evildoers will burn like stubble in an oven. Remember the Law or be utterly destroyed: this idea powerfully prefaces all of Jesus' teaching in Matthew's Gospel and is nothing new.

> The words of Jesus [in Matt 5:17-20], however filled with grace, are not by him construed as thereby novel with respect to the Law. In fact, so far is this from being the case that, like the prophets, he continually recurs to the Law to characterize such fundamental distinctions as that between true and false righteousness.[65]

Applying Jeffrey's observation (above) to the Matthew 19:1-12 passage, the Jewish leaders are rebuked for a false righteousness because "in the intensity of their concern for fine points... they fail to apply the plain moral sense of the law."[66] Indeed many others miss the plain moral *and legal* sense of "hardness of heart" (Matt 19:8), "sexual immorality" and "adultery" (Matt 19:9).

From Matthew's perspective, in every test Jesus is vindicated for his Law-allegiance; whereas the Jewish leaders and "the people" of Israel (Matt 27:25)[67] are eventually indicted for unlawfully shedding innocent blood.[68] For all the warnings that Jesus provided, Bolt observes "Israel was deeply in trouble; it was not a good generation, but an evil one. This

---

[64] D. Jeffrey, *People of the Book: Christian Identity and Literary Culture* (Grand Rapids: Eerdmans, 1996), 42.

[65] Ibid., 45.

[66] Ibid.

[67] In chapter 27, "Matthew changed his vocabulary from 'crowd' (vv 15, 20, 24) to 'people' (v 25), reinforcing that it was Israel – God's covenant people – who rejected their Messiah ...well aware of the blood of the Messiah now falling on their heads." Bolt, *Matthew*, 248.

[68] It might be said that this reflects the situation in a Matthean community at a later time of Christian-Jewish hostilities, but it is presented as the situation for Jesus' time. The text never presents the specific judgement on the people and religious leaders of that generation as applicable to any other generation.

generation would not go unpunished."[69] It was also an "adulterous" generation, which firmly links it to the μοιχᾶται of Matthew 19:9, with "hard-hearted" leaders, as judged by Jesus in Matthew 19:8. Bolt finds further evidence that Israel's religious leaders "showed themselves to be hard-hearted" in Matthew's account of Judas' return of the blood money,

> If Judas had 'betrayed innocent blood', then this would have been something that brought a curse down on all of Israel – polluting the land – and especially on the leaders, who were already implicated in his action... prophecy was once again being fulfilled... As these hard-hearted leaders of Israel still refused to change their mind, the promised judgement was about to fall.[70]

This pollution of the land connects with the apodosis of Deuteronomy 24:1-4, "you shall not bring sin upon the land that the LORD your God is giving you for an inheritance," integral to the only legislated command on divorce and remarriage in the Hebrew Bible. Not only was the land polluted, but the Temple too, for Judas had thrown the blood money into it before suiciding (Matt 27:5). Runesson sees that the Temple is so severely "defiled" (cf. Lev 15:31) that "the point of no return is reached."[71] This matches the defilement and "abomination"[72] of Deuteronomy 24:4, with terminal result: "to reject the Messiah... would be totally disastrous for this generation."[73] In doing so, "her 'house is left desolate', that is, this would prove to be their judgement (compare 1 Kings 9:7; Jeremiah 22:5)."[74]

Deuteronomic curses are enacted by the one who originally brought Israel "out of the house of slavery" (Exod 20:2; Deut 5:6) in a nation-birthing marvel that the people are reminded of every time the Decalogue is read. Not only will Israel be sent away ("divorced" or "separated") from her husband's house, "the house of God" (Matt 12:4; cf. Deut 23:18), for her evil and adultery, but the house itself will be destroyed (cf. Matt 23:37-39; 24:1-2)! This mirrors "the worst time of judgement experienced by Israel," the Babylonian Exile, "when the nation was 'handed over to the Gentiles' because of God's displeasure

---

[69] Bolt, *Matthew*, 127.

[70] Ibid., 247.

[71] Runesson, *Divine Wrath*, 436.

[72] This term usually refers to apostasy J. McConville, *Deuteronomy*, AOTC (Leicester: Apollos, 2002), 360. See also BDAG's second definition of πορνεία as cited in the exegesis of Matt 19:9.

[73] Bolt, *Matthew*, 216.

[74] Ibid.

(recall the significance of the exile for Matthew, see 1:11-12, 17)."[75] Bolt sees here that Jesus will be treated as if he deserved the curse and wrath of God (Matt 20:17-20), which is true, to the extent that he represents wayward Israel as her "king" (Matt 27:29, 37, 42). Yet the people, in their apostasy, swear a curse on themselves (Matt 27:25) and God's wrath will fall on them too, such that they will be killed and exiled, and the Jerusalem Temple will be destroyed. This catastrophic eviction has been foreshadowed and the "house of Israel" (Ezek 12:10; Matt 10:6) is forewarned.

While contending that "in the time of Jeremiah the death penalty was not normally carried out in cases of adultery or harlotry,"[76] Davidson writes

> The "divorce" that befell the northern kingdom was nothing less than a death penalty in practice. The northern kingdom of Israel was destroyed and ceased to exist; the majority of the population was either killed or taken into exile. So, although the terminology for divorce is utilized, in historical reality the punishment corresponds more precisely with the death penalty that was legally prescribed for adultery.[77]

However, rather than viewing divorce merely as a "substitute punishment,"[78] this divinely executed "death penalty in practice" captures *the full biblical meaning of divorce for adultery*: it is a sending (or loosing) away to destruction. In this instance, Israel was sent away from God (and his "house" / Temple and land) to be destroyed at the hands of Assyria. Judah was later sent away for the same infidelity. Contrary to cultural expectation, a "right to remarry" cannot be presumed.

Spadaro purports that "Matthew intentionally wrote what he believed to be Scripture" to produce "a polemical document that would demonstrate 'just cause' for the termination of the Levitical constitution and its house/temple."[79] Building on this interpretative lens of indictment, 'just cause' for God's separation or divorce of Israel (again) can also be found in the 'exception clause' of Matthew 19:9. Matthew's book itself might even be viewed as a divorce certificate or notice of separation *with handwritten* 'just cause',[80] yet simultaneously offering hope for revival from death (post-divorce, cf. the Assyrian Conquest)

---

[75] Ibid., 196.
[76] Davidson, *Flame*, 415.
[77] Ibid.
[78] Ibid.
[79] Spadaro, Matthew, 280.
[80] This may be a Matthean χειρόγραφον (cf. Col 2:14).

and reconciliation (post-separation, cf. the Babylonian Exile). A similar observation has been made concerning the book of Hosea:

> This reference to a divorce certificate in verse 8 (of Jeremiah 3) may be an allusion to the verbal divorce formula in Hosea 2:2 [MT 2:4], which becomes a divorce certificate by the act of Hosea writing it down.[81]

That the Pharisees "tested" Jesus (Matt 19:3) is significant given Jesus earlier cited the Deuteronomic command, "You shall not put the Lord your God to the test" (Matt 4:7). That the test subject is divorce increases the stakes, for God is in a marriage covenant with Israel (Isa 54:5; Hos 2:19–20), and being a jealous husband (Deut 4:24), God destroys the adulterous in hell (cf. Matt 5:27-30). While the Pharisees swing from hearing an absolute prohibition on divorce: "let not *man* separate" (Matt 19:6, italics added), to hearing one grave exception, they likely miss the terrifying ramification that *God* may separate what he has joined (Matt 19:6).[82] As God's marriage partner has committed "sexual immorality" (Matt 19:9), Israel is (again) guilty of a capital offence.

The prophetic tradition alone counts against any equivalence between the "sexual immorality" (*porneia*) of Matthew 19:9 and the "matter of indecency" (*'erwat dabar*) of Deuteronomy 24:1. The Hebrew prophets consistently warned of catastrophic national judgement for sexual immorality. Jesus warned of catastrophic national judgement (Matthew 23:37 to 24:14), and the historical fall of Jerusalem in 70CE – with multitudes slaughtered and cut-off from their land, the marvellous Temple destroyed and associated cultic practices terminated – begs far more serious grounds for judgement than a (trivial) matter of indecency. If justification for this judgement has anything to do with Matthew's purpose in writing, then theorising an insertion of the 'exception clause' (5:32; 19:9) for later Matthean community needs is totally unwarranted. Jesus' teaching befits early and universal needs – not merely local conjectures, and matches judgement prophesied centuries earlier.

---

[81] Instone-Brewer, Social and Literary Context, 41.
[82] "The very meaning of marriage will include: *What God has joined, only God can separate*" (italics original). Piper, *This Momentary Marriage: A Parable of Permanence*, 159. Piper notes this when asserting that God will never divorce the church (he avoids the idea that God did divorce Northern Israel).

General Application

Matthew 19:1-12 most immediately applies to religious leaders, for the passage centres on religious leaders who test Jesus (a religious leader), and Jesus' disciples (in training to be religious leaders) join the conversation. Large crowds of Jews look on, but probably only a few were privy to the whole conversation, and none might learn any lesson until Matthew later publishes his Gospel (that would likely be sent first to Christian religious leaders). Although the debate centres on a matter of Law, and terms within the debate (such as "sexual immorality" and "adultery") are best defined by the Law, the lesson has universal application because Jesus grounds his case in the Creation ideal, and just as marriage is universal, so are acts of sexual immorality and adultery. Once the immediate Jewish legal context is appreciated, moral principles may then be applied to all Christians, without imposing the Law's capital codes on non-Jews, or changing these codes (including the original meanings of terms therein) for anyone who remains subject to the Law.

Jesus directs his judgement of "your hardness of heart" (Matt 19:8) at the religious leaders, even if it has wider application to that generation (and Moses'). Likewise, the judgement would be directly applicable to religious leaders in any generation who do not practice what they preach, even when the wider audience also stands accountable (Matt 23:1-3). In Matthew 23, Jesus' fiercest judgement falls on the religious leaders, but the generation remains in trouble (Matt 23:36).

While the core pastoral lesson of this thesis can be concisely presented (centred on the permanency of marriage and the Law, and the premise that *mercy requires mercy*), with some risk of oversimplification, the wide-ranging pastoral applications – how the theology is applied to diverse situations involving marriage, divorce, remarriage, or non-marriage – must largely be entrusted to pastoral wisdom and God's good guidance. This is one reason why Christian leaders are held to extra account, "Not many of you should become teachers, my brothers, for you know that we who teach will be judged with greater strictness" (Jas 3:1). A more sobering verse is found in the lead-up to Jesus' teaching on marriage and divorce,

> Whoever causes one of these little ones who believe in me to sin, it would be better for him to have a great millstone fastened around his neck and to be drowned in the depth of the sea. (Matt 18:6)

Causing believers to sin, which would include a leader's false teaching and ungodly example regarding marriage and divorce, attracts greater judgement. The judgement falls on anyone ("whoever") although the context is that Jesus has exemplified a little child to teach his disciples (most of whom will become church leaders): "Truly, I say to you, unless you turn and become like children, you will never enter the kingdom of heaven" (Matt 18:3). "You will never enter" cannot be put more absolutely. The subsequent "let not man separate" (Matt 19:6) comes with an equally absolute indictment for those who show no mercy and never repent (cf. Matt 18:35; 19:8-9).

This is not to say that one mistake in the area of marriage and divorce is unforgivable! Rather, at the very heart of this (and any pastoral matter) is the question of humble obedience to God. Is a person really committed to following the way of Jesus, obeying him like a child, or essentially do they live their own way? Do they desire – above all things – mercy and forgiveness, or are they demanding of whatever they are owed or might feel a right to? "Blessed are the merciful, for they shall receive mercy" (Matt 5:7) stands in stark contrast to the fate of those who are merciless, who are hard-hearted and do not forgive others.[83] God will not forgive these people, and they will never enter his kingdom. "So also my heavenly Father will do to every one of you, if you do not forgive your brother from your heart" (Matt 18:35). It can be no accident that Matthew places Jesus' words on forgiving "from your heart" immediately before his words on marriage and divorce. *Divorce is ultimately about an unwillingness to forgive* – even if words of love are still spoken. Mercy is missing – even if parties appear to be amicable and far from ruthless. To divorce is to stubbornly separate what God has joined together, which only God should ever separate by death (under the Law, this could be by capital means). It is a rejection of the Creator's foundational command to always cleave, 'until death do us part'. The core pastoral implication then is to determine the state of each person's heart and to instruct on how crucial it is to show mercy.

Another related pastoral implication is to ensure that Scripture is handled correctly. Given that Matthew's Gospel addresses Law-keeping for those to whom the Law applies, then Christians can certainly observe that Jesus lived a totally lawful life, whereas his opponents acted unlawfully. Lawless people of Jesus' generation were judged, and

---

[83] It will be noted here that *no one earns salvation by works* (by what they do, or do not do), but when a person is saved by Jesus (in repenting from sins and believing in him, *they rely on Jesus' work* on the cross: his death to remove sin, and his resurrection to bring life), they follow Jesus, trusting and obeying God, and by their *fruit* (good works and character) they are recognised (Matt 7:16-20).

the Law remains unchanged for all generations. However, this does not mean that Christians must forever obey the Law – for they too would no doubt fail to keep every detail and commit capital offences (if only in the heart), including "sexual immorality" and "adultery" (cf. Matt 19:9); Christians must learn from the Law's principles and live by the love-principle, in fulfilment of the Law.

Whoever seeks to rely on Matthew's 'exception clause' as a reason to divorce should seek first to appreciate the lawful context in which it was given, and the author's purpose in writing it. If anyone remains adamant that Matthew 19:9 permits them to divorce (and remarry), it must be asked of them, are they wholeheartedly committed to seeking first God's kingdom and his righteousness, or half-hearted and anxious for other things of this world (cf. Matt 6:32-33)? Do they understand that God desires mercy (cf. Matt 18:21-35)? Or do they act in conformity with the hard-hearted of Matthew 19:8, whom God swore in his wrath that they will never enter his rest? At this point it should be emphasized, as before, that *not everyone who has divorced, or has been divorced, is necessarily hard-hearted*. However, forgiveness should be sought for any past action not sanctioned by God (one's divorce, or wrongdoing related to it), and commitment should be made to never wilfully do (or do again) what God has commanded married couples not to do (cf. Matt 19:6). Again, the heart is in prime focus: is it soft or hard toward God and his commands? Will a person repent, and forgive another who repents?

For a sinned against spouse, if the perpetrator earnestly repents (even seven times seventy times), then they are to be forgiven every time (cf. Matt 18:21-22). Such forgiveness sounds wonderful, but repetitive sin can hardly be easy to cope with. If the perpetrator only repents in pretence (the apology is not full and genuine, and no steps are made to make real change) – and extra discernment here is necessary, then safe distance may need to be maintained. God cannot be mocked (Gal 6:7) by falsity and treachery, what is sown will be reaped, and Israel's history provides stern warning for fake or half-hearted repentance, as Jeremiah 3:9-10 reveals:

> Because she took her whoredom lightly, she polluted the land, committing adultery with stone and tree. Yet for all this her treacherous sister Judah did not return to me with her whole heart, but in pretense, declares the LORD.

Precedent is set of catastrophic judgement for those who treat sexual immorality lightly, who are faithless, and who do not wholeheartedly follow the Lord. This is not merely an individual concern, but a corporate precedent: as a nation Israel was judged; so other nations may be judged, along with churches in those nations that follow the ungodly ethics of the status quo. In 'the first sexual revolution' the early Christians revolted against the corrupt sexual norms of Ancient Rome;[84] such godly revolt should continue.

Sometimes the evil in the church is worse than that in the world. Scandals involving paedophile religious leaders and child abuse are most obvious. Paul speaks of an odious case in the Corinthian church:

> It is actually reported that there is sexual immorality among you, and of a kind that is not tolerated even among pagans, for a man has his father's wife. And you are arrogant! Ought you not rather to mourn? Let him who has done this be removed from among you. (1 Cor 5:1-2)

If there is no repentance of sexual immorality (or other sin), and the person claims to be a Christian, then church discipline is necessary (1 Cor 5:1-12; cf. Matt 18:15-20). Mercy applies where forgiveness is desired, "Those who are well have no need of a physician, but those who are sick" (Matt 9:12). Peter's question in Matthew 18:21, "Lord, how often will my brother sin against me, and I forgive him? As many as seven times?" (Matt 18:21), is premised on a brother seeking forgiveness. The fact that a brother might need to be confronted first only enhances this, for positive action must be taken to effect reconciliation (cf. Matt 18:15, "If he listens to you, you have gained a brother"). It is not merely a matter of "reconciling" by vacuously declaring "I forgive you" when there is no knowledge and acceptance of the fault, and no repentance. The discipline of Matthew 18:15-20 is contingent on a godly process of confronting sin to bring about forgiveness and reconciliation, or non-forgiveness and disfellowship (mercifully undertaken with a view to finally restore the offender, but without any guarantee of this).

'The Story of the Unforgiving Servant' (Matt 18:23-35) likewise hinges on a servant pleading with God for forgiveness, and another servant pleading with his fellow servant for forgiveness. This all serves as prelude to Jesus' teaching on marriage in Matthew 19:1-12, so the same considerations for dealing with sin, desiring mercy and forgiving from the heart must apply. Automatic forgiveness is not the lesson taught, but certainly in view is a steadfast love that takes godly action, always desires mercy and is willing to forgive any debt.

---

[84] K. Harper, "The First Sexual Revolution: How Christianity Transformed the Ancient World," The Institute on Religion and Public Life, www.firstthings.com/article/2018/01/the-first-sexual-revolution.

Debts must be paid or forgiven. For all the debts of the world, there is a grand biblical narrative with a climactic fulfilment where one humble servant acts to pay the ultimate price. The hard-hearted refuse to comprehend and appropriate this, and they face God's anger and torment until they pay their own debt themselves. Good news of debt-release contrasts with bad news of debt-enslavement, as light (Matt 4:16; 5:14; 17:2) against darkness (Matt 8:12; 22:13; 25:30). Although the "gospel of the kingdom" (Matt 4:23; 9:35; 24:14) does not centre on earthly marriage, how one deals with sin and debt within this most intimate relationship on earth – and how one counsels others regarding it – certainly reveals whether one really knows the Gospel, is a member of this heavenly kingdom, and is right with the Lord and King who settles accounts with his servants.

A social rights mentality should be questioned, for self-denial and self-sacrifice are core to true love, and to the Gospel. With respect to an assumed cultural "right to remarry" (post-divorce on non-capital grounds), what is right by our generation – or any generation – is not always right, or righteous, by God. A "right to remarry" inexorably clashes with a *responsibility to remain married*, founded in the Creation command of God to cleave (hold fast) to a spouse – to steadfastly love our closest neighbour and God-given companion in marriage.

A commitment to permanent marriage is invariably expressed in wedding vows, with solemn promises to love and to cherish 'until death do us part'. On this wondrous occasion, severing the union on any grounds, let alone for a figurative death, would be far from the minds of most loving persons. Sam Crabtree stresses that straight truth-telling is needed and "anything more than this comes from evil":

> If anything but death is an option for ending a marriage, then don't say "until death" in your wedding vows. Tell the truth. Promise what is meant. Say something like "until adultery, abandonment, or abuse."
>
> Whether speaking of marriage or any other subject, it comes as no surprise that God expects people to say what they mean. The immediate context of Jesus's teaching about adultery includes his clarification that going back on your word (marital vow) is evil. (See Matthew 5:37.)[85]

To remember one's own solemn wedding vows, and to hear those of other couples, spoken before God, family, and friends, is of immense value. To support married couples in upholding these vows is vital too.

---

[85]   S.   Crabtree,   "Until   Death   Do   Us   Part   -   for   Real," https://www.desiringgod.org/articles/until-death-do-us-part-for-real.

Sundering or undermining what God has joined together attracts fierce condemnation:

> Let marriage be held in honor among all, and let the marriage bed be undefiled, for God will judge the sexually immoral and adulterous. (Heb 13:4)

God will judge. It is sobering to recall that "an evil and adulterous generation" (Matt 12:39; 16:4) was destroyed. Jesus' generation did not pass away until the judgement that he foretold was fulfilled (Matt 23:36); those indicted were sent away ("divorced") from God's house, banished from God's presence. Crowds of people who had followed Jesus, were healed by him, had other prophets and the Law point to him, and had heard the preaching of religious leaders who sincerely but wrongly taught on marriage and divorce, faced God's wrath.

"Deliver us from evil" (Matt 6:13) are words to pray to seek not only deliverance from the general evil of our time, but deliverance from the evil of breaking our own word and voiding the word of God. This is crucial, especially when many in our generation do not see the gravity in violating marriage covenants – whether for an exceptional cause, any cause, or no cause at all. It is better not to marry than to suffer divine judgement for stubborn rebellion and infidelity.

BIBLIOGRAPHY

Adams, J. *Marriage, Divorce and Remarriage in the Bible.* Grand Rapids: Zondervan, 1980.

Aland et al, B. & K. *The Greek New Testament.* Fourth ed. Westphalia: UBS, 2001.

Alexander, T. D. *From Paradise to the Promised Land: An Introduction to the Pentateuch.* Grand Rapids: Baker, 2012.

Allison, D. *The New Moses: A Matthean Typology.* Eugene: Wipf & Stock, 1993. 2013. Fortress.

———. *The Sermon on the Mount: Inspiring the Moral Imagination.* Companions to the New Testament. New York: Crossroad, 1999.

Arand, C., C. Blomberg, S. Maccarty, and J. Pipa. *Perspectives on the Sabbath: 4 Views.* Edited by C. Donato. Nashville: B&H, 2014.

Aune, D. *The New Testament in its Literary Environment.* Philadelphia: Westminster, 1987.

Banks, R. *Jesus and the Law in the Synoptic Tradition.* SNTSMS 28. New York: CUP, 1975.

Barth, K. *Church Dogmatics, Volume II.1: The Doctrine of God.* London: T&T Clark, 2009.

———. *Church Dogmatics, Volume IV.2: The Doctrine of Reconciliation.* London: T&T Clark, 2009.

Barton, S. "Can We Identify the Gospel Audiences?". In *The Gospels for All Christians: Rethinking the Gospel Audiences.* Grand Rapids: Eerdmans, 1998.

Batzig, N. "Israel and Typology in Matthew's Gospel." https://feedingonchrist.org/israel-and-typology-in-matthews-gospel/.

Bauckham, R. *The Gospels for All Christians: Rethinking the Gospel Audiences.* Grand Rapids: Eerdmans, 1998.

Baugh, S. "Marriage and Family in Ancient Greek Society." Chap. 5 In *Marriage and Family in the Biblical World*, edited by K. Campbell. Downers Grove: IVP, 2003.

Beal, E., and G. Hochman. *Adult Children of Divorce: How to Achieve Happier Relationships.* London: Piatkus, 1991.

Berger, K. "Hartherzigkeit Und Gottes Gesetz: Die Vorgeschichte Des Antijüdischen Vorwurfs in Mc 10:5." *ZNW* 61 (1970).

Berkovic, N., and E. Visontay. "Divorce Rate Drops, for Better or
    Worse." *The Australian*, 21 April 2018.
Betz, H. *The Sermon on the Mount*. Hermeneia. Minneapolis:
    Fortress, 1995.
Bibleworks: Software of Biblical Exegesis & Research Version
    10. BibleWorks, Norfolk.
Bird, M. *The Gospel of the Lord: How the Early Church Wrote the
    Story of Jesus.* Grand Rapids: Eerdmans, 2014.
Black, D., and D. Beck. *Rethinking the Synoptic Problem*. Grand
    Rapids: Baker, 2001.
Bloch, A. *The Biblical and Historical Background of Jewish
    Customs and Ceremonies*. New York: Ktav, 1980.
Block, D. "Marriage and Family in Ancient Israel." Chap. 2 In
    Marriage and Family in the Biblical World, edited by K.
    Campbell. Downers Grove: IVP, 2003.
Blomberg, C. "Marriage, Divorce, Remarriage, and Celibacy: An
    Exegesis of Matthew 19:3-12." *Trinity Journal* 11, no. 2
    (1990): 161-96.
———. *Matthew*. Nashville: Broadman, 1992.
———. "Matthew." In *Commentary on the New Testament Use
    of the Old Testament*, edited by G. Beale and D. Carson.
    Grand Rapids: Baker, 2007.
Bockmuehl, M. "Matthew 5:32, 19:9 in the Light of Pre-Rabbinic
    Halakhah." *NTS* 35, no. 2 (1989): 291-95.
Boice, J. *The Gospel of Matthew*. Grand Rapids: Baker, 2001.
Bolt, P. *Matthew: A Great Light Dawns*. RBT. Edited by P.
    Barnett. Sydney: Aquila, 2014.
Borg, M. *Jesus in Contemporary Scholarship*. Valley Forge:
    Trinity, 1994.
Bromiley, G. *God and Marriage*. Grand Rapids: Eerdmans, 1980.
Brown, J. "Matthew, Gospel Of." In *Dictionary of Jesus and the
    Gospels*, edited by J. Brown, J. Green and N. Perrin.
    Illinois: IVP, 2014.
Brown, R. E. *The Birth of the Messiah: A Commentary on the
    Infancy Narratives in the Gospels of Matthew and Luke*.
    ABRL. New York: Doubleday, 1993.
Bruce, F. F. *New Testament History*. London: Nelson, 1969.
Bruner, F. D. *Matthew: A Commentary. The Churchbook
    Matthew 13-28*. Vol. 2, Dallas: Word, 1990.
Burridge, R. *What Are the Gospels?: A Comparison with Graeco-
    Roman Biography*. New York: Cambridge University,
    1992.

Calvin, J. *A Harmony of the Gospels: Matthew, Mark and Luke*. Calvin's Commentaries. Vol. II, Grand Rapids: Eerdmans, 1972.

Cameron, A. *Joined-up Life: A Christian Account of How Ethics Works*. Nottingham: IVP, 2011.

Cameron, A., and B. Rosner. *Still Deadly: Ancient Cures for the 7 Sins*. Sydney: Aquila, 2007.

Carson, D. *Exegetical Fallacies*. Grand Rapids: Baker, 1996.

———. *From Sabbath to Lord's Day: A Historical and Theological Foundation*. Eugene: Wipf & Stock, 1999.

———. "The Jewish Leaders in Matthew's Gospel: A Reappraisal." *JETS* 25, no. 2 (1982): 161-74.

———. *Matthew*. Grand Rapids: Zondervan, 2017.

———. "Matthew." In *The Expositor's Bible Commentary Matthew & Mark*, edited by T. Longman III and D. Garland. Grand Rapids: Zondervan, 2010.

———. *The Sermon on the Mount: An Evangelical Exposition of Matthew 5-7*. Grand Rapids: Baker, 1992.

Carter, W. *Matthew and the Margins: A Socio-Political and Religious Reading*. JSNTS. Sheffield: Sheffield Academic, 2000.

Casey, M. *Aramaic Sources of Mark's Gospel*. SNTSMS 102. Cambridge: CUP, 2004.

Chapman, D. "Marriage and Family in Second Temple Judaism." Chap. 5 In *Marriage and Family in the Biblical World*, edited by K. Campbell. Downers Grove: IVP, 2003.

Christensen, D. *Deuteronomy 21:10-34:12*. 6 B WBC. Nashville: Thomas Nelson, 2002.

Ciampa, R., and B. Rosner. *The First Letter to the Corinthians*. PNTC. Grand Rapids: Eerdmans, 2010.

Cohick, L. *Women in the World of the Earliest Christians*. Grand Rapids: Baker, 2009.

Collins, J. "Marriage, Divorce, and Family in Second Temple Judaism." In *Families in Ancient Israel*. The Family, Religion, and Culture. Louisville: WJK, 1997.

Collins, R. *Divorce in the New Testament*. Collegeville: Liturgical, 1992.

Colson, C., and N. Pearcey. *How Now Shall We Live?* Wheaton: Tyndale, 1999.

Cooper, B. "Cedric E. W. Vine. The Audience of Matthew: An Appraisal of the Local Audience Thesis." *JGAR* 1, no. Sept 2017 (2017).

Cornes, A. *Divorce and Remarriage: Biblical Principles and Pastoral Practice.* Grand Rapids: Eerdmans, 1993.

Countryman, L. W. *Dirt, Greed and Sex: Sexual Ethics in the New Testament and Their Implications for Today.* London: SCM, 1989.

Crabtree, S. "Until Death Do Us Part - for Real." https://www.desiringgod.org/articles/until-death-do-us-part-for-real.

Craigie, P. *The Book of Deuteronomy.* NICOT. Grand Rapids: Eerdmans, 1976.

Cranfield, C. *The Gospel According to Saint Mark: An Introduction and Commentary.* CGTC. Cambridge: CUP, 1959. 1972.

Crossley, J. *The New Testament and Jewish Law: A Guide for the Perplexed.* London: Bloomsbury, 2010.

Crouzel, H. *L'eglise Primitive Face Au Divorce.* Paris: Beauchesne, 1971.

Culpepper, R. A. *Mark.* SHBC. Edited by R. S. Nash. Macon: Smyth & Helwys, 2007.

Danker, F. "Hardness of Heart: A Study in Biblical Thematic." *CTM* 44, no. 2 (March 1973).

Danker, F., W. Bauer, and W. Arndt. *A Greek-English Lexicon of the New Testament and Other Early Christian Literature.* Third ed. Chicago: UCP, 2000.

Davidson, R. *Flame of Yahweh: Sexuality in the Old Testament.* Peabody: Hendrickson, 2007.

Davies, W., and D. Allison. *The Gospel According to Saint Matthew.* ICC. Vol. III, Edinburgh: T&T Clark, 1997.

———. *The Gospel According to Saint Matthew.* ICC. Vol. I, Edinburgh: T&T Clark, 1992.

de Boer, M. "Ten Thousand Talents? Matthew's Interpretation and Redaction of the Parable of the Unforgiving Servant (Matt 18:23-35)." *CBQ* 50 (1988).

Derret, J. D. *Law in the New Testament.* Oxford: Alden, 1970.

"Divorce in Australia." Australian Institute of Family Studies, https://aifs.gov.au/facts-and-figures/divorce-australia.

Downing, D. *Marriage from the Heart.* Maitland: Xulon, 2012.

Dunn, J. *The Oral Gospel Tradition.* Grand Rapids: Eerdmans, 2013.

Dupont, J. *Mariage Et Divorce Dans L'evangile. Matthieu 19, 3-12 Et Parrallèles.* Bruges: Desclée de Brouwer, 1959.

Edgar, T. "Divorce & Remarriage for Adultery or Desertion." Chap. 3 In *Divorce and Remarriage: Four Christian Views*, edited by H. W. House. Downers Grove: IVP, 1990.

Evans, C. *Matthew*. New York: CUP, 2012.

Farla, P. "'The Two Shall Be One Flesh': Gen. 1.27 and 2.24 in the New Testament Marriage Texts." In *Intertextuality in Biblical Writings: Essays in Honour of Bas Van Iersel*, edited by S. Draisma. Kampen: Kok, 1989.

Farmer, W. *The Synoptic Problem: A Critical Analysis*. New York: Macmillan, 1964.

Fee, G. *New Testament Exegesis: A Handbook for Students and Pastors*. Louisville: WJK, 2002.

Filson, F. "Broken Patterns in the Gospel of Matthew." *JBL* 75, no. 3 (1956): 227.

France, R. T. *The Gospel of Matthew*. TNTC. Grand Rapids: Eerdmans, 2007.

Freyne, S. *Galilee: From Alexander the Great to Hadrian*. Edinburgh: T&T Clark, 1998. 1980.

Gaddy, C. W. *Adultery and Grace: The Ultimate Scandal*. Grand Rapids: Eerdmans, 1996.

Gagnon, R. "The Bible and Homosexual Practice: Key Issues." In *Homosexuality and the Bible: Two Views*, edited by D. Via and R. Gagnon. Minneapolis: Fortress, 2003.

Garland, D. "A Biblical View of Divorce." *RevExp* 84, no. 3 (Sum 1987): 419-32.

⸻. *Mark: From Biblical Text to Contemporary Life*. The NIV Application Commentary. Grand Rapids: Zondervan, 1996.

⸻. *Reading Matthew: A Literary and Theological Commentary on the First Gospel*. RNTC. New York: Crossroad, 1993.

Gehring, R. *The Biblical "One Flesh" Theology of Marriage as Constituted in Genesis 2:24*. Eugene: Wipf & Stock, 2013.

Goodacre, M. *The Case against Q: Studies in Markan Priority and the Synoptic Problem*. Harrisburg: Trinity, 2002.

Green, J. *Hearing the New Testament: Strategies for Interpretation*. Grand Rapids: Eerdmans, 2010.

Greeven, H. "Zu Den Aussagen Des Neuen Testaments Über Die Ehe." *ZEE* 1 (1957).

Grenz, S. *Sexual Ethics: An Evangelical Perspective*. Louisville: WJK, 1997.

Grundmann, W. *Das Evangelium Nach Matthäus.* ThHNT, 1. Sixth ed. Berlin: EVA, 1986.

Guelich, R. *The Sermon on the Mount: A Foundation for Understanding.* Waco: Word, 1982.

Gundry, R. *Matthew: A Commentary on His Literary and Theological Art.* Grand Rapids: Eerdmans, 1982.

Gushee, D., and G. Stassen. *Kingdom Ethics: Following Jesus in Contemporary Context.* Grand Rapids: Eerdmans, 2016.

Hagner, D. *Matthew 1-13.* WBC 33A. Dallas: Word, 1993.

———. *Matthew 14-28.* WBC 33B. Dallas: Word, 1995.

Hamer, C. *Marital Imagery in the Bible: An Exploration of Genesis 2:24 and its Significance for the Understanding of New Testament Divorce and Remarriage Teaching.* Apostolos Old Testament Studies. London: Apostolos, 2015.

Hamilton, V. *The Book of Genesis: Chapters 1-17.* NICOT. Grand Rapids: Eerdmans, 1990.

———. *Handbook on the Pentateuch.* Grand Rapids: Baker, 1982.

Harper, K. "The First Sexual Revolution: How Christianity Transformed the Ancient World." The Institute on Religion and Public Life, www.firstthings.com/article/2018/01/the-first-sexual-revolution.

———. *From Shame to Sin: The Christian Transformation of Sexual Morality in Late Antiquity.* Massachusetts: Harvard University, 2013.

Harrington, D. *The Maccabean Revolt: Anatomy of a Biblical Revolution.* Old Testament Studies. Eugene: Wipf & Stock, 1988.

Hartley, J. *Leviticus.* WBC. Edited by J. Watts. Dallas: Word, 1992.

Harvey, A. *Promise or Pretence? A Christian's Guide to Sexual Morals.* London: SCM, 1994.

Hauerwas, S. *Matthew.* BTCB. Ada: Baker, 2007.

Hays, R. *Echoes of Scripture in the Gospels.* Waco: Baylor, 2016.

———. *The Moral Vision of the New Testament.* Edinburgh: T&T Clark, 1996.

Heil, J. "Ezekiel 34 and the Narrative Strategy of the Shepherd and Sheep Metaphor in Matthew." *CBQ* 55, no. 4 (1993): 698-708.

Heine, R. *Reading the Old Testament with the Ancient Church.* Evangelical Ressourcement. Grand Rapids: Baker, 2007.

Heth, W. "Divorce, but No Remarriage." Chap. 2 In *Divorce and Remarriage: Four Christian Views*, edited by H. W. House. Downers Grove: IVP, 1990.

―――. "Jesus on Divorce: How My Mind Has Changed." *SBJOT* 6, no. 1 (2002).

―――. "Remarriage for Adultery or Desertion." In *Remarriage after Divorce in Today's Church: 3 Views*, edited by M. Strauss. Counterpoints. Grand Rapids: Zondervan, 2006.

Hill, D. *The Gospel of Matthew*. NCBC. London: Oliphants, 1972.

Himes, K., and J. Coriden. "The Indissolubility of Marriage: Reasons to Reconsider." *Theological Studies* 65, no. 3 (2004): 453-99.

Hoehner, H. "Dictionary of New Testament Background : A Compendium of Contemporary Biblical Scholarship." edited by C. Evans and S. Porter Jr. Westmont: IVP, 2000.

Holmes, M. *The Apostolic Fathers: Greek Texts and English Translations*. Grand Rapids: Baker, 1999.

―――. "The Text of the Matthean Divorce Passages: A Comment on the Appeal to Harmonization in Textual Decisions ". *JBL* 109, no. 4 (1990).

The Holy Bible: English Standard Version. Wheaton: Crossway, 2002.

Horder, J., and K. Fitz-Gibbon. "When Sexual Infidelity Triggers Murder: Examining the Impact of Homicide Law Reform on Judicial Attitudes in Sentencing." *Cambridge Law Journal* 74, no. 2 (2015).

House, H. W. *Divorce and Remarriage: Four Christian Views*. Downers Grove: IVP, 1990.

―――. "In Favour of the Death Penalty." In *The Death Penalty Debate: Two Opposing Views of Capital Punishment*, edited by J. H. Yoder and H. W. House. Dallas: Word, 1991.

Howard, L. "Quaker Marriage Ceremony and Records." *The Yorkshireman: A Religious and Literary Journal by A Friend* 3, no. 50 (1834): 17.

Hübner, H. *Das Gesetz in Der Synoptischen Tradition: Studien Zur These Einer Progressiven Qumranisierung Und Judaisierung Innerhalb Der Synoptischen Tradition*. Gottingen: Vandenhoeck & Ruprecht, 1986.

Hugenberger, G. *Marriage as a Covenant: A Study of Biblical Law and Ethics Governing Marriage Developed from the Perspective of Malachi.* Supplements to Vetus Testamentum. Leiden: Brill, 1994.

Instone-Brewer, D. "1 Corinthians 7 in the Light of the Graeco-Roman Marriage and Divorce Papyri." *TB* 52, no. 1 (2001): 101-15.

———. "1 Corinthians 7 in the Light of the Jewish Greek & Aramaic Marriage & Divorce Papyri." *TB* 52, no. 2 (2001).

———. *Divorce and Remarriage in the 1st and 21st Century.* Cambridge: Grove, 2001.

———. *Divorce and Remarriage in the Bible: The Social and Literary Context.* Grand Rapids: Eerdmans, 2002.

———. *Divorce and Remarriage in the Church.* Carlisle: Paternoster, 2003.

———. *The Jesus Scandals: Why He Shocked His Contemporaries (and Still Shocks Today).* Oxford: Monarch, 2012.

———. *Techniques and Assumptions in Jewish Exegesis before 70 C.E.* TSAJ. Tübingen: Mohr, 1992.

———. "Three Weddings and a Divorce: God's Covenant with Israel, Judah and the Church." *TB* 47.1 (1996).

———. *Traditions of the Rabbis from the Era of the New Testament.* 2a. Feasts and Sabbaths: Passover and Atonement. Grand Rapids: Eerdmans, 2011.

Janes, R. "Why the Daughter of Herodias Must Dance (Mark 6.14-29)." *JSNT* 28, no. 4 (2006): 443-67.

Janzen, D. "The Meaning of Porneia in Matthew 5.32 and 19.9: An Approach from the Study of Ancient Near Eastern Culture." *JSNT* 80 (2000): 66-80.

Jeffrey, D. *People of the Book: Christian Identity and Literary Culture.* Grand Rapids: Eerdmans, 1996.

Jerome. *Letters and Select Works.* Nicene and Post-Nicene Fathers: Second Series. Vol. 6, New York: Cosimo, 2007.

Johnson, E. "Aspects of the Remnant Concept in the Gospel of Matthew " PhD, Andrews University, 1984.

Josephus, F. *The Works of Josephus, Complete and Unabridged.* Translated by W. Whiston. 1987. 1991.

Keener, C. *And Marries Another: Divorce and Remarriage in the Teaching of the New Testament.* Peabody: Hendrickson, 1991.

————. *The Gospel of Matthew: A Socio-Rhetorical Commentary.* Grand Rapids: Eerdmans, 2009. A Commentary on the Gospel of Matthew (1999).

————. "Remarriage for Adultery, Desertion, or Abuse." Chap. 3 In *Remarriage after Divorce in Today's Church: 3 Views*, edited by M. Strauss. Counterpoints. Grand Rapids: Zondervan, 2006.

Kingsbury, J. *Matthew as Story.* Philadelphia: Fortress, 1986.

Kiuchi, N. *Leviticus.* AOTC. Edited by D. Baker and G. Wenham. Nottingham: Apollos, 2007.

Koehler, L., W. Baumgartner, and J. Stamm. *The Hebrew and Aramaic Lexicon of the Old Testament.* Vol. 2, Leiden: Brill, 1994.

————. *The Hebrew and Aramaic Lexicon of the Old Testament.* Vol. 1, Leiden: Brill, 1994.

Köstenberger, A., and D. Jones. *God, Marriage, and Family: Rebuilding the Biblical Foundation.* 2nd ed. Wheaton: Crossway, 2010.

Kuntz, P. *The Ten Commandments in History: Mosaic Paradigms for a Well-Ordered Society.* Grand Rapids: Eerdmans, 2004.

Lane, W. *The Gospel According to Mark.* NICNT. Grand Rapids: Eerdmans, 1974.

Laney, J. C. "No Divorce & No Remarriage." Chap. 1 In *Divorce and Remarriage: Four Christian Views*, edited by H. W. House. Downers Grove: IVP, 1990.

Lapide, P. *The Sermon on the Mount: Utopia or Program for Action?* Maryknoll: Orbis, 1986.

Lewis, C. S. *The Great Divorce: A Dream.* London: Geoffrey Bles, 1946.

Lindsley, A. "C.S. Lewis on Chronological Snobbery." *Knowing & Doing* Spring (2003).

Loader, W. *The Dead Sea Scrolls on Sexuality; Attitudes Towards Sexuality in Sectarian and Related Literature at Qumran.* Grand Rapids: Eerdmans, 2009.

————. "Did Adultery Mandate Divorce? A Reassessment of Jesus' Divorce Logia." *NTS* 61, no. 1 (2015): 67-78.

————. *Enoch, Levi, and Jubilees: Attitudes Towards Sexuality in the Early Enoch Literature, the Aramaic Levi Document, and the Book of Jubilees.* Grand Rapids: Eerdmans, 2007.

————. *Jesus' Attitude Towards the Law: A Study of the Gospels*. Vol. 97., Tübingen: Mohr Siebeck, 1997.

————. *Jesus and the Fundamentalism of His Day: The Gospels, the Bible and Jesus*. Melbourne: Uniting Education, 1998.

————. *Making Sense of Sex: Attitudes Towards Sexuality in Early Jewish and Christian Literature*. Grand Rapids: Eerdmans, 2013.

————. *The New Testament on Sexuality*. Grand Rapids: Eerdmans, 2012.

————. *Philo, Josephus, and the Testaments on Sexuality*. Grand Rapids: Eerdmans, 2011.

————. "Same-Sex Relationships: A 1st-Century Perspective." *HTS* 70, no. 1 (2014).

————. *Sexuality and the Jesus Tradition*. Grand Rapids: Eerdmans, 2005.

————. *Sexuality in the New Testament: Understanding the Key Texts*. Louisville: WJK, 2010.

Longenecker, B. "Evil at Odds with Itself (Matthew 12:22-29): Demonising Rhetoric and Deconstructive Potential in the Matthean Narrative." *Biblical Interpretation* 11, no. 3-4 (2003): 503-14.

Longman III, T. *Proverbs*. BCOTWP. Grand Rapids: Baker, 2006.

Luck, W. *Divorce and Remarriage: Recovering the Biblical View*. San Francisco: Harper & Row, 1987.

Luther, M. *The Christian in Society, the Estate of Marriage, Part 2, Luther's Works*. Vol. 45.

Luz, U. *Matthew 8-20: A Commentary*. Hermeneia. Minneapolis: Fortress, 2001.

————. *Studies in Matthew*. Grand Rapids: Eerdmans, 2005.

MacArthur, J. *Matthew 16-23*. The Macarthur New Testament Commentary. Chicago: Moody, 1988.

Macintosh, A. *A Critical and Exegetical Commentary on Hosea*. ICC. Edinburgh: T&T Clark, 1997.

Mackin, T. *Divorce and Remarriage*. Marriage in the Catholic Church. New York: Paulist, 1984.

Malina, B. *The New Testament World: Insights from Cultural Anthropology*. Third ed. Louisville: WJK, 2001.

Manson, T. *The Sayings of Jesus as Recorded in the Gospels According to St Matthew and St Luke*. London: SCM, 1949.

Martin, C. "Why Is Divorce Considered Worse Than Death?" Quora, https://www.quora.com/Why-is-divorce-considered-worse-than-death.

Mathew, S. "Law, Land, and Gender in the Hebrew Bible: A Postcolonial Womanist Reading." *ASJ* 30, no. 2 (2016): 177-92.

Mathews, A., and M. Hubbard. *Marriage Made in Eden: A Pre-Modern Perspective for a Post-Christian World.* Grand Rapids: Baker, 2004.

Mathews, K. *Genesis 1-11:26.* NAC. Edited by E. R. Clendenen. Vol. 1A, Nashville: B&H, 1996.

McConville, J. *Deuteronomy.* AOTC. Leicester: Apollos, 2002.

McGinn, T. *Prostitution, Sexuality, and the Law in Ancient Rome.* Oxford: OUP, 2003.

McIver, R. "The Sabbath in the Gospel of Matthew: A Paradigm for Understanding the Law in Matthew?". *Andrews University Seminary Studies* 33, no. 2 (1995).

McKnight, S. "Gospel of Matthew." In *Dictionary of Jesus and the Gospels,* edited by I. H. Marshall, S. McKnight and J. Green. Downers Grove: IVP, 1992.

———. "Matthew as 'Gospel'." In *Jesus, Matthew's Gospel and Early Christianity: Studies in Memory of Graham N. Stanton,* edited by D. Gurtner, J. Willitts and R. Burridge. LNTS. London: T&T Clark, 2011.

———. "Matthew, Gospel Of." In *Dictionary of Jesus and the Gospels,* edited by I. H. Marshall, S. McKnight and J. B. Green. Downers Grove: IVP, 1992.

———. *Sermon on the Mount.* The Story of God Bible Commentary. Grand Rapids: Zondervan, 2013.

Megivern, J. *The Death Penalty: An Historical and Theological Survey.* Mahwah: Paulist, 1997.

Meier, J. *A Marginal Jew: Companions and Competitors.* Vol. 3, New York: Doubleday, 2001.

———. *A Marginal Jew: Law and Love.* Vol. 4, New Haven: YUP, 2009.

———. *The Vision of Matthew: Christ, Church, and Morality in the First Gospel.* Theological Inquiries. Edited by L. Boadt. New York: Paulist, 1979.

Michaels, J. R. *The Gospel of John.* Grand Rapids: Eerdmans, 2010.

Milgrom, J. *Leviticus: A Book of Ritual and Ethics.* Continental Commentary. Minneapolis: Fortress, 2004.

Miller, P. *The Ten Commandments*. Interpretation. Louisville: WJK, 2009.

Milne, D. *The Westminster Confession of Faith for the 21st Century*. Strawberry Hills: PCA, 2001.

Moo, D. "Jesus and the Authority of the Mosaic Law." *JSNT 6*, no. 20 (1984): 3-49.

———. "Law." In *Dictionary of Jesus and the Gospels: A Compendium of Contemporary Biblical Scholarship*, edited by J. Green, S. McKnight and I. H. Marshall. Downers Grove: IVP, 1992.

———. "The Law of Christ as the Fulfillment of the Law of Moses: A Modified Lutheran View." In *Five Views on Law and Gospel*, edited by G. Bahnsen. Grand Rapids: Zondervan, 1999.

Moore, P. *Straight to the Heart of 1 & 2 Corinthians: 60 Bite-Sized Insights*. Oxford: Monarch, 2010.

Morris, L. *The Gospel According to Matthew*. PNTC. Leicester: IVP, 1992.

Mounce, W. *Mounce's Complete Expository Dictionary of Old & New Testament Words*. Grand Rapids: Zondervan, 2006.

Müller, S. "Adultery: IV. Christianity." In *Encyclopedia of the Bible and its Reception, Vol 1*. Berlin: de Gruyter, 2009.

Mullins, M. *The Gospel of Matthew: A Commentary*. Dublin: Columba, 2007.

Murphy, F. *Apocalypticism in the Bible and its World: A Comprehensive Introduction*. Grand Rapids: Baker, 2012.

Murray, J. *Divorce*. Phillipsburg: Presbyterian & Reformed, 1961.

———. *Principles of Conduct: Aspects of Biblical Ethics*. Grand Rapids: Eerdmans, 1957.

Nembach, U. "Ehescheidung Nach Alttestamentlichem Und Jüdischem Recht." *ThZ 26* (1970).

Neusner, J. *The Mishnah: A New Translation*. New Haven: YUP, 1988.

———. *The Rabbinic Traditions About the Pharisees before 70: The Masters*. Vol. 1, Leden: Brill, 1971.

Newman, B., and P. Stine. *A Translator's Handbook on the Gospel of Matthew*. New York: UBS, 1988.

Nolland, J. *The Gospel of Matthew: A Commentary on the Greek Text*. NIGTC. Grand Rapids: Eerdmans, 2005.

Nydam, R. "The Messiness of Marriage and the Knottiness of Divorce: A Call for a Higher Theology and a Tougher Ethic." *CTJ 40* (2005).

Olmstead, W. "A Gospel for a New Nation: Once More, the Ἔθνος of Matthew 21.43." In *Jesus, Matthew's Gospel and Early Christianity: Studies in Memory of Graham N. Stanton*, edited by D. Gurtner, J. Willitts and R. Burridge. LNTS. London: T&T Clark, 2011.

Orchard, B., and H. Riley. *The Order of the Synoptics: Why Three Synoptic Gospels?* Macon: Mercer, 1987.

Origen. *Ancient Christian Texts: Homilies on Numbers.* Downers Grove: IVP, 2009.

———. "Commentary on the Gospel of Matthew." In *The Ante-Nicene Fathers*, edited by A. Menzies. New York: Cosimo, 2007.

Osborne, G. *Matthew.* Zondervan Exegetical Commentary on the New Testament. Grand Rapids: Zondervan, 2010.

Osburn, C. "The Present Indicative in Matthew 19:9." *Restoration Quarterly* 24 (1981).

Pao, D. "Adultery, Divorce, and the Hard-Hearted People of God: The Function of the Matthean Exception Clause (Matt 19:9) in Its Literary Context." *Paradosis: A Journal of Bible and Theology* 1 (2014).

Parkinson, P. "Another Inconvenient Truth: Fragile Families and the Looming Financial Crisis for the Welfare State." *Sydney Law School Research Paper*, no. 12/05, January (2012).

Peabody, D. *One Gospel from Two: Mark's Use of Matthew and Luke.* Harrisburg: Trinity, 2002.

Pentecost, J. D. *The Words and Works of Jesus Christ.* Grand Rapids: Zondervan, 1981.

Perschbacher, W. *Word Pictures of the New Testament.* The Updated Classic Work by A. T. Robertson. Vol. 1, Grand Rapids: Kregel, 2004.

Peterson, D. "Divorce and Remarriage in the New Testament." *SMR* 115 (1983): 8-14.

Pharr, C. *The Theodosian Code and Novels and the Sirmondian Constitutions.* Union: Lawbook Exchange, 2001.

Philo. *Philo.* Translated by F. H. Colson. Loeb Classical Library. Vol. VI, London: Heinemann, 1984.

———. *The Works of Philo: Complete and Unabridged.* Translated by C. Yonge. Peabody: Hendrickson, 1993.

Pink, A. *An Exposition of the Sermon on the Mount.* Grand Rapids: Baker, 1979.

Piper, J. "Divorce and Remarriage." Minneapolis: Bethlehem Baptist Church, 1986.

———. *This Momentary Marriage: A Parable of Permanence.* Illinois: Crossway, 2009.

Powell, M. *Methods for Matthew.* Methods in Biblical Interpretation. Cambridge: CUP, 2009.

Powers, B. W. *Divorce and Remarriage: The Bible's Law and Grace Approach.* Preston: Mosaic, 2012.

———. *Marriage and Divorce: The New Testament Teaching.* Concord: Family Life Movement of Australia, 1987.

———. *The Progressive Publication of Matthew: An Explanation of the Writing of the Synoptic Gospels.* Nashville: B&H, 2010.

Powers, B. W., and J. Wade. *Divorce: The Bible and the Law.* Sydney: AFES, 1978.

Quesnell, Q. "'Made Themselves Eunuchs for the Kingdom of Heaven' (Mt 19.12)." *CBQ* 30 (1968).

Ranke-Heinemann, U. *Eunuchs for Heaven: The Catholic Church & Sexuality.* Hamburg: Hoffmann und Campe Verlag, 1990.

Reumann, J. *Jesus in the Church's Gospels: Modern Scholarship and the Earliest Sources.* Philadelphia: Fortress, 1968.

Richards, L. "Divorce and Remarriage under a Variety of Circumstances." Chap. 2 In *Divorce and Remarriage: Four Christian Views*, edited by H. W. House, 267 P 21 CM. Downers Grove: IVP, 1990.

Roberts, B. *Not under Bondage: Biblical Divorce for Abuse, Adultery and Desertion.* Ballarat: Maschil, 2008.

Robertson, A. T. *Commentary on the Gospel According to Matthew.* New York: MacMillan, 1911.

Robinson, J. A. T. *Redating the New Testament.* London: SCM Press, 1976.

Root, A. *The Children of Divorce : The Loss of Family as the Loss of Being.* Youth, Family, and Culture Series. Edited by C. Clark. Grand Rapids: Baker, 2010.

Rosner, B. *Paul and the Law: Keeping the Commandments of God.* Downers Grove: Apollos, 2013.

———. *Paul, Scripture and Ethics: A Study of 1 Corinthians 5-7.* New York: Brill, 1994.

Runesson, A. "The Audience of Matthew: An Appraisal of the Local Audience Thesis." *RSR* 41, no. 1 (2015): 24-25.

————. *Divine Wrath and Salvation in Matthew: The Narrative World of the First Gospel.* Minneapolis: Fortress, 2016.

Rushdoony, R. *The Institutes of Biblical Law: A Chalcedon Study.* Nutley: Craig Press, 1973.

Ryrie, C. "Biblical Teaching on Divorce and Remarriage." *GTJ* 3, no. 2 (1982).

Sailhamer, J. *The Meaning of the Pentateuch: Revelation, Composition, and Interpretation.* Downers Grove: IVP, 2009.

Sanders, E. *The Historical Figure of Jesus.* London: Penguin, 1993.

————. *Judaism: Practice and Belief 63BCE - 66CE.* London: SCM, 1992.

Sandvig, K. *Adult Children of Divorce: Haunting Problems and Healthy Solutions.* Dallas: Word, 1990.

Satlow, M. *Jewish Marriage in Antiquity.* Princeton: PUP, 2001.

Schaberg, J. *The Illegitimacy of Jesus: A Feminist Theological Interpretation of the Infancy Narratives.* Sheffield: Sheffield Phoenix, 2006.

Schachter, L. "The Garden of Eden as God's First Sanctuary." *JBQ* 41, no. 2 (2013).

Schnackenburg, R., W. Kruppa, and W. J. O'Hara. *The Gospel According to St Mark.* New Testament for Spiritual Reading. London: Sheed and Ward, 1977.

Schüssler Fiorenza, E. *In Memory of Her: A Theological Reconstruction of Christian Groups.* London: SCM, 1983.

Smedes, L. *Mere Morality: What God Expects from Ordinary People.* Grand Rapids: Eerdmans, 1983.

Spadaro, M. *Reading Matthew as the Climactic Fulfillment of the Hebrew Story.* Eugene: Wipf & Stock, 2015.

Spiro, K. "History Crash Course #29: Revolt of the Maccabees." Aish HaTorah, www.aish.com/h/c/t/h/48942121.html.

Sprinkle, J. "Old Testament Perspectives on Divorce and Remarriage." *JETS* 40, no. 4 (1997): 529-50.

Stanton, G. *A Gospel for a New People: Studies in Matthew.* Edinburgh: T&T Clark, 1992.

————. "The Origin and Purpose of Matthew's Sermon on the Mount." In *Tradition and Interpretation in the New Testament: Essays in Honor of E. Earle Ellis for His 60th Birthday,* edited by G. Hawthorne and O. Betz. Grand Rapids: Eerdmans, 1987.

Stassen, G., and D. Gushee. *Kingdom Ethics: Following Jesus in Contemporary Context.* Illinois: IVP, 2003.

Stegemann, W. "The Contextual Ethics of Jesus." In *The Social Setting of Jesus and the Gospels,* edited by G. Theissen, B. Malina and W. Stegemann. Minneapolis: Fortress, 2002.

Stern, M. "The Herodian Dynasty and the Province of Judea." In *The Herodian Period,* edited by M. Avi-Yonah. The World History of the Jewish People. Givatayim: Jewish History Publications, 1975.

Stott, J. *Divorce: The Biblical Teaching.* London: CPAS, 1972.

————. *God's New Society: The Message of Ephesians.* BST. Leicester: IVP, 1979.

————. *Issues Facing Christians Today.* 2nd ed. London: Marshall Pickering, 1984. 1990.

Strauss, M. *Four Portraits, One Jesus: An Introduction to Jesus and the Gospels.* Grand Rapids: Zondervan, 2007.

Strauss, M., and P. Engle. *Remarriage after Divorce in Today's Church: 3 Views.* Counterpoints. Grand Rapids: Zondervan, 2006.

Streeter, B. H. *The Four Gospels: A Study of Origins.* London: Macmillan, 1936.

Tanner, N. *Decrees of the Ecumenical Councils: Trent to Vatican 2.* Vol. 2, London: Sheed & Ward, 1990.

Tasker, R. *The Gospel According to St Matthew.* Tyndale. Leicester: IVP, 1983.

Thielicke, H. *The Ethics of Sex.* New York: Fortress, 1964.

Thompson, M. *John: A Commentary.* Louisville: WJK, 2015.

Treggiari, S. "Marriage and Family in Roman Society." Chap. 5 In *Marriage and Family in the Biblical World,* edited by K. Campbell. Downers Grove: IVP, 2003.

Turner, D. *Matthew.* BECNT. Grand Rapids: Baker, 2008.

Vawter, B. "Divorce and the New Testament." *CBQ* 39, no. 4 (1977): 528-42.

————. "Divorce Clauses in Matthew 5:32 and 19:9." *CBQ* 16, no. 2 (1954): 155-67.

Vine, C. *The Audience of Matthew: An Appraisal of the Local Audience Thesis.* London: Bloomsbury T&T Clark, 2014.

von Rad, G. *Genesis: A Commentary.* OTL. London: SCM, 1972.

Waetjen, H. *Matthew's Theology of Fulfillment, Its Universality and Its Ethnicity: God's New Israel as the Pioneer of God's New Humanity.* London: Bloomsbury, 2017.

Webb, W. "Unequally Yoked Together with Unbelievers: Part 2." *BSac* 149, no. 594 (1992): 162-79.

Wenham, G. "Does the New Testament Approve Remarriage after Divorce?". *SBJOT* 6, no. 1 (2002).

———. *Genesis 1-15.* WBC. Waco: Word, 1987.

———. *Genesis 16-50.* WBC. Dallas: Word, 1994.

———. "No Remarriage after Divorce." Chap. 1 In *Remarriage after Divorce in Today's Church: 3 Views*, edited by M. Strauss. Counterpoints. Grand Rapids: Zondervan, 2006.

Wenham, G., and W. Heth. *Jesus and Divorce.* BTCL. Carlisle: Paternoster, 1984. 1997.

Westbrook, R. *A History of Ancient Near Eastern Law. Volumes 1 and 2.* London: Brill, 2003.

Wevers, J. *Notes on the Greek Text of Leviticus.* Septuagint and Cognate Studies. Atlanta: Scholars, 1997.

Wiebe, P. . "Jesus' Divorce Exception." *JETS*, no. 32/3 Sept (1989).

Wilson, L., and L. Cornish. "Divorce Is Costing the Australian Economy $14 Billion a Year." News Corp, http://www.news.com.au/lifestyle/relationships/marriage/divorce-is-costing-the-australian-economy-14-billion-a-year/news-story/e5a101ea76351d4ba145279011b934ac.

Witherington III, B. *The Gospel of Mark: A Socio-Rhetorical Commentary.* Grand Rapids: Eerdmans, 2001.

———. *Matthew.* Macon: Smyth & Helwys, 2006.

———. "Matthew 5:32 and 19:9 - Exception or Exceptional Situation." *NTS* 31, no. 4 (1985): 571-76.

Woodhouse, J. "Divorce and Remarriage." In *The Priscilla & Aquila Centre Conference.* Sydney Moore College, 2014.

Wright, C. *Deuteronomy.* NIBC. Peabody: Hendrickson, 2007.

———. *Old Testament Ethics for the People of God.* Leicester: IVP, 2004.

Wright, N. T. *Jesus and the Victory of God.* Minneapolis: Fortress, 1996.

Yang, Y. *Jesus and the Sabbath in Matthew's Gospel.* JSNTS. Sheffield: Sheffield Academic, 1997.

Zodhiates, S. *What About Divorce? An Exegetical Study.* Chattanooga: AMG, 1992.

SCRIPTURE INDEX

Old Testament

New Testament

CPSIA information can be obtained
at www.ICGtesting.com
Printed in the USA
LVHW020747220721
693320LV00013B/227